Nicaragua in Reconstruction & at War: The People Speak

Sandinista militiaman on duty near the Nicaragua-Honduras border, July 1983. Photo by Loretta Smith.

Esteli, July 1983. Grieving mothers lead a religious procession honoring young men slain by the contras in fighting along the Nicaragua-Honduras border. Photo by Loretta Smith.

Assisting on Introductions, Chronologies & Notes:
Richard Grossman, with Rose Spalding,
Circe Ruiz, Dolores Quintela, Kate Pravera & Eric Berggren
Assisting on Poetry Selection & Translation:
Ellen Banberger, with Mirta Urroz, Eileen Sutz,
Karla Vanesa Sanchez, Judith Motyka, Katherine Malaga,
Carlos Eduarte, Patricia Carlos, Carlos Bauer & Beatriz Badikian
Assisting on Design: Estelle Carol & Bob Simpson
Photos by Vicki Grayland & Loretta Smith
Photo Processing Courtesy of Mickey Pallas

STUDIES IN MARXISM, Vol. 17

NICARAGUA IN RECONSTRUCTION

& AT WAR:

THE PEOPLE SPEAK

A Collage of Chronology/Analysis/Poetry/etc.
Portraying
Insurrection, Reconstruction,
Cultural Revolution & U.S. Intervention

Poetry by Gioconda Belli, Ernesto Cardenal, Rosario Murillo
& Other Nicaraguan Poets

Edited and translated by
MARC ZIMMERMAN

MEP Publications
Minneapolis

In the name of the Nicaraguan poets in this volume, the Nicaraguan government's Ministry of Culture retains rights to the Spanish originals from
which the translations herein were made. Writers of poems in English and
translators credited for specific poems retain the rights to subsequent publication of their work. Thanks to Ernesto Cardenal and Orbis Books for the
poet's poems and excerpts in translations by Marc Zimmerman *et al.* (©
Marc Zimmerman), from *Vuelos de Victoria/ Flights of Victory* (Maryknoll,
N.Y.: Orbis, 1985). Rights to visual materials are retained by their producers. Special thanks to Chicago's Casa Nicaragua, Committee in Support
of the Nicaraguan People and Rafael Cintron Ortiz Cultural Center (U. of
Illinois at Chicago); also Margaret Randall and Roberto Vargas.

Library of Congress Cataloging in Publication Data
Main entry under title:

Nicaragua in reconstruction & at war.

    At head of title: Gioconda Belli, Ernesto Cardenal,
Rosario Murillo & other Nicaraguan poets.
    Bibliography; p.
    1. Revolutionary poetry, Nicaraguan--Translations into
English.   2. Nicaraguan poetry--20th century--Translations
into English.   3. Revolutionary poetry, English--Trans-
lations from Spanish.   4. English poetry--Translations
from Spanish.   5. Nicaragua--History--Chronology.
6. Nicaragua--History--Revolution, 1979--Literature and
the revolution.   7. Nicaragua--History--Revolution, 1979--
Miscellanea.   I. Zimmerman, Marc.   II. Title: Nicaragua
in reconstruction and at war.
PQ7516.5.E5N53   1985   861   85-61046
ISBN 0-930656-41-5
ISBN 0-930656-42-3 (pbk.)

Printed in the United States of America
Cover Photo by Loretta Smith: Anniversary Celebration. Leon, July 19, 1983.

MEP Publications
c/o Anthropology Department
University of Minnesota
215 Ford Hall, 224 Church St. S.E.
Minneapolis, MN 55455

CONTENTS

*GENERAL INTRODUCTION: THIS BOOK &
NICARAGUA'S POLITICAL POETRY* 2

**BOOK I. NICARAGUA: YEARS OF INTERVENTION,
DOMINATION, STRUGGLE & INSURRECTION** 25

*INTRODUCTION TO BOOK I & PART I: NICARAGUA,
A HISTORY OF STRUGGLE* 26

PART I. 155 YEARS OF STRUGGLE (1821-1976) 35

Section 1. Early Interventions & Sandino's Campaign 35
Section 2. The Dynasty & the Sandinistas 39
Section 3. The Earthquake, the Quezada Unit
& the Death of Fonseca 44

PART II. YEARS OF INSURRECTION & VICTORY
(1977-79) 51

Introduction: Backgrounds to the Insurrection 51
Section 1. Solentiname & the Attack
on San Carlos (1977) 75
Section 2. The Uprising (1978) 78
Section 3. The Poet Combatants Who Fell (1972-1979) 91
Section 4. Final Insurrection & Victory (1979) 97

BOOK II. THE RECONSTRUCTION 119

*INTRODUCTION TO BOOK II: FOUR YEARS
OF STRUGGLE IN THE NEW NICARAGUA* 120
A. Political & Socio-Economic Developments under the GNR,
By Rose Spalding 120
B. U.S.-Nicaraguan Relations, Intervention
& Counterrevolution, By Marc Zimmerman
with Kate Pravera & Rose Spalding 126

PART I. THE FIRST YEAR (JULY, 1979 - JULY, 1980) 149

Introduction: Agrarian Reform, Mass Organization, Popular
Education & the Literacy Crusade 149
CHRONOLOGY 166
Section 1. First Celebrations & Commitments 167
CHRONOLOGY 172

Section 2. Remembering the Fallen 173
CHRONOLOGY 182
Section 3. The Literacy Crusade & Year's End 183

PART II. THE NEW ORDER & NEW CRISES
(JULY, 1980 - JULY, 1982) 191

Introduction: Internal Developments, the Church,
the Atlantic Coast, Health & Education 191
CHRONOLOGY 209
Section 1. The Army, the Police, the Militia,
Love & Revolution 211
CHRONOLOGY 217
Section 2. First Problems, Advances & Faith in the Future 220
CHRONOLOGY 225
Section 3. The Health Campaigns 228
CHRONOLOGY 233
Section 4. New Problems, Pastora, Education
& the Children of Nicaragua 236

PART III. INTERVENTION, DEFENSE & THE NEW
HEGEMONIC CULTURE (JULY, 1982 - JUNE, 1983) 241

Introduction: Developments During the Year, the New Poetry,
Solidarity & Women in the Revolution 241
CHRONOLOGY 256
Section 1. Defending the Revolution 256
CHRONOLOGY 261
Section 2. The Poets & the People 262
CHRONOLOGY 267
Section 3. Solidarity with Other Struggles 268
CHRONOLOGY 272
Section 4. Women & the Revolution 273

EPILOGUE (1983-85) 279

Introduction: Continued Intervention & Sandinist Legitimation
By Richard Grossman with Marc Zimmerman 280
Defense, the Election & the Future (July, 1983--) 288

BIO-BIBLIOGRAPHIES 308
BIBLIOGRAPHY 313

NICARAGUA IN RECONSTRUCTION & AT WAR:
THE PEOPLE SPEAK

Two women near the border. Jalapa, July 1983. Photo by Loretta Smith.

GENERAL INTRODUCTION. THIS BOOK & NICARAGUA'S POLITICAL POETRY

1. The Nature of this Book

In closing the "Prologo" of his anthology, *Poesia Politica Nicaraguense* (Mexico: Universidad Nacional Autonoma de Mexico, 1979, p. 18), Francisco de Asis Fernandez makes the following prophetic observations:

> Probably there is a need for a second volume which brings together the production of political poetry generated by the new crisis which faced the Somoza government starting with the action of the FSLN in December, 1974. ... The contradictions of the bourgeoisie with the dictatorial and genocidal government of Somoza have become more profound and irresolvable; the basis of support for the dictatorship is reduced now to the force of the National Guard's weapons and the support of North American imperialism. ... Now Somoza is carrying out his last battle as the people, with new points of view ... , advance toward the overthrow of the dictatorship in a process that involves national liberation, popular democracy and socialism. For the next volume, that will bring together the poetry generated in this historical moment, surely the title best able to characterize it will be ... *POESIA REVOLUCIONARIA NICARAGUENSE.*

Written in 1977, these words serve as an apt introduction to the poetic materials presented in this book. Obviously the nature of our book prevents us from using the precise title Asis Fernandez suggested. We have not been so foolhardy as to attempt bringing together "all the production of political poetry" from Nicaragua in recent years; we have only tried to fulfill the spirit and not the letter of the maximal project which the Nicaraguan poet and anthologist envisioned.

In fact, what we present here is not a poetry anthology at all, but rather an ample selection of poems, poetic excerpts and fragments mainly written during and dealing with the period of Insurrection and Reconstruction (1977-1985), with the materials so organized, edited and framed by introductions and chronological notes, that they render a coherent image of the period in question, both in function of the events which transpired, and how these events were seen by the social groups which the poets may be said to represent. As such, our book is a sequel, in a sense, to Asis Fernandez's volume, but it is even more directly a followup to a book I co-translated and edited with Bridget Aldaraca, Edward Baker and Ileana Rodriguez, *Nicaragua en Revolucion: Los Poetas Hablan/Nicaragua in*

Revolution: The Poets Speak (Minneapolis: MEP, 1980).

Unlike Asis Fernandez's volume, which is a standard anthology organized by poet, *Nicaragua in Revolution* is a text which initiates an experimental genre that finds another development in the volume we are presenting here. That is, the poetry is so cut, edited, organized and framed in *Nicaragua in Revolution,* as to constitute a history of Nicaragua from the end of the nineteenth century to the Sandinista victory of July 19, 1979. In a sense, the opening sections of this book go over the same turf as in the first volume. But several differences should also be noted.

First of all, *Nicaragua in Reconstruction and War: The People Speak* has sections which weave chronology and verse so as to provide a more readable text to those not used to reading large stretches of poetic material. Second, the poetic material of our new book is more specifically testimonial, more specifically poetry written either at the moment of the events or soon after. What we have, in fact, are not examples from the broad mainstream of Nicaraguan poetry (which is only overtly political in certain of its dimensions), but rather specifically political poetry which is in fact testimony to and constituent dimension of a social process. Third, with three very special exceptions, all of the many writers whose work is represented are Nicaraguan; that is, no attempt has been made to provide global, internationalist voices as in *Nicaragua in Revolution.*

Our intent here is to present the production of political poetry and poetic discourse internal to Nicaragua itself. Even the exceptions conform to the underlying principle, since all three poets have been intimately involved with the Nicaraguan social and literary process from within the national borders. Gaspar Garcia Laviana from Spain was a Sandinista combatant priest who fell in the struggle; Mayra Jimenez from Costa Rica directed the pre-insurrectional poetry work in Solentiname and developed the network of poetry workshops in the New Nicaragua; Margaret Randall, from the United States *via* Mexico and Cuba, worked and lived in Nicaragua through much of the Reconstruction period. A fourth writer, Claribel Alegria, known as a Salvadoran poet, was born in Nicaragua and has spent much of the Reconstruction writing about the process, as well as doing important solidarity work for all the Central American struggles.

A fourth difference, and one which we sorely regret, is that the text is in English only--and this because of our wish to provide as full a picture of the Nicaraguan Revolution as quickly and as economically as possible. Our emphasis on the "full" picture constitutes the fifth major difference from *Nicaragua in Revolution.* For we have gathered together *so much* chronology, commentary and analysis with respect to the total Nicaraguan process here, that the book probably constitutes the most comprehensive treatment of the country's recent development available at the time of its publication.

4

That is, beyond whatever value it may have as repository of poetic texts, this volume is probably one of the most thorough and useful orientations to the subject of Nicaragua that has yet appeared in English. This is not said to be boastful, but simply to delineate the total significance and scope of what is presented.

What we have in this book, above all, is a detailed treatment of Nicaragua's Final Insurrection against the Somoza dynasty and the first phase of the Reconstruction culminating with the elections and MIG scare in November-December, 1984, and the beginning of the Reconstruction with the elected government headed by Daniel Ortega. However, if there is something which does make us particularly proud of this effort, it is that the political, social and military dimensions of the Nicaraguan story are intermeshed with a presentation of cultural and ideological materials which are too often left to one side and treated as secondary or "superstructural" in other presentations of national development.

With respect to the poetry, our goal was to collect and select materials that could tell the story of the years in question, and could also serve as examples of the kind of poetry which the revolutionary process had generated. Thus, while Part I contains examples of Nicaraguan poetry throughout the entire century (including only a few post-July, 1979 selections), and while many subsequent parts and sections include work by the established poets (the "professionals" who exercise all their talent, technical capacity and experience to realize a maximal expression), such as Ernesto Cardenal, Ernesto Mejia Sanchez, Pablo Antonio Cuadra, Mario Cajina Vega, Fernando Silva, Jose Coronel, Jorge Eduardo Arellano, Luis Rocha, Julio Valle, Gioconda Belli, Rosario Murillo, Michele Najlis, Daisy Zamora, etc., the volume is mainly made up of the work of people who are or were not professional poets at all, but who were young participant-observers during the Insurrection and/or came to write poetry during the first years of the Reconstruction.

Many of the poets represented fought at the same time that they wrote. Some risked their jobs and their lives writing their poetry; others wrote from inside prison or in exile; others, between battles--in trenches, behind barricades, in dark rooms, where they hid from the Somocista Guards; some wrote projecting toward the early death they sensed would overtake them. Almost all the poets who survived the armed struggle now participate in the National Reconstruction process. Many carry out military, political, educational or cultural tasks that give them little time to write. But most of them continue with their poetry and in this way contribute to augmenting poetic production as a weapon of culture and consciousness in the New Nicaragua.

Of this group, in addition to the professional poets who also participated intensely in the struggle, we have some of the leaders, like Comandantes Tomas Borge, Daniel Ortega, Dora Maria Tellez, Hugo Torres, etc.; and we have young Sandinista soldiers, like Luis Vega, Bosco Centeno and many others. We also have those who died leaving a testimony of struggle and hope, like Jose Benito Escobar, Elvis Chavarria, Carlos Arroyo Pineda, Felipe Pena, Ernesto Castillo, Juan Carlos Tefel, and Garcia Laviana. However, we find, above all, the new beginning poets, poets without much literary experience who, inspired by the process, as well as by the poet combatants who preceded them, began to write their verses during the last stages of the anti-Somocista struggle or during the first phases of the Reconstruction.

Many of these young poets have been encouraged and promoted or at least influenced by the cultural, literary and specifically poetry workshops, contests and activities organized among all popular sectors of the new country: first mainly by the workshops established by the Ministry of Culture under the aegis of Ernesto Cardenal, and then more recently, by the programs set up through the Association of Sandinista Cultural Workers, including the Cultural Brigades developing in relation to the intensive and dangerous defense work necessitated by the counterrevolutionary incursions in the Honduran border areas.

As might be expected, this new poetry is of mixed quality, and we have chosen those materials which best fit the portrait we are trying to develop. We also felt free to cut this poetry as was demanded by the total scheme of our project; and, following a not uncommon Nicaraguan and Sandinista tradition (one already employed and extended in *Nicaragua in Revolution*), we sometimes took the liberty of adapting texts that were not formally poetry but which were similar in style, and written out of the same general elan as the poetic texts themselves, and which, cut in verse, could readily fit into and enhance our overall scheme. In effect then, we have a body of poetic material which typifies and is so organized as to highlight certain stages, aspects, events, and feelings of Nicaragua's revolutionary process; it is a selection which also demonstrates how in Nicaragua this process has implied in every sense a matter of letters as well as of arms.

2. *The Book's Genesis & Those Who Made it a Reality*

The story of how this volume came about is perhaps worthy of mention, first to give credit to all who participated in the process, but also to show how collective work may be promoted and how the enthusiastic participation of young, relatively inexperienced students may yield valuable results for themselves and for those who are the receptors of the final product.

First, as my collaborators and I were drafting *Nicaragua in Revolution*, it became increasingly clear to us that we were unable to portray the final years of the Insurrection with the detail we wanted because we had no access to some of the key poetic texts which in a country of young people inclined to writing poetry were surely being written at the time.

Our sense of the urgent need for a volume such as ours and our sense of imminent revolutionary victory, led us on to finish our text, even though we knew it would be least detailed where perhaps the greatest amount of detail was required. A near-final draft of the volume completed, I left for Nicaragua, where I soon found myself working in the Literature Section of the Ministry of Culture and indeed meeting several of the poets whose work was set to appear in our volume, as well as several others whose work might well have appeared if we had had knowledge of and access to their work. Very quickly word spread about the volume we had completed, which, so went the story, would be the definitive collection of Nicaraguan poetry dealing with the Somoza years and the Revolution.

People, including many of the important and lesser national poets, came by to peruse the manuscript, then being prepared for publication. Comments and criticisms abounded: Why hadn't we included their poems--or their friends' work? Or: "Look at the poems in Asis Fernandez's volume that are not in yours." No matter how often I explained that our book was not an anthology pretending to include everything, no matter how often I explained the haphazard process by which I had found the poems included in our book, the complaints and "helpful criticisms" came left and right. "Oh," I began to say, to cut off the discussion and get back to work, "All that material is going to appear in the sequel volume."

I really didn't mean what I said at the time. But my very work at the Ministry made it rather easy for me to start looking at a wealth of recent material I had never seen before, and of course a growing mass of new poems, dealing with the Insurrection and, increasingly, the Reconstruction that indeed were laying the basis for a followup volume. In fact I began working on the book, along with a junior member of the Literature Section, Karla Vanesa Sanchez, and a volunteer, my son, Carlos Eduarte.

At that time I envisioned a concise representative selection of about fifty to seventy-five poems, including older materials I had missed and newer ones that were coming to the Ministry, being written in the developing poetry workshops and, in some cases, being published in *La Prensa* and the new cultural page of *Barricada*. But already people were suggesting that it might be a good idea to do an another extensive English-language text that could serve literary and political functions in the English-speaking world, whether in the U.S. or Bluefields, Nicaragua. We began to think about this, as we finished our modest volume. However, the "clincher" came in March, 1980.

By then, the Ministry's new poetry workshops were well underway. An enormous poetry marathon had been held in Ciudad Dario (going from dawn to dusk, with each poet limited to two poems, the marathon-site filled to the hilt by townspeople, who listened intently through periods of scorching sun and pouring rain, while thousands of Nicaraguans, literate or not, listened to the radio version broadcasted throughout the country).

In the meantime, poetry manuscripts flooded our offices for consideration in the upcoming Ruben Dario poetry contest or for publication in the Ministry's new national journal, *Nicarauac*. The national literacy surveys and crusade preparations were almost complete, and the first pilot campaigns had not only produced people who could now read and write, but even some new, burgeoning poets. I personally was so inundated with masses and mounds of poetry that I, the only U.S. citizen working at the Ministry, decided to risk charges of "Yankee Imperialism" by calling for a national moratorium on poetic production.

It was at this juncture that Ernesto Cardenal revealed to the Section's staff that he intended to publish over eighty recently written poems in the first issue of *Nicarauac*. Seeing the standard anthology format given to texts that had perhaps more historical than aesthetic value, I protested to him, "*Poeta*, we're already doing a collection that will include many of these materials, but in an orderly, coherent and politically strong way as we did in *Nicaragua in Revolution*." "Good," he responded. "We're going to publish these poems as they are any way--we can't wait for you to finish off your careful text, because *we have to inspire our people to write more poetry--now!*"

I probably just stared at him open-mouthed as he said this, and he added, "I mean the new poetry, the Sandinista poetry we're just beginning to see ... But why don't you keep working on your project, and why not do it in English, so more people can learn what we're doing here." I could do nothing but stammer yes, I would do it. And work on the newly defined project continued from that point on.

That work was interrupted repeatedly, mainly because it was time for me to return to the U.S., and then followed a long period when I was looking for a job and reorganizing my life in this country. Meanwhile, the Reconstruction advanced, new programs and problems, as well as new poems, were emerging by the day. In fact, by the time I got back to working on the book, so many new things had happened and so much new material had appeared that the task at hand was clearly much larger and more complex than I had anticipated. It was especially complicated by my knowledge that as I worked, even more events and more poetic texts would

8

have to be incorporated into the final product.

One thing that helped along was my new position as the Coordinator of the Rafael Cintron Ortiz Cultural Center, a program and facility for well over 1,500 Latino students at University of Illinois, Chicago (UIC). One of my tasks was to organize campus/community projects under the aegis of "LUCA: Latinos, University, Community and Art"; and this book became one of the first LUCA projects initiated.

In the early phases students Patricia Carlos, Eileen Sutz and Mirta Urroz worked over my first draft translations of many of the poems. Then Ellen Banberger, a dedicated solidarity worker for Central American struggles, and a person with an excellent background in Spanish and literature, helped to re-draft much of the students' work and translated many new poems. Carlos Bauer, a professional translator of Spanish poetry, also drafted English versions of several poems, as did Katherine Malaga, a nurse and friend with a fine feeling for Latin American Literature, as well as Beatriz Badikian, a young Greek-Argentine poet from Chicago.

As the work went on, I redrafted and re-edited much of the material, receiving some help from Banberger in the selection process, as well as in the chronology weave for Part I of Book I and the sections dealing with the insurrections of 1978 and 1979. Then in 1981, after Ellen had to leave the project to one side, I continued seeking additional material and help to constitute a poetic text and the introductory materials which would finally make up the definitive volume.

As the penultimate version was nearing completion, solidarity worker Richard Grossman, Chairman of the Chicago Committee in Support of the Nicaraguan People (CC), introduced me to Linde Rivera, a Puerto Rican religious activist, who provided me with new materials, most of which went to constitute the section on women (see Book II, Part III), that I translated with Judith Motyka of the Ruiz Belvis Center in the Puerto Rican community of Chicago. Linde also provided me with a useful chronology of the first three years of the Reconstruction, and delivered a copy of much of the poetic text to Ernesto Cardenal for criticisms and suggestions. And Grossman continued to help, by providing me with new volumes of poetry appearing in Nicaragua and working on the bibliography for the volume.

Then as I was working on the introduction and notes for the Reconstruction, DePaul University Professor Rose Spalding and theological specialist Kate Pravera, both of them CC members who had made frequent visits to Nicaragua and had collaborated on *Voces desde Nicaragua*, a new journal I had helped get started in Chicago, agreed to write analyses of the Revolution's achievements and the U.S. intervention--analyses which I then reworked to constitute much of the general introductory materials for

Book II of our volume. Spalding's review of political and economic developments appears almost without change, as Part A of the Book II Introduction. Her passages on the Intervention were joined with a summary by Pravera and then integrated with my own detailed treatment of the Intervention to constitute Part B.

Pravera provided me with other important materials, as did Darlene Gramigha, a member of the Religious Task Force on Central America. Susana Picado, a Nicaraguan board member of *Voces desde Nicaragua*, also helped me with medical terms in the section on Health; Circe Ruiz, a UIC student from Colombia, helped translate and edit materials used in our chronologies of the Reconstruction and notes on the poets. Dolores Quintela, a UIC student from Bolivia, drew upon materials provided by Richard Grossman to develop first drafts for most of the Epilogue chronology entries; Grossman wrote up additional entries, and then drafted an essay which I first stripped to round out the chronology and which (in its slimmed down form) I then reworked slightly to constitute the final version of the Epilogue introduction. Grossman also drafted the bibliography and contributed a short resource list. In the meantime, student Eric Berggren gathered materials provided by Bob Simpson, Iris Blanco and other people recently returned from Nicaragua, and helped me in selecting, editing and then weaving them with the chronology and poetic materials I already had, to achieve the Epilogue chronology/collage.

Finally, I should acknowledge the continuing support of Walter Urroz, head of Chicago's Casa Nicaragua, in providing materials, advice and encouragement over the past several years. Thanks also to Mario Widel, Ester Soler and Ed Garay, as well as Otto Pikaza and my other colleagues in Latin American Studies and the students of the Cintron Ortiz Center, for their help and support during various stages of this project. Sonia Arvanitis word-processed several sections of the poetry, and Professor Hernan Vidal assured me of a home for the volume. No words can express my debt to Estelle Carol and Betsy Vandercook of the University of Illinois at Chicago Publications office and to Bob Hyman of the university computer center for invaluable advice, assistance and collaboration in preparing the manuscript for printing. Finally I wish to acknowledge the help of Todd Beja, Bill Rowe, Doris and Erwin Marquit, Mickey Pallas, Judith Sayad, Roberto Vargas, Anna Odegaard and Beto Barrera for their help in bringing this volume to press.

Poems from several sections of this text appeared in *Voces desde Nicaragua*, I, 1; most of the poems in the women's section appeared in *Voces*, I, 2-3. A whole chapter appeared in *The Minnesota Review*. Furthermore it should be noted that many poetic texts by Ernesto Cardenal that were to have appeared in this volume were relinquished in favor of a specific by-product of our total project, Cardenal's *Vuelos de Victory/ Flights of Victory*

(New York: Orbis Books, 1985). But those poems and excerpts by Cardenal that I considered as absolutely essential to this volume were retained. In this sense, the present text, even if it should appear before the Cardenal book, is a sequel to it as well as to *Nicaragua in Revolution* and offers, then, a wider view of the Insurrection and Reconstruction by joining to Cardenal's voice, the voices of many Nicaraguans involved in the making of a new country in Central America.

3. *Organization and Sources*

Aside from this introduction and closing materials, our volume is made up of two "books," each of which is divided into "parts" that are further divided into "sections." There is a general introduction to each book, and each part has its own introduction, the only variation being that Book I and its first part are both served by a single introduction. The purpose of these introductions is to provide key historical backgrounds and analyses that afford our full picture of the Nicaraguan process, as well as information about the poetic texts and their organization. Book I, Part I serves as a prologue, weaving chronology and poetry to provide a brief synopsis of Nicaragua's history from the Independence to the death of Sandinista leader Carlos Fonseca Amador in 1976. Part II details the major dimensions and events of the insurrectional period, extending from 1977 to July, 1979.

But while Book I more or less follows a chronological order, that approach could not be maintained as strictly in Book II, which describes crucial dimensions of the Reconstruction. The reason is simply that the period in question requires a grasp of "over-determined" processes and interacting forces, as well as an extended examination of given strands and dimensions, so that a rather complex and varied use of poetic and historical materials became necessary in the editing work. Thus, while each part attempts to deal with a given period of the Reconstruction, while there is a constant effort to create a sense of movement through time in each part's sub-sections, and while there are texts referring to major events at appropriate points, the main organizational principle is one of given themes and issues, interspersed with chronological and factual materials when deemed useful to providing a coherent picture for the reader.

The first part deals with events and issues keyed to 1979-1980; the second focuses on major concerns covering July, 1980 to July, 1982; and the third portrays key themes in relation to July, 1982-July, 1983. Internally to each part, the effort has been to alternate between roughly chronological and thematic sections; but clearly, for example the questions of health, women, solidarity and intervention, which dominate Part III of Book II, are matters germane to the entire Reconstruction period. They appear where they do because they are perhaps most appropriate there, but certainly some of these sections could have appeared elsewhere as well. In our Epilogue, all the themes of the Reconstruction return in a chronology-collage which provides a summation of events occurring during the period between the initial completion of the manuscript and its final preparation for the printer.

As suggested above, most of the poems and excerpts presented first appeared in Nicaraguan newspapers, especially in *La Prensa Literaria*, (a section of *La Prensa* that played an important ideological role during the Insurrection and in the period prior to the paper's overt problems with the Sandinistas during the first months of the Reconstruction), and in *Ventana*, the literary supplement of the Sandinista newspaper, *Barricada*. Subsequently many of them appeared in *Nicarauac*, the Ministry of Culture's national journal, or in *Poesia Libre*, a publication of the Ministry's Literature section disseminating poems by and/or for the young writers in the poetry workshops throughout the country. However, there are several other sources which should be mentioned.

First, while Part I of Book I provides a summary of the years covered in great detail in *Nicaragua in Revolution*, the poetic material is drawn from poems collected for but not used in the first book, as well as poems collected in the anthology by Asis Fernandez which did not appear in the bilingual collage. Finally, these poetic materials are weaved with excerpts from lyrics by the singing group, Pancasan.

The first section of Book I, Part II is based completely on texts appearing in *Poesia Campesina de Solentiname* (Managua: Ministerio de Cultura [Coleccion Popular de Literatura Nicaraguense, 4], 1980). Two of the poems by Garcia Laviana in Book I, Part II, Section 3 come from his book, *Cantos de Amor y Guerra* (Managua: Ediciones del Ministerio de la Cultura, 1979). Most of the selections by Gioconda Belli and Rosario Murillo were published in their respective books, *Truenos y arco iris* (Managua: Editorial Nueva Nicaragua, 1982); and *Amar es cantar* (Managua, 1980). Finally, almost all of the poems by my good friend Alejandro Bravo appear in his book, *Tambor con luna* (Managua, 1980).

For the factual and analytical introductions, as well as the chronological accounts employed throughout this volume, I have drawn as extensively as seemed necessary from whatever sources seemed most appropriate, always modifying them in function of the specific purposes of this project.

The introduction to Book I and Part I owes much to the article by Edmundo Jarquin C. and Pablo Emilio Barreto, "A Brief History of U.S. Imperialism and Class Relations in Modern Nicaragua," as translated from *Pensamiento Critico: La Lucha de Clases en Nicaragua* (Managua, 1979), in

Nicaragua: A People's Revolution, ed. Yvonne Dilling and Philip Wheaton of the Epica Task Force (Washington, D.C., 1980), pp. 1-8; but there are important extrapolations from the introduction to *Nicaragua in Revolution: The Poets Speak* and from the book by Claribel Alegria and D. J. Flakoll, *Nicaragua: La Revolucion Sandinista: Una cronica politica/ 1855-1979* (Mexico, 1982). These three books are also the primary sources for the chronology used throughout Book I, Part I. Except for the opening and closing sections, the Introduction to Book I, Part II is primarily indebted to *Nicaragua: A People's Revolution*, pp. 9-73; and the chronological material used throughout Part II is based on the same source, along with a day-to-day log of the Insurrection published by the FSLN in the first months of the Reconstruction.

The writers involved in the Introduction to Book II are specifically credited, but we should note that the prime sources used were the valuable analyses provided in *Envio/ Update*, published monthly by the Instituto Historico Centroamericano in Managua. These analyses are also the main sources for the introductions to each part of Book II, but they were supplemented by materials from the Epica book (pp. 76-91), as well as by *Nicaragua Fact Sheets*, published by the National Network on Nicaragua (Washington, D.C., 7/1/82). Other materials used include: various issues of the journal, *Nicaraguan Perspectives*; *Nicaragua: 79/82. Realizaciones Estatales en 3 Anos de Revolucion*, a review of governmental achievements in education, social welfare, etc., published by the Direccion General de Divulgacion y Prensa de la JGRN (Managua, 1982); Daniel Ortega's State of the Nation address delivered in May 1983; and Ortega's address on July 19th, 1983, "A Year of Struggle for Peace and Sovereignty," pronounced in the name of the FSLN National Directorate and the JGRN and published in *Barricada* on July 20, 1983.

For the month-by-month chronologies of the Reconstruction period used throughout Book II, I used the chronology, "3 Anos de Revolucion Sandinista," which appeared in *Amanacer: Boletin del Centro Ecumenico Antonio Valdivieso*, in a "special 3rd Anniversary Issue" (pp. 3-13); supplemented by Peter Crabtree's "Peace Efforts in Central America and the U.S. Response," from *Nicaraguan Perspectives* Number 5 (Winter 1983), pp. 18-19 and 33; and (especially for the fourth year) issues of *Envio*. The latter publication was also the main source for the Epilogue. Other materials, of course, were also utilized throughout the book; and in the last analysis, I must take responsibility for the use the sources were put to, their veracity and effectiveness with relation to this volume.

All the materials portray the immediate historical ambiance out of which the poetry in this volume grows, and of which the poetry may be said to be a dimension. Clearly the revolutionary process itself is the context of this book, to the degree that these pages are seen as a contribution to the dissemination of literature. However, it is also clear that that process, as reflected through literature is the object of our work. Ultimately, providing a dialectical unity between these two perspectives, is the view permeating this effort, that in Nicaragua, poetry and poetic discourse served as a specific constitutive force in the formation of the ideological and cultural practices necessary to the forging of a national revolutionary bloc. It is because of this view that within the context of Nicaragua's revolutionary history and the national Reconstruction process, the specific context of regional and national poetic practices must be underlined and examined.

As we pursue this theme in this introduction and throughout our volume, we should keep in mind that while all of the poetic texts used in the first half of this book deal with the revolutionary and insurrectional period of Nicaraguan history, and while several of the texts in Book I were written during the same period, most of the poetic material, including much of the insurrectional poetry and even some poems in Part I of Book I, were written after the July Victory, during the Reconstruction itself. Thus the principle substance of this volume is a testimonial poetry primarily of the Reconstruction.

From this perspective, the texts appearing which were written before the victory may be seen as instances of the poetic context from which the later poems sprang. Indeed, while we may say that the increasingly political tenor of all Nicaraguan poetry during the Somoza years provides the context in literary production (in approach, style, theme, *topoi* and the like) for post-victory poetic discourse, the poems most like the Reconstruction workshop poems which so dominate this volume are the ones written by the "professionals" under the pressure of insurrectional events, and by the combatants scrawling out their verses in between their confrontations with the National Guard.

The Sandinista victory not only gives hegemony to the revolutionary tendencies which have been accumulating in the country, but to the tendencies toward overt political poetry, which, born in pre-Columbian times, developing throughout the periods of Conquest, Colonization and Independence, reborn in the midst of supposedly anti-political modernism, nurtured even in the most reactionary valences of vanguardism, and reaching maturity in anti-Somocista exteriorism, had burgeoned in the young men and women of Nicaragua as an essential dimension of a new counter-culture seeking national dominance just when the revolutionary movement as a whole reached its culmination.

4. Nicaragua's Political Poetry

Poetry has a different specific gravity in countries like Nicaragua, which is the same as saying that it has a different class referent, a different relation to history... The political centrality of literature, and of poetry in particular, is due among other things to the paradoxical effects of capitalist combined and uneven development in Latin America, which, together with the introduction of a bourgeois commercial mass culture, leaves intact elements of earlier strata of cultural expression: for example, the rural tradition oral songs and storytelling with roots at once in the survivals of the pre-Colombian Indian civilizations and popular Catholicism; or the role of the writer consecrated by Liberal Romanticism in the epoch of the Wars of Independence as a sort of Moses, "informing" through his rhetoric the processes of national liberation and identity-formation.

In small rural towns, where TV has not yet penetrated, young people gather in the evenings to sing songs together and gossip. Where illiteracy, or marginal literacy, are still widespread, poetry and political rhetoric have the virtue of being susceptible to memorization and oral recitation. The spoken word conjures together the presence of the sacred (the sacred as produced *by* the people rather than *for* it), the communal and the erotic. This is difficult to understand "from the other side" of bourgeois modernism, unless like Chicano, black or proletarian poets you work in the context of a concrete social struggle. ... The task of elaborating that plain-speaking *Democratic Vistas* voice which was supposed to be the responsibility of the "great tradition" in U.S. poetry has now passed to those countries which are the main antagonists of U.S. imperialism.

We have quoted this passage, taken from John Beverley's illuminating review of recently published texts of Central American poetry in translation (including *Nicaragua in Revolution* and *Voces desde Nicaragua*, I), "Sandinista Poetics," in *The Minnesota Review*, ns 20 [Spring, 1983], pp. 127-134), because the passage, and the article as a whole, point to the total structural frame in which our consideration of Nicaraguan poetry and this entire volume may be best seen. The fact is that since Dario, poetry had been one of the intellectual and cultural modes in which many Nicaraguans (those who could write) gave expression to their sentiments and preoccupations. As Daniel Ortega told Claudia Dreifus in her *Playboy* interview with Sandinista leaders, "Nicaragua's great national poet Ruben Dario gave all of us an obligation to write. Nicaraguans *like* to write poetry. Given the culture, many sorts of poets emerge--good poets, all kinds of poets" (*Playboy* [September, 1983], p. 63).

To the degree that the force of historical transformations, fed by capitalist penetration and imperialist incursions, pushed intellectuals to consider and at times take political positions, to the degree that external pressures assaulted even the supposedly immune sanctuary of spiritual and cultural purity which the modernist aesthetic created, so (first, even in moments of the mature Dario himself), the tendency toward a social and political poetry became more pronounced.

As the most important Central American poet of his time, and as a figure who brought world-historical prestige to his area, Dario was able to establish poetry as the major mode of literary production and as the major vehicle of intellectual expression in the Central American area.

From this point on, a modern poetic system took form, and major changes in politics and ideology would of necessity register in transformations of the poetic system. Furthermore the system itself would serve as both a barometer of other changes and as a space for the generation of ideological and intellectual transformations which would be of importance in the political struggles affecting the zone.

In Nicaragua, itself, the change in literary systems evident in certain elements of Dario's work, when his modernist aesthetic seemed threatened from without, materializes in certain elements of the later post-modernists like Alfonso Cortes, Azarias Palais and Salomon de la Selva. But the change most fully manifests itself in the late 1920's with the almost concurrent emergence of Sandino and Nicaragua's vanguardist poetry.

Sandino's campaigns signalled a rupture in the classical struggles between Liberals and Conservatives, each vying for imperial support, which had dominated Nicaragua's political past. At the same historic conjuncture, Nicaraguan vanguardism breaks the vessel of modernism, to project an overtly national and historical discourse, as opposed to the "universal, culturalist and aestheticist" projections of modernism. While the Vanguardists espoused a corporatist, reactionary and ultimately proto-fascist world view which equated Somoza with Spain's Franco as the champion of national identity, still there were contradictory, communitarian and (in the work of Manolo Cuadra), even socialist valences in their poetic production.

The romance of Somoza fading with each new effort of the dictator to maintain and extend his power, the contradictory but at times progressive tendencies in Nicaraguan discourse and thought would ultimately turn the poets and their poetic system against the dictatorship, and, in conjunction with growing oppositional ideological and political tendencies, would make the Nicaraguan poetic system ripe for a radical transformation at once open to Sandinist influences and, those influences internalized, able to project them in such a way that they contributed to the constitution of Sandinism itself.

So much more central to national life was poetry in Nicaragua than it could conceivably be in an advanced technological society with its fierce division of labor and function, so much more was it a common mode of expression, that many of the anti-Somocista and Sandinist leaders wrote poetry.

Thus, Sandino not only spurred a movement that became the source of poetry; his campaign not only coincided with and influenced the vanguard poets's rebellion against modernism; but Sandino himself tried his hand at poetry, at least once. Thus, Rigoberto Lopez Perez and Edwin Castro, who carried out the assassination of Anastasio Somoza Garcia wrote political poetry, including works directly related to the preparations and repercussions of their act.

Pablo Antonio Cuadra and Ernesto Cardenal, ultimately coming to represent two very different political tendencies of Somocista opposition, were poets implicated in the political plots against the first Somoza and wrote poetry that influenced a whole generation of men and women who turned to the emerging Frente Sandinista in the 1960's. Student leaders Fernando Gordillo, Michele Najlis and Sergio Ramirez were among those so influenced. So were Sandinista leader Ricardo Morales Aviles, and finally a young poet who was to become the symbolic representative of the nexus between revolution and poetry, Leonel Rugama, writer of a few superb poems before falling in a shootout with the National Guard in 1970.

As our book shows, several of the Sandinista leaders wrote poetry. And while he himself did not write poetry, Carlos Fonseca Amador wrote of Dario and took the trouble to versify the letter Lopez Perez wrote to his mother, just prior to "executing" Somoza Garcia. The founder of modern *Sandinismo* showed thereby an instinctive grasp of the relation of Nicaragua's poetic traditions and discourse to central concerns of politics and revolution.

Clearly Pablo Antonio Cuadra, both as a poet and promoter of young writers, in his role as editor of *La Prensa Literaria* and the journal, *La pez y la serpienta*, did much to encourage young political poets and spur on the development of a poetry focused on the national problematic during the final years of the Somoza regime. But of still greater force was Ernesto Cardenal's influence as an anthologist and above all as a great poet whose increasingly radical views and poetic approach would be decisive in the emergence of the new political poetry that we find represented in the book---all under the aegis of *exteriorismo*.

In Cardenal's spiralling flights of poetic invention, the work of Nicaragua's vanguardists and their turn from Dario's *modernismo* to the national reality, the work of Ezra Pound with his method of collage, as well as his anti-capitalism (also his sense, however reactionary, of world-historical epic connections), and the work of Neruda with his comprehensive Latin American vision--all these come together with Thomas Merton and Tielard de Chardin and other masters of the spirit in a new synthesis which Cardenal called "*exteriorismo*," and which in its most advanced articulation came to be a *Sandinista* mode of concrete poetry.

Writing of this poetic mode in the early 1970's, and prior to his overt commitment to the Sandinista cause, Cardenal declared:

Exteriorism is a poetry created with images of the exterior world, the world we see and sense, and that is, in general, the specific world of poetry. Exteriorism is objective poetry: narrative and anecdote, made with elements of real life, and with concrete things, with proper names precise details and exact data, statistics, facts and quotations ... In contrast, interiorist poetry is a subjectivist poetry made with abstract or symbolic words: rose skin, ash, lips, absence, dream, touch, foam, desire, shade, time, blood, stone, tears, night... I think that the only poetry which can express Latin American reality, reach the people and be revolutionary, is exteriorist... Poetry can serve a function: to construct a country, and create a new humanity, change society, make the future Nicaragua, as part of the future great country that is Latin America.

--From *Poesia nueva de Nicaragua: Seleccion y prologo de Ernesto Cardenal* (Buenos Aires: Lohle, 1974), pp. 9-11.

John Beverley attempts to place Cardenal and exteriorist poetry in relation to Pound, Neruda and other "modernist" or "neo-barroque" tendencies in Latin American and other literatures. "Cardenal's poetry," he reminds us, "is unthinkable without the work of Pound and U.S. beat poets." Neruda is also important, but other poetic tendencies intervene to modify their syncretic resultant:

[The poetry of contemporary Central America] ... is rather "post-Barroque" in mood and composition. Gone is that sonorous, complex, vatic (and not incidentally patriarchal) voice that Neruda, for example, affected. ... Cardenal retains something of the Biblical sonority and the modernist taste for inter-textuality. But unlike his master Pound he keeps things simple, and lets bare physical or historical detail carry the weight of symbolism. ... Such a poetry--brittle, flat, direct, epigrammatic, alternating between irony and unforced lyricism, marked by what Robert Marquez calls "objectivistic immediacy"-- has its roots in two strains of post-Nerudian, post-magic realism Latin American writing. The first comes from the Chilean Nicanor Parra's "anti-poems' of the 50's, which consciously displaced Neruda's vatic Popular Front patriarch with the persona of the petty bourgeois everyman, *l'homme moyen sensuel*, cynical and prosaic in a cynical and prosaic world.

Parra's is the voice of a Latin American poetry no longer rooted in the land and peasant culture. The other is what Roberto Fernandez Retamar calls "conversational poetry," the fraternal and "grave but not solemn" mode of Vallejo's later, post-modernist poems (*Poemas humanos*) and of the majority of post-revolutionary Cuban poets, including Retamar himself. Unlike the anti-poem, which simply registers the experience of alienation, conversational poetry "tends to affirm its beliefs," according to Retamar, which are those of a Christian or Marxist humanism (or, characteristically, both). Set to music, conversational poetry is the *nueva trova* or "new song" movement in Latin America, exemplified by Victor Jara, the singer/poet killed during the 1973 coup in Chile. ... The irony in ... Central American poetry ... is not Baroque or "romantic irony" ...; it is rather a way of examining the gap between hope and immediacy, a revolutionary possibility (which it remains faithful to) and the frail achievements of revolutionary militancy. That is what makes it a weapon of struggle, rather than its antidote.
--From "Sandinista Poetics," pp. 129-30.

Exteriorismo became the poetry par excellence of a nationalist resistance to Somoza in the name of Sandino. It was a poetry that while influenced by the great vanguardists of Nicaragua (Coronel Urtecho, Joaquin Pasos, Pablo and Manolo Cuadra), was also influenced by the great revolutionary poets of other Central American countries (Otto Rene Castillo of Guatemala, Roque Dalton of El Salvador); a poetry referring to culturally loaded objects, national names and places, the most local *topoi* and linguistic idiosyncracies, all there to underline and counteract the incursions and distortions of destructive and lying masterpowers. The very prosiness of exteriorist poetry, its ever-open, narrative, metonymic mode of discourse, its very refusal of the overtly poetic, metaphoric, pristine and symmetrical made it the perfect vehicle for a realistic evocation of a horrendous reality. Indeed *exteriorismo* was the ultimate fulfillment of Huidobro's call, taken up by the Nicaraguan vanguardists and given new, radical meaning by Cardenal and the many young Nicaraguan poets who were to follow him:

> *Why sing of the rose, oh poets!*
> *Make it flower in your poems!*

This was to be the major task of *exteriorismo*: to convert the *vanguardista* project of concrete, objectivist poetry into one by which poetry transcended its own productive mode and helped transform the very world it sought to render: to bring the rose of poetry to the Sandinista struggle, transforming poetic expression by taking on the weight of the Sandinista historical experience, fertilizing the seeds of revolutionary aspirations that they might flower in the field of action.

Speaking of the ideological basis and role of exteriorism, John Beverley reminds us that most of the older Nicaraguan poets (e.g., major vanguardists Jose Coronel Urtecho, Joaquin Pasos, and Pablo Antonio Cuadra) came from "the conservative landowning oligarchy the Somoza dynasty displaced." Cardenal was no exception. However, Beverley continues,

> His achievement, essential to the development of Sandinista ideology, was to interpolate a Marxist vision of history and class struggle through the belief structures (and discursive practices: prayers, sermons, homilies, etc.) of popular Catholicism. This allow[ed] him to record in what [Robert] Pring-Mill ... calls his "documentary poems" ... not only history (the history of a dominated and dependent Banana Republic), but history seen in the light of a possible redemption. ...

> The concern with recovering and expressing a tradition of struggle reflects the experience of a history which has been falsified, mutilated, lost, driven underground. Imperialism implies in part the corruption of language and memory, its subjection to commercialization and commodity fetishism (an insight Cardenal gets from Pound's fascist anticapitalism). The sources of collective amnesia are various: the simple suppression of the past (...Sandino's epic struggle against the Marines [does not figure,] for example, in the "official" histories); the impact of advertising and the commercial mass media; the mendacious political rhetoric of the dictators and their ; sycophants; etc. ... The loss of the past is also the loss of revolutionary possibility, since the revolution is the return of the repressed, as in Cardenal's identification of communism with milenarian primitive Christianity.
> --From "Sandinista Poetics," pp. 132-33.

In the hands of Cardenal, Fernando Gordillo, the young Leonel Rugama and scores of now known and still unknown Nicaraguans who participated in the creation of an ever-more honed political/cultural instrument, exteriorism was, for all its surface realism, for all its materiality and concreteness the expression of a core idealism with respect to life, possibility and hope. The harsh sounds of torture sessions and shootouts, the glare of National Guard searchlights and raw-bulbed Sandinista cell meetings all came together and were explicitly juxtaposed to a standard of truth and humanity. The alienation of verses, like the alienation of objects, people, families, was the counterpart of a diametrically opposed vision, Rousseauesque in one dimension (the values of the seignorial countryside over the capital-penetrated cities) and of course in another dimension, deeply communal.

In the massive transmutation of values implicit in exteriorism's violent juxtapositions and montages, the native Calibans struggling to conquer over the imposed Ariels were the true keepers of a spirit that would shine like the light of Sandino over the sinister tropical nights of the Somozas. This light would rise from the inferno of dictatorships, repression and defeat, to illuminate a transcendent revolutionary force which would find fulfillment in the creation of a new and radiant humanity.

Probably the decisive rupture in an already politicized Nicaraguan poetic system that leads directly to the poetic material we find in this book is Cardenal's *La hora cero*, published in 1960 and dealing with Sandino's campaigns, as well as the rebellion of Adolfo Baez Bone against Somoza Garcia in 1954. *Canto Nacional* would mark another turning point. But perhaps the most crucial work is *Oraculo sobre Managua*, first because Cardenal leaves behind his views on passive resistance to the dictatorship and champions a national solution through the FSLN, and second because he accomplishes this by centering his poem on a heightened retelling and glorification of Leonel Rugama. In effect, the spirit of Rugama is rekindled in Cardenal's work and thought, and comes to pervade the spirit of the young people Cardenal inspires to write poetry in Solentiname.

Following the lead of Rugama and Cardenal, these young people move from passive resistance based on religious conviction to taking up arms against the Somoza regime. Their poetry and action form the link from Rugama and Cardenal to the poetry which emerges in the months and years to come. In fact, as the writings contained in Book I, Part II, Section 3 reveal in the most dramatic form, many young Nicaraguans sought to combine political and poetic activity. A veritable anti-imperialist counter-culture steeped in poetry and then in the music by Carlos and Luis Mejia Godoy based on this poetry, had come to a crystalization which, centered on the image of Sandino, ultimately united otherwise disparate sectors in a broad coalition that toppled the dictatorship.

After the victory, a key question was how long the broad-based unity could last; how long could the eupohoria of revolution keep together sectors which had ultimately different historical projects and goals. A related question, of course, was what would happen to the counter-culture itself,and to the foremost expressive mode of that culture. Given a religious dimension by Cardenal, and then becoming the basis for a popular musical movement through the work of the Mejia Godoy brothers, Pancasan and others, poetry had served as a key nexus between the radical, revolutionary middle sectors and the people. What would happen to poetry, to exteriorist poetry, when it was no longer a counter-cultural mode, when it was no longer only a force of opposition, and when its prime inspiration (the negative to Sandino's positive) was no longer in power.

With the Victory, Cardenal tried to develop the Solentiname model on a national level through his post as head of the *Ministerio de Cultura*. The Ministry's goal, said Cardenal, "is the democratization of culture. To bring culture to the people who were marginalized from it. We want a culture that is not the culture of an elite, of a group that is considered 'cultured,' but rather of an entire people... Our people have expropriated their culture, which is now their own, as they are owners of their land and their historical identity."

As for poetry, within a few months after the revolution, Cardenal commissioned Mayra Jimenez, his poetry specialist from Solentiname days, to launch a series of popular poetry workshops throughout the country. Shortly after, Cardenal could boast that many workshops had been established, and workshop poems had begun to appear in the major cultural organs of Nicaragua. And in the midst of all the challenges of Reconstruction, amidst all the internal struggles, the border menaces, the indirect and direct interventions and incursions, amidst all the problems that a small and poor country can have in developing a new system, the workshop program developed and thrived.

Indeed by the end of 1982, the workshops had entered into the postliteracy campaign areas and in the heart of every new structure created by the Revolution. Hundreds of young people took part in the workshops, giving expression to their perceptions, preoccupations and aspirations through their writings, and finding in their poetry a laboratory for ideological development and struggle. As workshop poems continued to appear and new centers continued to open, Cardenal could only remark:

> The production of new poetry is startling. There are poetry workshops in the poorest neighborhoods, in factories, in the Army and even in the police precinct offices. I think that Nicaragua is the only country in the world where poetry produced by the police is published.
> --From "Con Ernesto Cardenal," in *Amanacer: Reflexion cristiana en la nueva Nicaragua* (Managua, 1981), pp. 3, 15-16.

And yet like everything else that has emerged since the Revolution, Nicaragua's poetic production under the aegis of the Ministry of Culture is a matter for constant commentary and debate. Daily the controversy rages over the results of the workshops. Even confirmed Sandinists have complained about this poetic production, have said it's bad, artificial, too derivative of master-poet Cardenal, too prosaic, too propagandistic. Some have claimed that the uncodified and ever-changing principles of revolutionary *exteriorismo* have now taken on an academic, institutionalized air, and become a "prolet-cult"-style standard for the writing of poetry. Many young Nicaraguan poets intent on imitating every superficial aspect of Cardenal's poetic style and orientation, so that a rigid posture of "revolutionary virtue and commitment" is said to dominate and stultify national poetic production.

Cardenal himself has perhaps encouraged this view by his adamant defense of the workshops and his inculcation of a virtual formula for the writing of workshop poems, as set forth in his text, "Some Rules for Writing Poetry," first produced in mimeograph for the use of the workshop poets. Of this text, Robert Pring-Mill has written:

> The rules themselves seem a bit simplistic (the initial phrase, "It's easy to write good poetry," seems aimed at scandalizing the academic critic!), and great attention is paid to the document in workshop session--a fact which helps one understand why the poetry so didactically simplistic. It is natural that established poets, conscious of the existing danger of the over-literal application of Cardenal's rules don't embrace them. It is certain that some good poets will emerge from the collective experience of the workshop discussions, even if the result in the short run is the production of a young generation involved in the creation of "photographic" poems full of a message as direct (although in the majority of cases without the subtleties) as certain recent works of Cardenal. Nevertheless, one shouldn't judge the poetry workshops only in function of their poetry; the greatest cultural benefit resulting from this type of movement is the promotion of literary consciousness and confidence in oneself, in a generation whose civic and cultural consciousness was formed ...by their participation in the literacy campaign, as those teaching or learning literacy.
> --Pring-Mill, in "Poesia de la Nueva Nicaragua," in *Nicarauac*, VI, p. 152.

Truly there have been some imitation, posing and sheer banality in this new poetry. And yet some valuable work has already emerged from the efforts of the young poets. And their staunch champion, Ernesto Cardenal, has defended the workshop poetry as the enthusiastic expression of poor people who now have the opportunity to write and grow in a new society, and as representing the first and necessary stage in the development of a new revolutionary culture. Indeed, Cardenal is quick to point out how the publication and even criticism of these first poems by young men and women should lead to a deeper and more extensive development of the nation's cultural life.

In the volume at hand, readers may make their own judgements about Nicaragua's poetry of Reconstruction. And it may be that, arranged in function of chronology and theme, arranged as tiny pieces in the mosaic of revolutionary process, the poems take on greater strength and integrity than they have in isolation or as part of a disordered cluster. At the least, their relation to the political turn of the mainstream tradition of

Nicaraguan poetry may stand out in clearer relief as well. Indeed we should emphasize that just as most of the poems in Book I were written during the Reconstruction, so many of them, including one in Book I, Part I, were produced in Nicaragua's poetry workshops. Weaved with proto-workshop people's poetry and verse-cut political discourse by people participating in the revolutionary process, the workshop poetry touches on virtually every dimension of the Insurrection and every major theme of the Reconstruction. It provides a graphic and human portrait of a social process and the contours of a culture in transformation as its spokespeople give expression to it.

5. *Final Details, Acknowledgements & Closing Remarks*

To make matters somewhat easier for readers, the workshop poems themselves are always identified by reference to the particular workshop to which a given writer belongs. For the sake of brevity, however, subsequent references to writers already represented and identified in a given section are simply denoted by their last names; and in such cases, their workshop affiliations are not repeated. We should also note that there are two poets named Fernando Silva and two named Roberto Vargas. The Fernandos are father and son, and are so specified in the text. As to the Robertos, one is a young workshop poet, and is identified as such; while the second is the U.S.-based Nicaraguan poet currently serving as Cultural and Labor Counselor in Washington's Nicaraguan Embassy. A few poems, including two by the second Vargas and the one by Margaret Randall, were written in English and are so identified. Those passages initially written in prose and cut in verse form are indicated by means of an asterisk (*). But above all we should note that for the sake of producing this volume economically, we were compelled to modify line divisions so that we could double-column most of the poetic text; furthermore, we were forced into a mode of typesetting which did not allow for the Spanish accent marks needed for proper names and places, and we then decided against hand-writing in the accent marks to avoid producing a less attractive text. We deeply regret having had to take these steps, but they were ultimately necessitated by the current U.S. attitude toward the New Nicaragua which left us without a solid financial base for publishing this book in a more satisfactory way.

As I close these introductory comments, I wish to acknowledge the support of the Illinois Arts Council, which provided me with the financial support I needed to complete a draft of this volume during the summer of 1983. Furthermore, I should like to thank the Crossroads Fund and the Capp Street Foundation for backing *Voces desde Nicaragua*, where some of the sections of this book first appeared. And I should like to thank all the friends and colleagues who bore with me as I manically made my way along the five-year plus road to completing what was for me a difficult and sometimes painful task.

As I examine the manuscript and mark final corrections, I am overwhelmed by the number of people who, as poets, translators, researchers, commentators and collaborators, contributed to the making of this book. I am also struck by how, helped by all these people, I have kept my promise to Ernesto Cardenal and other poets in Nicaragua. I trust that the resulting text will meet all expectations and serve the vital promise of the Sandinista Revolution itself.

This volume of poetry and history is dedicated to *Ana Maria Andara*, a Nicaraguan woman who gave so much for the Revolution and the Reconstruction from her home in Ensenada, Baja California, Mexico. From this one dear human being, the volume then evokes the loftiest aspirations of all those who have struggled and all those who have fallen in helping to make National Reconstruction a reality, with the hope that Nicaragua's revolutionary voices may now ring out clearly to people whose primary language is English. The publication of this volume at a time when many are seeking to discredit and actually undermine Nicaragua and her Revolution, and when more people die each day trying to defend what has been won at so great a sacrifice, may be taken as a call to further solidarity with the cause of a beleaguered people.

BOOK I.
YEARS OF INTERVENTION, DOMINATION, STRUGGLE & INSURRECTION

Rubble remaining from 1972 earthquake. Downtown Managua, February 1977. Photo by Loretta Smith.

INTRODUCTION TO BOOK I & PART I.
NICARAGUA, A HISTORY OF STRUGGLE

1. Structural Perspectives

Nicaragua is the largest of all the Central American republics (130,000 square kilometers) and the least populated (2,500,000 by recent count). Except for gold, the country's natural resources are insignificant. The principal exports have been cotton, coffee, sugar, meat and bananas.

The most important geographical characteristics are its two great lakes: Lake Nicaragua, more than 100 kilometers long and 45 kilometers wide; and Lake Managua to the north, which is 38 kilometers long and 10 to 16 kilometers wide. Lake Nicaragua flows into the Caribbean Sea through the navegable San Juan River, and the distance from the east coast of the lake to the Pacific Ocean is only 18 kilometers at the widest point.

To these accidental geographical and ultimately geopolitical factors must be added another one: Nicaragua's proximity to the U.S., which gives it a strategic location in the U.S. empire's defense and security system. These factors combined to seal Nicaragua's historic situation from the time of independence and determined the future development of the country. Nicaragua's history would be one of struggle between the capitalist interests of the Republic to the north and, ultimately, the democratic interests of the Nicaraguan people.

Virtually corollaries to the nation's basic situation are the following dimensions of Nicaragua's history: 1) the ubiquitous threat and actuality of U.S. intervention (the *contras* are just the latest twist); 2) the national bourgeois liberalism of the Zelaya years; 3) the agonizing polemic over the feasibility of building a canal; 4) forty-three years of uninterrupted military dictatorship; 5) the semi-colonial status which this political structure imposed on the country; 6) a precarious economic development based on a narrow band of farm products and subordinated by the U.S.'s strategic interests in times of peace as well as times of war; 7) the Somoza family's monopolization of the nation's wealth and consequently the limited development of the national bourgeoisie; 8) the Nicaraguan people's constant resistance to U.S. invasion and Somocista tyranny.

The collage of chronology and poetry which constitutes Part I of Book I reviews several of the historical events that correspond to the factors cited. It sets forth the initial efforts of U.S. control and intervention, the transformation of the countryside in the late 19th Century, the Zelaya years and the direct U.S. intervention and control throughout this Century. Culminating fairly abruptly and negatively with the split of the Frente Sandinista into three factions and the death of their leader, Carlos Fonseca Amador, the material does set forth many of the salient points of modern Nicaraguan history, especially during the forty-plus years of the Somocista dictatorship and the first fifteen years of Sandinista growth and resistance.

What such a chronological treatment cannot do of course is provide a full sense of the deep structure of events in Nicargua, or a full picture of the complex interplay of forces that leads to the insurrectional, revolutionary crisis which, we know, was to overcome the country in the two and half years to be depicted in the subsequent part of our book.

That "deep structure" has to do with the conversion of the Nicaraguan economy and the stake of different national and international forces in the process. Liberals and Conservatives fought decade after decade in function of different developmental projects or their part in them. As the U.S became a major international force, its ability to influence the direction of national development came to dominate over local concerns. Clearly the implantation of the Somoza dictatorship was the cement required to accommodate and when necessary throttle the contending parties while keeping the country on a course relatively consonant with U.S. designs.

However, the dictatorship's internal momentum, its need for increasingly repressive functions to maintain its rule, and its need to extend national pillage to satisfy those whose loyalty it required, led to an ever-more precarious situation in which no dominant national bourgeois sector could find satisfaction (except the Somoza group itself) and in which the only viable, forceful opposition to the dictatorship came to lie in the hands of a small group of dissatisfied "middle sector" rebels who, capable over the years of attracting ever-larger numbers of people, finally threatened to upset the U.S. design and all contending national bourgeois projects.

The story in the first part of our volume is of the rise of this group, the Frente Sandinista, out of the early struggle against U.S. intervention and control (and most especially out of the campaign of Sandino himself, as well as the anti-imperialist ideology which began to accrue to his name), and then, directly as a response to the structural characteristics and evolution of the Somoza period itself.

To best round out and underpin the materials presented in our poetry/chronology collage, then, we will turn our attention here to certain crucial features of the Somoza period up to 1977.

2. The Somozas in Power

The Somoza dictatorship passed through several stages of development sustained by the family's monopolistic control of the economy and by the military force of the National Guard. Until the mid-1940s, the dictator held relative legitimacy among those sectors of society who, in their own self-interest, cloaked their leader with an image of "pacifier" and "innovator." By the mid-40s, Somoza's intentions to establish himself in perpetuity became clear, thus betraying the nationalist recovery goals of the Liberal Party, which the dictator now dominated. Furthermore, because of the democratic surge developing in Central America (emerging from the struggle against fascism during World War II), Somoza entered a period of isolation. The dictatorship lost its aura of legitimacy and maintained its control only through the coercion and power of the National Guard.

By this time large numbers of liberals had abandoned Somoza and formed the Independent Liberal Party, which together with the Conservative Party constituted a bloc of opposition to the dictatorship. This bloc, however, was far from solid, since members and sectors of each party could be led to accommodation with the regime for the sake of winning certain short term benefits for themselves or groups important to the maintenance of their own position. This situation, and the corruption it frequently implied, joined with the military might of the Guards to sustain the regime over the years.

Once the crisis of the second half of the 1940s had passed, a new stage developed. Worldwide economic recovery in the postwar period and technological developments in the area of agricultural chemicals facilitated the rapid expansion of cotton cultivation, which gave Nicargua a primarily agrarian export economy. The resulting profits led to a wholesale extension and diversification of the productive potential of the country.

Based primarily on cotton and secondarily on the expansion of coffee and beef exports, the national economy experienced significant growth and modernization. Capital accumulation, mainly agrarian based, was transferred to other economic sectors such as industry, finance and commerce. This new wealth was dominated by the Somoza family which had become synonymous with "the State." With this control over the expansion and diversification process, Somoza greatly increased his impact upon the social life of the country.

Economic changes led new social sectors to emerge, while others rapidly deteriorated. Cotton production, mainly in the departments of Managua and Masaya, as well as those along the West coast, accelerated a process of concentrating vast agrarian properties into a few hands. This same process converted large numbers of small farmers into plantation workers and produced a significant migration of other peasants off the land. These migrants converged particularly on Managua and the west coast cities of Leon and Chinandega, overloading the urban employment market, straining the weak social service structures, and creating widespread marginalization.

Meanwhile, expanded employment in industrial, financial and state bureaucratic sectors had given birth to a new salaried middle class, which grew so rapidly that its members failed to question the source of their genesis and tended to legitimize the dictatorship. Along with the new cotton producing capitalists, who were completely dependent on the financial and technical assistance of the State, the new middle class fortified Somocista control.

Nevertheless the older Liberal/Conservative conflict lived on during the 1950s. The conservative oligarchy kept its partial autonomy from the state through its coffee and beef production and sales. As the regime attempted to crack down on them, they and other opponents went so far as to involve themselves in coup and assassination plots (e.g., the abortive 1954 Baez Bone rebellion and the 1956 killing of Somoza Garcia by Rigoberto Lopez Perez). Only U.S. Ambassador Whelan's intervention in favor of Luis Somoza's coming to power dampened the growing conservative opposition to the dynasty.

The advent of the Central American Common Market in the early 1960s stimulated industrialization and modernization. The Somozas kept old and new bourgeois sectors at bay by their bureaucratic and military hold over industrial and agrarian structures, including the access to loans and export markets so crucial to bourgeois survival and growth. The share of national wealth controled by Conservatives became dependent on Somoza because all Nicaraguan industry was controlled through the State's fiscal, credit and commercial arrangements. Thus the Conservatives had to achieve accommodation with Somoza forces, which, developing from the late 1950s, ended Conservative independence and the resonance of the Liberal/Conservative rivalry.

The 1960s were the time of greatest Somocista power and legitimation. The parasitic economic groups in the apparatus controlled by Somoza and the economic growth of the period gave the dynasty immeasurable influence on all upper class sectors. Somoza's hegemony was assured through coercion, extortion and fraud, through the accumulation of family assets, innumerable links with U.S. capital, close ties with Central American oligarchs and bourgeois sectors and, all else failing, his U.S. backed National Guard, itself linked to other repressive Central American military machines.

However the very success of the Somozas produced social immiseration and opposition that were to bring down the dynasty. As old and new bourgeois elites prospered, broad sectors became ever poorer. An enormous unemployed work force emerged from population growth and the massive migration of dispossessed rural workers. Among those remaining in the countryside, a third were landless and another third barely survived on miserable low-yield plots. Administrative corruption blocked any adequate social service programs for an increasingly miserable populace. An ever greater unequal distribution of wealth crippled internal market expansion and general economic development. Nicaragua's agriculture and industry diversified, but the nation remained dependent on exported farm products subject to world price fluctuations. The poles of prosperity and misery were to prove essential to the dynasty's ultimate crisis.

By the late 1950s the Liberal/Conservative dichotomy in Nicaraguan politics was so debilitated, that opposition, resistance and rebellion began taking on a variety of new, tentative forms--including a series of skirmishes carried out by aging veterans of Sandino's campaigns, along with groups of younger people seeking some effective, militant mode of resistance to the regime. Certain of these young people, as well as others who left the reformist Nicaraguan Socialist Party, which they viewed as a dead end, found their place in a new organization, which in the early 1960s, took on the name of the Sandinista National Liberation Front.

As the fledgling organization served its painful, seemingly quixotic apprenticeship, often incurring terrible and tragic losses, other new groups and coalitions embarked on reformist projects that made occasional inroads but did not go very far, because of a fear of impairing their interests by granting concessions to popular demands or inciting Somoza's armed wrath. It was only the militant guerilla group which ultimately posed a dangerous threat to the order of things.

By the early 1960s, the United States, fearful of Cuban-style revolutions throughout Latin America, changed its overall strategy in an effort to conciliate the disenfranchised masses by a reformist campaign, the Alliance for Progress. In Nicaragua, the Alliance favored better income distribution, changes in tax structure, land distribution and a change of government from Somoza militarism to a charade of civil rule under Rene Schick.

The Alliance was in fact part of a counterinsurgency strategy operating on two different but mutually supportive levels: superficial pacifying social reforms, and intensified military control to halt revolutionary movements. This two-pronged strategy resulted in two new structures: the Central American Defense Council (CONDECA) and the Central American Common Market. The cosmetic quality of Alliance reforms was particularily visible in patterns of land distribution, which tended to focus on areas undergoing insurgency.

The Common Market spurred import substitution. U.S. multinationals profitting from "free zone" tax exemption seized the most important sectors of industry, installing premade factories that were easily transferable to other countries in case of labor or political troubles. Mainly involved in light industry, they took a share from the already precarious national bourgeoisie. United Brands acquired Corona Oil; Nabisco took over a bisquit factory; American Standard controlled ceramics.

Designed to operate in countries that had reached a high level of division of labor, the Common Market industries depended on semi-manufactured products and raw materials produced outside the country, thus intensifying decapitalization and dependency. From the outset, Common Market factories enjoyed rights to loans, free exchange, and freedom in determining export quantities, resulting in an absolute dependence on foreign loans to cover growing deficits.

Thus the plan to eliminate growing popular agitation through grandiose reform programs only intensified structural dependence on the metropolis. Furthermore, social and economic conditions were maturing which would only prepare the ground for even greater revolutionary violence. Indeed, the revolutionary movement deepened, especially after the Pancasan confrontation of 1967, when the FSLN, having survived its early period of difficulties, began a phase of consolidation. By that year, the U.S. strategy, albeit its short term successes, had lain the grounds for a situation in which, Nicaragua, its most loyal Central American client, would soon become the weakest link in the imperialist chain.

Believing their nation's vital interests to be menaced by increasing revolutionary activity, U.S. foreign policy-makers abandoned their reformist strategies. Nicaragua's democratic facade gave way to stepped-up military programs and counter-revolutionary violence. In 1967, Luis Somoza died, and the last phase of the dynasty began. Anastasio Somoza, Jr., educated militarily and politically in the U.S., took over the presidency and began reinforcing military rule. "Tacho" equipped the National Guard with modern arms, imported specialized personnel to provide counterinsurgency training, turned the police and security agencies into modern anti-subversive units, and coordinated National Guard activities with CONDECA.

The regime looked relatively secure, as Sandinista *foco* efforts failed, and as middle class sectors seemed to be caught up in a process of social and economic self-improvement. But the contradictions of the model of economic and social growth created conflicts that set the stage for crisis. The first crisis, one of the overall Central American Common Market (1969-70), coincided with a decline in international prices for primary agricultural and beef products. The result was a decline of economic growth and private investment. Unemployment increased and real income fell, as a general stagnation set in. Ironically, as our collage/chronology notes, the 1972 earthquake somewhat reversed the trend, especially when joined with favorable world market agricultural prices in 1974 and 1975.

However the earthquake and its aftermath deepened the conflict between the Somoza bureaucrats and other bourgeois sectors. Using State power, the Somoza bloc aggravated administrative corruption, and cut off other entrepreneurs from earthquake-related investment prospects. Somoza enriched himself by organizing his own bank, insurance company, finance and construction firms and taking over the most dynamic areas of capital accumulation. The government's failure to respond to the people's needs alienated middle class support and intensified opposition among the poor, leading to a widespread political radicalization.

To finance his post-quake projects, Somoza borrowed large sums and thus increased the rate of foreign indebtedness by 400 percent over a five year period. Furthermore, the debt was administered by Somoza's own corrupt, inefficient and almost bankrupt financial institutions. As his regime entered into crisis, growing numbers of Nicaraguans were faced with a choice of opposition in a young revolutionary movement still in the process of consolidation and a nebulous reformist sector seeking deeper social roots.

A major force in the growing opposition stemming from Somoza's earthquake bonanza was the Church sector, which was outraged by Somoza's post-earthquake dealings (see Introduction to Part II). Another source of growing opposition was the Democratic Union of Liberation (UDEL) which appealed mainly to those bourgeois sectors who felt their future menaced by Somoza's latest actions, and who united around a platform calling for the recovery of democratic rights and a social and economic transformation of the society.

But the third source was the FSLN itself, especially in the wake of the guerilla action of December, 1974. The Sandinistas were becoming increasingly associated with the struggle for democratic renewal, and especially with the immediate problems and demands of the poorest sectors of the populace. They began establishing bases among the people which in time helped the organization to overcome its earlier political and strategic isolation.

As the period described in our chronology/collage draws to a close, Somoza is still very much in power, but the bases of his support have eroded. They will further erode in the two and a half years remaining to the dynasty. The development of Church opposition, of opposition from the bourgeoisie and also a new U.S. administration whose human rights policy will cause it to fall away from Somoza as his efforts to hold power reach even newer levels of ruthlessness--all of these will be crucial in the fall of the dictatorship. But the most crucial factor will be the development of the Sandinistas and their relation to the increasingly organized rage of the people.

By 1976 the FSLN has split into three factions and the Sandinistas' most important leader, Carlos Fonseca has died. However, as Part II of Book I will show, the Sandinista split, while leading to differences in political line and practice that made it difficult for the three groups to reunite, served to strengthen the FSLN by broadening its perspectives and allowing for the full development of three positions which, when finally brought together, led to a successful synthesis. Perhaps it is an anticipation of ultimate synthesis which characterizes the final poems of this part of our book, referring to the fallen Sandinist leader and yet speaking of hope, joy and determination.

3. The Poetry in Part I

While most of the poetry in this volume was written during the Final Insurrection or during the Reconstruction, this part of our book presents fragments from the entire tradition of political poetry of Nicaragua, including a few post-victory selections and even one written in the Reconstruction's poetry workshops. As mentioned in our General Introduction, perhaps most worthy of note about the form of the section is the use of the lyrics from "The History of Uncle Sam," a spirited song about U.S. intervention in Nicaragua written and sung by the musical group, *Pancasan*, and very popular throughout Nicaragua in the first year of the Reconstruction.

But other pieces are also worth mentioning: first, the two selections by Ernesto Cardenal, one from his first great historical epic, *Hora Cero*, and then another from his post-victory opus; the excerpt from Francisco Hernandez Segura, an all but forgotten early champion of the FSLN; the poems by and about Leonel Rugama, the poet-revolutionary who would be the central inspiration for so much of the poetry written during the Final Insurrection and the Reconstruction; the selections by Michele Najlis and Gioconda Belli, anticipating the great number of women who would participate and write poetry in the years to come, and speaking for their presence in the pre-insurrectional period; and finally the poems by important historical figures--Edwin Castro and Rigoberto Lopez Perez, protagonists in the execution of Somoza Garcia; and then Daniel Ortega and Tomas Borge, representing different Sandinista tendencies in 1976 but together in the

Insurrection and the Reconstruction.

Different figures of the Nicaraguan poetic tradition appear: Dario, the great modernist; Pablo Antonio Cuadra, one of the leaders of Nicaragua's poetic vanguard (he represents the Conservative wing that first went with and then broke with Somoza, ultimately joining UDEL before the Revolution, and staying with *La Prensa* when it turned against the Sandinistas); and a fellow member of Cardenal's own poetic generation, Ernesto Mejia Sanchez. Several of these figures and others from Nicaragua's rich poetic tradition will reappear later in this book. But readers will be most struck by the dominance of new and younger voices expressing a sensibility forged in the fires of insurrection and reconstruction.

BOOK I, PART I. 155 YEARS OF STRUGGLE (1821-1976)

Section 1. *Early Interventions & Sandino's Campaign*

1821-1856: Nicaragua wins independence from Spain only to suffer from regionwide civil wars between Liberals and Conservatives struggling for economic and political hegemony in the new nation. With the "gold rush" in California, Nicaragua becomes a preferred route to the U.S. West Coast. Seeing the country's potential as a trade route, England and the U.S. sign the Bulwer Clayton Treaty of 1850, agreeing to share profits from any canal built on Nicaraguan soil. Six years later, U.S. southerner William Walker enters Nicaragua with his filibusterers, invited by the Conservatives to help them in their struggle against the Liberals. However, intent on setting up a slave state that could flourish through Atlantic-Pacific trade, Walker has himself elected President and rules for three years until ousted by a united Central American army.

1. Pancasan/ THE HISTORY OF UNCLE SAM

In 1856
pro-slavists from
the U.S. South
came to conquer
not to say rob,
led by William Walker,

and in San Jacinto they felt
the points of our shoes
and running like the devil
the imperialist gringos left.
This just marked the start
of their perennial intervention.

1860-1909: Nicaragua's large cattle-raising *haciendas* and grain-growing collectives are gradually replaced by large commercial estates, or *latifundia.* Large numbers of peasants are pushed off their small holdings and common lands, and into semi-proletarian status. Under the banners of Conservative and Liberal Parties, sectors of the bourgeoisie fight, compromise, then fight again, as they jostle for oligarchic status in relation to a new order which involves Nicaragua's entry into the world economy as a coffee producer. Finally, Jose Santos Zelaya becomes president in 1893 and initiates the Liberal Reform, strengthening the state and legal apparatuses, modernizing the financial and productive infrastructure, and incorporating the Atlantic Coast. But Zelaya also develops nationalist, protectionist policies which by strengthening new finance capital sectors, threaten Conservative projects and Dollar Diplomacy interests in a weak nation dependent on U.S. capital.

2. Pancasan/ UNCLE SAM

Zelaya came to power
through revolution
and the Creole bourgeoisie
took its first steps

when down came the big stick
courtesy of Uncle Sam
seems he blew his stack
when Zelaya wouldn't bow.

1909: Fomenting discord between Liberal and Conservative oligarchic sectors, the U.S. intervenes and helps Conservative candidate Estrada to overthrow Zelaya.

3. Ruben Dario/ THE SWANS

So many millions will we speak English?
Will we remain silent now only to cry later?

1912: Through Estrada, the U.S. begins eliminating Zelaya's protectionist barriers. U.S. loans and investments dominate over local bourgeois efforts. When Liberals, led by Benjamin Zeledon, seek to resist, U.S. Marines invade Nicargua through the Pacific port of Corinto, attacking the rebellious Liberals and executing their leader.

4. Jose Santos Rivera/ ZELEDON

He loved liberty more than life
and couldn't bear to see his
    homeland
stomped on by hooves of vile
    invaders.
So, seeing his flag trampled,
he left his protest hoisted

on murderous rifle barrels.

5. Pancasan/ UNCLE SAM

And for more than 13 Aprils
the Yankee invaders stayed.

1912-1925: The U.S. begins to control finance capital, monetary reform, the banks, customs and transportation. According to the Chamorro-Bryan Pact (1914), the U.S. pays $3 million for permanent rights to build a canal and establish military bases. Army occupation troops control key administrative functions; natural resources are exploited at will, and the national wealth is controlled by U.S. banks. The U.S. presence permeates the country at every level.

6. Ernesto Cardenal/ ZERO HOUR

They corrupt our prose
and corrupt our Congress.
Bananas are left rotting
on the plantations,
or in freight cars on the rails,
or they're cut over-ripe
so they're rejected
when they reach the dock,
or they're tossed into the sea;

the bunches declared bruised
or too small,
or spotted, or too green,
or too ripe, or diseased;
so there's no cheap bananas
or so they can buy bananas cheap.
Till there's starvation
on Nicaragua's Atlantic Coast.

1925-1927: During a brief absence of U.S. troops, Conservative General Chamorro breaks the U.S.-maneuvered oligarchic pact by denying Liberal Vice-President Sacasa his right to presidential succession and taking office by force. Under Liberal Jose Maria Moncada, a "Constitutionalist Army" fights against Chamorro's Conservatives, threatening U.S.-backed oligarchs and winning support from Mexico. As the struggle takes on a more popular character throughout the country and Chomorro's troops retreat, U.S. troops once again invade Nicaragua. They force Chamorro to hand over the presidency to Adolfo Diaz, and on May 4, 1927, get Moncada to sign a truce in return for controlled elections in 1928.

7. Pancasan/ UNCLE SAM

It was '26
when they came back
once more they had
to firm up their interests;
a great civil war

had just broken out
and at Espino Negro
a pact was signed
that was no more nor less
than a base betrayal...

1927: Constitutionalist Army General Augusto Cesar Sandino rejects the treaty, forms a peasant "Army in Defense of National Sovereignty" and begins a guerilla war against U.S. troops and Moncada's soldiers.

8. Leonel Rugama/ LIKE THE SAINTS

"There was a Nicaraguan from
 Niquinohomo
who wasn't a politician or soldier."
He fought in the Segovia mountains.

9. Pancasan/ UNCLE SAM

The traitor Moncada told
the Americans
all my men surrender
except one pain-in-the-neck
named Sandino...

10. Mario Cajina-Vega/ SANDINO

I was born in this countryside
that longs to be a country.
I come from the mountains,
from the heights I come,
I'm waiting here
to witness the miracle:
this countryside become
the homeland I hope for.
The one I dreamt of as a child
when the homeland was
the map of my house
and the town where I was born.
A town with flags
in peasant hands
with guns and tatters
and proud gestures
and shouts of protest
which I never heard again.
A tiny man
was the leader of them all,
he had a vibrant voice
with trumpeting echoes.
They fought for the Homeland
against the murderous Yankees,
their tiny leader
was named Sandino.

11. Rugama/ LIKE THE SAINTS

And once he wrote to Froylan
    Turcios
saying that if the Yankees
were to kill all his fighters
through some trick of Fate,
in their hearts
they would find the largest
treasure of patriotism,
and this would humiliate
    the chicken
the North American seal
passed off as an eagle.

12. Pancasan/ UNCLE SAM

And the guerilla fighter's campaign
made wondrous history
and in '33 the gringos left,
badly bruised,
once again in Nicaragua
the mouse beat up the cat.

1933-34: Before leaving, the U.S. military sets up a fully trained, equipped and funded National Guard under the direction of Anastasio Somoza Garcia, who then conspires with U.S. officials to do away with Sandino. On February 21, 1934, Sandino is assassinated. The process begins which brings the Somoza Dynasty to power.

13. Pancasan/ UNCLE SAM

...It couldn't last
so then came the disgrace
they had the heroic
guerilla fighter killed
by a butcherous tyrant
named Somoza
and his hated dictatorship
was born in '34
the work of Uncle Sam
to watch over his business
and for more than 40 years
we had to live in terror.

14. Edwin Castro/ AMBUSH

The dailies will no longer recount
his feats of war
nor will he return to his ranch
covered with medals.
The earth cradles him
in its dark arms,
and when the soldier quietly asks,
"Where is Mr. Sandino?"
the roadsides
will respond a thousand times:
Sandino is in the pines!
Sandino is in the mountains!
Sandino is in the rocks!
Sandino is in the rivers!
Sandino is in the towns!
Sandino is in the valleys!
Sandino is...! Sandino...!
Sandino is Nicaragua!

Section 2. The Somoza Heydays & the Rise of the FSLN

1934-56: After seizing formal power from Sacasa in 1936, Somoza Garcia establishes a long and corrupt dictatorship, sustained by monopolistic control of the economy, the National Guard's military power and overall U.S. backing. Until the mid-'40's Somoza holds relative legitimacy with most monied sectors; during World War II, he openly betrays his Liberal Party by making clear his plans for permanent rule. A new Independent Liberal Party emerges which often allies with the Conservative Party in opposing Somoza. There are attempted coups and rebellions. But the dictator survives, partially on the basis of the post-War economic boom but mainly through the force of his National Guard, which brings repression, oppression and assassination, sending some to prison, and others into exile, leading still others to desperation...

1. Ernesto Mejia Sanchez/ STAINS
   OF THE TIGER

We can't avoid revealing
the rancor our writing etches
and renders visible.
We decorate the mindless destroyer,
the decline of goodness.
We move forward on the wings
of delirious resentment.
We're carried off without
   consultation.
We're nothing more than stains.
   Pure stains taken off
and put on by the ungovernment
of the bloody one.

2. Mejia Sanchez/ TO THE POETS
   IN EXILE

We don't envy your comforts
nor your insults of the dictator
or your epic poems to Sandino;
such things are easy
outside our borders.
We prefer to be here, until
the dictator transforms
every word we haven't said
into a well-aimed missile;
we want Sandino
to be reborn among us.

1956: On September 21, rebel poet Rigoberto Lopez Perez, with the collaboration of Edwin Castro, Ausberto Narvaez and Cornelio Silva Arguello, brings Anastasio Somoza to justice. Lopez Perez is killed. The dictator's eldest son, Luis, takes power with U.S. backing. He captures and kills the "assassins" and unleashes a reign of terror worse than any known in Nicaragua up to that time.

3. Rigoberto Lopez Perez/
   ANXIETY

I am suffering.
I feel the pain of my entire
   homeland,
and in my veins roams
a hero seeking freedom.
My days' flowers
will always be withered
if the tyrant's blood
is in their veins.
I am seeking the fish of liberty
within the death of the tyrant.

4. Cardenal/ THE PORK
   RIGOBERTO DIDN'T EAT

Rigoberto Lopez Perez arrived
at the Central Park of Leon
September 21, 1956, in the evening
   and there he saw some friends,
and bought a fried pork
and set about eating the pork
with yuca in a banana leaf,
and he barely ate anything,
only some two mouthfuls,
he wasn't hungry, and he threw
the pork with yuca to the ground
with the leaf, and saw a worker
who was very drunk and a beggar,
and he said: "This is going
to come to an end now."
   And he went where he had to go.

5. Pablo Antonio Cuadra/ IN THE
   HEAT

...The excited birds
dance with ingenuous joy
around the serpent's cadaver,
as if with its death,
Evil had ended forever.

So the people leaped into the streets,
jubilant, waving flags,
believing that a single man
summed up their wrongs
dancing in the sun
while in the dark crevice
of one or two hearts
the new tyranny quietly nestled...

1957-60: In answer to the new regime and the failure of individual acts of heroism, groups of guerilla fighters, inspired by Sandino and recent events in Cuba, begin to organize and confront the Somocistas. In 1958, battles in Los Encinos, Jicaro and El Dorado culminate with the costly struggle of El Chaparral. In 1959, student orgzanizations demonstrate, only to be cut down by the Guards. But clearly a new generation is on the move.

6. Francisco Hernandez Segura/
   EL CHAPARRAL

Guerilla fighters who stayed behind
under the skies, in Chaparral,
on warming your blood,
the sun became a wheat field!
From your blood, spilled
for the homeland, guerilla fighters,
comes so much light on the roads:
a treasure of stars.

7. Pancasan/ CONCERNING THE
   PEOPLE'S FREEDOM

During nineteen hundred
fifty-nine, the police
fired on the students' march
since then we began
to prepare our offensive
because you overthrow a system
of violence with violence.

1961-64: Learning from these experiences, Carlos Fonseca Amador, Silvio Mayorga and Tomas Borge form a new organization which comes to take the name of the "Sandinist Front of National Liberation" (FSLN). From 1962 on, guerilla struggle intensifies, with confrontations in Coco, Bocaycito, and Bocay, in a failing Sandinist effort to establish a rural base.

8. Michele Najlis/ TO THE MARTYRS OF BOCAY

With all the outrage of your death
with all the blood of your life
with all the love of your struggle,

with all the clay of your land,
and with the water of your rivers,
with air, with fire,

with the children of your blood,
with what you have left us

with all this and what we have;
we shall build our world.

1964-67: The FSLN cooperates with traditional left parties, concentrating their efforts on urban organizing committees in the poor barrios. As a response to the growingly organized opposition, Luis Somoza collaborates actively in the formation of the Central American Defense Council (CONDECA), which will coordinate counterinsurgency actions for the area. In spite of this, the FSLN reacts against the move of left parties into electoral politics by intensifying their agitational work in the cities and returning to the mountains to organize the Pancasan guerilla group. In the Pancasan campaign, 20 of 35 combatants fall, but the FSLN claims to have succeeded in establishing a rural base. Entering into a strategic period entitled, "the accumulation of forces in silence," they begin to establish intermediate organizations of students, workers, Christian and cultural groups as "the umbilical cord" between themselves and the people. Somoza suddenly dies, and his West Point-trained brother Anastasio, Chief of the National Guard, takes power to direct the nation's repressive apparatus against the forces of revolution.

9. Ricardo Morales Aviles/ PANCASAN

We were on night's edge
and abandoned our useless
   meekness
bent on conquering power
by using rifles.
What happened while
some combed their hair,
chewed gum or slept indifferently
in their beds?
We opened huge holes in the silence
and dented the chariot of war,
we marched like those
who never question the trees
along a different path where
unknown scandals of the soul
   circulate;
because we were nothing
but the guerilla fighter's passion,
two, three or more whistles
giving clear notice to the stars.

We died so many times
that we closed our eyes to memory
and bandaged our million wounds
   with dreams,
so that death no longer exists,
that we overcalculate fear's
   magnitude
and that no joy will suffice
to celebrate the arrival
of so many thousands and
   thousands
of waving arms and of so much
   hatred
to hammer among the thorns.
A gesture to hang on humanity's
   pulse
PANCASAN!
A people illuminates its history.
The north wind is red
And here it blows bright red.

1967-71: Under "Tacho," Somoza power and wealth increase. The FSLN advances and retreats in the mountains and the cities. Many young revolutionaries (key figures of their generation) are consigned to prison and torture chambers, or are killed in battle. Among the former is Ricardo Morales Aviles, who survives only to be killed in 1973; among the latter are Jorge Navarro, Julio Buitrago, Selim Shible and poet Leonel Rugama.

10. Rugama/ LIKE THE SAINTS

Jorge Navarro

He had an accordion
but knew that it's one thing to sing
and another to die,
he died with his feet worm-infested
from the mud of Bocaycito
but was reborn
on the same day
every where.

Selim Shible

You knew Selim
You knew he once plugged
a secret police agent
in the secret police office itself
if you didn't know that
you didn't know Selim
when he came to live with us
he died in the same perfect way
he was born
but long before that
he was born forever

Julio Buitrago

No one answered a thing
because the heroes never said
they would die for their homeland
they just died.
In July Julio was born
he was born killing hunger
he was born fighting alone
he was born without a shirt
and singing while he fired his M-3
he was born when they tried to kill
him
with National Guards
with tanks, with airplanes
he was born when they couldn't kill
him
and tell the whole world about it
always tell them harshly
always harshly
with club in hand
with machete in hand
with gun in hand.

11. Napoleon Fuentes/ A FLAME IN SPACE

To poet Leonel Rugama
dead rejoicing in the promised land
with no other choice but to struggle

Fire in the heart
that inhabited his body
in his eyes

that saw all
that felt all
fire in the last corner

of his hands on the earth
which received his blood.
He didn't have to talk
or not talk
it was enough that he was among us
with his everyday blue jeans
with his dawning face
with his revolutionary outrage.
Like a ray of light in the dark
everything went so fast
that we don't know if now
he's closer than before
in the closeness that was so much
ours
and in the closeness, so distant.
Actually, in spite of everything
he's here
like the first day
like every day
nothing's changed
only his feet
set off sparks higher
than the Empire State's top floor
on this unique
and irreplaceable path.

1971-72: The Somoza dynasty survives the foco-style uprisings of the young Sandinists. In spite of revolutionary developments on several fronts and a growing economic stagnation, the third Somoza and his dynasty are more entrenched than ever.

12. Fanor Tellez/ GOD AMONG US

God presided over his Convention
talking of unintelligible things;
God heard the praises of his adorers
the blow of wings
of his ferocious birds of prey.
God who has sent the shadows of
    death
        to the Hades jail
God who has sent many rebelling
angels
to the shadows of death
comes down from his throne
garnished by exterminating
    cherubim,
    God will govern eternally
climbs into his fiery chariot
Somoza forever is the motto.

*Section 3. The Earthquake, the Quezada Unit & the Death of
Carlos Fonseca*

1972: Economic stagnation increases throughout the country, when an earthquake destroys downtown Managua killing 10,000 and dislocating over 100,000 people. The national economy actually benefits as the destruction of housing, buildings, roads, etc. create new investment and production opportunities, and as insurance and international aid creates the financing needed for new investments. However, Somoza and his gang further alienate the people and sectors of the bourgeoisie by appropriating aid for the poor sent from abroad and expropriating the holdings of Managua merchants.

1. Gioconda Belli/ WHAT ARE YOU, NICARAGUA?

What are you
but a tiny triangle of land
lost in the middle of the world?
What are you
but a flight of birds?
What are you
but the sound of rivers,
sweeping along brilliant, uprooted
    stones
leaving trails of water in the
    mountains?

What are you
but the breasts of women made of
    earth,
smooth, pointed and menacing?
What are you
but the song of leaves in giant trees,
green, vined and filled with doves?
What are you
but a clenched fist and a loaded gun?
What are you, Nicaragua,
to make me ache so much?

1973: U.S. "Rangers" are invited into the country under the pretext of the emergency situation created by the earthquake but with the intent of crippling the Sandinist Front. Miguel Obando y Bravo, Archbishop of Managua, breaks openly with the Somoza regime and calls for a new order. But meanwhile the old order continues.

2. Cajina-Vega/ THE CHIEF

His home is the biggest
    and plushest
in the best spot in town.
He had dealings
    with Somoza Garcia.
He got on well with Luis Somoza
and always gets his way with
    Tachito.
He's a well-placed man in the
    Government
    in Industry/ in Society

He makes recommendations
    and his word is heard.
He decides municipal and judicial
    matters.
And he has a large group of
    sycophants
who regularly pay him homage.
    He can grant favors
    and throw
        anyone
            in jail.

1973-74: The exploitation and repression intensify, especially among the peasants who support or join the FSLN in the rural mountain areas. Many are indeed thrown in jail; others are murdered.

3. Cuadra/ CATALINO FLORES

Habeas corpus
for Catalino Flores.
Three women come down
crying from Susuli.
They come dressed in black
at dawn.
They go to the garrison,
to the judge,
to the jail,
asking his whereabouts.
  The Union fearfully
  writes the telegram:
  Habeas corpus
  for Catalino Flores,
  a thirty year old farmworker,
  married, with five children,
  he organized
  the Peasant League

he read and taught
reading under the trees.
A patrol arrested him
one night.
Passersby heard shots.
Habeus Corpus
  for Catalino Flores,
  missing
  from the Garrison,
  from the Court,
  from the Jail.
The three women crying
go down to the cementary.
They come dressed in black
at dawn.
They are looking
for his body.

1974: Protestant and Catholic opposition, growing especially since Somoza's handling of the earthquake, reaches new levels. In politics, the Democratic Union of Liberation (UDEL) forms as an oppositional force led by the editor of *La Prensa* Pedro Joaquin Chamorro, and representing conservatives, liberal democrats, Chistians, social democrats and the Nicaraguan Socialist Party. Nevertheless, the Somoza gang feels secure, as overt revolutionary activity continues to be limited. Then, on December 27, the Juan Jose Quezada comando unit, led by Eduardo Contreras (Comandante Marcos), occupies the house of Dr. Cheme Castillo Quant, an important Somicista "cacique," and demands freedom for fourteen political prisoners, five million dollars, broadcasts of a Sandinist message to the people, and free passage to Cuba. The action is a complete success, as the regime shows its growing weakness by acceding to the FSLN, and many new young people are inspired to join the Sandinist movement.

4. Emilio Miranda Ramirez/ SUDDENLY...THE 13 KIDS ARRIVED

The "bacchanal" had begun
music, highballs,
snacks made in USA,

Giggles, jokes, tricks,
Political promises.
The ruling bourgeoisie's

"cream" laughing,
the crystal glasses
filled by the minute.
Some came and others left.
The foreign fat cats left early
but the national fat cats stayed on,
and the party went on
and the people went on
putting up with the dictatorship,
and more cars arrived,
and the party was at its best
wasting the people's money.
And suddenly...some one said,
"Okay, the party's over.
This is a political assault."
All the big shots,
full of food and whiskey
turned pale facing the rifles
of the thirteen
young guerilla fighters.

Many of those present hid
in the mansion's giant rooms,
and at the sound of freedom's shots
they ran out like frightened rats.
In a matter of minutes,
all was under control.
The tyrant recognized
the affront to his lackeys
and came to the capital
to fix things all up
and was humiliated and forced to
    deal
with the 13 guerilla fighters.
They set forth their demands
and the tyrant accepted
for he knew they would only say
FREE HOMELAND OR DEATH!
The baccanal had begun,
it was December 27, 1974.

1975: After the December action, Somoza imposes martial law and press censorship, and begins to deploy CONDECA forces (including U.S. as well as Central American soldiers) to wipe out armed FSLN units in the north. An intense internal struggle develops in the FSLN among those who stress "prolonged popular war" involving a permanent mountain military base (the Guerra Popular Prolongada or GPP tendency) and those who stress urban working class organization (the Proletarian tendency, or TP). But in the early months of the year, both tendencies are carried out, as Somocista repression spreads and intensifies and FSLN ranks swell.

5. Carlos Rapacciolli, Carlos Aguero Military School
Poetry Workshop/ 1975

The dark night.
The silence broken only
by the frogs' croaking
at that hour coming from the
    puddles
surrounding the house.
The clock on the wall struck two
    a.m.
Rolando and I didn't sleep.
I didn't look at him

I only heard troubled and broken
    breathing.
Suddenly those bangs on the door
and the shouts,
"Open in the name of the National
    Guard,
we know you're in there.
We have you surrounded. Open up
or we'll shoot our way in."
We hid. Aunt Margarita opened the

door
and we heard the rapid steps
of people coming in.
A Guardsman asked,
"where are those sons-of-bitches?
Don't say you don't know who."
She didn't answer.
Only sobs came out.
All of a sudden a bulb lit up the
  room.
Afterwards all was violence,
one blow followed another,
they pulled us out into the street
where a wind
began to stir rustling and icy.

I saw how they dragged Rolando
barefoot and shirtless through the
  mud.
I fell and got up.
We arrived at the garrison,
they tied us up,
they threw us in the cell
and we stayed there
stretched out in pain.
In those moments Rolando maybe
  thought
the same things I did
yes, my very thoughts,
about the triumph
of the Nicaraguan Revolution.

1975-76: The GPP sanctions the TP, which refuses to accept discipline. The CONDECA "Aguila Sexta" operation claims many FSLN militants and forces countless others into exile. Among many of those outside of the country, a third (or *tercerista*) position emerges vis-a-vis the GPP-TP split: an "insurrectionalist stance" arguing that Somoza has become so weakened that bold attacks against the National Guard could win support from sufficient forces to bring the dictatorship down. As the debate rages and schisms deepen, some of the most important leaders die in encounters with the National Guard. Included among the fallen are Comandante Marcos (Eduardo Contreras) and Carlos Fonseca, who die within forty-eight hours of each other in November, 1976.

6. Daniel Ortega Saavedra/ TO EDUARDO CONTRERAS, "COMMANDER ZERO"

Troubled and twisted streets
dust
flies
bright sun
noon full of sadness.
Here the flowers buried
the fighter's bow and arrows
buried.
Here, time stopped
the chief reincarnated
the voices of the tribe

Here the neighborhood:
in a hearth
burnt rice
the little houses
rats
cockroaches and moths.
A steaming plate of beans
a tortilla
10 kids ready for war.
COMMANDER MARCOS
Your people receive you.

7. Julio Valle Castillo/ NICARAGUAN OPTICS

"Carlos Fonseca...came to us with his brusque and near-sighted blue eyes... Carlos died with gun in hand, with his heart overflowing with love toward humanity, with his blue eyes aiming toward the future."--Tomas Borge

Put yourself in his blue eyes
they say were myopic,
but trespassed the light
of the present day
as if they were the very light
of the light;
because not all that's seen is felt,
because not all that's in view is in
　view
and we sorely need his glasses, his
　eyes.
His eyes fix the sight,
his glasses are contact,
and so your gaze
becomes one long unending caress
and where you put it,
you'll place bullet or life.

Seeing will then be like hearing,
tasting, smelling, touching

and seeing once again, loving
and loving is the only sense
that is all sense.
You'll see that Sandino is not a
　man,
but a path, a road with mowed
　grass
and the crickets ordering silence:
"There goes an underground
　people."
Nicaraguan, inevitable compatriot,
whoever you may be,
look for those glasses, put yourself
in the eyes of Carlos Fonseca.
There's still time.
Remember that man was never
　permitted
to shut his eyes,
not even when he was already dead.

8. Guillermo Rothschuh Tablada/ EVERYTHING PLUS ONE

If you build a monument to Carlos
in the middle of the public plaza,
don't make it of metal or marble.
Put five million feet on top
and you'll see how he gets up and
　walks.

9. Gioconda Belli/ OF COURSE WE'RE NOT

Of course we're not a funeral
　procession,
in spite of all the swallowed tears

we're filled with the joy
of building new things
and enjoy the day, the night
and even weariness
and we harvest laughter
from the high wind.
We use the right to happiness,
to find love in distant lands
and to feel lucky
at having found a partner
and share bread, pain and bed.
Although we're born to be happy
we find ourselves surrounded
by sadness and dullness,
by death and forced hideaways.
Fleeing like fugitives,
we see how wrinkles

are born on our faces
and we grow serious, but always
the rite follows us tied to our heels
and we know how to have a good
     laugh
and be happy
in the deepest and darkest night,
because we're made of a huge hope,
and we go around
hanging from victory's neck,
ringing its bell ever more
     rhythmically
and we know that nothing can
     happen
to stop us;
because we're seed and habitat
of an intimate smile

that will burst out soon now
in every one's face.

10. Tomas Borge/ OF SALT AND WATER

I don't want tears,
I   want avenues, machine-gun fire,
rains of laughter and words.
Maybe a contribution
of salt and water in tenderness
a bit of rancor
hate
but tears no
only blows.

BOOK I, PART II. YEARS OF INSURRECTION & VICTORY
(1977-1979)

INTRODUCTION: BACKGROUNDS TO THE INSURRECTION

1. The Formation of a Revolutionary Bloc

In spite of all the good justifications that existed for a revolution in Nicaragua, Central American specialists will generally agree that the Revolution itself still awaits adequate theorization. What seems perfectly clear, and is inscribed in all post-Gramscian Marxist thought, is that the supposedly "objective pre-conditions" for revolution (overall economic crisis, the progressive immiseration of the people, etc.) are not adequate to the generation of a successful revolutionary struggle. If only such objective pre-conditions mattered, revolution would be a common experience across the globe. But even adding such "factors" as "the international conjuncture," a possible "crisis in the structures of power," "organization of the working class and working class parties," etc., cannot provide the full solution.

In the Nicaragua of 1976-77, the economy was going through one of its better times. While the immiseration of large numbers was at a high level, many stages of the immiseration process had come and gone in the past, and in itself there was no reason why this particular phase should produce a revolution. As it turned out, the international conjuncture was a good one, long enough for the development of a particular approach to revolution-making; and the structures of power, especially in terms of legitimacy and in ties to new middle and capitalist sectors generated by economic development, were soon to enter into a severe overt crisis which had perhaps been delayed but was then intensified by Nicaragua's post-earthquake period.

However the very nature of Nicaragua's laboral structure, the force of Nicaragua's repressive apparatuses, and, it must be added, the relative failure of the FSLN to organize peasants, workers and other immiserated sectors (here, the source for the split into tendencies), seemed to preclude the possibility of a successful revolutionary movement in the near future. Events in 1977 and 1978 were to change all that very rapidly. But they were not to occur simply in function of the "objective pre-conditions."

What seems to shine through all the accounts of the Nicaraguan revolutionary process, including, we hope, the account which is presented in this book of our volume, is the crystalization of a vast, multi-class social consensus rife with contradictions and distinct projects, but united enough for a brief historical moment to constitute, in relation to a growing, militant vanguard force, which ultimately becomes its only adequate organizational form and effective practical means, an insurrectional bloc capable of overthrowing a State which, for all its military might and destructive will, is no longer able to muster the minimal legitimizational base necessary to its survival.

Finally, an essential corollary to all this is that the emerging bloc shared as a feature of minimally necessary and provisional unity an ideological and more generally cultural "macro-vision" or "world view" which, rooted in the structural development of the nation over the decades, and in spite of all the specific differences among classes, sectors and groups, was sufficiently promoted by the FSLN and sufficiently accepted by large enough numbers to serve the given historical moment. That macro-structure bears the name of *Sandinismo*, a national and in some ways regional construct. And an important material contributant in the constitution of Sandinism as the multi-valenced revolutionary force adequate to the historical moment was the exteriorist poetic system, and its impact in the formation of the revolutionary counter-culture, especially among the young, that was able to overthrow the Somoza regime.

To be sure, the regime's ever greater dependence on its repressive apparatus signalled the crisis of its "ideological" ones. Never having had a sufficient consensus to institutionalize its power at any great depth, and never having fostered a significant national ideology and culture of its own (beyond paternalistic misappropriations of Dario, folk culture and the like), and yet attempting to block or restrict ideological and cultural manifestations which might prove threatening, the regime in fact forced people toward producing a culture which opposed it and gave these producers no other choice but to "sell out" or join an increasingly radicalized opposition.

When the regime no longer had the flexibility to tolerate a Cardenal's space of Solentiname, when it cracked down on dissident priests and no longer respected church sanctuaries, when it was forced to kill off the figure-head of semi-legal and respectable opposition (Pedro Joaquin Chamorro), when it had to close schools and universities, and sent its death squads after the students, it completed the process of displacing all oppositional intellectual and cultural work towards the overall production of a revolutionary rupture.

In his previously-cited article, "Sandinista Poetics," John Beverley formulates the matter in ways which further illuminate the view expressed here:

If there were not a relation, in process between (proletarian) "class partisanship" and an anti-imperialist "multi-class synthesis,"... [there would be no emerging, united force which could] represent and mobilize the struggle of a *people* (which includes women, children, the unemployed, students, poor farmers and small business people, etc.); only the sort of chemically pure "proletarian" vanguards whose dogmatism stifle[s] the growth of the revolutionary movement. Imperialism creates not only a proletarian relation of production; it creates a whole dependent and distorted social mechanism, which dominates everyone not in the immediate power bloc of the comprador bourgeoisie. That is why, as Ernesto Laclau has argued, the normal form of socialist revolution must be populist. *The people* is the revolutionary subject in the concrete; the revolutionary class acts as/through the people. ...

Sandinismo ... is undeniably a form of revolutionary populism, but one with a marxist core. This was already implicit in the figure of Sandino himself, on the one hand a typical product of the frustrated Jacobin nationalism of the provincial petty bourgeoisie in Central America, on the other hand aware from the start that his war against the U.S. Marines and the comprador bourgeoisie depended on the peasants, artisans and workers of Nicaragua, that it would have to be not only an anti-imperialist war but a "revolutionary anti-imperialist war," to use a central slogan of current Sandinista ideology, activiating both modern (socialist and anarchist) and traditional (Catholic and pre-Colombian) images of collectivism. The specific form of imperialist penetration and "modernization" of Nicaragua was the Somoza dictatorship, which shrouded itself in a quasi-Liberal (in the Latin American sense) ideology of law and progress. That meant that Catholicism, even in the patrician and reactionary forms left over from the feudal phase of Nicaragua's political economy, came to constitute an ideological space where an anti-capitalist ethics could be preserved and expanded.
-- *Minnesota Review, ns 20*, pp. 132.

Poetry itself, of course, was another related space in which anti-capitalist and ultimately pro-revolutionary ideology could develop, and which, in a country giving a certain structural privilege to poetry, could contribute to the politicization of a whole generation of urban young, literate or not. It was the particular contribution of Carlos Fonseca Amador to realize that a standard Socialist Party could not forge a revolution in Nicaragua, and to tie his socialist aspirations to the specifically national anti-imperialist campaigns of Sandino. Carlos Fonseca invented modern Sandinismo as a political and ideological force. However, that force has a pre-history in the 1930's, including the work of Manolo Cuadra, but also the reactionary vanguardists; and that work, given new direction by the FSLN, was carried on by Cardenal and those who followed him. Indeed, Beverley notes, "Cardenal's poetry has been an invaluable ideological weapon for

Sandinismo."

What we see in the four parts which comprise this book is the final emergence of the revolutionary bloc out of many disparate social elements. And we also see how revolutionary poetry and poetic discourse not only describe the process but are a constituent part of it. To the extent that the poetic material we have found enables us to do so, we attempt to give a very detailed picture of Nicaragua's great insurrectional period from 1977 to the July, 1979 victory. However a sparsity of poetic material dealing with 1977 and a need for tracing certain underlying structures and patterns not easily articulated in a chronology/collage such as ours require our presentation of certain matters here to enable readers to better understand our text and the Insurrection itself.

2. The Events of 1977

By 1977, with major Sandinista leaders dead and the FSLN itself split into three seemingly ever more divergent tendencies, the Somoza regime, in spite of its deepening structural economic crisis, seemed relatively secure. The bourgeois opposition rumbled, appealed for U.S. pressure to loosen up Somocista restraints, but generally accepted the dictatorship as a necessary evil, to be endured until a new regime, perhaps headed by Chamorro's UDEL party, could come to the fore and avert a worsening of the situation which could only play into FSLN hands.

In the Frente, the rift among the tendencies deepened, and any member of one of the three factions which sought to bring about a reconciliation of another tendency risked being called a partisan of that tendency and a traitor to his own. Thus, a tactical split seemed to be hardening into something deeper and more serious. On the positive side, each tendency brought its own energy into recruiting new cadres, developing alliances, finding financial support. While there could be little question that unity was essential for any ultimate victory, perhaps the split enabled the development of resources which would never have come into play had there been a relative consensus of direction.

The GPP seemed the most quiet, seemingly stunned by the disaffection from the traditional Sandinista stance and by the recent loss of so many important leaders. But the GPP was laying the seeds for forming important mass organizations that would be significant in the final victory. Meanwhile the Proletarian Tendency (PT) was busily doing political work in the cities, in the work centers, the schools, the neighborhoods. True to their name, the Insurrectionalists were intent on international fundraising to buy the weapons to carry out actions that would show the growing vulnerability of the Somocistas.

At the begining of 1977, the Catholic Church, student organizations, unions and UDEL raised a growing clamor to put end to the state of siege and martial law Somoza had imposed after the events of December 27, 1974. Pedro Joaquin Chamorro's *La Prensa* reported that the State had borrowed millions of cordobas from a Somoza-owned company to cover its external debts. The Social Security Institute was nearly bankrupt; the Power and Light Company lacked operating funds; 300,000 cordobas were missing from the Bank of America. International protests put additional pressure on Somoza to modify his rule, as the new Carter administration informed Somoza that he could receive further military credit only if civil liberties and overall human rights improved.

On June 24, Tacho suffered a heart attack and went to Miami where he spent five weeks recuperating. Meanwhile UDEL used his time of absence to put forth a program for democratization in Nicaragua: general amnesty for political prisoners, lifting press censorship, ending the state of siege, political and union freedom. UDEL also suggested that Somoza leave office. As these demands received growing support, a CIA publication indicated there were only 46 Sandinistas left in the country after the CONDECA operations of 1976-77. Apparently seeking to quell rumors of failing health and a weakened hand, and apparently with a false sense of security about the militant left, Tacho lifted the state of siege. But this only made the opposition feel freer to renew their campaign against the dictator.

Christian organizations and members of the women's organization, AMPRONAC began a publicity campaign demanding that the regime account for missing peasants. *La Prensa* stepped up their campaign against Somocista corruption. However, as mid-October approached, it was the left, represented by the Insurrectionalists, who dispelled CIA rumors and Somoza illusions, to show that the FSLN and the spirit of revolution were still very much alive in Nicaragua.

On October 12, a group of well-armed Insurrectionalist guerillas, working with the young people of Ernesto Cardenal's Solentiname community, launched an attack on the San Carlos Garrison and military installations on the southern coast of Lake Nicaragua near the Costa Rican border. The San Carlos Guards were defeated and the town fell into FSLN hands. But very shortly Somoza launched an indiscriminate land and aerial counter attack which placed all civilian life in jeopardy. The Sandinists decided to retreat to avoid a massacre. In this action, some of the Solentiname young people died, others went to prison, still others sought refuge in Costa Rica. And Cardenal's religious commune was liquidated.

The anti-Somoza attacks were part of a larger plan designed to strike blows against the National Guard in various parts of the country simultaneously with the intent of showing that the Frente still had power and that the Guard was vulnerable. The new Carlos Fonseca Amador Northern Front attacked Monzonte near Ocotal on October 15; and there were significant attacks on Masaya, Esteli and San Fernando, Nueva Segovia in the days that followed. But there was poor coordination, and clearly the townspeople in the areas were unprepared for what took place.

Many of the plans fell through; the effort to rally the people and to arm them never came to much. In each instance, no matter how great the surprise and initial success, Somoza's troops were able to rain such havoc and such casualties on the insurgents and the civilian population, that the enterprises and the total military operation collapsed.

While praising the courage of the combatants, both the GPP and TP condemned the October uprisings as adventuristic and detrimental to the developing struggle. However, in retrospect, the failed Insurrection achieved certain ends. The military failure helped in the development of more successful future strategies which would be guided by at least one concept gleened from this insurrection: that relatively weak forces could conquer over the stronger Guard by simultaneously attacking at several points at once.

Indeed, in their October "adventures," the Terceristas had shown their ability to launch armed assaults in distinct parts of the country, make strategic retreat when faced with superior numbers without suffering many losses and regroup themselves for renewed attack. Above all, the insurrection succeeded in alerting people in Nicaragua and the world that with popular support, insurrectional struggle could be waged and might succeed in Nicaragua.

Immediately after the San Carlos attack, a group of twelve respected Nicaraguans (including priests Miguel D'Escoto and Fernando Cardenal, novelist Sergio Ramirez, businessmen Arturo Cruz, Alfonso Robelo and Joaquin Cuadra, etc.), brought together as an Insurrectionalist FSLN strategy, to represent the kernal of a provisional government (indeed many were to participate in the first post-Somocista administration) and known simply as "The Twelve," left the country for San Jose, Costa Rica.

Shielded from Somocista reprisals, the Twelve announced their existence to the world and called on all sectors of the country to become involved in a process which would lead to "a national solution to the anguishing problem of Nicaragua," and which would necessarily involve the participation of the FSLN. La Prensa published their manifesto on October 21, and UDEL supported their demand for a new government, as members of the group travelled throughout Latin America and Europe making the whys and wherefores of their position known to the world.

The continued military attacks by the FSLN after October 15th not only created internal pressures on Somoza, but tensions developed with Costa Rica and Honduras, which Somoza blamed for harboring the Sandinistas. The National Guard reinforced and tightened its military patrol over all highways, reinstating a surveillance which had been relaxed when the state of siege was lifted. Then too, the Mexican government protested when the Guard tried unsuccessfully to kidnap a group of Sandinistas who had taken refuge in the Mexican embassy.

In the midst of this situation, the Twelve began demanding substantial changes in the government. When they stated that the FSLN had matured politically and should be considered a legitimate part of the opposition, Somoza declared them guilty of criminal acts and had them condemned to prison in absentia.

Archbishop Obando y Bravo called Somoza and the opposition to "constructive dialogue." And UDEL officially invited all opposition parties to participate in a Commission to Promote a National Dialogue, to be headed by the Archbishop. But the FSLN declared that such a dialogue made sense only if Somoza left power. More important to the FSLN was its own effort to build the mass organizations that would provide the support for any insurrectional moves. Thus in October, the United People's Movement (MPU) began to function and organize city barrios, factory workers, etc. and to integrate them into a national collective that would include workers, peasants, professionals, intellectuals, women and students.

Somoza responded with a new wave of violence directed against FSLN support in the countryside. Between mid-October and late November, hundreds of campesinos were tortured, imprisoned or murdered. The Permanent Commission on Human Rights in Nicaragua, the women's organization, AMPRONAC, and student groups protested, and in fact mass organization began to spread throughout the countryside. In December, inhabitants of a poverty development project rallied against their conditions and were beaten and arrested by the Guards. Responding to this, 6,000 hospital workers joined AGROTEX textile workers in a threatened walkout. As the government cracked down again, "The Twelve" withdrew from the Dialogue and UDEL began expressing doubts about it.

Then too, La Prensa began uncovering new examples of national fraud. Three million cordobas had disappeared from a school construction fund; monies were transfered from funds for the rural poor to cover the city ripoff. In the cities and the towns, a spiral of protest, repression and more protest was met with another spiral of fraud, discovery and more fraud or coverup, to create a growing national crisis. UDEL announced its pre-conditions for dialogue with the government in late December: investigation of the missing, freedom for political prisoners, investigation of government agency fraud, guarantees against media censorship, freedom of political activities, union rights, and an end of persecution against "The Twelve." These demands published in Chamorro's own newspaper, became the basis of renewed attacks on him, his political organization and his newspaper. In a matter of days, as Chamorro pursued his investigations of fraud and other illegalities of the regime, he was assassinated. At this point, the forces of Insurrection swung into intensified action.

3. Political Organization, Religion, Women and International Forces during the Insurrectional Period

Underlying the events of the insurrectional period are developments on several fronts which must be mentioned for a full understanding of what took place. Perhaps the most significant factor in the overall collapse of the dictatorship was the growth of popular organizations, especially among peasants, students women, and the development, as well, of the FSLN itself. The role of religion and the efforts at international intervention and mediation were also important factors worthy of some note.

A. The Peasants

Gradually after 1976, the PT began working to build up peasant associations. The process was difficult because of the Somocista repression unleashed throughout the countryside, but workers' associations began to spread, especially throughout the Pacific region. In 1977, the Sandinistas formed the Association of Rural Workers (ATC) which united the committees existing in Managua, Masaya, Chinandega, Leon and Carazao. While organized around demands for bettered living conditions, year-round employment and an end to repression against farm workers, the ATC came to stand increasingly against the regime and with the FSLN.

By the fall of 1977, ATC members met in public rallies to denounce the disappearances of northern farmworkers. In October, they carried out a campaign against conditions on sugar and coffee plantations. Gradually they joined other burgeoning organizations in protests against the regime's repression. They often provided clandestine asylum for guerilla fighters and, as the insurrection came on, many actively joined in by taking up arms. After Chamorro's assassination, they increased their protest actions, and their level of insurrectional militancy, at least in the key Pacific region areas, became more intense. As the number of strikes and subsequent repressive acts by the Guard continued to multiply in 1977-78, more and more of them joined popular militias intent on ousting the dictatorship.

B. *The Students*

During the same period, student organizations, always a factor in anti-Somocista developments over the years, became increasingly militant, especially during the disturbances of April, 1978. Whereas in the 1950s and 60s it was almost exclusively the college students who joined in, now high school and even elementary students became steadily active in the struggle against the dictatorship. and in support for the FSLN. The student movement, centered in Managua and Carazao, gradually grew stronger in Leon, Chinandega and Esteli. High school and university organizations began to coordinate their work, so that by the end of 1977, they could mobilize a few thousand students for major demonstrations.

The first key student-led action was the protest against the Somoza-sponsored bus fare hikes in the summer of 1977. This protest involved picketing, lightning meetings, spray painting of political slogans, tire air-bleedings, bus window busts, etc. But in December, the students became involved in the more serious popular campaign against political prisoners and peasant repression. Students carried their protests from the streets and into churches and schools, holding buildings for days on end. They learned hit and run tactics against the Guards, learned to build barricades out of Somoza's post-earthquake streetstones, out of tires and sandbags.

In the wake of Chamorro's assassination three pro-Sandinist organizations, the Revolutionary Student Front (FER), the Nicaraguan Revolutionary Youth (JRN) and the University Center for Popular Solidarity, became active. The organizations integrated their work ever more fully with trade union and other worker groups, participating in work stoppages and demonstrations. In retaliation the National Guard increased their use of BECATs (Special Brigades Against Terrorist Acts), groups of four armed soldiers travelling in jeeps, arresting and shooting students and young people on sight. But the use of BECATs only led to more sophisticated tactics and more intense commitment on the part of increasing numbers of students.

During the intense actions of spring, 1978, students and young people became the vanguard of uprisings in many cities. In March, Albertina Serrano, a widow, began a hunger strike to protest the confinement of Marcio Jaen and FSLN co-founder, Tomas Borge. First supported by AMPRONAC, this hunger strike soon won crucial backing from students at the National Institute in Masaya, who added to the demands that teachers serving as Somocista spies be expelled from the faculty, On April 6, the most massive student strike in the nation's history began. By April 8, some twenty schools throughout the country had been taken over.

An open struggle began between the students and the Guards, with the latter retaking schools and converting them into military headquarters. As other people joined the hunger strike, students throughout the Pacific area developed ties with progressive teachers, developed parent-student militant organizations and in effect became the vanguard of the popular struggle in the cities.

More than 60,000 students were involved in the strike of this period. In spite of Somoza's fear of alienating additional social sectors by cracking down too fiercely on the young, the National Guard did react ruthlessly in Diriamba, Jinotega and Esteli. But students continued to organize and act, staging key demonstrations in Esteli during May and in Managua during July. Perhaps more than any other sector, it was the students who built the momentum for what culminated in the September, 1978 insurrection. They were, of course, to play a major role in the Final Insurrection as well, continuing in the student sector and joining in the direct war against the dictatorship in city street wars and, as members of the Sandinist Army, in the battles against the National Guard throughout the country.

C. The Women

The rise of organized women's opposition to the dictatorship accelerated throughout the 1970s, and became a significant factor in the groundswell leading to victory. Women were the major wage earners of families, but they received lower wages, long working hours and fewer opportunities. Increasingly they demanded decent wages, better housing, health care, education for their children and equal employment opportunities. After 1972, they began to organize, first in the Association of Nicaraguan Women Confronting the National Problem (AMPRONAC) and then in other organization forms.

Composed mainly of middle class women, and becoming an official organization on September 29, 1977, AMPRONAC gradually grew and diversified in membership, and rapidly became a political force. In the charter meeting of September 29, 1977, AMPRONAC denounced violations of women's and human rights. Subsequently the group investigated and denounced the disappearance and imprisonment of women and children. It carried out women, citizen and human rights campaigns in *La Prensa*. These efforts culminated in a religious service on November 19, 1977, where AMPRONAC denounced major atrocities against women and children.

From this point on AMPRONAC broadened its base, establishing chapters in urban and rural areas, holding assemblies on cases of imprisonment, torture and death of peasant victims of the National Guard. After Chamorro's assassination, women from the Atlantic Coast region occupied

United Nations offices in Managua to protest National Guard murders, kidnappings and rapes. Lasting two weeks, the takeover allowed AMPRONAC to dramatize and publicize their overall campaign. After a direct attack on AMPRONAC demonstrators on January 30, 1978, the organization radicalized. More and more working class women joined the organization.

By March AMPRONAC's membership had grown to over a thousand. That month, AMPRONAC staged an International Mothers Week program, calling on all women to join the struggle. By early April, the organization reached new levels, joining the ATC in a massive hunger march in Diriamba. The march directly challenged Somoza, and the Guard attacked the marchers. killing an AMPRONAC member. This action won the organization new respect, as women joined in hunger strikes throughout the nation.

Gradually AMPRONAC had successfully linked the women's rights struggle to popular opposition to the dictatorship. Within the organization and without, on the field of battle and in other functions, women were intensely involved in all phases of insurrectional struggle which contributed greatly to the revolutionary triumph.

D. The Church

Since the Vatican Council II and the Latin American Episcopal Conference in Medellin, Colombia, the Catholic Church had been redefining its goals and reordering its hierarchy, declaring a new commitment to defending the rights of the poor and to fostering grass-roots religious organzations. This profound shift in the definition of the pastoral mission was an impetus for the transformation of Nicaragua's Catholic Church.

During the 1960s the new "theology of liberation" had spread throughout Nicaragua. Notably, Ernesto Cardenal had founded his lay community in Solentiname, while in the barrios of Managua, Father Jose de la Lara, a Spanish priest, was creating Ecclesiastical Base Communities. in which poor people were asked to discuss the relevance of the Bible's teachings to their own lives and suffering. The Jesuits founded the Ecclesiastical Committee for Agrarian Progress (CEPA) as a training center for campesinos in rural community organizing. In Zelaya Province, Capuchin fathers sent out 900 lay persons as Delegates of the Word whose purpose was to teach literacy, health and "consciousness raising" in previously neglected rural areas.

The earthquake was a turning point in religious opposition to Somoza. Much of the international relief money was at first administered through the churches. The Protestants formed CEPAD (Evangelical Committee for

Aid and Development) four days after the earthquake to help those who were left homeless. Somoza soon demanded control over the international aid. His subsequent embezzlement and abuse of these funds increased the alienation and opposition of the Catholic and Protestant hierarchies to his rule. Under Somoza, other avenues of organizing (political parties, unions, etc.) were repressed, leaving the Churches as a major outlet for dissent and challenge to the dictatorship. In 1976, the U.S. based Capuchin order exposed internationally, for the first time, Somoza's human rights violations. But as the Churches became more and more vocal in their denouncements of Somoza, they began experiencing greater repression at the hands of Somoza's National Guard.

Many Christian activists joined the FSLN. Rural leaders from CEPA started working with the ATC, the Sandinista Rural Workers Association, while others took up arms with the guerillas. In Managua, Christian youth organizations were challenging Somoza's rule by protesting increases in water rates and bus fares. As the fighting progressed to the final stage of the insurrection, Church buildings were used as centers for medical aid and food distribution. Clean water for drinking filled Church baptismal fonts during the refugee crisis. Church members published newsletters and served as a communications link for the FSLN combatants.

In a landmark development within the Catholic hierarchy, Archbishop Obando y Bravo announced that armed struggle was a legitimate form of resistance under the following specific circumstances: 1) the existence of obvious and extreme injustice; 2) a proven failure of all forms of peaceful solution; and 3) when armed resistance will produce fewer deaths than the existing injustices. In doing this, the archbishop was repeating the traditional--if often ignored--church teaching on the right of a people to overthrow a tyrant. Under Somoza, these circumstances certainly existed.

E. The Consolidation of Popular Forces

By mid-1978, the popular forces had merged in a single bloc called the United People's Movement (MPU), an alliance of popular organizations including women, students, workers, peasants, trade unions, political parties and revolutionary groups. Given direction by the FSLN and legitimization by the emergence of "The Twelve," the MPU worked through innumerable internal contradictions and became an effective force during the September, 1978 uprisings.

They initially called for massive popular mobilization to overthrow the dictatorship and an achievement of unity among revolutionary forces. They rejected the unpopular composition and agenda of the Broad Opposition Front (or "FAO"), a businessman's organization seeking a moderate solution to the national problem; and they brought virtually every grassroots people's organization, including Marxist-Leninist, Church-based, student and women's groups into their fold. Furthermore, they had a clear political program, pointed toward a future government of national reconstruction which would liquidate the National Guard, carry out land reform, confiscate Somocista holdings, provide broad organizational rights to workers and in effect create a people's government. It was by offering a broad-based program that the MPU was able to outflank the FAO and play its considerable role in September, 1978.

Learning from the lack of coordination and firm organizational struggle which played such a role in the uprising, the MPU, even while forced into hiding, was able to work with the FSLN to set up the Civilian Defense Committees (CDS's) which would play a major role in the Final Insurrection. The CDS's were designed to provide grassroots support and cooperation for a pending insurrection. They were organized by block and coordinated by neighborhood and zonal steering committees, with the goals of coordinating urban defense, placing all resources and forces at the service of FSLN combat units, and insuring the people's power in a new socio-political structure. Intensive organizing occurred in Fall, 1978, when direct confrontations seemed to be ebbing.

In the months which followed, the increasingly well organized CDS's collected medicines and supplies, set up a network of "security houses" to provide meeting places and protection for combatants, and carried out a number of educational and propaganda tasks that prepared the ground for the coming insurrectional phase. Thus while the FAO and upper bourgeois opposition consolidated bourgeois forces, the MPU and CDS's formed a unified, underground civilian and political force, prepared to battle the National Guard in the streets, and prepared to struggle against any reformist compromises which the bourgeoisie sought to work out with the U.S. government.

F. The FAO & U.S. Efforts

By early October, 1978, the U.S. set up a "Trinational Commission for Friendly Cooperation" along with trusted allies, Guatemala and the Dominican Republic. This commission was meant to mediate between Somoza and the "legitimate opposition," i.e., the FAO, in seeking an alternative to the Somoza dynasty while leaving *somocismo* intact.

FAO business supporters endorsed the new commission, seeing this as the only means to avert a major revolutionary victory by radical forces. The U.S. viewed matters in similar fashion, seeing that Somoza was finished and the future of U.S. interests very insecure. The strategy of Carter and his advisors was "the application of pressures and incentives to force our erstwhile client dictator to go into early retirement." This meant cutting off military aid, blocking IMF loans and threatening to cut diplomatic ties. If Somoza would leave, he would be granted asylum in the U.S. and be able to take out part of his fortune.

However, Somoza would not cooperate with this plan, and it fell to FAO to try to keep the internal pressure on the dictator, without yielding to pressures from the left. Indeed, FAO's major concern was to contain the rapidly spreading radicalization process that moved through urban and rural areas of the nation, as bourgeois unity collapsed and popular revolutionary unity was being forged. Faced with this situation, FAO moved slowly and thus enabled Somoza to re-establish military consolidation over rebelious forces; meanwhile the U.S. funnelled arms to Somoza through Argentina and Israel. Underplaying the leftward momentum U.S. officials favored the conservative business wing of FAO. The more progressive sector, and then "The Twelve" broke with FAO by late October, charging the organization with attempting to impose a reactionary U.S. solution on Nicaragua.

Abandoned by all its most respected supporters, FAO could only count on U.S. legitimization for its continued existence. But by late November, the conservative FAO was almost completely discredited by popular forces. At this junction, Somoza called for a plebiscite, and the remainders of FAO and its U.S. backers jumped at the chance, assuming that a plebiscite could counter the impact of the September uprising, discredit the divided FSLN, and sow division among urban and rural popular sectors. The U.S. underplayed popular suspicion of an electoral process which had only been a farce throughout all the years of the dictatorship. Those still in the FAO tried to tie the elections to Somoza's departure, but Somoza insisted on staying in power until 1981.

The FSLN then countered the shadow play over elections by creating a strategy of "parallel power," that is of providing a real alternative to the FAO through the creation of the National Patriotic Front which united the FSLN, the MPU and the progressives who had left FAO in November. In December and January the MPU sought to mobilize its organizations around the new Front.

The popular mobilization against pacts and plebiscites led Somoza to reject all pleas that he leave Nicaragua, and to attack the U.S. for its betrayal. Somoza wanted arms and money, not mediation; and mediation had virtually no support in the country.

G. The FSLN Reunification & Insurrectional Preparations

Gradually the three FSLN tendencies came together after September 1978. Most of the leaders recognized that the uprising proved that insurrection could work, but only if the popular forces were better organized and if the vanguard could overcome its fragmentation. Mass reorganization came gradually through the MPU structure, but FSLN reunification was another matter. By December 7, 1978, representatives from the three tendencies were able to hammer out an accord of unity on the bases of Sandino's initial program as interpreted in light of the current historical conjuncture: rejection of imperialism and Somoza, as well as foreign intervention; rejection of pacts or plebiscites betraying the people's aspirations; dismantling of the National Guard and support for the MPU as an expression a unified expression of broad sectors of Nicaraguan society.

However, achieving sufficient unity for concerted action took far more than an agreement on principles. Intense Somocista repression in early 1979, as well as the need to bring various FSLN factions together, delayed the effective unity of the three tendencies until March 8. The formal agreement on this date established a provisional government of national unity, a program of National Reconstruction, a national army (without *Somocistas*); a non-aligned foreign policy, and an expropriation of all of Somoza's holdings by the new government.

Other agreements sealed the pact for the military and diplomatic campaign necessary to achieve these goals. In fact, several months went by to further solidify Sandinist unity and forge this unity with the growingly organized popular forces, to finally launch the definitive offensive against Somoza. In effect, FSLN unity was no easy accomplishment, and it did not happen a moment too soon. That unity was forged out of necessity, out of the will of Sandinistas and the Nicaraguan people to bring a hated regime and system to an end.

H. Political and Diplomatic Manuevering During the Insurrection

With the formation of the Provisional Government of National Reconstruction on June 16, 1979, all was in readiness for a political transition if victory could be obtained on the military front. The governmental composition resulted from months of FSLN negotiations with all opposition sectors. It included Sergio Ramirez, representing "The Twelve"; Alfonso Robelo from the FAO; Moises Hassan from the MPU; Daniel Ortega from the FSLN; and Violeta Chamorro, widow of Pedro Joaquin. Once inside the country, the PGR would call for the expropriation of Somoza family property, the dissolution of the National Guard (with guarantees for Guardsmen who defected) and recognition from democratic governments throughout the world.

The FSLN timed the announcement of the new government to coincide with the re-opening of their Southern Front. With the Battle for Managua raging, Somoza could not afford to send his troops south. The Sandinistas announced they would take Rivas and install the provisional government there. Their announcement coincided with breaks in diplomatic relations with Somoza made by Mexico, Panama, Costa Rica and Ecuador. In fact, on June 16, the countries of the Andean Pact granted the FSLN "belligerent force" status, thus challenging Somoza's legitimacy, opening the way for military support to the FSLN and creating a context in which additional countries would soon break with Somoza.

Earlier, on June 4, the Organization of American States (OAS) had dismissed Somoza's appeals for help, arguing that his government was crumbling. In a June 11 OAS meeting in Washington, Somocista delegates accused Cuba and Panama of gunrunning only to be shouted down by pro-Sandinist Nicaraguan exiles who went on to argue in favor of the revolutionary forces. A few days after the formation of PGR, the U.S., now fearful of an allout Sandinist victory, called an emergency OAS meeting and set forth a proposal that included Somoza's resignation, the sending of an inter-American peace keeping force to Nicaragua, and the establishment of a government of "national reconciliation" which completely ignored the PGR. On June 22, Venezuela and 12 other OAS members put forth another proposal much more in line with the FSLN's own position. Acknowledging defeat in their efforts, the U.S. voted with the majority in a 17-2 vote favoring the Venezuelan initiative.

But the U.S. continued interventionist efforts. If they were to have any voice, they had to first scuttle Somoza. U.S. Ambassador Pezullo began negotiating for this, while refusing to contact the PGR and merely suggesting that the PGR would "play a role in developing the eventual political solution." Junta members responded to this effort to marginalize them, and U.S. officials added insult to injury by seeking a cease-fire with a governing junta different from those in the PGR. and including representatives from two forces now repudiated by the people, Somoza's party and the National Guard. Moderate PGR groups resisted U.S. efforts to win them to the new plan and all PGR groups joined in charging the U.S. with attempting to subvert Nicaraguan unity. Indeed on June 27, FAO and the Superior Council of Private Enterprise (COSEP) endorsed the PGR, thus exposing the U.S. effort as aimed at denying FSLN military victory and political power.

Next the U.S. sought to enlarge and water down the PGR. by adding more conservative elements. This tactic failing, they tried three others. First they sought to convice centrist Latin American nations to condition support for the PGR until it had more moderate elements; second they promised massive aid to the new government if the FSLN role were reduced; third, they backed up the Somoza claim of massive Cuban aid to the FSLN. The first two measures failed, and U.S. officials finally had to admit that there was no basis for the third claim, and that Cuba was far less involved than were other Central American countries. In effect, by mid-June most Latin American forces saw the U.S. as the major factor holding up an FSLN victory and the overthrow of Somoza. However reluctantly, the U.S. was forced to accept the PGR's makeup. But U.S. efforts at manipulation continued to the day victory. What the U.S. did during the Reconstruction period is another story.

4. About Part II Itself

Part II is divided into four sections, describing crucial moments and processes leading to the July victory. Sections 2 and 4 are collage/chronologies featuring poetry written during and after the events described. Sections 1 and 3, however are portraits, first of an event, the 1977 attack on the San Carlos garrison, and second, of a phenomenon, the many combatants FSLN combatants who wrote poetry only to die before the July victory. These sections, and indeed all of part II, require commentary with respect to their significance as history and as poetry.

Of all the events of 1977, only the San Carlos assault is the subject of a sustained body of poetry. This is because of the participation in the assault of young people from poet-priest Ernesto Cardenal's Solentiname community. Under the influence of "Liberation theology," Cardenal established a religious community parish in the Solentiname archipeligo during the 1960s. There he taught a new interpretation of the Gospel, calling for an active struggle against worldly evil and the establishment of the "Kingdom of Heaven" on the earth. Peasant families from the various islands of Grenada Lake participated in Cardenal's religious masses, and in the cultural and educational programs established in Solentiname as a kind of model for a future Nicaragua based on communalism, justice and love. Gradually, crafts and poetry workshops developed in the community, as more and more people sought to express their new found sense of life in all forms possible.

The poems in Section 1 are examples of the work created in Solentiname. But taken in sequence, they also represent the gradual evolution of consciousness on the part of this special community. If in his early work in Solentiname, Cardenal preached non-violent resistence, he gradually came to the conclusion that in many parts of Latin America, such as Nicaragua, non-violence was impossible; the same shift in viewpoint occurred for many of Cardenal's impressionable disciples. Thus in our selection, we first see them reacting to conditions in their home area; gradually, they begin to see the political sources of their problems. Then they spring into action as idealistic militants in an action that at least overtly is doomed to failure. Finally, in the aftermath, we read of those in exile, in prison or in the grave; we read of the regret for the fallen Solentiname community, and also of commitment to continue the struggle for a new Nicaragua.

The poetry in this section, then, portrays the story of Solentiname's young people, their sense of place, their growing sense of their role in their local, national and universal history. However, the poetry is not only important in its particularity but in its symptomatic value of a pattern of growing consciousness that will take place in Nicaragua in the coming months. Indeed, many of the Solentiname poets who survived the San Carlos assault appear in other parts of this book, writing as combatants in later phases of the struggle, or as young militants (some of them in poetry workshops) in the process of Reconstruction. In fact, the poetry here is the precursor of the workshop poetry that will become so important in Nicaragua after July 19, 1979. Above all, the poetry constitutes a coherent body exemplary of the kind of writing which dominates this book: poetry by the young, by combatants, and by those who give their lives in the Nicaraguan revolutionary process.

Mayra Jimenez, a Costa Rican poet/teacher who came to Solentiname to develop the commune's poetry workshop and who later established the poetry workshops throughout Nicaragua in the Reconstruction, makes the following observations about this poetry and the poets (in "Poesia Libre," literary page of *Barricada*, [April, 1980]):

> It can be said that the first poetry workshop that existed in Nicaragua was the Solentiname workshop founded at the end of 1976 and the beginning of 1977 (there on the island and later in exile)...The first poems written in the "Workshop" reflected the real world in which the poets lived: the lake, the sky, the moon, ... the island, the guitar and the future. Later, when the assault on the San Carlos garrison occurred (in which all the people participated except the very old and the very young), they had to go into exile and then the themes of their poetry were combat, jail, exile, memories, love, repression, etc.... This poetry from Solentiname is known in many countries of the world...; it is an excellent example for the peoples of America because it is written by peasant people and it is a very revolutionary poetry. Of the poets that are here included, Donald Guevara and Elvis Chavarria were last seen in San Carlos after the assault as they were escorted away by the National Guard toward the Frio River; and Felipe Pena wrote his poems before and during the insurrectional process until he fell in combat in Nueva Guinea. Currently [many of the other] Solentiname poets

are to be found in Nicaragua fulfilling various tasks in the revolutionary process.

Later, in her August, 1980 preface to *Poesia campesina de Solentiname* (Managua, 1980), Jimenez added the following reflections worthy of note:

[These] poems are full of the people, of the natural elements that make up their world, without artifices, without metaphysical images, without literary niceties. This peasant poetry will be an example for the proletarian classes of the world. This poetry is an excellent example of what is the true function of art and its approximation to the interests of the people. ... Poetry in Solentiname emerges as a collective artistic product. In the first sessions we dedicated ourselves to reading the great Nicaraguan poets...and to universal literature. We read and commented texts from the earliest hours of the afternoon until dusk. ... I never asked any one to write.

The poetry began to emerge very quickly and in a natural way among the people. ... The first poems they wrote were discussed between the author and me but always in the presence of other members of the group. Immediately we began to discuss them with every one, as to what seemed good and what didn't. Sometimes the authors defended their positions, sometimes, they modified their work, and there were times when they eliminated their original version and began once again from scratch.

The important thing to underline is how the poetry was among them and appeared--as Ernesto Cardenal says--like a miracle. That is, it's a peasant poetry, from and for the people and therefore is an eminently social, political and human production. Above all, revolutionary and testimonial. ... [With San Carlos] the poetry took a positive leap: it went from dealing with the relations between man and nature to the relations between humanity and insurrection. But it always maintained its literary quality, ... its political function. ... They have published the poetry of these young people in Venezuela, Costa Rica, Mexico, Espana, Cuba, and Nicaragua itself. ... It constitutes a good example for the working classes who have never had access to art.

The poets lived in Solentiname and were fishermen/agriculturalists/ primitivist painters/craftsmen and then combatants. The majority of them were young people between seventeen and twenty-two years old, but there were also children of five, seven and ten years old and also older persons like Olivia, mother of six Sandinist guerrilleros, Donald among them. ... Today those who survived the war are all over the national territory working in the reconstruction. We may say that with the Solentiname poems a given stage of Nicaraguan poetry draws to a close: the peasant poetry of Solentiname and simultaneously a new time opens, with the creation of the Poetry Workshops where poets from the neighborhoods and from all the peoples of Nicaragua are joining to develop their work. They are now creating the new revolutionary poetry written since the triumph.

Of Section 2, little need be mentioned except the presence of poems by famous combatants such as Dora Maria Tellez, Hugo Torres, Daniel Ortega and Daisy Zamora, as well as poets from the great Nicaraguan tradition (Pablo Antonio Cuadra, Ernesto Mejia Sanchez, Ernesto Cardenal and others), poets from Solentiname, and other poets who would later participate in the Final Insurrection and the Reconstruction. Perhaps of special note is the collage use made of certain poems by Ortega, Cajina Vega and Fernando Silva, son of the famous Nicaraguan doctor-writer. Also, we should note the poem by Michele Najlis, really Nicaragua's first important female political poet, and also the poems by Daisy Zamora, whose participation as a militant began to transform her poetic production in the late 1970s. Finally we should note the Claribel Alegria poem on Esteli. As mentioned in our General Introduction, Alegria, though raised to identify as Salvadoran, was born in the Nicaraguan town about which she writes. Also, the translation of Alegria's "Esteli" is the only one in the whole volume that was not done by the editors (it appeared in a publication by the women's organization, WIRE).

The increasing volume of poetry by women, represented in this section, even more than the first, is a prelude to Section 4, and to all of Book II, just as it is an anticipation of the events those portions of our volume describe: the victory and the reconstruction. As elsewhere we have cut and spliced poems to present as rich a picture of the 1978 insurrection as possible, and we have tried to depict every key event as fully as our poetic materials would allow.

But on the verge of portraying the Final Insurrection, we encounter an interlude, a selection of poetry by combatant-poets who fell between 1972 and 1979. We have already had examples of such figures: Edwin Castro, Rigoberto Lopez Perez, Ricardo Morales Aviles and Leonel Rugama appear in Part I; Felipe Pena, Elvis Chavarria and Donald Guevara appear in Part II, Section 1. Morales and Pena reappear here, but they are joined by several other writers who would not live to see the final triumph, but whose lives and poetry would serve as examples during the anti-Somocista period and during the Reconstruction.

Putting aside the literary quality of the work included, we may find this body of poetry worthy of presenting here because it represents the dedication, the aspirations and ideals of many who, writers or not, struggled and died, and yet lived on as poets. Addressing this theme with reference to

Latin and Central American situations, John Beverley observes:

> No one is ashamed of idealism; without it, it would be impossible to fight against very long odds and win. ... A poet like Roque Dalton represents a new type of Latin American writer: no longer the genial "fellow traveler" of revolution..., but rather the rank and file activist for whom the intricate cabbala of clandestine struggle--slogans, passwords, safe houses, sectarian squabbles, weapons know-how--is as familiar as the world of French surrealism. This is a dangerous and difficult profession, in which the event that seals a poet's reputation is more often than not, as in Dalton's own case, precocious martyrdom.
> --"Sandinista Poetics," in *Minnesota Review*, ns 20, p. 128.

In his preface to a book of poems by Edwin Castro, *Y Si No Regresera...?* (Costa Rica: EDUCA, 1979, pp. 9-10), Jose Coronel Urtecho makes several points which elaborate the Nicaraguan dimension:

> In a country like Nicaragua, ... poet heroes and martyrs are hardly few in the ... martyrology of the struggle for liberation. The ... already sacred list of youths or kids dead in this struggle, who if not all figured exactly as poets, nor were generally recognized as such, wrote verses to express their revolutionary sentiment or their attitude of rebellion, up to now goes from ... Lopez Perez to Gaspar Garcia Laviana... All of them were, naturally, poets in their way, or as Nicaraguans tend to be, more or less poets, in the sense of a little more or a little less poets, as also in the sense of some more poets than others, all of them at different levels of quality, and although the majority didn't even dedicate or define themselves as poets, they all had the natural disposition or predisposition that is the fate of poets. In reality, all people are born more or less poets and Nicaraguans are almost all natural poets, who stop being poets to the degree that life deforms them or separates them from poetry.

> This means that ... the system, or if you wish the regime, is of itself a war against the poets and the poetry of Nicaraguan life or of human life itself. It is, in any event, a struggle against the poets, and all those who fight the system which in Nicaragua has taken the worst form imaginable, are poets. At least this is one way one could describe ... the Nicaraguan struggle against imperialism. This is, without doubt, the enemy of all Nicaraguan values. In Nicaragua, the well known motto of the dark rightwing, "Death to the intelligentsia!" becomes "Death to poetry!" It is therefore almost natural that in this struggle not only do young people recognized as poets die, but all those who struggle or die, die or struggle as poets.

Coronel Urtecho's words, written in April, 1979, of course have more significance and resonance after the final offensive and victory, because it is now known how the last years of the anti-Somocista struggle produced more poet-combatants than he knew about. Thus our selection of poems written by the poet revolutionaries who fell represents all the fallen combatants who, writers or not, known or not, are present in the Reconstruction.

We begin with Ernesto Castillo, a young man who died fighting at the age of twenty, in Leon, during the September, 1978 insurrection. "Seeing that the tanks of the enemy had been rendered useless, he launched an attack, crying FREE HOMELAND OR DEATH. At the same time that he shouted the motto, a bullet penetrated his head." Castillo was to become especially important in the Reconstruction, not only as the nephew of Ernesto Cardenal, but as the direct link in the Final Insurrection to the poet-revolutionaries like Rugama and Morales Aviles in a previous period. The poems of his we present explain why he wrote, what he thought of life and the struggle and what he hoped for in the future he sensed he would not live to see. We include one poem by Morales not included in *Nicaragua in Revolution: The Poets Speak*, which seems particularly appropriate to the portrait we undertake in this section, but we also include a poem and a versified letter from another leader of the pre-earthquake struggle, Jose Benito Escobar.

In a rather special instance, we present a poem written by Felipe Pena, one poet-combatant who died, describing the death of another poet-combatant, Father Gaspar Garcia Laviana. Although born in Spain, Garcia Laviana was a priest who became so identified with the Nicaraguan struggle that, like the seminary student Rugama some years earlier, he joined the guerilla struggle. Indeed, as Pena's poem indicates, he was an important Sandinista leader who lived on after his death in combat as an example of the relation between religion and liberation struggles. In the earliest days of the Reconstruction, Ernesto Cardenal chose to publish Garcia Laviana's terse and often moving poems as the first publication of the new Ministry of Culture, in the volume, *Cantos de Amor y Guerra* (Managua: Ediciones del Ministerio de Cultura, 1979).

Cantos explains the priest's life and death, his combative Christianity, his critical solidarity with the peasantry, his growing conviction of the necessity of armed struggle against the landowners and oppressors of the people, his vision of a time after the victory which his own sacrifice would help to make possible. We take two poems from this volume, but we have also chosen to versify one of the priest's letters, which expresses his motivations so well that it, like many previous expressions of commitment by Nicaragua's great revolutionaries, merits entering the poetic canon.

Pena of course was one of the poets from Solentiname who survived the San Carlos assault only to die at a later stage of the struggle. Of him Mayra Jimenez writes (in her preface to *Poesia campesina de Solentiname*, pp. 7-8):

> I think of Felipe, so disciplined in combat, so constant in his poetic efforts. He wrote while he made ready for war, he wrote in break times during the combat, he wrote while he was in jail, he wrote in exile, and his last poem he carried in his heart. ... But it would be more just to say that he realized the poem, because Felipe, so wise in life, was ingenious in death. His company launched an attack in Nueva Guinea, and the enemy fatally wounded a companero. Every one retreated but him. He couldn't leave the wounded man alone and concerned himself with recuperating his body with the hope of helping and saving him. He was last seen dragging a wounded man ... We don't know where he was buried ... [but] ... he died cursing his assassin. Felipe knew he would die for Nicaragua. Many times he was at the point of being assassinated during torture sessions. His poems today, after his death, have a prophetic dimension, such as when he says goodbye to his father, or when he says to a young woman, "What can I offer you/ when I have offered my life to the people."

Finally, our selection includes work by lesser known figures. Oscar Antonio Robelo, nephew of Alfonso, but a firm FSLN militant, wrote his anti-Somocista poem before falling in combat in August, 1978. Ricardo Su Aguilar left at least three poems, before dying in the Masaya struggle during the very last days before the victory. We conclude our selection with a poem by Juan Carlos Tefel who also died during the Final Insurrection, on July 14, 1979 in La Calera, on the Southern Front. His poem and his life are a direct expression of many of the young people from "good families" who joined the Sandinist struggle, except that, contrary to the opening words of his poem, we may surmise that he and other young people in Nicaragua, did indeed read Ernesto Cardenal or at any rate partook of a revolutionary culture much shaped by Cardenal and the other famous poets of Nicaragua.

After death, the victory. In the final and longest section of Part II (itself divided into four sub-sections), we present a detailed, step-by-step depiction of the period from January to July, 19, 1979. Mixing poetry, versified prose document and slogans with our chronology, we try to present a rich, action-filled, moving and comprehensible picture of the struggle, of the combatants, of their feelings, their hope and despair. We present outraged expressions about the past, hopes for the future; and above all we see examples of an attitude of compromise in the creation of a new world and a new humanity in Nicaragua.

Formally, we introduce each subsection with a passage from Luis Rocha's poem which he designed to cover the insurrectional period. As in Part I and Part II, Section 2, we have works by famous major poets of Nicaragua. Cardenal, Mejia Sanchez, Cuadra and Cajina Vega are present, as are younger but important writers like Gioconda Belli, Rosario Murillo, Alejandro Bravo, Julio Valle-Castillo and others. And there are even excerpts from a poem by long-exiled poet Mario Lugo. But here, as in the book as a whole, the major portion goes to young, virtually unknown writers: the poets from Solentiname, many poet combatants, and many others who did not write until the Reconstruction made possible the poetry workshops in which they could learn to write and express their experience of the war.

Of the poetic materials, we should just mention the poems by Mario Cajina Vega, "written while he participated in the defense and liberation of Masaya, to inspire his companeros," and "dedicated to those who stayed in Masaya without giving in." And we should also note the poems from Esteli by Magdalena Rodriguez, written as an almost day by day account of the events taking place in her town; also the poem by Luis Vega which we have broken into parts to maintain our chronology while detailing the street-fighting in Managua, the strategic retreat to Masaya and the victorious return to the capital after Somoza's departure.

Worthy of special citation is the brief selection from another mainstay of the Nicaraguan poetic tradition. Known mainly for her surrealistic poetry in the past, Mariana Sanson finds her poetic vein appropriate for presenting us a crucial vision of Nicaragua some days before the victory. "Here they are giving birth to a primary liberty," she tells us. With the older woman poet are the younger ones. Rosario Murillo's voice begins to be heard, as she grows impatient with the slow march to victory. Winner of the 1978 Casa de las Americas prize for her poems of struggle, Gioconda Belli gives us an ample expression of her feelings on the day that victory finally comes. And Vida Luz Meseses makes an analogy between the revolutionary struggle and "writing a poem."

All told, the voices of women, almost silent in the early political poetry of Nicaragua, have grown louder and louder throughout the years of revolutionary struggle. Those voices reach a new peak in the Final Insurrection. And they will achieve still newer levels and richer nuances in the period of Reconstruction when they, and all the poets of Nicaragua, including many represented in our chorus of victory, participate in the making of Nicaragua's poetry of reconstruction.

Section 1. Solentiname and San Carlos (1977)

1. Bosco Centeno/ SOLENTINAME WAS

Solentiname was Julio Guevara
with his strawberry-wood fishing
  pole
and his laugh, catching fish in the
  lake.
It was the girls with their rowboats,
dressed up like bouquets, going to
  mass.
And the herons on the shore which,
as Alejandro says: "From the
  distance
you can confuse them with a
  virgin."
And the parties with drinks
under the mango tree in front of the
  church
playing Chono's phonograph. It was
the town discussing the gospel on
  Sundays
And the trips to catch turtles and
  gather
carob for our communal breakfasts.
And the music of Elvis, William
and little Adan on Sundays.
And the children's noise in the boats
on their way to school,
scaring ducks that fly off shitting.
Solentiname was our pledge
to a Free Homeland or Death.
And Ernesto prophesizing
about new times and lands.
And paintings full of life
by peasant painters.
Solentiname is Julio Guevara
in exile with his smile
catching glimpses of the future.
It's Elvis and Donald, captured,
wearing bloodied hoods, tossed like
  sacks

onto a boat and taken to Managua
(we never heard from them again).
It's Felipe in prison in San Carlos
like a bird in a cage, unable to write.
It's Sunday being one more day.
It's Jose and Oscar
tortured by Ranger Franklin
  Montenegro.
It's the memory of our islands.
(It's the heron on the shore
that from a distance
you can confuse with a virgin.)
It's our houses where they satisfied
their impotent and abusive rage.
It's the children at home
because there's no school.
It's the pain you need to give birth.
Solentiname is Julio Guevara
with his smile and grandchildren
catching fish in the lake
And the herons looking like
small virgins from a distance.
It's the children's shouts on their
  way
to the school of revolution.
It's the Company's lands made
into cattle cooperatives. And "Yes,
companero land-clearer; and yes,
companero fieldworker; yes,
  companero"
Everyday will be a Sunday and a
  mass,
It will be/ it will be
  It will be/ it will be to each one
  according to each one's needs.

2. Johnny Chavarria (age 11)/ PEASANTS

The peasant works,
the rich see the poor suffer.

While the peasant eats beans,
the rich eat meat everyday and
whatever else they want.
The poor wear torn clothes,
the rich wear linen.
The poor live in cardboard homes,
and the exploiters laugh at the
     peasant.

3. Olivia Silva/ MARCOS JOYA'S CHILDREN

The children of Marcos Joya
die without medicine,
for the children of Ricardo Reyes
and the elderly can't eat well
but Somoza has the latest arms to
     kill.

4. Elvis Chavarria/ SAN CARLOS

The rain falls on rotted roofs.
An old lady hawks her wares,
"Fried fish, fried fish."
Dogs, cats, pigs,
on a really dirty street.
A cart with a bell, and an old man,
"Come and see, come and see,
here are the cones."
Bars, barbershops, billiard parlors,
gas stations, eateries, whorehouses.
Swallows, ticks, flies, stench,
merchandise, more stench,
more merchandise, shit.
Full clotheslines--sheets, shirts,
     pants,
the noise of the women, "pon-pa,
     pon-pa,"
washing and washing.
The suckers, the apples, the
     mangoes,
the cheese, the tripe, the
     watermelon,
the cold drinks, the rice water.

More merchandise, more ticks,
     swallows,
more shit, more posters.

5. Donald Guevara/ IN THE DARK NIGHT

In the dark night
one star or another;
the phonograph sounded
rather far away,
while I gave you a hand
to get in the boat
which was still empty.
And slowly, like arrow-grass,
you went out of sight
without saying when
we would see each other again.

6. Gloria Guevara/ THE GUERILLA-FIGHTER

You who left the warmth of your home
to seek true love.
If they kill you your death won't be
in vain
because you'll live in the memory
of the people.

7. Elena Pineda/ WHEN THE KIDS OF SOLENTINAME ATTACKED SAN CARLOS

The small blue and white boat
color of sky and water
left the dock and for the last time
I stole a glimpse of my lovely
archipeligo Solentiname.
And at last we left the lake
we entered the river
on the route towards Costa Rica.
Night falls, you only hear the song
of crickets in the silence

and once again I begin
to recall the song of
all the birds of Solentiname.
And all at once they startled me:
the bam, bam, bam, the r-r-r-um
r-r-r-um of distant machine guns.

8. Pedro Pablo Meneses/ IN
   NICARAGUA, THE GREAT
   ATTACK

In Nicaragua the great attack
on the San Carlos garrison
that cold dawn.
From the fort, on the twelfth,
I looked at Solentiname.
Time passes like a shooting star.
We'll go on till the final victory.
We'll be free or we'll be martyrs.

9. Centeno/ BROTHER

Brother guardsman, forgive me
for having to aim
with care while shooting at you,
but on our shots depend the
   hospitals
and the schools we didn't have,
where your kids will play with ours.
You know they will justify our
   shots,
but your deeds will be
the shame of your generation.

10. Myriam Guevara/ TO CHATO
    MEDRANO, FALLEN IN THE
    SAN CARLOS ASSAULT

That October dawn
wearing bluejeans and an azure
   jacket
carrying an assault gun,
you fought next to us.

When you entered the old barracks
they wounded you in your right leg,
dragging yourself with the help
of a companero you reached us.
Your face handsome but pale,
you shouted, "Maintain your
   positions!"

11. Silva/ DONALD AND ELVIS

Donald and Elvis were captured
   together,
later they separated them.
I know they're alive and that
the National Guard denies holding
   them,
but history will absolve them.

12. Felipe Pena/ SOMOZA'S
    MAGAZINE

I'm sitting on the cement floor
of the Bartolina prison
and the guard cautiously
gives us the magazine
which shows old Somoza and his
   sons,
the one who had
the General of Free Men murdered
and the one
who murders our people today.
I look at Somoza Debayle
riding a Peruvian horse,
I wanted to read but my vision
   blurred,
I saw the letters as black stains.

13. Meneses/ IN EXILE

All day long cars go by
contaminating the air.
The mountains full of fresh air,
small birds singing at dusk,

the river flowing
I remember my Solentiname
with its calm lake and the
    blackbirds
heading toward the fields.
But one day I'll return
to Nicaragua without Tacho.
I'm living in exile.

14. Silva/ IN SOLENTINAME

Nothing's left in Solentiname;
Ernesto's not there
discussing the Gospel with us.
That lunch among family has ended.
Ernesto isn't directing painting
Only the birds' song has stayed
    behind
with the repugnant presence
of the National Guard.

15. Ivan Guevara/ TO MY NICARAGUA FROM EXILE

Nicaragua, Nicaragua cries
like an abandoned girl, Nicaragua
    cries.
But the day isn't far off when we
    won't
have to live underground or in exile
nor pass clandestine leaflets
and documents from hand to hand.
The day will come
when thousands of heroes will be
    reborn,
those still unknown by the people.
The day will come when we can
    shout
in the middle of the street
LONG LIVE THE SANDINIST
    FRONT!

Section 2. Towards The Final Victory

1. Pedro Xavier Solis/ IN MY COUNTRY

In my country
the vultures flutter in the air
in the stench of crime,
rotting bodies scattered
on the ground.
Already the dry echo of bullets
has become a habit.

In my country
crosses project
extended black wings.
    ...Soon other birds will
come to my country.
There'll be other breezes,
not those of death.

January 10: In the midst of his press campaign exposing the dealings of Somoza's son with rightwing Cuban exiles, *Prensa* editor and UDEL leader Pedro Joaquin Chamorro, the only viable non-Sandinist alternative to Somoza, is assassinated. His burial leads to massive demonstrations against the dictatorship, and the deepening of opposition to Somoza throughout the country.

2. Pablo Antonio Cuadra/ THE GOURD

A hero rebelled against the powers of the Black House.
A hero fought against the lords of the House of Bats.
Against the lords of the Dark House
   ...in whose interior only sinister thoughts are thought.
He went up front. And it was his daring foot which opened
   the way.
And many times he astutely mocked the oppressors
but in the end he fell into their hands...

January 22-Feb. 2: Fearful of the political vacuum caused by the death of Chamorro, the private sector calls a work stoppage and goes on strike, demanding Somoza's resignation. The Catholic Church supports the strike, and soon many parts of the country are paralyzed. Venezuela boycotts petroleum exports to Nicaragua and the U.S. cuts military aid to Somoza. Esso workers strike, as do bank employees. Somoza declares a state of "public calamity." Announcing his decision to reinstate the National Emergency Committee which had operated after the 1972 earthquake, he calls on all sectors to return to work. But by month's end, protests break out in Matagalpa, Diriamba, Managua, Masaya and San Carlos. The National Guard attack women demonstrating at the United Nations building with tear gas; they brutalize 3,000 students protesting at the national university. In several towns, women march through the streets beating pots and pans, as young boys burn tires and build barricades. BECAT patrol units sweep through the streets, beating and sometimes shooting protestors on sight. AMPRONAC, the women's organization, begins to grow in size and strength, relatin more concretely to the struggles of workers and peasants.

3. Michele Najlis/ PROVERBS AND SONGS

Silent seamstress
between the noise of machines
that devour kilometers of cloth.
Hammering shoemaker
tired over the nail.
Miner, daily resurrected
from the firelamp.

Mortar mason of the future.
Peasant who works another's land
without wife and without sons
without harvest.
Proletarians of the world
let's unite.

February 3-19: By February 3, it is clear that the work stoppage and initial protests have failed to bring down the dictatorship. The businessmen warn they will continue their attack on Somoza, but they open their doors for commerce, and it is clear that the limits of liberal pressure have been reached. As organizing among peasants and workers, women and students continues to develop, the Sandinists take up the initiative, attacking Granada, Rivas and counter-insurgency training camps in Santa Clara, Nueva Segovia. Then, on February 10, the people of Monimbo, joined by large numbers from Masaya, baptize the San Sebastian plaza with Chamorro's name. At 5 p.m. two thousand people occupy the plaza. The National Guard attacks, but the people fight back, building barricades and trenches. By the 19th, the town is in full rebellion, fighting against the Guards for an entire week. The people suffer great losses, and are beaten back. But the spirit of Monimbo persists throughout the growing national insurrection. As poet Mario Cajina Vega explains, "Monimbo is Nicaragua!"

4. Alejandro Bravo/ MONIMBO

1978 saw them raise
their fists and pistols
their 22s and contact bombs
their barricades made with tires
their trenches made with
   streetstones
against forty years of evil.
And the machine guns
sang for Monimbo
the song Somoza

knows how to sing.
And Somoza is strong
like strong rocks.
And Monimbo is weak
like a drop of water.
And Lao-Tse taught us
so very long ago
that...by pounding
the drop of water
beats the rock.

Late Feb.-Early March: Subtiava, an indigenous community near Leon, rises in arms. On March 8, AMPRONAC initiates International Mothers Week, calling all women to struggle for a free country. Masses are held in memory of the many mothers killed by the Guards. The Leon chapter joins with the Central University in collecting medicines and monies for Monimbo. The chapters in Jinotepe and Diriamba also respond. In Managua, the Guards attack students at the National University, killing two, arresting many; in Leon, protests, Guard violence and more arrests. In the countryside, EEBI forces terrorize peasants, raping women and arresting ATC members, as the prison population swells.

81

5. Ivan Guevara/ IN LA BARTOLINA

The cells are filled
with political prisoners,
in the mountains
peasant women are raped
by the National Guards
the children are hung and burned
together with their parents...

Late March-Early April: In Diriamba, the ATC calls a hunger strike and march to discredit government claims of improved rural conditions. Protesting peasant starvation and persecution, 1,200 members and supporters assemble in the streets, only to be confronted by National Guardsmen, who block the key intersection of the march. As demonstrators shift their point of mobilization, the Guards attempt to disperse them again with tear gas bombs. Diriamba's residents open their doors to the marchers and offer to relieve their burning faces. Meanwhile, the Guards open fire on those unable to find refuge, killing several demonstrators, including AMPRONAC members. This "victory" earns Somoza the rage of the women, who join with students throughout the country in hunger strikes expressing solidarity with the ATC and the peasants.

6. Rosario Murillo/ POINT NUMBER 1 ON THE AGENDA

I imagine the face of the assassins
I imagine their faces in the night
like a fist, like a shadow
like a hammer on the breast
marking blow after blow
more now than ever, because
eye for eye, tooth for tooth
here the rage of the people
here the demand of the mother
without sons
eye for eye, today, tooth for tooth
there is no ill
that will last a hundred years
there is no people that will endure
    it.

Early to Mid-April: From this point on the ATC participates in the formation of Sandinista popular militias, and peasant homes become FSLN refuges. Student mobilization rises, and AMPRONAC completes the process of linking women's and human rights issues with popular opposition to the dictatorship. Supported by AMPRONAC and students of Masaya's National Institute, widow Albertina Serrano goes on a hunger strike to protest the solitary confinement of her son, Marcio Jaen, and FSLN leader Tomas Borge. The students also demand the dismissal of teachers serving as Somoza spies, and attack the National Guard's efforts to bribe young people into passivity with marijuana. By mid-April, the nation's largest and longest student strike is underway, as young people take over 20 schools and battle with soldiers who attempt to retake the schools and convert them into military posts. 38 people join Albertina Serrano's fast, and more than 60,000 students join the student struggle, which develops alliances with trusted professors and parents.

7. Sergio Vizcaya, Condega Poetry Workshop/ 1978

The school and church
were taken at dawn.
Over the megaphone, the voice of
  Alcides:
Stop the repression.
Land for the peasants
  of Tonala and Sirama.
Freedom for Tomas Borge and

Marcio Jaen.
It was the first time we heard
Carlos Mejia's Peasant Mass.
The damp tires burned
and the smoke hung
in the laurel trees of the park.
With bad hand writing, on the walls:
SANDINO AND THE FSLN LIVE.

Same Period: Somoza tries to moderate the counter-attack for fear of further alienating his class allies by slaughtering their children. But in Diriamba, Jinotega and Esteli, the Guards employ tear gas, mustard gas and shooting to break up pickets and drive students out of the buildings they hold.

8. Vizcaya/ 1978

Join us, Guards!
And the reply was tear gas bombs.
The son of Candida cried out:
  Here they come.
The people ran to their refuge,
the BECATs in pursuit.

The streets with barricades,
the barricades with barbed wire.
You could only hear the BECAT
  motors
the barking of the dogs
and the uproar from the bar.

May 16: In prison, Jaen and Borge hold a hunger strike of their own to break their isolation and join the general population's protest of the treatment of political prisoners and the peasants.

9. Daniel Ortega/ IN THE PRISON

The shit and piss,
hot damn, so many people...
Jailman!
Don't let nobody talk with this man,
  ...let 'im sleep on the floor

and if he makes a move, belt 'im
  one...
The galleys, Auschwitz, Buchenwald
Nicaragua.

May 17-26: Workers and students intensify their solidarity with Borge and Jaen by once again occupying churches and schools, striking and demonstrating in the streets.

10. Fernando Antonio Silva/ DEMONSTRATION

We all shouted
we ran
we blocked corners
1 truck

1 jeep
they went that way
they'll come out this way
so we have to go over there...

Late May: Families of political prisoners join in hunger strikes. The treatment of prisoners worsens as Somoza tries to break the spirit of the strikers.

11. Ortega/ IN THE PRISON

Kick him this way, like this,
in the balls, in the face, in the ribs.
Pass me the hot iron, the billy-club.
Talk! Talk you son-of-a bitch,

try salt water,
ta-a-alk, we don't want to mess you
up.

Early June: During the installation of the National Congress, Monsenor Miguel Obando y Bravo asks the government to cease the terror and persecution against the Nicaraguan people. Chamorro's widow demands international diplomatic isolation of the Somoza regime. Arrests and prison brutality continue.

12. Ortega/ IN THE PRISON

Most Honorable and Reverend
    Archbishop,
Most excellent and illustrious
Ambassador.
Peace, respect for the people,

abundance, democracy.
Handcuff him.
Put him in the Chiquita prison,
you're going to eat your own
shit, you bastard.

June 29: In protest against the repression, thousands of elementary and high school students join with striking university students in massive demonstrations that are again met by violence.

13. Silva/ DEMONSTRATION

We came together again
  on another street
  2, 3 tear gas bombs
  we all dispersed
  handkerchiefs damp

with bicarbonate powder
covering nose and mouth
we all came together
on another corner...

July: The Group of Twelve arrives in Nicaragua saying, "The dictatorship is a cadaver, we are here for its burial." The Guards occupy Carazao and spread their violence to Esteli. But in late July, the Front counters, attacking the hated EEBI secret police from the Intercontinental Hotel, attacking Los Sabalos and El Castillo in the Department of the San Juan River.

14. Ortega/ IN THE PRISON

Keep your eyes and ears open.
Yesterday there was a battle
in the mountains,

keep your voice down,
the thing is getting hot.

August 1-21: The Twelve and the Church denounce the increasing collaboration of the major Nicaraguan capitalists with Somoza and his army; they call for strikes to force Somoza's resignation. Rumors circulate that the Sandinists are planning a major move, as demonstrations, strikes and armed confrontations multiply throughout the nation.

15. Mario Cajina Vega/ BALLAD OF MONIMBO

The time that's coming
is already turning the corner.
The time that's coming
is a social fist.

16. Dora Maria Tellez/ WE LIVE IN A RUSH

We live in a rush
that's why
I can't write

to say that when I stayed home
in the mornings
I felt your presence
in the folds of the sheets.
Maybe I'd remember
that time
we cried on duty
thinking about Ocotal,
when we went together
to fetch water
from the little ravine,
when we planned
that search;
when we began
to discover our caresses

in the barn at Don Teyo's,
the barn full of fleas
but full of love.
  Or I could go even further back
when I met you again
and we talked about boxing
the division,
the comrades;
that afternoon we ran

out of cigarettes
but not words.
  Or that time in San Fabian
When it was our turn at the M-30s
shooting and shooting.
  I can remember more...
Today we have to put
together a small document
and it's already night.

Mid-August: Dora Maria and other Sandinists of the Rigoberto Lopez-Perez Unit draft plans and make final preparations for the rumored action. On the morning of August 22, a group of twenty Sandinists, led by Eden Pastora, Hugo Torres and Dora Maria leaves the house of Daisy Zamora.

17. Daisy Zamora/ COMMANDER TWO

Dora Maria Tellez
           twenty-two years old.
Small and pale,
wearing boots, black beret
the guardsmen's uniform
           very loose.
Behind the fence
I watched her talk to the kids
under the beret the nape of her neck
white and her hair recently cut
(before she left, we hugged).
Dora Maria
the war-hardened girl
who made the tyrant's heart
tremble with rage.

Polo adjusted the olive green awning
(that turned out to be too short
at the last minute
and we covered the holes with two
    boards
nailed to the frame).
Polo, who's now dead.
The companeros
 began to take their places
wearing new uniforms and carrying
    guns
in two tight lines.
(A neighbor went out
to the patio next door.)
And Augusto in the cabin
of the truck waiting
for the order to move out.

18. Zamora/ THE RIGOBERTO LOPEZ PEREZ UNIT

I still vividly remember
the extreme paleness,
the berets, the frightened eyes.

19. Guevara/ THERE ARE DISCOURSES LIKE THESE

They're all together, all of Somoza's
liberals and assassins.
Suddenly...

August 22, 12:30 p.m.: The Commando occupies the National Palace during a session of Somoza's Congress, demanding liberty for many of the political prisoners, $10 million, and a plane to leave the country. This daring action receives international attention and awakens greater numbers of Nicaraguans to the key role of the Sandinists in the struggle against the dictatorship; it also brings the three Sandinist tendencies, which have existed since 1976, into closer coordination. The Ample Opposition Front (FOA, an organization of businessmen) and the legal opposition parties join with unions and popular organizations in calling for a massive strike of the people...

20. Bravo/ MANIFESTO

Those who weave
colored blankets.
Jewelers who fashion bracelets
    and rings
priestly goblets

and ceremonial breastplates.
Those who plant corn
    and cocoa.
Those who cut
white cotton...

August 25-30: As the strike movement grows and pressure mounts from international sources as well, Somoza accedes to the Sandinist demands, and they leave for the airport. Thousands risk death by taking to the streets and cheering them on their way. Somoza demands that things return to normalcy, but his vulnerability has become apparent, and by the end of the month, work stoppages are virtually total throughout the country. Finally, young people in Matagalpa begin what becomes a national offensive, attacking the National Guard barracks and taking areas vacated by the retreating troops.

21. Bravo/ MANIFESTO

Makers of cups and mats
for hammocks and cords.
Those who play flute and drum.
Vendors in the market.
Fishermen of rivers and lakes...

22. Cajina Vega/ BALLAD OF MONIMBO

The time that's coming
is Brotherly Sun.

Machetes come to life
in the cotton fields.

23. Guevara/ THERE ARE DISCOURSES LIKE THESE

Meanwhile, Somoza...
nervous, kept on speaking,
"Calm down people,
everything is peaceful.
I'll put everything in order,
don't be afraid.
Here there is freedom, love..."

September 1-9: The national strike continues; priests all over the country protest the repression of the people. International solidarity mounts, and the case of Nicaragua goes before the Organization of American States. The Front launches a coordinated offensive, taking Ocotal in the north and Penas Blancas in the south. Popular insurrection spreads from Matagalpa to Masaya, Chinandega, Leon and Esteli, and the Guards are forced to retreat. Somoza compares the total national mobilization to the 1968 Tet offensive in Viet Nam.

24. Cajina Vega/ BALLAD OF MONIMBO

The time that's coming
    is a communal voice

25. Bravo/ MANIFESTO

Those who work
rare feathers
And those who make
verse and history
            in manuscripts
have said ENOUGH!
No more chiefs
No more gentlemen
at the gathering.

September 10-18: Sandinists simultaneously attack five police stations in Managua. Somocista planes bombard Costa Rican border towns, wounding innocent civilians. Fierce battles continue in Masaya, Chinandega and Esteli. The work stoppage continues with demonstrations and fighting throughout the country. Somoza declares a State of Siege and employs massive force against the national uprising, placing his major emphasis on Esteli. He cuts off the city's communications and access to Red Cross aid, while launching fierce aerial bomb attacks.

26. Guevara/ THERE ARE DISCOURSES LIKE THESE

Suddenly we hear contact bomb explosions
terrified the people run
shouts of women and children...
This is the peace of Nicaragua.

September 19-25: The O.A.S. steps up its pressure on Somoza and his allies; the International Monetary Fund agrees to hold off promised aid to the regime. Undeterred, the Somocistas continue their attack, bombing out sections of Leon and Chinandega. Both cities fall; and finally, Esteli, subjected to the most ruthless bombings for many days, gives in before the devastating air attack.

27. Claribel Alegria/ ESTELI

Esteli
Eastern river
after forty years
of drought
of plunder
of deception
of predatory rulers
your bed no longer dry.
With slime and blood
it has been filled
with empty cartridges
and with blood
and shirts
pants
and corpses
sticking like algae
to the rocks.
A suffocating stench
rises from the river.
Esteli
Eastern river
your shipwrecked
can't find employment
they walk downcast
marauding
searching the rubble
for those broken scissors
that Singer sewing machine
The river Esteli
is spurting blood
and it was your step-sons
your step-sons dressed
as national guards
your step-sons unleashed
by Somoza
trained
tamed
by Somoza
and mercenaries hired
and castrated
by Somoza
your step-sons underpaid
by step-son Somoza
who opened fire
and destroyed
Esteli
Eastern river
you are weeping blood.

(Translated by Electa Arenal and Marsha Gabriela Dreyer)

Late September-Mid-October: The popular uprising of 1978 is defeated. National Guard planes drop leaflets on the people warning them against further resistance; they bomb and strafe thousands of refugees fleeing to Honduras and Costa Rica. Several Latin American and European countries condemn Somoza's campaign in the U.N. The negative international reaction spreads as reports and statistics appear which make a baleful, insidious poetry of National Guard achievements for September...

28. Permanent Commission on Human Rights/ FORMS AND LEVELS OF HUMAN RIGHTS VIOLATIONS IN NICARAGUA*

Arrest without accusation
disappearance of prisoners
appearance of cadavers of prisoners
in deserted areas
death from torture in jails
civilians murdered without cause
in the streets
sexual abuse of women
bombing whole neighborhoods to
ruins

Late October-Late December: It becomes clear that Somoza's victory is just a further step in his ultimate undoing. Fearing the worst, the U.S. cuts off direct aid and works with FAO to build pressure for elections that would replace the dictatorship with a more "moderate" and less murderous government less likely to incite insurrection while maintaining a power and investment base agreeable to U.S. and Nicaraguan business interests. Starting with "The Twelve", one moderate group after another deserts the FAO to side, however reluctantly, with the Sandinists, who repudiate FAO's dealings and their U.S. fabricated formula of "Somocismo without Somoza." As the days go by, there are many maneuvers and countless encounters. Above all, ever-higher levels of unity are achieved among Sandinist tendencies, and more and more sectors join in new, ever-multiplying organizational forms, such as the United People's Movement (MPU) and the Civilian Defense Committees (CDS's), which will come to constitute the victorious insurrectional bloc. Meanwhile, a more profoundly revolutionary spirit comes to permeate consciousness and every day life (including the very nature of family and love relations) for increasing numbers throughout Nicaragua.

29. Alba Azucena Torres/ COMMUNIQUE NUMBER 1,000 FOR MY LOVE

I write you this poem
so that one of these days
they'll give it to you and a friend
will tell you that I still love you
or he'll tell you that here in
    Nicaragua
we no longer write romantic poems
and that things are still a mess.
Don't write me.
I know how to decode the clouds
and the strangely human signs
that sometimes appear in the
    afternoon
silent with illusions apt for
    dreaming.
Here in your country bombs are
    heard
every few minutes and there are
    thousands
of guards who ardently seek their
    fate
(and you know, my love,

the green of the uniforms
reminds me of the green of hope)
and they go on like blind creatures
or zombies.
Love, you've heard of voodoo,
here the dead are alive and the
    living are dead
and we're not in Brazil or Africa.
Perhaps this friend will tell you
that in Nicaragua
we no longer write love poems
except when we give our lives.

30. Ernesto Castillo/ IN THIS COUNTRY

If we had been born
in another country,
if we had known
another type of society,
we would be a happy couple,
making plans for the future,
writing poems and love letters,
and all our problems
would stem from our relationship.

But we were born in Nicaragua,
we met each other
and love each other
in this country.
We write each other
letters and poetry.
not about love,
but about struggle,
letters that talk
about murdered companeros,
poems that are published
   underground.
Our problems
are the problems of our people.
However, I'm sure
that our love
couldn't be greater,
since besides being ours,
it belongs to the whole people,
and that's enough.

31. Bravo/ LETTER

Tell your parents that I love you.
That I bring strong hymns
for the worker's struggle
and the sailor's travel,
that I can sing
old ballads to Sandino
full of the scent of pines
and trills of quetzales
for the peasant's battle.
For you flowers
and sweet songs I have.
But they must not ask where
   or how we'll live.
Tell them that we come from the
   people
      and we'll go to the people.

32. Zamora/ A TIME WILL COME

A time will come when
   love will be the only language.
And we will remain alone:
brother with brother
sister with sister
hearing the dark throbs of the earth.
Sometimes we'll remember
the ancient objects
and their reign on the earth
   --and perhaps we'll laugh--
But no one, no one will look
for them again.

33. Cajina Vega/ BALLAD OF
   MONIMBO

The time that's coming:
Total justice.
Guitars, marimbas
and national peace.
The time that's coming
the Muse that thunders!

34. Francisco de Asis Fernandez/
   LET'S GO, COMRADES

Let's go comrades,
let's assault the heavens
to live in them fully;
but let's be clear about one thing:
no region of earth
has such riches
or makes them bloom so.
Lovingly and sadly
we have to accept the fact
that our abundance of gifts
resides within us.
The chosen ones are within us,
the mob, the people.

Section 3. The Poet-Combatants Who Died (1972-79)

1. Ernesto Castillo/ JUNE 18, 1978

Save these poems with care,
the originals, the copies,
because one future day
I'll ask you for them
or others will ask for them,
so they may be published
when the conditions
we're creating
with our struggle
make it possible.

2. Ricardo Morales Aviles/ WHEN
THE BOURGEOISIE LOSE
THEIR HAIR

"When the Bourgeoisie lose their
hair..."
Capital

When dawn comes
and the bourgeoisie lose their hair,
will you still love me as you do now
and will your eyes still shine
as they do today?
If by then I've found a place to rest,
will you still need me
and want to stay with me?
We'll be older
and have more dreams than today
but maybe we'll be able
to stroll through a garden
talk under a tree or I'll sing you a
song
you can watch me
through a window pulling weeds
or if you wish, play with the
children
clinging to your skirt
or we could read the stars

or find the thread
and the rhythm of poems
or travel to some solitary planet on
Sundays
or slowly walk in the afternoon on
warm sands,
or we could invite some friends
and not say goodbye until dawn
or be very serious, study and learn.
Together we could watch
the world's darkness change to light.
Could we ask for more? When this
time comes,
will you still need me and keep me
company?
I'll wait for your answer,
the rifle has fired, I have much to
do.

3. Carlos Arroyo Pineda/ I
REMEMBER YOU

I remember you in this hour of
happy distance:
radiant, fresh like an early winter
morning
which makes one find a sweet coat.
I remember you next to me:
delicious, smiling
waking up like a little girl in my
arms
and your inevitable clamor
for the first kisses at dawn.
I remember you in the busy hours
we lived:
hours of sweaty fires and speeches
ablaze
with the red and black verb
hours of huge walks at double time
guided by our flag of proletarian
freedom.

I   remember you in the routine: quick
your hair tossed by the wind
giving gifts of smiles to the work,
following the precise instructions
in block letters that Anselmo sent
   us.
And I remember you on slow
   morning walks
looking for you in the bed we built,
burying my head on your beautiful
   belly
as if to discover the secrets of your
   soul
and that way love you in happiness
   and anguish.
I remember you
in the daily communion
of ideas and actions
which illuminate the future: there
   where
our child will grow healthy, strong,
   happy.
And summing up memories:
I think of you so much
that time when from deep inside me,
from my depths,
with veins raised and fists
clenched more than ever,
out burst the words over the heads
   of men
and women in the neighborhoods:
FREE HOMELAND OR DEATH!
with that I also wanted to tell you
That I love you,
I love you, Luisa, don't forget it.

4. Arroyo Pineda/ FOR MY SON*

Brother, try to give
my son when you can
the kisses and embraces
I won't be able to give him.
If I fall in this struggle
then I want you to help

form him as he should be formed,
educate him in solidarity,
humility and the virtues
to which we aspire
and for which today
we are ready to give
the little we can:
our very lives.
I want nothing of riches
and luxuries for him;
I fight and will fight
for a different tomorrow
in which he can live with dignity
in harmony and happiness.
Where homes are not filled
with mourning and tears.

5. Castillo/ EVEN THOUGH MY LIFE MAY NOT LAST

Even though my life may not last
until the day of victory,
my struggle won't be in vain,
since in the happiness of the people
will be a feeling of sadness
mixed with hope,
and then they'll say,
"companeros,
let us remember those
who fell in battle."
Then everyone will know
that mine was not a useless act,
nor were the acts of many others,
we know that even if
we don't see it,
the day is near.

6. Castillo/ WHERE THE UNKNOWN

Where the unknown
spilled their blood,
there where they left
a reminder

smelling of gunpowder,
there I'll start
to build
joys and hopes.
There where the Guardsmen
burnt ranches,
where the planes destroyed
towns,
we will build schools,
cooperatives,
hospitals,
with the names of those
who died without seeing them.

7. Jose Benito Escobar/ LIKE THE
   MOUNTAIN
   (To Eulalio Lopez)

My poems are sad
like the afternoon,
like the peasant's face haggard
    from hunger,
like the wind's song
sad like the creek
which goes to the ravine
and from the ravine to the river,
the river is noisy,
it's a giant
    it's a murmur
a sad song.
The mountain is sad
    without skyscrapers,
    without mercury
    or neon lights,
    without discotheques
    or psychodelic colors,
    without restaurants
    or beauty parlors,
    without countryclubs
    or the Terrace club,
    or other crappy joints
    where the rich
    go to play.
Everything, everything is sad
at the peasant ranch

(quaint say the sons-of-bitches
who live in mansions),
sad the mat where they sleep
    and even sadder
    what they eat,
    and sadder still
    when they don't have
    anything to eat!
    the face of a child
    who died of hunger,
    and the face of the mother
    who conceived him while hungry,
    raised him while hungry,
and saw him die while hungry,
    her tears
    aren't from grief,
    they're from hunger.
Paradise
    say the bastards
but they don't know
    how a peasant is born
    grows
    lives
    dies.
What are they going to know
    about hunger?
They don't even have
to live off the catch.
They know about...
    about Chevrolet,
    about Cadillac,
    about coffee,
    about cotton,
    about meat
on the world market,
about bank accounts,
    about whisky,
    about champagne,
    about perfumes
    and refined whores,
they know nothing about hunger,
    nothing
    they don't even know what it is,
it's "society"
    the aristocracy
yes, it's them

receiving communion
  everyday
  and crossing themselves
  to go to sleep.
They're afraid of death
  but they use it
  like a medicine.
Eulalio didn't die of hunger,
  he was in Pancasan
  and died in Zenica,
  fighting those who
  prescribe hunger,
  nakedness,
  ignorance,
  misery, death.
Eulalio roams the mountains
  he's a path
  he's a footprint,
  he's a shadow,
  he's a creek,
  he's a ravine,
  he's a river,
  he's a violent
  storm.

8. Oscar Antonio Robelo/ THE
   ACCEPTED WHORES

I'm sitting here
like a fool
thinking
without thinking
about anything
my mind's blank
like this sheet of paper
before I started writing,
from that moment
it also started
to get lines.
I'm surrounded by whores
by people who sell
their ideas
their way of life
"they" don't sell their
bodies like the saintly women

in the neighborhood brothels
and the society of the
marginalized class.
They're the real whores
and for their brothel they have
the government, the ministries,
the work centers
and houses of study.
Day after day
class society
manufactures more whores,
meeting its needs that way.

9. Felipe Pena/ A GOOD LEADER

I met you at the beginning of
    September;
we were in a column of 35 soldiers
in the people's army;
you were in the rearguard
with companera Marta and me.
Your pseudonym was Martin.
We heard rockets explode 400
    meters away.
They gave the order to advance.
We went into some pastures;
the brush barely reached our knees
and the planes came in close.
"This is murder," I shouted angrily.
"They take us from our cover
to a place where there is none.
And, Martin, you shouted: "Don't
    be afraid,
when the plane comes near,
sit down and don't move.
Running and sitting we got to the
    ravine
there you took off your shoes
and seeing our desperation,
you said with all the tranquility in
    the world:
"If a bomb hits us that's as far as
    we go,
but not one of us is going to run."
I was afraid and I asked you

timidly,
"Aren't you going to do
anything to these people?"
And you answered firmly: "No."
The next night on the road
the Civil Guard took you prisoner
and deported you to Panama,
then I saw you again in the camp
directing drills from five to six
in the morning.
I remember that because of you
they didn't send me to another
    camp.
After that I heard nothing about you
until I heard the news
that the guardsmen had killed you
    in battle
with your priest's name, Gaspar
    Garcia Laviana.
When I met you I didn't know you
    were a priest;
to me you were just a good leader
giving body and spirit
to the people's struggle.

10. Gaspar Garcia Laviana/ ANGUISH

The afflictions
of my heart
are not lightened
by the Rosary,
nor mass,
nor the Brevary.
My afflictions
are lessened
by schools
in the valleys,
by the peasants'
well-being,
by freedom
in the streets
and peace
on the roads.

11. Garcia Laviana/ WHY A PRIEST FIGHTS*

It fell to me to see perhaps
the most shameful
the most miserable
the most oppressed
of Nicaragua.
I tried to save this situation
in a Christian way
peacefully;
seeking to raise this people
by their own means
or with the means of the
    government.
But I realized that all this
was a lie, a deception.
I began to lose heart
seeing that so much work
was completely useless
that so many dreams
were left in the air
because the people kept on
living as before.
That is why I joined
this violent movement
since I realized
that nothing peaceful
was possible.
Any other way
would have been dishonest
to an entire people
and to myself.

12. Garcia Laviana/ WHEN I DIE

When we win the war,
don't come remorseful to my grave
with roses and carnations
red like my spilled blood.
I swear I'll rise up
and whip you with them.
I'll only allow violets
like my bruised flesh,
like my mother's pain,

like the peasant's hunger
in my Latin America.

13. Ricardo Su Aguilar/ LETTER
    FROM A SANDINIST*

From this cold and wet cell
I wanted to write you these verses
and tell you, my mother,
that I'm a prisoner
not to make you suffer;
that's never been my intention.
I don't want to see you cry
I would like you to be proud
of "your little boy"
as I am of you
and not be ashamed
of having a revolutionary son
a Sandinist proletarian son
because I aspire to that honor,
to give testimony, to fight and,
if necessary, give my life.
I ask you, my mother,
think instead that your sons are all
those who struggle
and that I'm in everyone of them.
In jail, in the mountains
and in the fields and anywhere
think of me as the son who loved
    you
as he won't be able to love anyone
    else,
more than any woman,
that's how much I love you.
I know you're suffering
because I was captured.
maybe they could have killed me
but I got out already, I'm free.
Free to struggle and to love you,
to live and die

and keep on living and keep on
    dying
because I'm sure
that if I die in battle, my mother,
you will be able to say,
"I had a revolutionary son,
and in spite of everything,
in spite of the repression and vices,
he preferred to follow the path
    which every honest man should
    follow."

14. Juan Carlos Tefel/ THE
    DAMAGES WILL BE PAID

I didn't throw bombs in Masaya
or Esteli, or in Leon or Monimbo,
but I've felt the tremor caused by
the explosions of the Revolution.
I haven't read Cardenal's poems,
but I've felt the flame
which ignites outraged desire
singing songs of death.
And rocket and tank explosives
and the murderous fire
which machine-guns our brothers
and erupting volcanoes and
    earthquakes
which rise from within me
when I pull the trigger.
Don't cry, market woman, you'll
    soon see;
nor you, poor kid.
Don't cry, drink-vendor;
The kingdom of Nicaragua belongs
    to you,
we only have to wait,
mother of five dead sons
and two in the hospital,
the damages will be paid.

Section 4. The Final Insurrection & Victory (1979)

A. *First Phase: Preparations and Early Moves (January-May)*

1. Luis Rocha Urtecho/ YOU STILL HEAR THEIR VOICES IN THE WIND

You hear roosters
at dawn.
   No.
It's their voices
in the wind
because not even death
stops us from hearing them

one more time.
Their steps in the night
approach on the run
in the dark cold their bodies
erupt
pure, cool and tremulous
in our troubled dream...

January-February: The political turning point in the popular resistance. Various mass organizations take form, and Somoza's efforts at repression only make them grow. Commemorating the death of Pedro Juaquin Chamorro, the organizations mobilize, as 30,000 march in Managua and demonstrations take place in many cities, including Bluefields. The Health Workers Federation (Fetsalud) stages a three-week hunger strike, and teachers join with students to demonstrate against announced plans for massive university funding cuts.

2. Jose Maria Lugo/ ENOUGH

And the lips of the oppressed
   said: Enough.
And the hearts of those
who came to break

in the earth said: Enough.
And the greed of the ruler
who sidetracked the people's will:
   Enough.

February: The FSLN-backed United Popular Movement (MPU) moves to create the National Patriotic Front (FPN), which unites all democratic forces, including liberal groups which have withdrawn from the discredited FAO. In the FPN are the Independent Liberal Party (PLI), the Group of Twelve, the Nicaraguan Workers' Confederation (CTN) and the Managua Radio Reporters Union (SRPM); the Popular Social Christian Party and the Nicaraguan Democratic Movement (MDN) attend as observers of sessions in which the joining groups hammer out a program involving commitment to bring down the regime, oppose foreign intervention and establish the bases for effective democracy. The FPN sets up a National Secretariat and a series of commissions, which provide the FSLN's transitional political alternative to the dictatorship and a basis for insurrectional mobilization. Meanwhile guerilla activities break out on the Southern Front; the National Guard carries out various atrocities in Leon and elsewhere; and the still-divided Sandinist "tendencies" move closer to internal unity while leading an ever-more-unified national movement.

3. Roberto Vargas, Nicaraguan Embassy (Washington, D.C.)/ IT'S TIME

It's time that we get
more serious.
If we're more serious, it's time
that we get braver, it's
time that we get
stronger. If we're stronger

it's time that we unite.
If we're united,
it's time we should be fighting.
If we're fighting
serious/brave/strong and united
we will win!

March 11: Representatives of the three Sandinist tendencies sign a unity pact, firming up the strategy to overthrow the dictator and establishing a general program of reconstruction.

4. Conjoint Leadership of the FSLN/ COMMUNIQUE*

Fellow Nicaraguans
with revolutionary and Sandinist
joy,
we announce to the world
what every one awaited:

the irreversible and unbreakable
unity
of the Sandinist Front
of National Liberation.

March 26-30: Led by Commander German Pomares Ordonez ("El Danto"), Northern Front combatants take El Jicaro. England recalls its ambassador in protest against Somoza's human rights violations; and the national clamor against the regime grows more organized. New volunteers join the FSLN for further action on the Northern Front and elsewhere, as part of a plan to divert the Guards toward greatly separated parts of Nicaragua.

5. Juan Ramon Falcon, Tenderi Nueva Macatera Poetry Workshop/ AND YOU LEFT FOR THE NORTHERN FRONT

The last time I saw you
you were wearing a simple dress
I meant to ask you for a kiss
but I was afraid

that's why I left
without saying goodbye
and without seeing you again.

April 1-16: Increasing military activity throughout the country, as the FSLN tests its new unity. During Holy Week (April 8-14), the Front attacks Guard outposts in the North (El Sauce, Rio Grande, Achuapa, Condega, Ducali, Yali and Esteli) in a series of hit-and-run assaults. In Esteli itself, guerillas strike the city to collect weapons; the people rise up, take over the city and ask the FSLN to stay and support them. They hold the city for some days, as the total of FSLN fighters rises to roughly 200, but they are surrounded by 2,000 Guardsmen. The Sandinists drive a wedge through the Somocist guards, and most of the fighters escape. The Guards retake the city, but most of them are drawn toward the north, where the young Sandinists prepare themselves for combat.

6. Olivia Silva/ TO MY FOUR CHILDREN IN THE MOUNTAINS

In the mountains they
don't have blankets,
they sleep on the ground
next to their companeros.
On winter nights
the wet grass
wets their tired bodies;

and breakfast doesn't come to them
in a helicopter
as it does to the guardsmen.
But with their lives they
will give these blankets
and that breakfast
to others in Nicaragua

April 17-30: Fierce combats in southern and northern towns. Fifty Sandinists attack the National Guard garrison in Catarina. Armed actions and arms recuperations in Diriamba, Jinotepe and San Gregorio; bombings in Esteli. On the Costa Rican border, Sandinists battle 3,000 Guards and decide to open a new front in Nueva Guinea, east of Lake Nicaragua. In late April, 140 Sandinists make a surprise attack, but are cut off and massacred by 1,000 Guards diverted from the Southern Front. A terrible loss, which shows, however, that the Sandinists can open new campaigns at will. May comes with the expectation of insurrection.

7. Pablo Antonio Cuadra/ MAY

In May the dead soldiers
play their drums in the distance.
But in Sandino's camp, at dawn,
the trumpet doesn't play reveille
nor does the rooster crow
(the guerilla war is silence).
"Children," the teacher tells us,
"You must stand up!"
The guerilla fighter has prepared an
   ambush
for the words which oppress, has
   overthrown
the names which shame us!
In May the peasants look for
the guerilla fighter's grave with
   flowers.
And in his notebook the child's heart
hurriedly writes a word: Freedom?
or Death? ... Don't interrupt him!
Don't you see that the child
is learning to write a Republic?
In May words fall in the furrows.
In May verbs begin to be
   conjugated.

Early May: The cordoba is devaluated; prices soar and wages fall further behind. The bourgeoisie no longer supports Somoza. A FAO representative states: "The country is moribund: a street without any exit." Venezuela and Panama end diplomatic ties with Nicaragua, and Costa Rican support for revolution grows. As the time for the Final Offensive approaches, the FSLN makes plans to integrate the three tactics they had formerly employed separately: national strike, popular insurrection and military attack. More and more young people leave the towns and go to the mountain guerilla posts; others participate in urban skirmishes which test and probe the enemy. A communications network is set up between rural guerillas and urban militia, between the MPU and the Civilian Defense Committees, between the FSLN and the people.

8. Luis Alfonso Velazquez, age nine (killed May 2)/ CALL TO ARMS*

Companeros,
now it's time to wake up.
We can see the peasant children
sleeping in their wooden bunks
and eating tortilla with salt,
that's why I tell you
that we fight for a Free Homeland.

9. Alba Azucena Torres, Juigalpa Poetry Workshop/ THE DAWN OF MAY 5TH

You came running sweaty
your dust-filled white t-shirt
which read INCH
   (National Institute of Chontales)
carrying a pistol between your skin
and your pants,
you came by the house that night
and I gave you the package
I was afraid to open that afternoon
   (it was ammunition).
Alone you went away,
the stars illuminated you
and the road was clear, clear.
The dog's barking
went with your quick steps
and then just like you
thousands of kids moved by quickly

throughout Nicaragua
to take their places in the trenches.

10. FSLN/ COMMUNIQUE*

We'll fight in the moutains,
    fields and cities
Till the poor have roof, bread,
work, peace and liberty.

11. Ivan Guevara/ WHEN YOU
SEE THIS POEM

The wind blows here in the
    mountains
where we guerilla fighters
make camp next to a river,
its water flows on and on
it goes far and yet
there's always water in the river.
The road can't tell the guardsmen
where we've come from
or where we're going;
mountain, you who have seen us
sleep on the ground
under a tree at the edge of a hill,
you also have your law
according to the legend of Chief
    Nicarao;
mountain, keep us hidden
and keep our secrets of war.

12. Guevara/ AFTER THE
AMBUSH

It gets dark quickly, starts to rain
    and
the guerilla fighters' tracks are
    erased.
We're tired;
the plains we have to pass are big,
the mud and water reach our waists
and everything's dark, not even a

star
can be seen in the sky;
the column walks in silence.
Only one guerilla fighter
thinks about writing a poem.
It continues to rain,
the mosquitoes come out of the
    swamps,
the hunger and sleepiness are
    intense.
I curl up and feel
pins-and-needles numbing my body.
No shots are heard,
now we're close to a camp...

13. Bosco Centeno/ ON THE
SOUTHERN FRONT

Sweaty and muddy
three days marching and four
    ambushing
pale, bodies full of insect bites,
the backpack weighing down like a
    cross
passing camp watch-posts slowly,
companeros ask us with just a look,
"All here?"
"Companero, not even one shot in
    seven days.
Nothing new."
Other companeros will leave
tomorrow to set ambushes.

14. Jaime Buitrago Gil/ TIRED
AND DIRTY

On returning to camp
we were all soaked,
people came to the door
to look at us.
It had rained all morning.
Arriving at the barracks
the wet and tired troops
sat on the floor,

we saw how dirty we were
and started to laugh.

along with the birds.
I have a rifle frozen in my hands.

15. Guevara/ A WATCH AT DAWN

Five in the morning.
The forest is still dark,
all the companeros are asleep
only those of us on duty are awake.
The birds begin to sing
throughout the forest.
My companeros start to get up
full of enthusiasm

16. Fernando, FSLN Combatant/
LETTER TO MARCOS

The hammocks are being made,
though I don't think
they get much use,
since we won't remain
long in the mountains.
The insurrection is upon us.

May 9-24: The FSLN launches attacks in Matagalpa, Masaya, and other northern towns trying to disperse the Guards as much as possible. On May 19, German Pomares and Javier Carrion lead the Oscar Turcios Column in an assault on Jinotega with the aim of taking pressure off the combatants in Nueva Guinea. The battle rages for five days, as Mexico breaks ties with the Somoza government and Sandinists attack Posoltega and Rivas. By May 22, the Guards retake Jinotega, and German Pomares falls. Jinotegan refugees join the FSLN in a successful retreat.

17. FSLN Combatant/ ON THE
DEATH OF "EL DANTO"*

He was wounded on May 22
between three and five in the
    afternoon.
On Thursday morning at three
when I approached him,
he was already dead;
and we formed an escort around him
so that no one would know
what had happened
and morale wouldn't flag.

18. Hugo Torres/ POMARES

You
who conquered diarheas,
rheumatism

arthritis
ignorance
the lag of centuries
You were
worker, electrician,
peasant, baseball player,
singer, guerilla fighter,
LEADER.
Faithful sign of joy
in the future,
you
who made us conquer our fear,
the shitting in our pants,
the trembling,
the weak nerves.
You who continue your life
your history in us.
You will defeat the enemy of Today,
of Tomorrow, of Whenever.

19. Lugo/ ENOUGH

And the dead soldiers in their landings said: Enough.
And the news agencies that foresaw it all: Enough.
And the friend obliged to betray a friend: Enough
And the man forced to confess through tortures:
Enough. Enough. Enough.

B. *Second Phase: Late May-June 8*

20. Rocha/ YOU STILL HEAR THEIR VOICES IN THE WIND

From their young throats
come shouts
slogans speeches
from their chests
exposed to horror.
Nothing stops their advance

their panting their ideals
their march toward victory
under a sister moon
which proclaims a tomorrow
under freedom's sun.

May 25-31: The difficulties in Jinotega and Nueva Guinea show that the FSLN must attack on many fronts at once and that an "internal front" of popular forces must lead urban insurrections which give the Sandinist columns enough time to regroup for renewed attacks. Heavy fighting breaks out on the Northern Front between Condega and Esteli; coordinated assaults on Rivas, El Naranjo and Colina 155 by the Benjamin Zeledon Southern Front. Fighting also in the mountains--in Bonanza, Rosita, Siuna--and in the two major cities, Managua and Leon, as the internal urban fronts begin to mobilize and as core Sandinist units prepare to move out in the general insurrection that is announced for the first days of June.

21. Anibal Falcon Vilchez (11 years old), Condega Poetry Workshop/ YOU LEFT SECRETLY

Your folks, your brothers, your
   girlfriend,
no one knew you were going.
You kissed them one last time
without saying a thing,

off to the Cantagallo commando post
to join the guerilla army.

22. Mario Bolanos, FSLN Traffic Police (Subtiava)/ THAT KISS

Carmen, your tears, your look
and the planes launching rockets

over Leon
near the Guadalupe neighborhood
for a short time they keep me put
but we say goodbye.

For me it was hard to leave
without turning to see you
for the last time, perhaps.

June 1-2: The mass organizations join the Sandinist call for a popular national insurrection, and the Episcopal Conference ratifies the insurrection's moral and juridical legitimacy. The Rigoberto Lopez Perez Western Front sets out from Leon to attack Chinandega and thus divert guards from Leon, as part of a plan for that city's uprising.

23. FSLN Leaders/ SANDINIST
  PROCLAMATION*

WORKERS, PEASANTS,
NICARAGUAN PEOPLE
EVERY ONE JOIN IN
THE REVOLUTIONARY
GENERAL STRIKE.

24. Daisy Zamora/ DEPARTURE II

In a yellow shirt
  --ready to change--
Augusto drove.
And when I gave
the signal for the departure
he passed by saying goodbye
with his smile.

25. Juan Velazquez/ LEON, JUNE
  2, 1979

Suddenly the kids knocked on our
  door,
a rainy night, the second of June,
  1979.
They came out from their hiding
  places
onto the street,
like a wild animal that first searches
for a scent in the air and quickly
  goes.
The sparks of drops
shining in their beards.
Jets of water
falling from the brims of their hats,
the mahogany butts, the steel like
  lead
each one like a storm made into rage.

June 3-4: In Leon insurrection is total. Whole neighborhoods are up in arms; fires, bombings, demonstrations and confrontations rage throughout the city, as Western Front troops begin to move back toward Leon to attack the Guards from without. Meanwhile, the Sandinists assault Matagalpa, and the general strike spreads throughout the country, paralyzing more than 80% of businesses in the rural areas and all but cutting off commerce in Managua, where street fighting continues to intensify.

26. Zaida Dormuz (12 years old),
San Judas Barrio Poetry
Workshop (Managua)/ THE
FINAL OFFENSIVE

On Monday, June 4th, 79,
no one went to work.
The streets deserted.
The stores, the factories,
the market

--everything was closed.
Only Somoza's Guards
were to be seen.
The pillage of the supermarkets
(the people hungry).
The neighborhoods, the suburbs,
the cities joined in the struggle,
even the boys and girls like me,
11 and 14 years old, we said,
"Free Homeland or Death."

June 5: In a multitude of neighborhoods, the people begin to construct barricades by piling up streetstones manufactured by Somoza's construction company in the years following the earthquake.

27. Luis Vega/ CHRONICLE OF LA BARRANCA, I

I started the first day
of the Big Strike
putting up barricades
in my neighborhood.
I stayed up that night
with just a machete
while the "beasts" with modern
rifles waylaid us.
We kept the neighborhood awake
and the dawn found us
taking up bricks
and putting them one on top of
    another
a meter high
so the "dogs" couldn't pass.
But, in spite of everything,
they entered
and the horror of Operation Cleanup

forced me and my young companeros
to retreat to El Dorado,
where for 22 days Somoza's
    National Guard
couldn't enter in spite of the planes,
the rockets, the 500-pound bombs,
the tanks, the M-50s,
the Uzi machine-guns,
the high-powered Fal rifle, the silent
Galil, the destructive mortars,
and the thousands, thousands and
    thousands
of capsules which remained strewn
like yellow worms around San
    Cristobal,
El Eden, El Paraisito,
Larreynaga and Bello Horizonte.

June 6-7: Intense fighting continues in Matagalpa and Leon, where the FSLN now has virtual control. They close in on the Leon National Guard garrison, and, through the CDS's, institute a socialist-model community, distributing food and medicines on an equitable basis. Fighting begins in Masaya, where the Guards control by day and the Sandinists control by night. Meanwhile, his appeal for help to the Organization of American States rejected, Somoza declares a state of siege, steps up aerial bombings in Masaya, Leon and other points, and intensifies the slaughter of youths in those towns still under Guard control. His goal is clear: to seal off and devastate the taken towns and thus spread terror throughout the nation. Hundreds die, including many "kids," are massacred in Managua, Masaya, San Juan de Oriente and other points.

28. Juan Jose Jimenez, San Juan de Oriente Poetry Workshop/ SERGIO

On June 7, 1979 at dawn
we heard Garand, Enfield and
   machinegun blasts
and also shots of 22 rifles.
We heard the slogans
and then everything grew silent.
In the morning all the people
of San Juan de Oriente
looked at the corpses.
You had a bullet

in the right side of your chest.
Pedro and Jose, machine-gunned,
a Guardsman still kicked at them
   and said
"Fucking sonsovbitches, this is how
I pay back the shots I missed."
Then he stripped off your watch,
asked if we knew you.
We didn't answer.

C. Third Phase: June 8-24th

29. Rocha/ YOU STILL HEAR THEIR VOICES IN THE WIND

Drops of sweat dampen their
   breasts
and perhaps even the rain
evaporates a little
on making contact
with the rushing flow
of the blood in their veins.
Close now to the relentless dawn
of the final triumph or death
their words take flight
   --hearty birds--
against a sky lit

by lightning rays and flashes
and an anxious earth shaken
by its thunder.
But the only thing heard is
their words, their voices, their lives
fluttering in the shadows
and one feels a burning mixture
of thick fear
of the unknown
and the just arrogance
of unfaltering bravery.

June 8: Matagalpa, Leon and Chichigalpa are in Sandinist hands, but under constant Guard attack. Battles rage in Esteli and Masaya. Managua fighting grows more intense, with the Guards roaming the streets, and the guerillas slipping into town at night. This phase of the Final Insurrection is marked by struggles in Esteli and Masaya, complex maneuvers on the Southern Front, and above all, the battle for Managua. Radio Sandino, the clandestine Sandinist communications network, links all insurrectional sectors.

30. Ernesto Cardenal/ FINAL OFFENSIVE

"Workshop here." "Come in,
  Assumption."
"Come in, Cornfield." "Workshop"
  was Leon;
"Assumption," Masaya; "Cornfield,"
  Esteli.
And the calm voice of the girl
Dora Maria from "Taller"
saying that enemy reinforcements
were surrounding them
  dangerously...
And Ruben's voice in Esteli.

Joaquin's voice
in "Office." "Office" was Managua.
"Office" would be out of ammunition
in two more days ("Over.").
Serene, calm voices, crossing over
each other on the Sandinist
  frequency
And there was a time in which
the balance of forces stayed even
and stayed and it was very
  dangerous.

June 9-19: The Battle for Managua rages day after day, as the Sandinists control a fourth of the streets, houses, stores and supply centers. The "kids" take over the city at night, building barricades and shooting it out with the Guards. For their part, the Guards conduct house-to-house searches, finding and killing many young people. Managua civil life is completely disrupted; food, water and other supplies are scarce; hunger, disease and looting escalate, as the numbers fleeing the city soar. Meanwhile, fighting continues throughout the country. Cities taken are then lost and taken again. The struggles around Leon and Matagalpa continue; Esteli, Rivas and Masaya are once more sites of intense fighting.

31. Magdalena de Rodriguez/ JUNE 10TH

The city of Esteli
woke up taken by the kids.
All the roosters crowed
"Free Homeland or Death"
and a huge tremor
went through the ruins and rubble
that the barbarians left twice.
There's a party in the ruins

and a party in the souls.
They came and with them
the voice of patriotism
has grown more robust and louder
and travels on all roads, climbs the
  trees,
and enters houses and the rubble
  blooms
and the jasmine trees
and rose bushes also flower.
Every one sings. The Fal rifles,

the elderly, the adults, the children
 sing.
It rains and in the puddles the frogs
 sing.
In the streets the barricades which
tireless hands build, flower.
A fine party in the streets.
 Afternoon falls.

32. Guevara/ A HILL IN THE
     BENJAMIN ZELEDON
     SOUTHERN FRONT

And here I am in my trench
camouflaged with freshly-cut grass.
I have twenty companeros on the hill
all in their trenches,
in place, watching attentively.
The "suck-blow" passes over
 quickly,
further behind is a D43
 reconnaissance plane.
Mortars are heard all over the
 place,
120 and 82 cannon and mortar-fire.
The "push-and-pull" zig-zag one
 after another
machine-gunning the hills,
rocketing Penas Blancas and Sapoa,
the helicopter hovers up there
and drops 500-pound bombs,
bombs supplied by the U.S.
to kill our population. We're all
 hungry.
It's been three days since we ate
And the condensed milk and tuna

that arrived today aren't very much,
our hair is all dirty, our faces dirty,
our clothes have been on us for a
 week.
The afternoon has been seemingly
 calm,
the guerilla fighters are hidden
in the bush, waiting.
From the high hill,
I can see the whole valley
and the roofs of all the houses
in Sapoa and Penas Blancas.
The roofs' colors look like
those the sun makes when it sets.
My FAL has a bullet in its mouth
aimed straight ahead, since there
 are
hundreds of guardsmen in the zone.

33. Mario Cajina Vega/ SOMOZA'S
     UMBRELLA

Israel's push-and-pull planes, all the
 T33s,
C77s, F80s, B26s from Uncle Samuel,
Pinochet's sulphur rockets,
the Huey helicopters and the new AC's
from the King's Spain
pass over Masaya time and again
on their way to the Southern Front
 or to Esteli,
Matagalpa, Leon, Jinotega, New Guinea
where they bomb, bomb, bomb
while Nicaragua buries the sons of
 bitches.

Meanwhile, Somocist tank operations intensify in Managua. Now the
Guards no longer take prisoners; they shoot civilian suspects on sight. The
nations of the Andean pact recognize the FSLN as a legitimate army, and
the new provisional government council is proclaimed.

34. Provisional Government of National Reconstruction/
PROCLAMATION*

In the moment of assuming
the historical responsibility
of heading the Government
of National Reconstruction,
that will return freedom,
justice and democracy
to our homeland,
and when our people in arms
are burying forever
the Somocist dictatorship
and all it represents
in crimes, repression
and exploitation,
we direct our first call
toward the total unity
of Nicaraguans,
the indispensable basis
of the process of reconstruction
which this government
must carry forward.
We announce that the government
that is herewith constituted
with the full support
of the SANDINIST FRONT
OF NATIONAL LIBERATION
and the other democratic forces
of the country
fully committed
to the final struggle
against the dictatorship
will put in march a plan
of national reconstruction,
fundamentally aimed at
strengthening our sovereignty
and our self-determination,
the country's economic recuperation
and the organization
of a truly democratic
system in Nicaragua.
Finally we wish to make a call
to all the democratic governments
of Latin America and the world,
to extend their diplomatic
recognition
to this GOVERNMENT
OF NATIONAL
RECONSTRUCTION
which represents
the legitimate interests
of the people of Nicaragua.

June 20-23: Sandinist advances around Leon and Diriamba. The Guards assassinate U.S. television reporter Bill Stewart, an action filmed and televised around the world. Somoza argues he "never wanted this to happen." But U.S. Secretary of State Cyrus Vance urges him to step down, as U.S. proposals for an Inter-American peace-keeping force are roundly defeated by the OAS, and fourteen member countries vote a peace proposal that excludes Somoza and calls for non-intervention. Somoza desperately keeps on, naipalming FSLN-held zones of Managua and escalating attacks on all fronts. Helicopters bomb several neighborhoods. And the FSLN leadership debates retreating from Managua, as part of a regrouping strategy they hope will end the war. Fighting continues in Esteli and Masaya, as well as on the Southern Front.

110

35. de Rodriguez/ JUNE 23RD

At noon
a frightful battle
between Somoza guardsmen
and the guerilla fighter kids.
Fifty yards from my house
there was a trench.
In a moment of fatigued rest
a guerilla fighter leaves the
    barricades.
"Water, please," he says to me.
I fill his small canteen to the rim.
He drinks like a guzzling Bedouin.

"How old are you?" "Fourteen."
He's a fierce angel.
His rifle looks like
a little-league bat to me.
He drinks so avidly
that I tell him I'll fill his jar up
    again.
When I return with fresh water
my ineffable fighter is impatient.
"Hurry, ma'am," he tells me,
"I'm missing the action."

D. The Final Phase: June 24-July 19

36. Rocha/ YOU STILL HEAR THEIR VOICES IN THE WIND

Nothing stops their advance
their panting their ideals
Close now to the relentless dawn
of a final triumph over death...
You hear footsteps
you hear birds
you hear gunshots.
You hear bodies
that fall
forever
on this

our earth.
You hear roosters
at dawn.
        Yes.
They're roosters
it's them
it's their voices
in the wind...
because not even death
stops us from hearing them
one more time.

June 24-26: Chichigalpa is liberated. Somoza continues his campaign in Managua, and the FSLN orders the strategic retreat to Masaya. Within two days, guerillas, militia, streetfighters and civilians leave Managua by night.

37. Luis Vega/ CHRONICLE OF LA BARRANCA, II

They ordered us to retreat
to Masaya,
"a strategic retreat" they told us
(I found out later that it was
  intelligent)
"whose results we don't know"
(and the "beasts" found the eastern
neighborhoods desolate, only their
  guardsmen
dead and rotting in the sun)
"but that's the best" they told us.

That night about 5,000 of us young
  people
started the march
over paths, puddles, mountains,
fences and mosquitoes.
The march was hurried
and the wounded slowed us down
but at dawn we arrived
at Masaya's outskirts
and there I had my first serious
  encounter...

June 27: In Masaya, Managua Sandinists join the local resistance and begin the final stages of liberating the city.

38. Cajina Vega/ THE PLEDGE

House by house
we'll defend this city of Masaya ...
We'll tie our feet together
for the final battle
from street to street

we'll blow up tanks with contact
  bombs.
We're still here!
In Masaya, teeth
bite powder and bullets.

June 28-Early July: But the Guards maintain their positions in the old prison on Coyotepe hill outside Masaya, shooting on the city and on the soldiers still coming in from Managua.

39. Luis Vega/ CHRONICLE OF LA BARRANCA, III

La Barranca is a place
on the way to Masaya, near
  Coyotepe,
there Benjamin Zeledon made his
last stand against the Yankee
  invaders,
in 1912,
the "horses" controlled the hill
and from there they laid out
their ambush against us
and when remembering it
I don't hide my sadness

since it was there
that I lost my best friends.
We were all tired, soaked;
you could only hear our boots
  sloshing
and the mosquito's air song in your
  ears
when gunfire broke out
from where we didn't know.
It took us so much by surprise that
Commander Martin fell dead next to
  me

and further ahead someone else fell.
We hit the ground
and the mud hit our faces.
We stayed on the ground
almost without breathing
(nobody breathes in that position,
   I swear)
wanting to discover with our eyes,
noses, all our senses,
what had hit us,
where the shots were coming from.
We heard the groans of our
   companeros,
someone shouted, "Shoot me."
The enemy surrounded us,

and forced us toward a small
   orchard,
I felt death's carress,
I knew by its taste that it was
   blood
but I didn't feel pain
only the anxiety to escape the
   blockade.
Someone shouted we should shoot
   someplace
and we went out that way,
dragged between barbed wire fences
until reaching a passageway
which led down to the lagoon
where shots couldn't reach.

Early July: The FSLN gradually consolidates a hold on Chinandega and Somotillo in the west, on Ocotal and Esteli in the north, and on Granada and Rivas in the south. Matagalpa is already liberated, and the Carazao region of Diriamba and Jinotepe begins to fall under FSLN control.

40. Rosario Murillo/ ILLUMINATION

Slow the caravan and the night
large the fingers grasping the rifle
a rage in the soul

and victory now near
almost caressable.

July 10: The Guards are forced to retreat to Managua, while some hold out on Coyotepe hill. They begin to succumb to the constant ebb and flow of the war. Many Somocistas begin to make plans for departure. But the U.S. continues to recognize Somoza, desperately trying to arrange favorable terms of settlement, and Somoza continues bombing raids and murders.

41. Roberto Vargas, German Pomares Battalion
Poetry Workshop/ THE INSURRECTION OF JULY 11TH

Orders to advance
on the Coyotepe hill outside
   Masaya.
Encouraging voices
(the peasants with faith).

Our column prepared for the
   struggle.
We advance, we fight.
We succeed in repelling the enemy...

July 12-14: The war is virtually over. Radio Sandino announces that Leon, Chinandega, Esteli, Matagalpa and Masaya are liberated. The Sandinists begin to group for their final drive on Managua. Somoza makes some last desperate efforts to secure U.S. help; the U.S. fails to "broaden" the Provisional Government, which names twelve of its proposed eighteen-member cabinet.

42. Mariana Sanson/ JULY 14, 1979

Here they are gestating
a primary liberty.
A new word.

The air is suspended
by the hand of humanity
that is barely a child.

July 15-16: Final bombings over Esteli.

43. de Rodriguez/ ESTELI 79

Today is Sunday.
It's now noon.
Only ten minutes ago
the air bombardment ended...
Three new Israeli airplanes,
frightening, spraying bullets from
    the air
throughout the widow-city of the

people.
We are some thousand civilians and
    some
one hundred thousand guerilla
    fighters.
The spirit of this people is
    inexhaustable.

July 16-17: Esteli is liberated. Many small towns follow the example of Leon in electing local provisional juntas to work with the Sandinists. The Guards only control Managua; they fight on in terror for their lives. It is clear that Somoza must go. Even the U.S. finally accepts the Provisional Government's "Four Step Plan to Achieve Peace." For days, top officials have been preparing to leave, gathering all their spoils together. Somoza makes no public announcement of Guard resignations, nor does he announce a cease fire. But shortly before midnight, the Liberal Party Secretary announces Somoza's resignation to the waiting National Congress. With a few family members and one hundred Guard officers, Somoza departs for Miami in a private plane, shortly after 5:00 a.m. on July 17.

114

44. Ernesto Mejia Sanchez/
BEFORE SATURDAY
Every pig gets his Saturday
(Popular Saying)

The beast is leaving; leave, leave.
It should have left with its heart
    wounded.
It's going.
It's leaving in a state of
    decomposition,
when it could have left
without need of transfusions,
of plasma and rice-water, and died
    happy
in Houston, Rochester, Miami.
But it wanted her sauna, hot-blood
    bar,
highballs of boiling bile,
cocktails of melted eggs with
    oysters.
This is what the antediluvian beast
    wanted:
pickled child's liver,
pus-milk from a poisoned prostitute,
double-yolked balls
of an unwashed guerilla fighter,
a virgin's menstruation,
a priest's saliva genital,
poets' urine and diarrhea.
With this menu it could well
have lived and died anywhere,
but not in your mother's Nicaragua.
Salvadorita, Salvadorita,
Save your soul first.
You shameless, burst-bellied pig's
    heart,
for being a sonuvabitch and a
    shiteater,
for Dinora, for Junior,
for Cosiguina, for Asososca and for
    Tiscapa,
for Matagalpa and for Monimbo, for
    Granada,

Managua and Leon, for Solentiname
and San Carlos, for Chinandega,
    Telica,
El Viejo and Las Segovias,
Yali, Esteli and Tipitapa,
Boaco and Chontales, Santo
    Domingo,
Gracias a Dios and La Libertad and
    Siuna
and Rama, Acahualinca and Quilali,
for Telpaneca, Masaya, and me,
every last one, you and you.

45. Vega/ WHEN SOMOZA
ARRIVED IN MIAMI

When Somoza arrived in Miami,
and in America
there was dancing in the streets,
the ex-tyrant had a dream.
He dreamt about his father's dead,
about his brother's dead
and when he dreamt about the dead
he had to kill
he woke up.
He took a drink and went on
    dreaming:
he dreamt about Augusto Sandino
he dreamt about Carlos Fonseca
and when he started to dream
about Pedro Joaquin Chamorro
he woke up.
He took a pill and went on
    dreaming:
about the property he left behind
about his old party
about his old National Guard
about bombs falling on him
about legs, arms and ears.
When he awoke,
the blood choked him
in one fell swoop.

July 17-19: The Congress elects Francisco Urcuyo Malianos as interim President. According to plans, Urcuyo is to relinquish power immediately to the Provisional Government. But Urcuyo shocks the world by announcing his intention to serve out Somoza's presidential term and by commanding the Guards to keep on fighting. This bizarre maneuver quashes the U.S. plan to have the war end without a clear Sandinist victory and Guard surrender. The Sandinists order the people to keep armed and begin advancing on Managua. Junta members fly from Costa Rica to Leon to meet with Daniel Ortega and declare Leon the provisional capital. Guards surrender *en masse* throughout the country. The Somoza army falls apart in a matter of hours. The night of July 18th is one of the worst during the entire insurrection, with heavy fighting and casualties, as the Sandinists advance on Managua and call for unconditional Guard surrender, and as massive looting takes place in almost every populated area. But by the morning of the 19th, the victory is assured, as Radio Sandino declares the nation liberated. The Junta and indeed people from all over the country make their way to Managua, going to the plaza outside the National Palace. It is the greatest day of rejoicing in the nation's history.

46. Luis Castro, Sandinist Airforce Poetry Workshop/ I WAS ALIVE

On July 19th I was in the Plaza
of the Revolution, and from a
    military truck
we captured from the Guards in
    Leon,
I was watching the children
who mixed in the multitude, free.
Alberto greeted me with surprise
because he never imagined
that I was a guerilla fighter.
I thought of my family
and I looked for them among so
    many people.
Before we left once again for Leon,
my cousin Juan Jose arrived,
and I went away happy
because he would tell my mom
that I was alive.

47. Gioconda Belli/ JULY 19, FREE HOMELAND

It's strange to feel this sun again
and to see the joy
in the streets crowded with people,
red and black flags everywhere
and a new face to the waking city,
still smelling like burnt tires,
the barricades still in place.
The wind hits me full in the face
where dust and tears freely roam,
I breathe deeply to convince myself
that this is not a dream,
that there's the Momastepe,
the Momotombo volcano, the lake,
that we finally did it,
that we made it,
so many years of going against the
    grain,
believing this day was possible,
even after hearing about the death
of Ricardo, of Pedro, Carlos...
of so many others they tore from us,
eyes they gouged out,
without ever being able

to blind us to this day
which today bursts forth in our
  hands.
So many deaths crowd my throat,
beloved dead ones with whom
we sometimes dreamt this dream
and I remember their faces, their
  eyes,
the confidence they had in this
  victory,
the generosity with which they built
  for it,
positive that this happy hour
lurked in the future
and that it was well worth dying
  for.
This happiness hurts like giving
  birth.
It hurts that I can't wake them up
  to come see
this giant of a people coming out at
  night,
with faces so fresh
and a smile so on their lips
as if it had been building up inside
  them
and they suddenly release it in
  droves,
all at once; there are thousands of
  smiles
coming out of drawers, out of burnt
  houses,
out of the streetstones,
smiles dressed in colors
like pieces of watermelon,
of cantelope, of medlar fruit.
I feel like enjoying myself and
  rejoicing
as my sleeping brothers would have,
to enjoy this triumph which is so
  much theirs
so much a child of their flesh and
  blood
and in the midst of the noise on this
  day
so blue, riding on a bus,

passing through the streets, in the
  midst
of my people's beautiful faces,
I wish I could sprout arms to hug
  them
and tell them that I love them,
that blood has made us all siblings
with its painful link
to learn to speak again, to walk
  again,
that in this future
  --inheritance of death and sighs--
we'll hear the nosy volleys
of hammers resounding
flashes of lathes,
buzzing of machetes,
that these will be the weapons
to get light from the ashes,
cement, houses, bread from the
  ashes,
that we won't be weak-hearted,
we will never surrender,
that like them
we'll think of the beautiful days
other eyes shall see.
And this drunkedness of freedom
which invades the streets, stirs the
  trees,
blows the smoke away from the firs,
which accompanies us
    tranquil,
      happy,
    ever-living
    our dead ones.

48. Manuel Adolfo Mongalo, Camilo
    Ortega Saavedra Poetry
    Workshop, Diriamba/ JULY 19

The sky was clear
it was cold
and us Sandinists embraced each
  other
for the victory that just a few hours
  before

we had won from the National
  Guard.
It was July 19th, 1979.
We came in a caravan of trucks
hundreds and hundreds of happy
  combatants.
We entered the city of Granada
  at two in the morning
the people awoke,
gave us coffee, tamales, beans and
  cheese.
The girls ran from one place to
  another.
The mothers peered at us
looking for a certain face.
Others cried (some companeros
  stayed behind).
This night was all excitement,
joy, triumph, Revolution.
I arrived at the Alhambra Hotel
and I saw everything sad
the rocket shots, burnt houses,
  estates.
In the middle of the street
a dog cried and cried, his death was
  near.
I walked on on with my eyes
  tearful
for the death of the animal
who before dying licked my hand
as if to tell me he couldn't die.
The same thing happened to my
  friend
Victor, when we were in the same
  trench
out there in Ostayo.

49. Pancasan/ JULY 19TH

July 19th means
an end to death and misery
a black and red bull which destroys
the foundation of an inhuman
  tyranny.
July 19th means

a hand raised proud and free
grasping homeland and machine-gun
showing our organized strength.
July 19th means
our struggle reaching a goal,
let's continue down this road
sprinkled with the fallen's blood.
July 19th means
that we have land for every one
and these hands that were tortured
  before
are today owners of their labor's
  fruit.
July 19th means
hospitals, houses and schools,
the entire people defending our
  conquests
bringing about another war just
  beginning.
July 19th means
a transcendent advance in the
  process
demanding our effort and struggle
to build the homeland for the
  worker.
July 19th means
an end to death and misery,
a hand raised proud and free,
our struggle reaching a goal,
that we have land for every one,
hospitals, houses and schools,
a transcendent advance in the
  process
of building the worker's homeland.

50. Luis Vega/ CHRONICLE OF LA BARRANCA, IV

When we were returning to
  Managua,
the revolution triumphant,
we passed through La Barranca
and we buried the dear companeros
who gave their lives for our
  brothers.

One day I'll go get them
with my own hands
and kiss the earth
and I'll give some to my children
for them to kiss too,
even though they might see me cry
as I'm crying now.
I write these lines
from my place in the Bunker
(I know they're going to rename it
the Chipote in honor
of the first Sandinist garrison)
which now belongs to the people,
and I think about my friends,
about my parents
and about the streetstones
which ended my childhood
and began my destiny as a man
of the Revolution, headed
toward the reconstruction
of the Free Homeland
about which Sandino dreamed.

51. Julio Valle-Castillo/ THAT'S THE WAY IT IS

*"Humans claim as their undeniable
right,
making their heavenly kingdom here
on earth."*
                    --Heinrich Heine

Here in Nicaragua
the stars are within your hands'
    reach.
Of course it cost and is costing a
    fortune,
one ball and half of the other,
half of Masaya, one and a half
    Leons,

all of Esteli,
but we were able to bring heaven
    down to earth.

52. Vida Luz Meneses/ IN THE NEW COUNTRY

Pain was a challenge
and the future, hope,
building the same way you write a
    poem
creating, erasing and writing again.

53. Murillo/ DAGUERROTYPE OF A MOTHER

A rooster sings
announcing the start.
Ending the night.

54. Guiselle Morales/ FROM THE NORTHERN POST: WORMS AND DEATH

SANDINO-SUN
lights up the song
of the crickets and zenzontles
the flight of the butterflies
and the pure smell of the seeds that
    burst,
    that shout
    that scream
    that write...
The dawn was slow but it came.

FSLN Comandantes and children at ceremony honoring militia combatants. Nicaragua-Honduras border, July 1983. Photo by Loretta Smith.

INTRODUCTION TO BOOK II: FOUR YEARS OF
RECONSTRUCTION & INTERVENTION

A. Political & Economic Developments (1979-1983)

by Rose Spalding

1. Initial Perspectives

In the period following July 19, 1979, Nicaragua experienced a process of fundamental change. As with other revolutionary struggles, major accomplishments went hand in hand with major problems. The government's most important and hard won accomplishment was its continued survival. Especially since the winter of 1982, Nicaragua fell under systematic military attack. The Sandinists were menaced by counterrevolutionary groups on three fronts, and contingents from all of these groups operated periodically within Nicaragua's national territory. Ex-national guardsmen attacking primarily in the north-west and center, Indian separatists concentrated in the Atlantic Coast region, and supporters of ex-Sandinist Eden Pastora fighting in the south created a continual state of military emergency. Backed and organized by the Reagan administration, these forces took a toll on the Revolutionary process.

This difficult situation was exacerbated by international economic pressures. Coming to power at the beginning of a deep and durable global recession, suffering a dramatic drop in the value of their major export products, the Sandinists were faced with monumental problems from the outset. The U.S. cutoff of Nicaragua's sugar export quota in 1983 only compounded these problems and alluded to pressures which had yet to develop fully.

The new government's task of mobilizing Nicaraguan society required the creation and development of revolutionary organizations for mass participation. This entailed not only institutionalizing and strengthening the forces that participated in the overthrow of the dynasty, but rousing even those who were not previously engaged from their traditional passivity and distrust of political authorities. Faced with limited resources as well as internal and external media criticism, this organizational push was difficult. Simply sustaining the revolutionary process in the face of massive and frequently mounting obstacles, a spate of defections, and growing international hostility was a major task. Yet survive the revolution did, and in some ways it even flourished. An overview of changing political and economic conditions can illustrate the major areas of progress and development.

2. Changing Political Structures

The political system during the Somoza period was characterized by highly concentrated political power and an essentially privatized state. The family had traditionally exercised power directly (or through a close political proxy), with the "Presidents" dominating the process. This control over the state facilitated personal family enrichment through the sale of contracts, kickbacks, or outright theft. Instead of serving a public, developmental function, the Nicaraguan state served a highly private purpose. Public services and development programs were sorely underdeveloped, even by Central American standards. Education, welfare and health programs were limited, mainly serving the rich and middle sectors; in spite of the presence of decent and talented individuals, the programs were systemically inefficient, exclusive and corrupt.

The Sandinist government was committed to a radical restructuring of the Nicaraguan state. It took on the task of both promoting political pluralism and giving the state more of a public service orientation. On the one hand, this entailed a diffusion of political and economic power, but a diffusion in which relatively privileged groups retained considerable influence. On the other hand this situation required the construction of a forceful and activist state that was capable of pursuing national development and addressing fundamental social problems.

This dual commitment proved virtually impossible to achieve in practice, even before U.S.-sponsored aggression turned the border into a battlefield. Recognizing the primacy of their commitment to integrated development and redistribution, the Sandinist forces assumed hegemonic control over the State within the first six months of the Reconstruction. Yet simultaneously an effort was made to preserve an important element of political pluralism and responsiveness to various groups.

The initial arrangement under which the new government was constituted in July 1979 entailed a sharing of power between Sandinists and more traditional political elites. In the original junta, only one of the five members, Daniel Ortega, overtly identified with the Sandinists. While two other members were closely tied to Sandinist organizations, the remaining two members, Violeta Barrios de Chamorro and Alfonso Robelo, were clearly not part of the FSLN. Likewise many members of the original cabinet were not Sandinists. For example the past president of the Chamber of Commerce was made Minister of Industry, and a former colonel of the National Guard (who acquired credibility through his involvement in a stillborn coup affair in 1978), was made Minister of Defense.

This inclusionary approach, however, complicated the process of revolutionary change and diluted the power of the state. Shortly after the takeover, tensions within the government became visible, and by the end of the year, the Sandinistas had consolidated their control over the key ministerial positions. Comandante Jaime Wheelock, for example, assumed the leadership of a consolidated Ministry of Agriculture and Agrarian Reform, while Comandante Tomas Borge was placed in charge of the Ministry of the Interior.

At the mass level too, the FSLN proceded with the organization and integration of the population. Following the expropriation of the holdings of the Somozas and Somoza allies, workers on the newly created state-owned farms were encouraged to participate in the Agricultural Workers' Association (ATC) that the Sandinists created during the insurrection. By the end of 1980, membership in this organization had grown considerably. Industrial workers were also encouraged to organize into unions. A variety of unions were created or expanded, but participation in the Sandinist-sponsored CST was particularly encouraged. This organization came to represent a clear majority of organized labor. In the second year of the Reconstruction, a new organization, UNAG, was created to better integrate peasant producers and small farmers into the Sandinist Revolution. UNAG was involved in the distribution of credit, hearings about land expropriations and the organization of agricultural cooperatives. It functioned as an alternative to UPANIC, the private sector's established agricultural organization.

The Sandinists also built on the Centers of Sandinista Defense, the CDS's, established during the war, and sought to extend the CDS network throughout much of the country. AMNLAE, the heir to AMPRONAC, the women's organization during the Insurrection, also expanded and received financial and institutional support from the government. Young people were organized to support the process through participation in the Sandinist Youth Organization, the Literacy Crusade, the voluntary work and health campaigns, the cultural brigades and of course the regular army and militias.

Indeed, almost the entire population was mobilized to participate in the struggle for national defense. A new armed service composed of around 25,000 troops was raised, trained and deployed, and a reserve force of over 80,000 was also created. The degree of mass mobilization broke down the barriers that had separated the government from the society.

During 1982-83, the government became involved in the development of the political parties law. This law was designed to specify the roles political parties should play in Nicaraguan politics, the requirements for legal recognition and the operating procedures they could use. Delays in drafting and promulgating this legislation alienated members of the four informal political parties that constituted the conservative opposition, and to a lesser degree, the two leftist parties that criticized the Sandinists for excessive moderation. The completion of this legislation paved the way for additional mass organization by both the Sandinists and others. This continued mobilization reached a culmination in preparations for national elections during 1984.

The establishment and expansion of multiple mass organizations by the FSLN and the assumption of control over the state apparatus raised the charge of betrayal by some non-Sandinist organizations which were reduced to minority status within (or even excluded from) the revolutionary coalition as it maintained its hegemony in the Council of State inaugurated in the Spring of 1980. But while the Sandinists' determination to lead the revolution was unwavering, they were also reluctant to monopolize the political life of the country.

However, the government periodically sanctioned opposition leaders; and as the military crisis escalated, the dangers posed by the opposition became more palpable. As a result of these problems, several leaders of both the Communist Party's labor affiliate and COSEP, the major private sector business organization, were briefly imprisoned in the Fall of 1981 for violations of a new Social and Economic Emergency Law. Beginning in the following Spring, prior censorship was imposed on the press, and two of the three major newspapers were closed on several occasions for one or two days following the publication of material deemed a threat to national security.

Yet, in spite of these tensions and limitations, which were widely publicized in the U.S. as examples of "Sandinist leftist totalitarianism," a diverse political opposition continued to exist in Nicaragua. COSEP, the opposition business group, continued to operate freely; La Prensa, the opposition newspaper, continued to circulate widely. Furthermore, six of the ten political parties being organized were clearly opposition parties. The reports by international human rights organizations such as Amnesty International indicated that civil liberties violations were infrequent and not part of the institutional structure. Even in the middle of a struggle for survival, the government consistently avoided the kind of repression of opponents that characterized the military regimes of El Salvador and Guatemala. And there was no comparison between the restrictions of the post-1979 period and the systematic violence that was routine in the last years of the Somoza dynasty.

3. Changing Economic Structures

Major changes were also made in the structure of the Nicaraguan economy. Under the Somoza dynasty, control over economic resources had become highly concentrated in the hands of a small number of economic groups. The family rose from fairly modest beginnings in the 1930's, to control vast resources at the end of the 1970's. Their holdings included coffee and cattle farms, financial institutions, construction companies, major media firms, transportation enterprises and many others. By the time the dynasty was overthrown, the family's wealth was estimated at over $400 million.

One of the Sandinist government's first actions was the expropriation of all the property owned by the Somoza family and their close political allies. The state also took over the country's banking system and agreed to assume responsibility for meeting its obligations. As a result of these changes, the state's economic controls and resources were substantially increased. Yet the new government neither desired nor was capable of full control of Nicaragua's economy.

Even after these expropriations, private businesses and farms still controlled 60% of the nation's production, while the state's portion was 40%. The Sandinist government was committed to the concept of a "mixed economy," in which both the public and private sectors play important and complimentary roles.

Since the 1979 victory, the Nicaraguan government used its economic resources to produce social change as well as economic growth. In every area where the government assumed more control, it pushed to increase the resources that were made available to the less advantaged groups. Using its control over the banking system, for example, the government increased the amount of credit available to peasants.

Between 1979 and 1981, the amount of real credit for small peasant producers more than doubled. Furthermore, the interest rates charged for this credit were kept far below the inflation rate. For peasant cooperatives, the interest rate was 8 to 10%, only about half that charged to medium and large farmers and to industry (17%). Instead of being used to increase the wealth of the economic elites, the new banking system was designed to provide special assistance to the poor and promote more balanced national development.

The new government was also addressing the problem of land distribution. One of the features of the Somoza period was the increasing concentration of land under the control of a smaller and smaller number of grand estates. This process was accompanied by the displacement of small farmers from their land and their movement into the cities or relatively isolated interior part of the country. One of the most important pressures the new government faced was the pressure for an agrarian reform program that would provide land for the growing number of displaced peasants.

In order to respond to these pressures, the government allocated a portion of the land it expropriated from Somoza to these peasants. However, much of the expropriated land was organized into large modern farms, and the government decided that their production would be best maintained by not breaking them up. Still, many smaller plots and unused lands were set aside for redistribution to peasants and peasant cooperatives.

Legislation was also passed allowing for the expropriation (with compensation under most circumstances) of land that was left idle on farms larger than 850 acres (or 1,200 acres in the less densely populated interior part of the country). This law also allowed the government to take over land that had been abandoned for two years or farms that were run down by owners who were not maintaining production. While the amount of land that was expropriated under these provisions had not been that extensive, these developments indicated the government's effort to require producers to use their property in a productive manner or risk losing it to others who would. Beginning in the Spring of 1982, some of this land was retitled over to individual peasants or, more typically, to peasant coops. Progress on handing land over to the peasants was slow, but the process continued from year to year.

In part because of these efforts to stimulate the economy, the GNP growth rate was remarkable after the war. This was especially so during 1980 and 1981, and indeed certain areas of production, especially in essential staples, were to continue at impressive growth rates even with world economic problems and interventionist destabilization efforts. Under the dynasty, the food sector had been steadily eroded as the nation's resources (land, credit, labor, etc.) were increasingly channeled to export crops or beef production. This made certain staples scarce and expensive, and contributed to widespread malnutrition. The Sandinist government gave special attention to increasing food production; and within a short period, it had increased the supply of beans, chickens, eggs and other basic foods.

In spite of this progress, the country also experienced major and mounting economic difficulties. Thus, in 1982, after two years of rapid growth, economic problems began to challenge hopes and projections. The *per capita* growth rate dropped sharply, the inflation rate began to rise again, and it was difficult to continue reducing the unemployment rate. Payments on the foreign debt (which had been renegotiated in 1980 and 1981 on generally favorable terms) were difficult to meet. The supply of certain basic goods became inadequate to meet the increasing demand; and the government was forced to introduce rationing of sugar, rice, soap, oil and gasoline in order to hold down prices and prevent shortages.

The causes of these economic problems were multiple. In part they were due to the sharp and sustained drop in the international prices for many of the products that Nicargua exports (cotton, coffee, beef and sugar). Global recession, combined with specific acts of economic sabotage (such as Reagan's cutoff of a wheat shipment in 1981 and of sugar imports from Nicargua in 1983), reduced Nicaragua's export earnings and made it difficult for the country to secure needed supplies.

These international problems combined with disinvestment and decapitalization by many of Nicargua's economic elites to produce economic stagnation. Acting on motives ranging from a commitment to the counterrevolution to general fear and uncertainty, many business leaders and large farmers were unwilling to reinvest and maintain production. This undermined the government's program for national economic reconstruction and increased the tension between the Sandinists and the bourgeoisie.

Production was also hurt by natural disasters like the combination of flooding and drought that hit the country in 1982. But one of the most important factors contributing to these economic difficulties was the military pressure being placed on the country through the intervention of the Reagan administration. This required the Nicaraguan government to shift its scarce resources away from social and economic development programs to national defense programs. And this was in turn retarding the process of revolutionary reconstruction while undermining Nicaraguan development. In spite of these problems, the agrarian reform program was making progress, and the general push for redistribution and growth continued.

B. U.S.-Nicaraguan Relations, Intervention & Counterrevolution

Written with the Collaboration
of Kate Pravera & Rose Spalding

1. The First Year

Book I of this volume portrays the intimate ties between the U.S. and the Somoza dynasty, which did not end until the final months of the Insurrection. Given this history, it is little wonder that the Sandinists viewed the U.S. government with serious suspicion from the outset.

Early into the Reconstruction period, the GNR began to diversify its international relations and establish its new foreign policy direction. New embassies opened in Managua, including those of both socialist and non-aligned countries. Indeed, Nicaragua joined the Non-Aligned Movement, participating in the sixth summit conference in Havana, held during September. Addressing the conference, in which Latin American/Caribbean representation had risen to over 10%, Daniel Ortega asked for the solidarity of the other nations in overcoming the problems he predicted the U.S. might make for his country. Then, addressing the UN, Ortega defined the new framework of Nicaraguan foreign policy as non-alignment, diversification of diplomatic and economic relations, and support for self-determination. Ortega sprinkled his speeches with attacks on the U.S. right and support for leftist revolutionary movements throughout the world. Furthermore, visits to Nicaragua by the likes of Morris Bishop from Grenada and Phan Van Dong from North Viet Nam, as well as the arrival of Cuban teachers, doctors and technicians, only intensified the image of Nicaragua as a new leftist country in Central America.

On the occasion of the transfer of the Canal Zone to Panamanian control on October 1st, the Nicaraguan delegation was greeted by a stirring 15-minute ovation. And the possibility of Nicaragua serving as a catalyst in the region became a preoccupation of U.S. foreign policy, as El Salvador's Romero government collapsed and a reformist junta came to power. Then, in the months which followed, as the first junta collapsed, El Salvador's four prime leftist militant organizations formed a strategic alliance called the *Coordinadora Nacional*; and in Guatemala, 150 organizations joined in creating the Democratic Front Against Repression, to coordinate opposition to General Lucas.

The Nicaraguan process involving the unification of militant sectors and the formation of a broad popular bloc which the united sectors could vanguard seemed to be serving as a model for regional strategies that could only alarm those with a stake in maintaining U.S. hegemony in the area. The first junta overthrown and a less progressive one in power, the situation in El Salvador became steadily aggravated, as Archbishop Romero was assassinated, and the supposed Agrarian Reform turned into a series of massacres, reaching one of its many crescendos in the slaughter of peasants attempting to find refuge in Honduras by crossing the Simpul River.

Meanwhile, in Guatemala, Quiche Indians fleeing from a massacre in their village found refuge in the Spanish Embassy only to be slaughtered by a a military which stopped at nothing to defend the ever more more discredited Lucas dictatorship from a growing opposition that was quickly spreading to the nation's indigenous majority. Even the supposedly stable Costa Rican economy suffered severe shocks, as the *colon* was devalued, and the government moved increasingly to the right as it sought to fend off the possible emergence of any revolutionary movement.

From the start, these and other developments in the Central American and Caribbean area were sources of increasing concern on the part of the Carter administration, especially as Ronald Reagan and those supporting his bid for the presidency steadily confronted Carter on the purported calamity brought on U.S. vital interests from his soft-minded emphasis on Human Rights.

At first Carter tried to implement an officially tentative and neutral policy toward Nicaragua, showing considerable signs of distrust but also willing to grant some emergency help through AID and to seek approval for a $75 million assistance package. Nevertheless, weakened by the Tehran hostage crisis and then the Afganistan situation, the administration attempted to fend off Reaganite attacks by progressively hardening its Central American stance. In September, Carter attacked a purported military buildup in Cuba; in the weeks which followed, he sent military advisors and roughly $7 million in military sales and credits to El Salvador.

By January, the U.S. stance toward Nicaragua began to harden. Strong debates raged in Congress about different alternatives for imposing conditions on the $75 million aid package, so that it was directed mainly toward helping the private sector, as the open hostility of Reagan supporters to Nicaragua began to condition government stances. As the Polish crisis began and over one hundred thousand refugees left Cuba, the propaganda war against the FSLN began to concentrate on Nicaragua's relation with the Socialist bloc, the buildup of its army (as if there were no clear signs that the new country would have to defend itself), the development of mass organizations which scandalously reduced bourgeois political power to only several times its population base in the country, and the expressed FSLN solidarity with other Central American revolutionary movements. As the first year moved to a close, ex-Somocista National Guard border attacks increased, and it was becoming clear that developments in the Honduran military infrastructure across from Nicaragua were not being funded by the Honduran government itself.

2. Reagan & First Efforts at Destabilization

During the summer and fall of 1980, U.S. policy further hardened, as Carter fell under the constant fire from Reagan and his campaign staff, who continually drafted ever more hostile position papers on the Administration's handling of Central America. Violating the 1794 Neutrality Act, the administration tolerated the establishment of training camps by Somocista ex-National Guard in the Miami area, and the polemic over U.S. economic aid to Nicaragua continued, with AID in favor and the CIA opposed.

The Reagan platform had called for avoiding another Nicaragua in El Salvador and Guatemala, by increasing military aid to these countries and embarking on an aggressive anti-Sandinista campaign which linked the FSLN to Cuba and ultimately the USSR, while it portrayed the revolutionary struggle in the area as a creature of worldwide Soviet and Cuban aggression. When Reagan triumphed and assumed office, his State Department immediately published its "White Paper," which claimed to prove that Nicaragua was serving as an arms conduit to Salvadoran guerillas. Within a few days, Reagan suspended the remaining $15 million from the $75 million Carter administration grant; and in March, Reagan suspended credit for the sale of $9.6 million of U.S. wheat to Nicaragua. Secretary of State Alexander Haig and UN ambassador Jean Kirkpatrick joined Reagan in making creasingly hostile attacks on the GNR. But these hostile acts were just the surface manifestations of a more pervasive strategy aimed at fomenting economic and political crises leading to the destabilization and possible overthrow of the government.

The U.S.'s initial Central American priority was "normalization" in El Salvador, coupled with improved relations with the Lucas Garcia regime in Guatemala. With respect to Nicaragua, the plan was to carry out a program of harassment that would culminate in economic and military blows aimed at weakening grassroots power and strengthening internal opposition so that the FSLN would fall and a new regime would emerge willing to serve U.S. interests and help deter revolutionary victories in other area nations. In addition to cutting off needed emergency monies and food supplies, the program involved resistance to Nicaragua's requests for developmental credit from multi-national banks, as well as efforts to pressure allies like the Netherlands, West Germany, Spain, France, Venezuela and Mexico to reduce their substantial developmental support by pointing to the growing levels of assistance Nicaragua was receiving from East Germany, Libya, Cuba and the USSR, and by pointing to claimed repression of internal opposition groups having ties with important parties and organizations that were influential in the ally countries.

By isolating Nicaragua, Reagan could further discontent among sectors in the country and could then hope to link dissidents with a U.S.-funded counterrevolutionary force that could grow to the degree that the discrediting of Nicaragua and Central American revolutionary organizations allowed Reagan to drum up support for his Central American war at home and abroad. Finally, to make the overall strategy fully effective, the administration joined its diplomatic attack with a propaganda campaign aimed at damaging Nicaragua's image throughout the world.

As the Reconstruction's third year began, the Reaganites urged France's Mitterand not to sell arms to Nicaragua, and they tried to pressure Mexico's Lopez Portillo into taking a less friendly stance toward the

FSLN and Salvadoran rebels. Then, at an OAS meeting in Santa Lucia, where the U.S. threatened to invoke the Rio Treaty, Nicaraguan Foreign Minister Miguel D'Escoto had fierce confrontations with Haig and Kirkpatrick. Meanwhile, Honduran and U.S. military carried out joint *Halcon Vista* exercises in Honduras to test their capability and send a message to the Central American left; and Somocista Guards, receiving ever more U.S. support, built their military strength and made ever more frequent raids into Nicaraguan territory from their various border camps.

As our Introduction to Book II, Part II details, anti-Sandinista forces and their U.S. allies invested considerable energies in exploiting the historical, cultural and geographical isolation of the Miskitus and other Indian groups from Nicaragua's Ladino majority. In their border actions, the Somocistas counted on support from anti-FSLN Miskitus, but they also set about killing large numbers of Miskitus who supported the Revolution or at least remained neutral in the struggle. The killings began to extend from individual Miskitus to government health and education workers and then to whole Miskitu villages accused of FSLN sympathies. Then, when the Sandinistas uncovered the "Red Christmas" plot, and made their painful decision to relocate several thousand Miskitus from their homes along the Coco River, the U.S. stepped up its propaganda war, charging the GNR and FSLN with gross acts of tyranny against the Miskitus, but also stressing the Sandinistas' press policy, their relations with Church and private sector groups, their close ties with Cuba, their aid to Salvadoran insurgents, and, as always, their "unnecessary" military buildup."

As 1982 began, the State Department's Central America mouthpiece Thomas Enders rejected the GNR's appeal for bilateral U.S.-Nicaraguan negotiations, insisting on an area-wide negotiation process that would by its structure prove favorable to U.S. interests and not those of the revolutionary organizations. The U.S. spurned peace efforts by France and Mexico and had some success in winning further support for its policies from Costa Rica, Venezuela and Panama, as well as increased direct participation in the Honduran border campaigns by soldiers from Argentina and elsewhere in Latin America.

3. *The Intervention Deepens*

Throughout the winter of 1982, the Administration went beyond its earlier verbal and economic assault on Nicaragua to an increasingly escalating attack on political and military fronts, with ever more direct support and coordination of counterrevolutionary activities affecting every aspect of Nicaraguan life.

Consisting mainly of diplomatic actions damaging Nicaragua's credibility with other democratic states, the political aggression was backed up by an intensified campaign of misinformation. On the economic front, the U.S. tried to convince international money sources to cut off aid, and resorted to financial, technological and commercial pressure to create a situation of crisis in the country. It became clear that the U.S. was extending its financial support to anti-Sandinista political groups, as well as conservative Church forces, while it supported anti-Sandinist training camps in Florida and Miami, as well as at least three ex-Somoza National Guard companies in the Panama Canal Zone, and roughly ten in Somocista bases in Honduras.

However, perhaps most notable between December and April was rise in direct military action. The Somocista border raids, so frequent in December, only increased throughout the winter. In addition there were acts of terrorism against the National Airport in Managua and against an Aeronica plane in Mexico City, as well as over forty violations of Nicaraguan air space by the U.S. Air Force and numerous actions by the Honduran Navy against Nicaraguan ships. Meanwhile, a plot was uncovered in which the CIA channeled funds to anti-Sandinista groups through Argentine and Venezuelan government officials for the purpose of blowing up Nicaragua's only cement factory and oil refinery.

As the GNR charged, these plans showed how the administration was interested not so much in stopping alleged arms traffic to El Salvador, as it was in bringing about the total collapse of Nicaragua's economic infrastructure. And as if to prove the point, an ex-National Guard took credit for blowing up two key bridges over the Rio Coco and the Rio Negro during early March. As this final attack took place, and as the systematic nature of the overall U.S. campaign became ever more apparent, a rash of articles appeared in the U.S. indicating Reaganite backing for 500 Honduran-based guerrillas. This press barrage reached its culmination on March 9, 1982, when *The Washington Post* published a story which confirmed the approval of a $19 million CIA fund for overt action against the Nicaraguan government. Only a few days later, on March 15th, the GNR declared a state of national emergency.

4. The Covert Action

Although announced to the world in March, the CIA Covert Action Plan had been agreed upon in December. Furthermore, while the plan centered on funding a para-military contingent of 500 Latin Americans on the Honduran side of the border, it really embodied a broader set of considerations, and indeed was only a key piece in a much more elaborate overall strategy to which far more than $19 million was committed. All of the winter aggressions against Nicaragua were an integral part of U.S. policy aimed at defeating the area's revolutionary movements by military means. But whereas earlier policy stressed Nicaragua as adjunctive to the struggles in El Salvador and Guatemala, the new policy direction seemed most centered on Nicaragua itself. Along with other measures, the covert action was meant to disrupt the economy and strengthen anti-Sandinista political forces. The hope was that the external influences would generate such internal discontent that sufficient sectors would come to support an armed overthrow so as to make a Chile-style coup or counterrevolution possible.

Shortly after the key *Washington Post* story, senior officials in the Reagan Administration confirmed the president's authorization of the paramilitaries. Senator Barry Goldwater, Chairman of the Senate Committee on Intelligence, admitted, "Everything in the *Post* story was true. They didn't have everything, but everything they had was true (*Time*, 3/22/82).

In that same month, Assistant Secretary of State for Inter-American Affairs, Thomas Enders, informed members of the House and Senate Committees on Intelligence that the CIA was already secretly providing training, money and weapons to former members of Somoza's National Guards. The monies were being funnelled through "friendly Latin American countries" with the aim of inciting unrest in Nicaragua by supporting both dissident elements in Nicaragua and exile groups in the U.S. (*The Nation*, 3/6/82).

One of the main goals of the covert operation was "to build popular support in Central America and Nicaragua for an opposition that would be nationalistic, anti-Cuban and anti-Somoza." Beyond the $19 million in covert aid, U.S. anti-Sandinista support took the form of covert CIA financing of anti-Sandinist political parties, as well as business and labor organizations, including the Superior Council of Private Enterprise (COSEP) and the Confederation for Trade Union Unification (CUS), which had long been receiving funds through AID.

5. *The State of Emergency*

Clearly a response to the announced covert action plan and the events that occurred under its aegis, Nicaragua's State of Emergency implied a national mobilization not unlike that of the final insurrection. The Sandinista army, militia and other forces went on a state of alert, and largescale recruitment and training for additional fighting forces went into immediate effect. Citizens participated in voluntary vigilance over farms, factories and means of communication. A national emergency law was passed to prevent internal acts of destabilization and sabotage. Every means was used to instruct the populace in what it should do before, during and after aerial bombardment and how to minimize damage to the national infrastructure. Nevertheless, while all sectors were warned against carrying out activities that could increase tensions in a time of crisis, and while prior censorship was imposed on the media, the majority of basic rights for Nicaraguan citizens remained in full effect.

Meanwhile the GNR pursued international, diplomatic and political channels to air its grievances and seek a solution to the crisis. Four days after the State of Emergency was declared, Comandante Daniel Ortega approached the U.N. Security Council to denounce U.S.-sponsored military attacks and economic destabilization tactics against Nicaragua. The aggressions were classified by Ortega as verbal ones in Reagan administration official pronouncements, support to forces preparing to invade Nicaragua and blanket approval of covert actions aimed at destabilization.

Subsequently, Mexican President López Portillo proposed a peace plan calling for a negotiated settlement of the Salvadoran conflict, dialogue and normalization of Nicaragua-U.S. relations through a series of mutual accords and Cuba-U.S. negotiations.

Ortega's talk led to the passage of Nicaragua's anti-imperialist resolution in the U.N. Security Council; the Mexican initiative won support from a number of democratic governments, the Parliament of the EED, the Socialist International and 106 U.S. Congress representatives. But the U.S. voted against the Security Council Resolution, rejected the Mexican proposal and continued to press the anti-Sandinist war. In fact, that aspect of the CIA plan stressing the effort to discredit Nicargua came more and more into play with each passing day, as operatives worked to intensify its public relations campaign aimed at creating an atmosphere in which stern action against Nicaragua might be supported. First, Reaganites capitalized on the State of Emergency their own actions had necessitated, interpreting it as a "state of siege" illustrating the repressive and dictatorial nature of the FSLN; they stepped up their charges of FSLN atrocities against the people, and especially the indigenous population; their charge that Nicaragua was supplying Salvadoran rebels became a ubiquitous one.

Many of the efforts in the U.S. misinformation and distortion campaign misfired. Haig's attempt to pass off photos from the Somoza era as though they represented Miskitu Indians being burned alive by the Sandinistas was exposed; photos claiming to portray FSLN violence were revealed to have been taken of Somocista guards before the Revolution; a young Nicaraguan set up by the State Department to provide eye witness of Salvadoran-bound Nicaraguan supply shipments embarrassed the Reaganites by stating the facts, exposing the setup and denying the charges. Then in April, U.S. human rights and American Indian groups sent representatives to Nicaragua and declared that they found no evidence for administration charges of abuses committed against the Miskitus or the overall population.

Even U.S. embassy officials complained that "the administration's tendency to exaggerate, distort or ignore information" about Nicaragua only exposed U.S. intentions before the world.

But embarrassments and complaints did not cause any abatement of the covert action. Indeed, at times they seemed part of the overall strategy.

Most important to the U.S. plan was the search for a means of increasing coordination among the fragmented forces opposing the FSLN, and of syphoning off the Somocista stigma attached to much of the opposition. This approach also meant winning support for a growing U.S. involvement in the continuing militarization of Honduras, and even for a possible war between that country and Nicaragua.

It is only to be surmised that the Administration concluded it could only pursue these goals effectively by becoming more open about them, and by attempting to manipulate anticipated Sandinista reactions to this situation in ways that would further justify the plan. This would seem to be behind the comment of a White House official quoted in *The Washington Post* that Reagan "was not especially upset about the news leaks about covert operations, because the reports convey the President's determination to counter what he considers aggression in Central America (3/13/82)."

It is very probable that the administration had engineered the leaks in the first place, or that it quickly sought to capitalize on them. Why it might have chosen to do so in the month of March, risking reproaches from its less bellicose allies, may be explained by the failure of its earlier ploys and strategies. The Christian Democrat experiment collapsed in El Salvador and the war between left and right intensified. The Lucas Garcia regime collapsed in Guatemala, and an unpredictable rightwing fanatic who made genocide a matter of holy war came to power. The country's four political-military organizations unified into the URNG, and famous Guatemalans from diverse social sectors formed the CGUP.

In spite of all the problems it faced, the Nicaraguan process was consolidating, growing stronger with each effort to make it weaker. A final, not inconsiderable factor was the outbreak of the Malvinas war and the U.S.'s subsequent support for the British. Nicaragua supported the Argentine government, in spite of the fact that the latter was involved in the intervention from Honduras. The U.S. option of a strong Argentine presence in attacks on Nicaragua dissipated, and the Reaganites had to seek another approach to their plans for the area, short of direct intervention.

The Somocista stigma which seemed to impede U.S.-Nicaraguan plans could only be countered in the Honduras area by stirring up

Sandinista-Miskitu tensions. But the war could only be successfully pursued by attempting to further involve Costa Rica in the process, and by joining this effort to one that would establish a clearly non-Somocista opposition to the FSLN. The re-emergence of ex-Sandinist Commander Eden Pastora (Comandante Cero) in Costa Rica during April, 1982 seemed to fit the U.S. bill to perfection. The popular leader of the National Palace assault of August, 1978 and the Southern Front in the 1979 Insurrection had left Nicaragua Che-style with Commander Jaime Baldivia in the summer of 1981, supposedly to fight for liberation in other parts of Latin America. Now, ten months later, Pastora declared his opposition to the Sandinistas, complaining about the "Cuban influence" and vowing he would take up arms to overthrow the government.

Baldivia, who repudiated Pastora's stance and returned to the FSLN fold, revealed that Pastora had had regular contact with U.S. officials. And Pastora's anti-Cuban, anti-Somoza and nationalist rhetoric matched the CIA's requirements for an alternative to the FSLN. In June 1982, Alfonso Robelo, leader of anti-Sandinist business and political groups under the banner of his DMN Party, went in to voluntary exile, declaring his support for Pastora's armed struggle. Reports circulated that both Pastora and Robelo were receiving CIA funds and advice.

Meanwhile, responding to the increasing Honduran border raids and destabilization efforts, the State of Emergency, initially announced as a thirty-day measure, was renewed in April, May and June, as it would be renewed month after month so long as the covert action and intereventional crisis was to continue. With each renewal, U.S. propaganda took on new life, as every dimension of the crisis seemed to escalate with each action and reaction.

By the third anniversary of the Revolution, in July, 1982, it was absolutely clear that the military activity against Nicaragua was reaching the point of being not a matter of random aggressions, but a "silent, bloody invasion." Speaking at the Masaya anniversary celebration, Vice Minister of the Interior Luis Carrion asserted, "The aggression has already begun. We can no longer talk of preparation for war because the war is underway."

From May to July, more than fifty armed attacks had been carried out on Nicaraguan soil by counterrevolutionaries crossing over from the Honduran border. The attacks had resulted in roughly 100 Nicaraguan military and civilian deaths.

The largest, most successful of the attacks took place just five days after Carrion's speech, in the border town of San Francisco del Norte. A well-equipped unit of 100 *contras* crossed the Honduran border and then quickly retreated. But before they were finished, they had killed fifteen Nicaraguans, torturing eight of them first, and kidnapping eight others in the process. This kind of "foreign policy", elaborated in the winter and spring of 1982, was to continue as the basic Reagan approach throughout the fourth year of the Reconstruction.

6. Continued Incursions & U.S. Maneuvers (Winter, 1983)

During the summer and fall of 1982, counterrevolutionary attacks continued in the border areas and in such towns as Puerto Cabezas and Corinto. Evidence of U.S. participation in the coordination, training, supplying, financing and control of the counterrevolutionary forces became more and more an open matter. The U.S. Congress passed the Symms Amendment which empowered the President to send troops to Central America and the Caribbean in the case of an emergency. And U.S. military aid to the Honduran armed forces increased markedly. Congress softened a bill which would have prohibited the covert actions against Nicaragua and passed one which only prohibited CIA action to overthrow the GNR. Media sources leaked news of Reagan administration plans for a stepped up cross-border intervention in December. And in November, the GNR decreed a Military Emergency in one fourth of the country.

The emergency was called because of U.S. diplomatic moves and military show-of-force exercises throughout the Central American/Caribbean area (and especially in Honduras) planned for in the month of December, and also because of the growing organization of counterrevolutionary forces, which created a greater threat of more coordinated incursions into the country.

In October, Standard Fruit abandoned Nicaragua, thus increasing the country's economic problems. In November, a united force of various contra groups under ex-National Guard control attacked Jinotega, Madriz and Nueva Segovia with the aim of sabotaging coffee and cotton harvests. In early December, 800 contras entered Nicaragua and tried to take Jalapa, while Reagan's visit to Central America strengthened U.S. influence aimed at destroying the Salvadoran guerillas and defeating the Sandinista government behind the facade of his proposed Pro-Peace and Democracy Forum.

On the other hand, the U.S. postponed their announced military maneuvers until February, and spent much of January making preparations for a new stage in the war against the Sandinista Revolution. Thus Reagan representatives traveled to various European and Latin American countries attempting to cajole and coerce allies to fall in line with U.S. policies.

Following up Reagan's December trip, Jeanne Kirkpatrick visited Venezuela, Honduras, El Salvador and Costa Rica seeking to bolster the Reaganite Pro-Peace and Democracy Forum. Thomas Enders travelled to Spain for the same reason, as well as in an attempt to win support for a Central American "zero option" which saw the regional problem as part of the East-West conflict, without recognizing underlying causes, and proposed the withdrawal of all foreign military advisers and military aid for both warring parties. In January also, diplomats from Colombia, Venezuela, Mexico and Panama met on Contadora island off Panama and began work toward posing an alternative to the U.S.'s one-sided Central American peace plan.

Working under a "super-directorate" of CIA and North American military advisors coordinated from the U.S. Embassy in Tegucigalpa, the *contras* had two objectives: to occupy positions in the north of Jinotega and Nueva Segovia and to penetrate Zelaya Norte as a diversionary tactic subordinate to the first goal. During January, six task forces totaling roughly 2,000 armed *contras* began penetrating into Nicaraguan territory, one contingent of 200 reaching Northern Jinotega and another reaching Nueva Segovia, with some getting as far south as Matagalpa, were they attempted to reach Boaco and Chontales, and to take the Rio Blanco. In late January an opposition task force entered Bismuna, Northern Zelaya in an attempt to take the town, move into the mining areas and possibly take over Puerto Cabezas. They were driven from Bismuna into Honduras, suffering more than eighty casualties.

From February 1-5, more than 1,600 U.S. troops joined over 4,000 Honduran soldiers in the $5.2 million Big Pine Operations on the Atlantic Coast of Honduras; on February 11-17, in Panama, several thousand U.S. troops participated in military exercises. Other operations were slated off Puerto Rico and the Central American coast during February and March.

The Administration denied it was attempting to overthrow the GNR; rather it insisted it was attempting a "harassment action" aimed at making arms supplies for El Salvador too costly a business. When newspapers reported little solid evidence for Nicaraguan military aid to Salvadoran guerillas, the U.S. charged that "massive amounts" were going across the Gulf of Fonseca by "dugout canoes." The harassment action included the installation of a huge $5 million radar facility and plans to build a large military training base in Honduras.

The CIA asked for continued covert action funding into 1984, and the number of CIA personnel in Honduras rose to well over 100. The fighting in January and February had left a death toll of fifty-six Nicaraguans, including 17 youth and 3 children. Moving into the final week of February, as preparations were being made for the Pope's visit to Nicaragua, counterrevolutionary guerilla attacks began to escalate, and it became apparent that a major anti-Sandinista campaign was about to begin.

The tense situation in Nicaragua just prior to the Pope's visit goes a long way to explaining the reception his harsh words about the Revolution received in Managua. The fact that the Pope made no mention of those who died or their bereaved families, the fact that he in no way condemned the counterrevolutionary attacks or the U.S. intervention stirred great bitterness in the country. Within a couple of days of the Pope's departure, as the U.S. propaganda machine stepped up its campaign in view of the papal reception, fierce battles began to rage on the northern borders, the Atlantic Coast and several other points in the north. The "silent invasion" became very noisy indeed.

On March 10th, five peasants and three soldiers were killed. On March 20th, the border observation post at Vado Ancho, Chinandega was attacked from Honduras. On March 22nd, there was a large deployment of Honduran troops in the Palo Grande border area. Then in the final week of the month, various technicians and volunteer workers, including peasants, children and Sandinista soldiers were killed in a series of raids and attacks. Among those killed was French volunteer doctor Pierre Grosjean, whose end became a matter of international concern.

As March drew to a close and April began, the Sandinistas destroyed a landing strip being used for supplies by the *contras*; and they killed roughly fifty Somocistas in battles around Chicahagua, El Cacao, the El Limon northern border zone, the Rio Coco area and Zelaya Norte. They also defeated the task force operating in the Matagalpa area, encircling the survivors in Muy Muy and Matiguas.

In sum, a two-pronged coordinated military operation could be observed in the accelerating attack on Nicaragua. One, carried out by Somocista units, consisted of 1,200 to 2,000 combatants organized in task forces that had been penetrating Nicaragua and terrorizing peasants throughout February. The second was carried out by Somocistas and Honduran solidiers in the border zone. The effort was intended to draw FSLN military forces to that area and to have a psychological effect on a civilian populace forced to live in a permanent state of alert. In addition to terrorizing rural towns, the *contras* sought to sabotage important infrastructural facilities, recruit ex-National Guard members and kidnap peasants. The *contras* also sought to improve logistical support and restructure their high command.

In spite of exaggerated claims by invading *contras*, repeated in anti-Sandinista articles in the U.S. and elsewhere, the GNR did not seem to be facing any overwhelming military threat. No towns had been taken, nor did the *contras* have any broad-based support among the population. What seemed to be occurring was a greatly accelerated continuation of the terrorism and selected assassination that had been going on for some time. But now, there was danger of a war with Honduras, along with the *contras* attacking on various fronts.

Indeed, Humberto Ortega stated at a press conference, "We consider the situation to be critical. Yet from a military point of view, the real danger is not with the *contras*, whom we are now defeating, but rather in the possibility of a war with Honduras."

Asserting his view that the recent escalation was designed to divert international attention from El Salvador and facilitate U.S. political moves in the region, Ortega nevertheless pointed out that the Reagan administration could encourage border conflicts between Nicaragua and Honduras which could then lead to war. Presumably, if that failed, the U.S. itself might be forces to intervene. The question was that of the ultimate stake of the U.S. in the struggle and the degree to which they would be able to wield the various *contra* sectors into a coherent force sufficiently purged of Somocistas and yet sufficiently strong and convincing to win over Nicaraguan dissidents and international support.

7. The Continuing War & Reagan's April Speech

During the month of April and into early May, attacks against Nicaragua continued in the north and began developing in the south as well. The northern border mountain range summit was occupied by invading forces, only to be reoccupied by the Sandinista army in an extensive area 13 kilometers northeast of Jalapa and 5 kilometers from the border. Efforts by the *contras* to control the road from Jalapa to the border were also turned back although they attacked a bus traveling from Ocotal to Jalapa and a small passenger vehicle of the latter city, injuring some and kidnapping others. Also, in early April, two to three hundred *contras* entered Zelaya Sur from Costa Rica along the Indio and Maize Rivers. They remained in Nicaraguan territory receiving supplies from Costa Rica.

During the second week, two technicians and one Nicaraguan solider were kidnapped in Tasba Parni, two of them later discovered dead. From mid-April to early May, there were twelve identified violations of Nicaraguan air space on the southern border. Meanwhile, there were attacks on border posts in Halouver, Sarabiqui, La Esperanza and Fatima, as well as on the rural communities of Cruz Verde, El Papayo and Las Azucenas.

On April 27, as the battle with the *contras* continued to rage, Reagan delivered a major speech against the Sandinists: "They were Marxists; they were becoming a Cuban and/or a Soviet military base; they were encouraging revolution throughout Central America; they were undemocratic; they hadn't held elections yet... 'The government of Nicaragua ... has seized control of most media and subjects all media to heavy prior censorship; it denied the bishops and priests of the Roman Catholic Church the right to say mass on radio during Holy Week; it insulted and mocked the Pope.' ... In light of all that, Reagan announced, 'We should not--and we will not--protect the Nicaraguan government from the anger of its own people.' What he was saying openly was the United States of America would be happy if the Sandinists were overthrown (*Playboy* [September, 1983)], pp. 57 and 68."

While receiving support from his own party, five of the six Democratic presidential candidates sharply criticized the speech, and Senator Christopher Dodd delivered a televised response. While major newspapers and magazines agreed with Reagan's goals, they disagreed with the military means he was employing. They tended to argue that Reagan policy ignored root causes for Central American violence and prevented a negotiated solution, and also that covert and military activities did not best serve U.S. security interests. Clearly, the *The New York Times* opined, military responses in Central America would fail without a national commitment behind them that was unlikely to come.

Within a week, the House Intellgence Committee voted 9 to 5 to halt U.S. aid to covert paramilitary groups in Nicaragua, but the Committee authorized $80 million assistance aimed at interdicting military equipment supplies from Cuba and Nicaragua. In effect, Reagan interpreted the vote as allowing the covert action to become officially open, and even allowing the Central American regimes receiving U.S. aid to pass part of it on to the Nicaraguan "freedom fighters."

Two days after his speech, Richard Stone, a hardline rightwinger, was appointed by Reagan as "special envoy to Central America." And within two weeks, as the fighting again heated up in El Salvador, *Time Magazine* reported how the Sandinistas shipped arms to rebels along routes that were so complex and surreptitious as to explain why Reagan simply could not flesh out his charges in this regard. The sense was of a hardening of U.S. resolve to carry on the war against Nicaragua. Indeed, within a few days of the Reagan speech, counterrevolutionary groups in Honduras and Costa Rica announced their alliance, Sandinista troops clashed with guerrilla units under Eden Pastora in the south, and a new rebel force of 1,500 men crossed the Honduran border into Nicaragua, backed by a barrage of artillery fire from the Honduran military.

8. The Contras & their Development

In 1982, as many as nine distinct, organized groups of counterrevolutionaries were enumerated by spokespersons for the Nicaraguan government. But during late 1982 and on into the new year, the groups tended to consolidate into two main contingencies, the Nicaraguan Democratic Forces (FDN) stationed in Honduras, and the Democratic Revolutionary Alliance (ARDE), operating out of Costa Rica, claiming more than 6,000 armed guerillas in its ranks. The FDN was organized by Jose Francisco Cardenal in 1981 and quickly became the dominant counterrevolutionary force. Its political directorate included a former National Guard colonel, a former Vice President under Somoza and a former Coca Cola franchise manager who was also a Conservative Party leader during the Somoza regime. In addition, the organization counted with Steadman Fagoth Mueller's Miskitu dissidents. With a military leadership largely composed of former National Guard members, they claimed to secure their weapons through the Black Market in Florida, as well as from Honduran army "donations." Formed in the Fall of 1982 as the umbrella organization for four counterrevolutionary groups operating in the southern border area, ARDE included Alfonso Robelo's MDN (Nicaraguan Democratic Movement), the UDN-FARN, led by "Negro" Chamorro-Rappaccioli, the MISURASATA contingent led by Brooklyn Rivera, and Eden Pastora's FRS (Sandino Revolutionary Front).

Throughout the fall and on into 1983, FDN forces led the incursions into Nicaragua. But during this same period, the organizations suffered from internal weaknesses and contradictions which impeded their unity and their ability to coordinate efforts with each other.

FDN members and contingents jockeyed for power and influence, vying with each other in either disassociating themselves from or identifying themselves with Somocismo. Eden Pastora was viewed suspiciously by the other ARDE members for his flamboyant statements, and his unpredictable, adventuristic activities, as well as his former association with the FSLN. Meanwhile, Pastora complained bitterly about the lack of funds coming to his forces as compared with the others. Then too, ARDE had difficult times working with the FDN, first because of the Somocista ties of the latter group, and second because Fagoth and Rivera, both claiming to be the authentic leader of dissident Miskitus, were unable to work together. In late March, Chamorro's UDN-FARN broke with ARDE and joined with the FDN, claiming that the Somocistas had been purged and that they hoped to maintain close contacts with Fagoth, the "authentic leader of MISURASATA."

Later in the year, Pastora withdrew from ARDE for lack of funds, only to return a few days later, but always refusing to work with the Somocista-infested FDN and always running into trouble with the Costa Rican government, being forced to abandon the country at the end of March, only to reappear there some time later, presumably jumping back and forth between Costa Rica and ARDE's southern front. Even as it launched its southern campaign, ARDE began to unravel and its alliance with the FDN broke down.

Directly or indirectly, and irrespective of their claims or wishes, the FDN and ARDE were absolutely dependent for support on the U.S. and the CIA for their arms, their logistical base and their very existence. The FDN suffered from additional difficulties as well. They were attempting to move on foot in difficult mountainous terrain; although they received limited supplies by helicopter, their supply route from Honduras was repeatedly cut off. Finally the fact that they were National Guardsmen and used brutal terror tactics limited their possibility of ever developing a social base.

News reports that the FDN had taken over such towns as Matagalpa and Esquipulas were false, but they continued to be broadcast and heard on short wave in Nicaragua, and to circulate internationally. These reports were part of a campaign to undermine the legitimacy of the GNR, to further isolate the government and cut off tax credits. Throughout the period of their organized invasions, from Fall, 1982 through mid-summer, 1983 and beyond, they did not have the ability to take a single town, nor were they able to establish bases from which they could carry out operations against the Nicaraguan army. Their only significant offensive was their attack on a reserve battalion in San Jose de las Mulas on February 28, where they killed 17 members of the Managua's Sandinista Youth Association chapter. Whereever they went, they attempted to play on the peasant, private sector and ethnic discontents which they themselves had helped to generate.

But what the FDN was really capable of was the implementation of a terror campaign that spread fear and destruction by continual kidnappings and murders of peasants, local government officials and technicians. Contrary to U.S. and *contra* claims, then, there was never a civil war in Nicaragua, but rather a vicious and destructive intervention financed and executed by a powerful nation against a weak one through the mediation of a group of experienced, bought and self-interested assassins.

9. From Mid-May to July 19th: Continued Attacks, U.S.-Nicaraguan Relations & the Contadora

From Mid-May to early June, the war against the Revolution continued on the level of rhetoric, economic reprisal and military action. Reagan, Kirkpatrick, Enders and company kept up their verbal war against the GNR, and the administration ordered a reduction of U.S. sugar importation quota by 90 per cent. However the cruelest aggression was military, as the *contras* continued to war on fronts in the north, north-Atlantic and south, attempting to consolidate their spring operations and making the military question the most important and determinate one facing the GNR.

In the north, alongside the ongoing Jalapa operations, the *contras* began attacking the Mcarali area, only to be repelled in a few days. In the second week of May, the task forces that had been trying to get a foothold in Matagalpa and Jinotega since March were repelled with 243 dead, 60 wounded and 12 taken prisoners. By mid-May, 500 *contras*, mainly Miskitus, attempted to invade Llano de Bawisa in the north-Atlantic zone under the direction of Fagoth. Meanwhile, it was reported that Pastora was leading ARDE forces in the San Juan River area. As the war forced the GNR into domestic moves that looked ever more radical and dictatorial from the outside, the government pursued diplomatic channels to end the process of intervention and destabilization.

The GNR filed complaints in meetings of the U.N. Security Council, the OAS and the Latin American Economic System. Furthermore the government kept in touch with the Contadora group which had been seeking a negotiated resolution of problems in the area since January. While such moves forced U.S. officials to deal on diplomatic levels, and to make some tentative gestures of encouragement to its allies involved with the Contadora, nevertheless U.S.-Nicaraguan relations reached a new low in early June, as the GNR expelled three U.S. diplomats for their participation in a CIA plot to poison Foreign Minister Miguel D'Escoto, and the U.S. retaliated by closing all U.S. based Nicaraguan consulates except the one in Washington, and by giving Nicaraguan consuls twenty-four hours to leave the country.

From that point on, the U.S. harped on all the ills of the Sandinists, giving special emphasis to private sector and ethnic repression, railing against the many political prisoners in the country, while the U.S.-backed ex-National Guardsmen, many of whom had been released and pardoned by the GNR, continued to wage war against the country. Above all, the U.S. advanced the line that the conflicts in Nicaragua and El Salvador were both civil war situations between left and right, which required "one regional solution," especially since the Soviet Union was really the source of all problems. Clearly the Sandinistas were being asked to sit down with the anti-Sandinista *contras* and denegotiate the people's revolution. To back up U.S. wishes, governments bowing to Washington (El Salvador, Costa Rica, Guatemala and Honduras) formed a bloc to isolate Nicaragua and serve as intermediary with the Contadora group.

In their initial alternative to the Pro-Peace and Democracy Forum, the Contadora group proposed dialogue and negotiations to resolve the Central

American conflict, expressing a willingness to consider multinational and/or bilateral talks, but leaning toward the latter. They rejected the view of the conflict as one between East and West, proposing that all outside forces worsening the area's internal situation be eliminated, perhaps through the intervention of the Non-Aligned Movement.

In May, the Contadora group sent observers to the Costa Rican-Nicaraguan border and held meetings in which they renewed their peace efforts. Wracked with internal contradictions, the Contadora was nevertheless strong enough to resist Costa Rica's efforts to call on an OAS "peacekeeping force," a move that would have lent credence to the *contra* claims of having launched a generalized war in the south, and that would have subordinated Contadora decisions to the U.S.-dominated OAS. The Contadora group also resisted U.S. efforts to "integrate" itself with the U.S. bloc, and thus neutralize the group's potential effectiveness. In spite of the group's weaknesses, then, Nicaragua came to see itself as representing the only viable hope for dialogue and negotiation in the region. As the Colombian representative stated in Panama, "If the current peace efforts of the Contadora fail, the only alternative left is war."

In his State of the Nation speech in May, 1983, Daniel Ortega pointed to the toll of the Reagan war as of that time: 500 Nicaraguans killed in 1983 alone, including 58 specialist/technicians, 23 professionals, 73 workers and 34 adult education teachers; 549 Nicaraguans (mainly peasants) kidnapped in the past twelve months; over 7,500 government employees called into reserve battalions, and 3,200 more protecting strategic economic posts in the same period; 113.4 million cordobas in destroyed machinery, vehicles, equipment, schools and health centers; 119.8 million lost due to delays in development projects, roads, agriculture, hydropower, forestry and social services; 224.2 million in forest fires, coffee and tobacco field destruction and cattle losses; 104 million in goods that could not be exported, gold that could not be extracted.

By later that month, the number of U.S. personnel in Honduras had grown to 120, including military technicians, advisors and Green Beret counterinsurgency soldiers, and it was reported that the U.S. was preparing to open a major military base in Northern Honduras with an "advisory staff" of one hundred. By that time, another 600 Nicaraguans, mainly civilians, were dead. Speaking to these maters once more in his address at GNR's fourth anniversary victory celebration, Ortega mentioned even greater losses, including those accrued through the sugar quota reduction. While pleased to report on the failure of the military attacks and the overall intervention up to this time, Ortega was quick to point out that the intervention continued and might get far more severe. In the concluding portion of his talk, he turned to the question of the Contadora group's proposals made the previous week in Cancun. Nicargua, he said, "shares the

Contadora's criteria that 'force does not solve, but rather aggravates underlying tensions.' Central American peace can only be reality [if] ...fundamental principles of co-existence between nations are respected: non-intervention, self-determination, the sovereign equality of states, cooperation for economic and social development, peaceful solutions to controversies, as well as the free and authentic expression of the popular will."

Reemphasizing the GNR's wish to build a free, democratic, pluralistic society based on a mixed economy and benefitting the large majority of people in the country, Ortega set forth a new peace proposal, for consideration by the Contadora group. The proposal included the following points: 1) an end to war through the signing of a non-aggression pact between Nicargua and Honduras; 2) an end to all military support, through arms supplies, training, use of territory to launch attacks or any other form of force adverse to any of the Central American government; 3) an end to all weapons supplies by any country to the forces in conflict in El Salvador so that the people may resolve their problems without foreign interference; 4) commitments to insure absolute respect of Central American peoples' self-determination and non-interference in the internal affairs of each country; 5) an end to economic discrimination against any Central American country; 6) no installation of foreign military bases on Central American territory and the suspension of military exercises which include non-Central American armies.

Even as Ortega spoke, however, Ronald Reagan, criticized for his policies at home and abroad, began setting up a special commission on Central America to be headed by none other than Henry Kissinger, and he ordered the preparation of another massive Big Pine military exercises in Fonseca Bay and Honduras. Reagan's Central American War would continue; the *contras* would continue to enter the country and cause havoc; Nicargua's class polarization would intensify, through a spiral of strong economic measures and general conscription, non-cooperation and betrayal, imprisonment and confiscation. And still, only the Contadora group stood as a hope for peace in the area.

10. *Final Perspectives & What Follows in this Book*

In his speech on the State of the Nation in May of 1983, Daniel Ortega, speaking for the Junta of the GNR and the FSLN, reviewed the state of the economy (see the Introduction to Part III of this book), and reaffirmed the goals of the economy for the future: 1) to obtain self-sufficiency in basic food products; 2) to obtain vitally needed foreign exchange credits by increasing agricultural production and agro-exports; 3) to transform industrial structures, developing new basic domestic consumption article industries dedicated to using and refining Nicaragua's own raw materials; 4) to increase the population's purchasing power through the minimum wage; 5) to diversify international market relations, avoiding the one-sided arrangements of the past and finding trading partners willing to provide credit and technology transfers.

On July 19, Ortega indicated that immediate priorities included stimulating basic foodstuffs and food production necessary to the people's well-being; severely penalizing "hoarding and trafficking in the people's hunger and needs"; and guaranteeing, as primary, food for children and for the people mobilized in defense.

These goals and orientations guided the GNR's 1983 Economic Plan and would be the touchstones for every concrete measure taken in the months to follow the fourth anniversary celebration. The four years of Reconstruction had already entailed tremendous socio-economic and political transformation, the breakup of the initial bloc which made the revolution and the formation of a new more militant social coalition able to combat native opposition and the powerful external force that attacked the country with increasing tenacity. Inevitably, the years to come would require greater sacrifices, more intense work, to maintain and develop international support to keep the enemies of revolution at bay, while extending and deepening the new bloc in a struggle for a society truly representing and able to meet the needs of a long oppressed and needy people.

But just as in the four years of Reconstruction past, so the crucial period of material, objective organization and activity ahead would require a complementary development of a revolutionary consciousness and a revolutionary culture. In his fourth anniversary talk, Ortega addressed this very issue:

A new consciousness bloomed on July 19th: A consciousness that tells us that individualism, selfishness, greed, demagogy, and lies must be eradicated. A consciousness that readies us to work at any time, in any place and on any task. A consciousness that tells us, with Che, that we cannot feel totally happy and tranquil while there are barefoot children without schools in our Homeland or in any corner of the world. A new consciousness in a limitless war against the vices of the old consciousness. A new consciousness that readies us to give our lives in defense of the interests of the people. A new Sandinist consciousness that makes us worthy children of Sandino.

Building on the tradition of political poetry, the new poetry of the Reconstruction would play a significant part in the elaboration of the new revolutionary culture that would both express and help form the committed consciousness necessary for the first four years of the new society. In a nation where poetry plays so much more important a role than in technologically advanced societies, in a nation, too, where literacy and education programs, as well as the specfic promotions by the Ministry of Culture, could only lead to even more people reading and writing verse, poetry could only be expected to continue playing and developing its role throughout the country. It is this poetry, as it emerges in relation to Nicaragua's concrete circumstances, that is central to the pages which follow.

"Everything for the combatants!" Young woman in demonstration against U.S.-supported contras. Managua, December 1984. Photo by Vicki Grayland.

BOOK II, PART I.   THE FIRST YEAR (JULY 20, 1979 - JULY 19, 1980)

Introduction: Agrarian Reform, Mass Organization,
Popular Education & the Literacy Crusade

1. The First Weeks

The weeks after the victory were ones of jubilation and chaos, as the new government attempted to bring order and launch its program of national reconstruction. Efforts were made to clean up the bombed out and looted factories and businesses, to tear down the barricades and repave the streets with the streetstones, to begin controlling food distribution, to stabilize prices, and establish a minimal structure for policing and ordering civic life. At first, these tasks were difficult. The majority of people were caught up in block parties (or "kermesses"), and other celebrations. Unprocessed Somocistas and other counterrevolutionaries came out at night to commit petty thefts or simply to kill a few Sandinista sympathizers. The latter held onto their guns, and in the midst of the celebrations, more than one person was killed by accident.

The Sandinista military was itself a problem. Consisting mainly of young people who were now armed war heroes considered worthy of respect and admiration, they were a difficult group to control, as they roamed around in groups, or in confiscated Somoza jeeps and trucks, waving at the people, but sometimes drinking a bit too much or asserting an authority that no longer applied to the situation. Meanwhile, pro-Sandinista peasants carried out their own land takeovers without any due process, and at times unjustly according to the standards being set by the GNR. Sandinista *compas* were often too eager to help in these confiscations, and when they didn't help, there were usually "*milpas*" on hand, that is bands of young extremist leftists who saw the Sandinistas as moving too slowly in the making of a people's revolution.

Gradually the new government worked with neighborhood Sandinista Defense Committees and other grassroots organizations to bring order to the process. Most of the remaining Somocistas were arrested or fled the country, currency and gun control went into effect, unjustly confiscated houses and lands were returned to their owners, the *milpas*, as well as other ultra-left elements (national and internationalist sectors who wanted an immediate Socialist state), were put in their place, and the young war heroes were subjected to discipline, some leaving the military to return to community work and school, others remaining in their uniforms to become part of a new, peacetime regular Sandinista army or the new Sandinista Police. The new GNR was able to assess the state of the nation and begin ordering the countless tasks at hand.

2. The State of the National Economy in July 1979

Forty thousand (1.5% of the population) dead, 100,000 wounded, 40,000 orphaned, 200,000 families left homeless, 750,000 dependent on food aid were among the human costs of war. Commercial zones throughout the country were in shambles, the treasuries looted and more than one third of the labor force was out of work. In more general terms, the Somoza regime had left Nicaragua an inefficient, bankrupt and scarred economy.

Structured around the narrow goal of enriching a small minority within the country, the nation's limited industry was centered on consumer goods production, and the domestic business sector had stopped investing in 1975-76. During the war, Somoza borrowed heavily from private foreign banks, double-mortgaged his businesses and left countless unpaid bills from multinational corporations which the new government would have to pay before receiving new credits. Furthermore, Somoza slaughtered and exported the bulk of the nation's cattle holdings; and in the final hours, he ripped off a $33 million loan from the International Monetary Fund, wrote large sum personal checks and gave the green light to cronies as they stripped inventories from port warehouses and went off with them on their private boats. When Somoza himself left, there was only $3.5 million in the national treasury, and a $1.6 billion foreign debt.

In Somoza's final days, his air force razed entire neighborhoods and 25% of industry, including 33% of Managua's major northern highway manufactures, and major portions of every other city's industrial area. The industrial/manufacturing infrastructure suffered from destroyed buildings and machines, depleted inventories, uncollectable outstanding accounts, raw materials shortages and a technical exodos that had begun with the 1978 uprising. Furthermore, the war had devastated the harvest, limiting agricultural production for consumption and exchange. Roughly 70% of the important export exchange cotton crop and the year's corn, bean and rice staples had gone unplanted. The country's main sugar mill was destroyed before harvest time, and a major coffee plant blight control program had been halted by the war.

In social terms, the Somoza regime had left the nation with an infant mortality rate higher than India's and an illiteracy rate of 53.3%. The social service system was generally deficient in housing, health care, basic services and urban infrastructure; and the war had destroyed or damaged hospitals, schools and social service centers that were sorely needed to serve the wounded, malnourished, diseased and psychologically traumatized. Medical personnel declined by 15% and there was a further exacerbation of the already alarming pre-war doctor/population ratio of 6.5 to 10,000.

The GNR sought to strengthen national self-determination through a policy of diversified, as opposed to U.S.-centered economic dependency; it hoped to foster economic recovery through a mixed economy; and it sought to develop a truly representative pluralistic political system. But first it had to meet emergency needs: feed the hungry, heal the sick, bury the dead, and, in the process, organize and mobilize the people for all the tasks at hand. Doing all this required at least initial steps in renegotiating the Somocista international debt, the government finally agreeing to honor all but Nicaragua's outstanding military contracts with Argentina and Israel for $12.5 million in Somocista arms, ammunition and aircraft.

The GNR's new economic plan, aimed at developing a system ending with exploitation and corruption and the wide gap between rich and poor, included a provision expropriating all Somoza-owned and controlled properties and businesses. This made the state immediate overseer of 50% of the nation's arable land and 155 companies--i.e., one third of the country's assets. The state also nationalized banking, mining and other key sectors. But it would take infrastructure, system building and trained personnel to manage these holdings well; and the government took every step possible to spur the private sector to full production as soon as possible.

Credit institutions were created or revamped to steer private sector production toward the Reconstruction's goals. Credit went to small businesses and industries as well, if they areed to generate maximum employment, use domestic raw materials, and minimize any new foreign indebtedness. Then, after a review of its initial steps, the GNR drew up its 1980 "Emergency Economic and Reactivation Plan" which gave a key role to the private sector, including 75% ownership of industry and 60% part in the GNP. All of this was a recognition of the country's continued commitment to private ownership as it sought to develop the skills to manage the large, nationalized sector.

In the meantime, paralleling the effort to structure the nation's overall economic functioning, the government sought to improve the people's standard of living and quality of life by carrying out a series of institutional and financial measures aimed at stabilizing the course for future changes. Reconstruction of the government apparatus began, as new ministries (Economic Planning, Culture, Domestic and Foreign Commerce) came into being, and as institutes of energy, water works and insurance were consolidated.

The GNR nationalized the banks, and implemented rational and financial concentration policies. Striving for less bureaucracy and greater popular participation, the GNR replaced municipal government structures with local juntas; it also created special Courts of Justice to try Somocista prisoners, while abolishing the death penalty. A patriotic tax was created and imposed on real estate so that the government could receive the inital minimum resources to get the economy going. The Central Bank took away legal tender from bills of the highest denomination and gave 48 hours to change them in the banks so that the vast sums of Nicaraguan currency which Somocistas took out of the country would lose their value.

Meanwhile, as the GNR took steps to develop the 1980 Economic Plan, inflation and unemployment rates declined markedly, and economic activity went through a phase of apparent normalization. The GNR called on the private sector, except the Somocista fraction, to join in reconstruction efforts, encouraging investment and offering financial aid for industry, trade and agriculture. And although investment continued to lag, numbers of business people applauded the overall direction of measures to be incorporated into the Economic Plan.

In sum, all government efforts were directed to create the minimal circumstances necessary to carrying forth the most important programatic goals: implement land reform, develop free health care, eradicate illiteracy--that is, accomplish all that was necessary to create a new and free society. To meet these goals in the midst of economic and social survival problems, the GNR depended on the efforts of the FSLN and the many mass organizations developing throughout the country.

3. The Sandinista Defense Committees

The most important mass structure was the network of Civilian Defense Committees, or CDC's, which had played such an important role in the final weeks of the Insurrection in feeding militants, caring for the wounded, setting up supply centers and meeting all emergency needs. Renamed 'Sandinista Defense Committees," (CDS's), these organizations now acted to coordinate neighborhood defense, health and hygiene, as well as to distribute food, medicine and information and to bring suggestions and complaints to the attention of the FSLN and the GNR. Food distribution was vital in the first weeks, until the government was able to issue the first salaries and begin normalizing the food supply infrastructure. Health and hygiene coordination was also a crucial matter in this early period, to prevent and identify malnutrition and diseases and tend the wounded.

The CDS's worked with the FSLN to identify Somocistas, some of whom, dressed as Sandinistas went out on night sniper raids. They also supervised exit visas, reviewing applications to prevent National Guards-men and *Somocistas* from fleeing the country, often with unearned fortunes. Gradually the CDS's extended to all over the country. Overcoming initial organizational problems, they became centers of recruitment and organiza-tion for revolutionary tasks. They brought neighbors together to solve common problems and involve every one in the work of reconstruction. As focal points for information and organization, they provided the base for recommending and discussing new policies and laws. Not only did they organize demolition and cleanup campaigns, but in every way, they pro-vided the base from which the country dug itself out of the rubble and debris of the past and moved to create a new future.

4. Early Stages of Agrarian Reform

In winning the Revolution, the FLSN promised to bring economic devel-opment and justice to the countryside through agrarian reform. A 20% infant mortality rate, a 94% rate of families with no access to safe drinking water, and a 78% illiteracy rate were just three of many alarming integers of rural conditions under Somoza affecting more than half the nation's pop-ulace. Most of the people lived as landless farmworkers or smallholders who produced corn and beans for their own consumption during the rainy season and migrated to crucial export cotton, coffee and sugar plantations in the winter. Increasingly the smallholders were being pushed off their lands by the expanding cash crop production, so that by the 1970's 2% of landowners controlled half of all cultivated lands.

Agrarian reform would unfold in two stages during the first four years of the Reconstruction, the second phase beginning with the implementation of the 1981 Agrarian Reform Law. The first stage, already in full swing during 1979-80, involved reactivating production on what were *Somocista* lands, promoting a cooperative movement among peasant smallholders and landless peasants, and unionizing rural wage workers.

Immediately after the Victory, the GNR established the Ministry of Agricultural Development (MIDA) to coordinate state and private agricul-tural development. MIDA mainly dealt with the private sector (including 80% of cotton and 55% of coffee production), providing investment credit and tax credit, pressuring recalcitrants to invest in and use their lands. Meanwhile, it established the National Institute of Agrarian Reform (INRA) to administer the confiscated *Somocista* lands, including some of the most highly mechanized sugar and rice production centers. In effect, INRA was given charge of the essential revolutionary tasks affecting Nicaragua's impoverished rural sector.

One of the first problems faced by INRA was staffing the new state farms and preparing for the 1979-80 harvest. Former owners showed little concern for efficient production or the welfare of workers on these farms. But the new managers INRA brought in were often young and inexperienced, and lacked seed, fertilizer and farm equipment. Once these problems were somewhat resolved, INRA turned to improving the lot of peasant smallholders by promoting agricultural cooperatives, beginning a process that would organize over 70% of this sector by 1981. Two types of cooperative emerged. In credit and service cooperatives, smallholders cultivated their own lands, but joined together for credit and technical aid. In production coops, formerly landless workers rented idle state or private lands at drastically reduced prices, mainly for collective development.

The problems for INRA in initiating and developing these new structures were numerous, as impatient workers tore down fences and forcibly collectivized lands they wanted, as some smallholders resisted external organization and as all the difficulties attending social changes on more traditional sectors manifested themselves. However, INRA's early work was greatly eased by the development of mass organizations and then by the literacy crusade. Founded during the Insurrection, the Rural Workers Association (ATC) played a key role in organizing rural wage workers and peasant cooperatives, fighting against continuing exploitation and for new benefits, serving as the mediator between the workers and the government, and establishing ties with the Sandinista Workers Confederation. The literacy crusade provided the FSLN with a better understanding of rural values, attitudes and needs; it brought the rural populace a heightened political consciousness, as well as the minimal reading, writing and arithmetical skills for future agricultural modernization and fuller civic participation.

Even with all the positive developments in the agrarian sector, multiple problems would continue to plague reform efforts. Lack of farm machinery and replacement parts, inadequate technical knowhow, resistance and decapitalization on the part of private owners (including threats by Standard Fruit and other large growers to abandon the country--Standard Fruit would soon do so), and cumbersome government bureaucracy were serious concerns. Problems with smallholders indicated that they would need their own organization.

Most of these problems would be fully addressed during the second reform stage begun in 1981 with the establishment of the National Union of Farmers and Ranchers (UNAG) and the National Food Program (PAN) in April and then the passage of the Agrarian Reform Law in July.

UNAG built on prior ATC work to organize smallholders, and it sought to bring in those still under the sway of the large producers. PAN was undertaken as part of the growing national emergency over U.S.

destablilization efforts (especially the $9.6 million wheat credit cutoff), with the goal of achieving national self-sufficiency in basic foods, mainly through the efforts of UNAG's constituency, which produced over 80% of Nicaragua's beans and corn. The program entailed more productive use of idle lands, use of technology to build adequate local grain storage facilities, and distribution control to prevent hoarding of foodstuffs brought to market.

Finally, the Agrarian Reform Law represented the impact of the rural poor, including UNAG members, on government policy, in that the law shifted emphasis from state farms to optional organizational patterns. Expropriating idle or poorly used lands, the law guaranteed rights to landed property for all who worked their land well, and slated 160,000 rural families, including smallholders with insufficient lands and workers without any, to receive new holdings. Furthermore, while the GNR urged cooperative formation on the affected lands, they were to be distributed to individual families, especially in thinly populated rural areas.

During the first year of the Reconstruction, the FSLN had envisioned a mixed farm economy, with 50% of the land in independent coops, 30% in private holdings of varying size and 20% owned by the government. The basic structures established in the first stage and then modified in 1981, went a long way to revolutionizing Nicaraguan agriculture. The question would increasingly become whether U.S. destabilization and actual armed incursions into rural communities would create conditions that made continued agricultural progress impossible. In the meantime, and in spite of the many problems, the revolution had begun, and increasing numbers of peasants and workers had assumed increasing control over their work and their lives.

5. *Organizing Youth, Women and the Urban Work Force*

In addition to initial CDS and developing institutional structures, countless other organizational forms developed in the first year, many in conjunction with and some in growing opposition to the FSLN. Youth organizations such as the Revolutionary Sandinista Youth and the Federation of Revolutionary Students grew quickly in size and were ultimately incorporated in the July 19th Sandinista Youth (*Juventud Sandinista*), which, steadily growing in numbers, sent brigades out to the poorest areas to help with food distribution and neighborhood cleanups, help register poor children for the first post-Insurrection school year and spread the *elan* of the Revolution all over. The pre-victory women's organization, AMPRONAC, changing its name to the Luisa Amanda Espinoza Association of Nicaraguan Women, launched cleanup and health campaigns, developed plans for public laundries, cafeterias and "child development" centers, and strove to incorporate increasing numbers of peasant women from both Pacific and

Atlantic areas into their ranks.

Both youth and women's sectors, working closely with the CDS's and other organizations, gave their major attention to participation in the developing literacy crusade which would be the central mobilizing force for all mass work in the second half of Reconstruction's first year.

Three major labor organizations existed under Somoza: the Nicaraguan Workers Confederation, affiliated with the social democratic Latin American Workers Confederation (CLAT) based in Caracas; the General Labor Confederation (CGT), a Marxist-oriented group affiliated with the Permanent Congress of Trade Union Unity, based in Europe; and the Confederation of United Trade Unionists (CUS), a pro-capitalist union affiliated with ORIT (AFL-CIO) based in the U.S. These organizations only represented 8% of the labor force. The first two were considered oppositional and operated in quasi-clandestine modes; the third was allowed to operate openly because, even when it joined the FAO in 1978, it never functioned as a genuine opposition of any sort.

With the victory, the Sandinista Workers Confederation (CST) quickly formed and came to represent 90 trade unions. Structurally independent from the FSLN, the CST stressed trade union democracy and won support by convincing union rank and file that it could provide a genuine vehicle for their interests.

Along with the ATC, the establishment and continued growth of the CTC led to opposition charges, first by CLAT and its CTN affiliate, that free trade unionism had ended in Nicaragua. But in fact the CTN had been busily organizing since July 19, with monies coming from Venezuela and West Germany. The same could be said for CUS, which served as a virtual AFL-CIO bastion for leveling attacks at the FSLN. As the year drew on, the CST joined the Council of State and, in the midst of growing protests from the right, continued serving as a key popular force in the Reconstruction.

6. Growing Opposition at Home

As the GNR decreed its initial measures and carried out the first stages of Agrarian reform, and as the FSLN regular army and FSLN inspired mass organizations developed, a variety of international and national forces came to the fore which generated oppositional tensions that were soon to crystalize in the first crisis of the new government.

In the face of basic problems, the GNR and the FSLN had to balance establishing order with demonstrating their will to political pluralism. Such a stance led quickly to the emergence of particular obstructionist tendencies which threatened to throttle the work of social transformation. First, the Simon Bolivar Brigade, including members from a variety of Latin American countries who arrived shortly after the victory, and then the Nicaraguan Workers Front (*Frente Obrero*), which had fought hard against the dictatorship, caused problems by calling for immediate socialist revolution, fearing that reactionary elements would co-opt the Reconstruction. The GNR was forced to deport the first group and crack down heavily on the second, especially as the Front refused to disband its rural "*milpa*" troops who incited unlawful peasant land takeovers and published libelous materials in its newspaper, *El Pueblo*.

From the right, in addition to *Somocista* sniper killings and thefts, the FSLN was met with fierce criticism when it reacted to middle class commercial and political opportunism by restricting the use of the term, *sandinista* to itself, and when it chastised participants in a September regional meeting of CLAT for referring to the victory as an achievement of "the people" without reference to the FSLN. Severe criticisms against the FSLN and virtually every new decree and government policy mounted throughout the first year among members of the private sector, and their twin national allies, the Church hierarchy and the newspaper, *La Prensa*, as they watched the Sandinistas consolidating their position as the hegemonic force in the nation.

Early discontents perhaps first crystalized in December, when the GNR junta announced a shakeup of ministries which led to placing FSLN leaders Tomas Borge and Henry Ruiz in key positions. Then, as literacy crusade preparations moved along, junta member Alfonso Robelo, speaking for the business sector, complained bitterly about the pro-FSLN political content and mass organizing the campaign was being planned to promote.

Undoubtedly a key issue was the GNR's announcement of its plans for establishing the Council of State, a quasi-legislative body set to begin operating in the spring of 1980 and to be made up of representatives of political, trade union, business and religious organizations from all sectors of Nicaraguan society. Eight political parties were to have seats in the Council, but it differed from traditional Western parliaments by its reliance on direct representation of social groups instead of the mediating role of political parties alone. This was the basis for the controversy over Council formation and representation, in that the GNR gave representation to mass organizations that the conservative factions saw as creatures of the FSLN, to the degree that they dominated the Council. These protesting factions held that their membership in the Council was merely lending legitimacy to FSLN power without their having a genuine voice in the future of the country.

It was this structuring of political power which, on the wings of the midyear government shakeup, probably had the most to do with the resignations of Violeta Chamorro and Alfonso Robelo and the first political crisis of the Reconstruction. Immediately feeding into this crisis was the strike held by 90% of the staff of *La Prensa*, opposing the growingly anti-FSLN policies of the editorial staff, and ultimately resigning to form an independent, "critical" but ultimately pro-Sandinista paper, *El Nuevo Diario*.

While Communist Party leadership was in and out of trouble (and jail) at the same time as these confrontations with the bourgeoisie, still the latter sector, through their leading voice, Robelo, spoke of a growing Communist drift in the government. Also, while many private sector members continued to support the GNR, and while the crisis in junta composition was resolved by the appointments of Arturo Cruz and Rafael Cordova Rivas (respectively representing the private sector and the traditional political parties), still bourgeois opposition continued to mount in the weeks preceding the Revolution's First Anniversary.

Unsurprisingly, joining bourgeois protests were those from the Church hierarchy and the United States, which, in addition to opposing FSLN moves toward national hegemony, became increasingly concerned about the role of Nicaragua as a model and catalyst for other struggles in Central America.

7. The Revolution & Church in the First Year

Long before the July Victory, the FSLN leadership knew that the truly intense class struggle in Nicaragua would only take place after the anti-Somocista bloc had ousted the dictatorship, and that religion would constitute one of the most heated fronts of contention. The most atheistic and religiously cynical Sandinistas were careful to respect religious sentiment and to cultivate accord with the radical religious tendencies that had been developing in the county since the early 1960's. Priests Miguel D'Escoto and Ernesto Cardenal were assigned Cabinet level positions from the start; the poet's brother Fernando was charged with coordinating preparations and carrying out the national literacy crusade; other priests (including Edgar Parrales, later to become Minister of Social Welfare) also filled key posts. Priests and radical religionists of all denominations built on Insurrection-period work with the the nation's poor to develop support for Reconstruction tasks and establish an identity between Christian and Sandinista aspirations.

The Catholic hierarchy was inevitably disturbed by a priesthood more inclined to heed revolutionary imperatives than the Church's discipline, especially when the bishops of Nicaragua were suspicious of Sandinista plans for the country.

At the end of July, the bishops wrote a pastoral letter which was very guarded in relation to the jubilant mood prevalent at the time. But in November, they followed with a pastoral letter which openly supported the Revolution and the first steps taken by the GNR while affirming that there was no necessary contradiction between Christianity and a truly democratic socialism. Meanwhile, the apostolic nuncio Montalvo, very much identified with Somoza, left the country and a *charge d'affaires*, Pietro Sambi, arrived from the Vatican with experience in dealing with revolutionary situations from his service in Algiers and Cuba. The traditional *Purisima* and *San Domingo* pre-Christmas holidays were celebrated with splendor and relative harmony, with only some minor complaints that the FSLN was politicizing these events.

But this period of relative hiatus came to an end as the government shakeup in January left FSLN priests in office, and Sandinista hegemony asserted itself more fully with every passing day. The developing literacy crusade also served to strain relations between the hierarchy and the government, as national religious agencies and Christian relief organizations were mobilized to give material and human resources to a process which the bishops viewed as becoming progressively politicized. As Robelo and his supporters denounced the campaign as anti-Christian indoctrination, the hierarchy published a tentative letter of support. And their unhappiness with the government grew as the non-Sandinists resigned from the GNR junta and the dispute over *La Prensa* developed. Then in the midst of the tensions of May, the hierarchy added fuel to the fire, as Bishop Obando y Bravo voiced his support for *La Prensa*, while declaring unilaterally that the national state of emergency had ended and that those priests with government posts should resign. By the time of the Revolution's first anniversary, the bases of future discord between Church and State were well established.

8. Mass Education, the Formation of a Revolutionary Culture & the Contents of Sections 1 & 2

In the face of problems stemming from internal conflicts and a growing threat from without, the Sandinistas recognized that beyond developing organizational power they had to build on and deepen their popular consensus through the development of work in culture and education. Indeed, such work could not only create an overall aura of revolutionary culture, but could actually serve as a motive for developing new organizational forms and further consolidating the overall revolutionary process. In the first months of the Reconstruction, as the revamped Ministry of Education and the new Ministry of Culture developed their programs, trained their workers and carried out their first pilot projects, the dominant cultural and educational forms for the people consisted of the countless concentrations and rallies, and above all, ceremonies to bury and commemorate the fallen.

Then, within a few months, political education seminars and orientation sessions began to proliferate in neighborhood centers and worksites throughout the country. The Sandinista newspaper, *Barricada*, as well other publications, served educational and cultural functions for all who could read them or hear them read. *Television Sandino* and *Radio Sandino* provided other means for cultural and political education. The new Nicaraguan film production unit, INCINE, developed some important documentaries, including Sandinista newsreels seen before feature films at the nation's movie theaters.

Public poetry readings and recitals were a common occurrence, and the new political song movement, extending from music of the Insurrection, was the source for countless new songs and performances which reached literate and illiterate alike in every rally, as well as on radio and television. The poetry and song movements, as well as developing work in the plastic arts, theater and dance, found their framework for development and dissemination in the Ministry of Culture. The Ministry also carried out training seminars for "cultural promoters" and set up plastics arts and poetry workshops, as well as cultural houses, in many city neighborhoods and rural centers. The varying forms of political and cultural education initiated in the first year of Reconstruction are simply too numerous to detail or even mention. Of special interest to us here, however, because of the proliferation of poetry with respect to them, are the public celebrations, the burial of martyrs and the ultimate, culminating education program of the first year, the one which overshadowed and conditioned the functioning and effect of all other cultural and educational projects: the literacy crusade itself.

It is perhaps not surprising that the poetic material produced in Nicaragua about this first year of revolution does not begin to deal with all the dynamic events and processes which are set forth in our introductory materials, and which underpin and are the generative context for every cultural manifestation of the first year. While it is true that some of the combat poetry presented in previous sections of this book dates from this period, even more dates from from 1980-82, and it indeed may be that the aura of celebration, the sense of accomplishment, sacrifice and commitment temporarily overwhelmed the exteriorist bent toward dealing with particular issues and events, and the space of poetry was inevitably one primarily of lyric exclamation, of rhapsodic testimonials to insurrectional heroism, of eulogistic dedications to countless fallen heroes, of hopeful and ecstatic visions of the future in a newly liberated nation.

It is only when the initial structures of the Reconstruction are in place, when initial problems crystalize in the May crisis and when the nationwide literacy crusade mobilization is well underway that we find the poetry itself focusing on particular and everyday dimensions of the political and social process. Thus it is that poetry of celebration and dedication dominates the first section of Part I, that eulogistic poetry to the fallen is the substance of the second section, and that only in the third section do we begin to move from celebratory verse to a poetry focused on a specific process--in this case, the literacy campaign itself.

However, taken as a whole, the poetic material does constitute a profile of several dimensions essential to the newly emerging Sandinista culture that will be vital to the future of the Revolution. The initial celebrations and ceremonies brought together people from diverse social and ethnic sectors from various parts of the nation to voice their support of the new government and dedicate themselves to the organizational tasks multiplying themselves in every Nicaraguan community. In addition to the stirring speeches by the comandantes, public rallies included new, half-improvised plays, regional dances and presentations of the most popular and recent compositions emerging from the revolutionary new song movement.

The poems in Section 1 show the sense of optimism and dedication which the Nicaraguan masses brought to the tasks that lay before them. One poem, Cardenal's "Waslala," is especially significant. At a December "Assembly of Campesina Women," sponsored by AMNLAE as part of their organizational drive, women from the Waslala area spoke not only of their past tribulations at the hands of the National Guards, but of their current problems in the new Sandinista framework. However, Cardenal's poem reflects only the early, naive optimistic faith of the Sandinistas in the Revolution's reception by peasants and the indigenous population, without registering even the slightest critical or doubtful note about matters that were to plague the Reconstruction during the next few years. Gioconda Belli's anniversary poem at the end of Part I alludes to the coastal peoples, but again without registering much anticipation of the serious problems to come from the Atlantic Coast.

In the first months after the victory, Nicaraguans marched in solemn processions, stood in somber meetings, and carried banners through their streets and neighborhoods honoring and grieving for the many who had fallen in the struggle against Somoza. There can be no doubt that the FSLN and GNR used these services for mass political education and organizing. In Matagalpa during August, members of the FSLN high command marched with 3,000 townspeople in tribute to Carlos Fonseca Amador. At the memorial service, the leaders declared Matagalpa a national sanctuary.

On the same day in Managua, the residents of *barrio* San Judas gathered to inaugurate a Gallery of Martyrs in honor of a neighborhood woman who helped found the CDS's and coordinate local MPU activity. But the revolutionary leadership had to move the people beyond reflection on the past. On August 16, the great peasant leader Commander German Pomares Ordonez was hailed as "a symbol of all the heroes of the Revolution and above all a symbol of the most oppressed and exploited sectors of our country." At his funeral, Daniel Ortega turned the eulogy from personal lament to political projection, speaking of the need to dedicate "all our energy, all our capacity in the great task of national reconstruction."

There can be no doubt that mourning in Nicaragua was great, and that it came to serve a political purpose in winning commitment for struggling against the Revolution's enemies and for undertaking the difficult tasks that lay ahead. This concern with the dead emerged in every demonstration, march and rally, as the people called out the names of their favorite fallen heroes and responded, *Presente, presente!* The concern surfaced in the poetry of reconstruction as well, in a vast body of work dedicated to recalling the fallen, whether famous, barely known or completely unknown. No selection of the poetry of the Reconstruction could be complete without presenting examples of this poetry of remembrance and dedication. Section 2 does just this, its samples so arranged as to recapitulate the story of key figures and events throughout the history of Nicaragua's struggle. The presence in this section of so many poems from Nicaragua's newly founded poetry workshops indicates some of the thematic concerns of the younger writers and their part in the developing Sandinista culture.

However, both the celebrations and memorial ceremonies, as well as the poetry written to give expression to these historical dimensions, were all part of the total cultural and educational process, part of the formation of the new revolutionary cultural synthesis. And it was the mobilization and implementation of the national literacy crusade, its texts and lessons based on a Sandinista interpretation of the national history, which, more than any other single force during the first year, crystalized the new culture both for the bourgeois and church sectors growing ever more uncomfortable with the Revolultion and for the thousands of workers and students who gave the crusade their full and enthusiastic participation.

9. *The Literacy Crusade & Section 3 of Part I*

So much has been said and written about the crusade that it would seem unnecessary to devote several pages to it here. Clearly, the FSLN had established the campaign as a national priority long before the victory; the problem of illiteracy and the dream of its end were inscribed in Sandino's own reflections and reiterated frequently in the writings of Carlos

Fonseca. Only fifteen days after the victory, the FSLN and GNR set in motion plans for a national crusade, appointing Father Fernando Cardenal as coordinator. From the start a goal of the campaign was to reduce the national illiteracy rate of 50.35% by a considerable margin, to extend native language literacy not only to the Spanish-speaking majority but to the Indian and Black populations as well, and to establish a solid base for a subsequent adult education program.

Carrying out the Crusade depended on mobilizing Nicaraguan youth, with the goal of contributing to their formation as people willing to use their knowledge for the common good in helping to transform the harsh conditions in which the country's majority lived. Furthermore, literacy workers were to collect information about agricultural areas, flora and fauna, and the health, educational, cultural and economic characteristics of each social group encountered; they were to develop oral history projects, transcribe legends and popular songs, locate archaeological sites, provide basic health and preventive medicine information and help eradicate malaria.

In sum, the campaign was designed to provide the total population with the tools needed for the restructuration and modernization required to spur on production and national progress on all levels; it was also designed to to teach the people about their own history and reality so they could participate more adequately in the revolutionary process. The charge that the FSLN was using the campaign to spread its propaganda and galvanize thousands into organizational structures aligned with it was not without justification, and was a source of open pride for those committed to the Sandinista vision.

In the months prior to March, the Ministry of Education invited mass organizations, political and administrative bodies, private sector businesses, religious organizations and the Sandinista military to participate in a National Literacy Commission designed to carry out the work of the Crusade on a national level. This group established commissions to analyze the literacy experiences that had taken place in many other parts of the Third World. On the basis of these studies, the group elaborated a model appropriate to Nicaraguan conditions, and drafted various pilot publications, including textbooks for reading, writing and arithmetic, as well as a teachers' manual with methodological and didactic information and an explanation of the political themes to be discussed with the people as part of their lessons. Indeed, the textbook titles, "The Sunrise of the People" and "Mathematics to Reactivate the Economy" directly set forth the political education involved in the Crusade. The first word of the reading material was in fact not a word, but the first name of the founder of the FSLN (Carlos); the math book developed its pedagogical materials in function of the 1980 Economic Reactivation Plan.

As preparations for the crusade went forward, the CDS's and other mass organizations helped in a census and literacy worker recruitment campaign to determine the exact level of illiteracy in each area of the country, and to list the names and addresses of those who would learn and those volunteering to teach. At the same time, preparations were made to teach the future literacy workers. First, 80 people were trained who in turn taught 560, who in turn taught 10,000, who in turn taught the 200,000 who would carry out the task. From November on, pilot projects in different parts of the country tested the effectiveness of the methods and materials so they could be improved before being used on a mass scale.

The literacy workers were organized into a "Popular Literacy Army" in a new "war against ignorance." Army divisions included The Popular Literacy Army, students sent to teach in the mountains with their teachers; the Workers Literacy Militia, workers who taught in the mountains and their work centers; the Urban Literacy Guerillas, people who taught in their own towns and cities; the Rural Literacy Militia, those living in the countryside who knew how to read and write and who taught others where they lived; and the "Red and Black" Brigades, teachers affiliated with the National Teachers Association who were sent to the most distant, difficult and dangerous areas of the country. On March 23rd, the first contingents of this army came from all over Nicaragua to gather in Managua's main plaza and receive a tumultuous sendoff as they made their way onto the buses that soon wound their way out of the city and off into the fray of battle.

The major campaign lasted until August, as teachers and workers went through an intense and difficult process of mutual learning and aid. The poetry in Section 3 portrays the March departure and several typical moments of the crusade through July 19th, 1980. Depicted are the anxieties and hopes of parents, the hopes and travails of the young, their feelings on separation from loved ones, their sense of idealism and dedication. We see the workers in the mountains doing work chores, teaching their lessons, carrying on flirtations, falling in love. We get glimpses of rural conditions, of peasant life. And we receive also a verse record of workers killed by counterrevolutionaries in the mountains, a prelude to events that would come to the fore in the years to follow. The military elan and language of the workers also anticipates the future, just as it expresses a continuity with the insurrectional past.

In June a National Congress of Evaluation was held in Managua to resolve crusade problems and develop new methods for the remaining period. On July 19th, many of the workers returned to the city to join in the first anniversary celebration, and to receive a roaring ovation of recognition, anticipating the ceremonies that would conclude the major phase of the Crusade in the following month.

The efforts of the literacy workers reduced the national illiteracy rate to roughly 12.9% among those over ten years of age. More than 406,000 people were successfully educated, and many literacy workers and learners were selected and trained for followup adult education program scheduled to begin in the fall of 1980. Also, the campaigns slated to begin on the Atlantic Coast in English, Miskitu and Sumo were already in full preparation. In retrospect, it becomes clear that the campaign was the successful bridge from the Insurrection not only to future education programs, but to the health campaigns and all the activities that became part of the national defense against intervention and counterrevolution. Above all, in its mobilizing and organizing force, the Crusade succeeded in bolstering the revolutionary bloc which had suffered from middle sector, bourgeois and Church hierarchy fallout. Again, it contributed to forging the revolutionary culture as found in the poetic materials presented--in such concrete terms that some of the poems to be found in this book were written by those made literate in 1980.

Even before Helen Solberg-Ladd used Coronel Urtecho's poem as the *leit motif* for her film, *From the Ashes*, excerpts from that poem were so used in the first drafts of our poetic treatment of 1979-1980, to sum up the sentiment which even in the memorials and eulogies for the dead crystalized as the dominant attitude of the period that would remain crucial in the years to follow: "The Past Will Not Return."

CHRONOLOGY: JULY - OCTOBER, 1979

July: First laws of the Government of National Reconstruction (GNR) published. They include a law confiscating Somocista holdings, as well as laws establishing the new ministries and security forces; also laws derogating repressive Somocista laws. The private banks and financial sectors are nationalized. Many National Guardsmen and Somocistas who did not flee the country are now in detention or have been permitted to seek asylum with the Red Cross and foreign embassies. The GNR establishes "Emergency tribunals" in local neighborhoods to deal with assassins.

August: Agrarian Reform Minister Jaime Wheelock distributes 2,400 hectars of land among peasants in the areas of Cuajachillo and Nejapa. The GNR issues a decree over the "Law of the Special Tribunes" that establishes a complete apparatus for the fair trial of Somocistas in captivity. The Sandinistas' humane policies toward the Guards will later come to haunt them. A unified health system eliminating class differences in the rights to medical aid is proclaimed. The International Fund for the Reconstruction of Nicaragua is established to channel loans and donations coming in from all over the world. *La Prensa* comes out with its first post-victory issue. And the GNR decrees a provisional law over means of communication. In late August, "The Voice of Nicaragua," the GNR's official radio station, begins operations, and the Popular Sandinista Army is officially formed.

September: Daniel Ortega represents Nicaragua at the sixth meeting of the Non-Aligned Countries in Havana. Nicaragua officially joins the organization. A new Urban Reform Law regularizes confiscations and returns improperly seized property to their owners. Members of the GNR hold discussions with President Carter in Washington. One member, Sergio Ramirez, addresses the United Nations about Nicaragua's problems. The "Sandinista Youth, 19th of July" is established. Harsh and unsanitary conditions are reported by ATC workers at the Standard Fruit banana plantation near Chinandega. The company threatens to leave Nicaragua as ATC members protest. In the cities, the CST reaches new organizational levels, now representing more than 90 trade unions. The GNR decrees that only FSLN organizations can call themselves Sandinistas. This move raises the ire of organizations like CLAT (the AFL-CIO-based Latin American Workers Confederation) who join with the Social Democratic Party in proclaiming, "Sandinismo, Yes; Communism, No." Christians attend a seminar entitled "Christian Faith and the Sandinista Revolution," at Managua's Catholic University. The aim is to "help Christians in Nicaragua understand how to make sense of their Christian faith and experience in the Revolution." Late in the month, Sandinista Oscar Rivas Gallard is killed by para-military *somocistas* who have been attacking people in the Monsenor Lezcano neighborhood.

October. Prices of basic grains are frozen in the fight against price-gouging and hoarding. *Noticias Nueva Nicaragua*, a new news agency, begins its work. Discontents against the Romero government in El Salvador culminate in a coup which brings a reformist junta to power. Under pressure from the Right, the Carter Administration shows increased concern over Central American developments, and immediately recognizes the new government, as the slogan, "If Nicaragua won, El Salvador will win," spreads throughout the region. The Interamerican Press Society (SIP) claims the GNR's new press law limits freedom of expression. The Carter Administration, fearing the spread of revolution, steps up its attacks on Cuba and Grenada. At the ceremony transferring U.S. Zonian-held property to Panama, a crowd of 400,000 cheers the Nicaraguan delegation, alerting the U.S.

1. Carlos Mejia Godoy/ HYMN OF SANDINIST UNITY

Let's march forward, companeros,
let's advance to the revolution...

2. Rosario Murillo/ THE REUNION

And now peace arrived
and now we are the dawn.
Now it's time to reunite the pieces,
give back each place its shadow,
each hour its rite,
each step its fleeting wonder.
And this new suit,
these shined shoes,
this luster of ceremony.
The streets smell of earth,
of sweat, of sacrifice.
The streets still dark.
The war still whistling over us.

3. Jose Coronel Urtecho/ THE PAST WILL NOT RETURN

The past will not return
Everything has already changed
Everything another way
Not even what was is now as it was
Now nothing of what is
will be what it was
Now everything is something else
It's another era.
It's the beginning of a new era
It's the start of a new history
The old history ended, it can't
    return
This is already another story
another story distinct from history
another history contrary to history
Precisely the contrary of history
Precisely the contrary of the past.
The past will not return.
The past will not return.

4. Vida Luz Meneses/ MINIMAL
   HOMAGE

With production on the ground
without enough desks
or typewriters,
we're taking on the challenge
of the second stage
of your work, Carlos,
and it's like when
you went to the mountains
with a few companeros, minimal
   weapons
               and a flag.

5. Ernesto Cardenal/ VISION OF A
   FACE

Sun and flags,
        first hymns,
     sun and slogans,
        signs and loudspeakers,
applause and slogans,
                    sun and smiles
eyes of every color
     every tone of skin,
               every kind of hair,
each smiling mouth distinct,
  each nose a little different,
(eyes: light from countless colors
  framed in white)
long, short, straight, curly, afro
  hair,
young people, a fat man,
a woman with a small child,
an old wrinkled woman, little kids...
And suddenly from the stand I saw
  one face
with thousands of smiles
and thousands of pairs of eyes,
a Face of faces, a Body of bodies...
   The face was still blurry
but it had a kind of halo...
I saw that this united flesh
was the victory over death.

Photographers flashing away.
The people squeezing together,
and you could see the unity of
   everyone,
Unity the only guarantee of Victory.

6. Alejandro Bravo/
   COMMUNIQUE

The same force
we used to raise
the barricades
 and dig up streets and highways
The same drive
we had to silence
the cannons
the planes
the defenses of the tyrant
The same love
we gave to protect
each other
in the clandestine semi-dark
The same precision
 we put
in each bullet we fired
The energy
 the joy
 the rage
and the hatred
we spent to overthrow
this tyranny
we'll apply to each street
we clear
to each brick
we put in place
to each piece
of the new homeland
we reconstruct.

7. Carlos Calero, Monimbo Poetry
   Workshop/ IN NICARAGUA

You start to hear work tools
around seven in the morning

throughout Nicaragua.
(At the Augusto Cesar Sandino
    Airport
the planes arrive, go down the
    runway--
through the windows the passengers
red and blue flags--
the turbines' roar is overwhelming;
some are ready to leave or are
    leaving.)
The boats are anchored in the
    Pacific
or the Atlantic
and shake the ports with their
    hoarse horns.
The teletypes cross space to all
    countries
with news of the Revolution's
    advances
and the international news agencies,
as with everything else,
contradict the stories
about the advances of the
    Revolution.
Everything's begun to be different in
    Nicaragua
(To make the Revolution among
    everyone.
It belongs to everyone and is for
    everyone).
Alert, consistent, full of solidarity,
ready to work.
And the student has begun to write
with books, pencils, notebooks
and a new commitment:
    Revolution, study and work;
the unionized worker
marching to the shop, the plant, the
    factory
with proletarian enthusiasm;
the coal-sellers, the kids who sell
    candy
on the buses and streets
(while the Revolution struggles
  so they can study and work);
revolutionary secretaries,

peasants heading to the farm
    cooperatives,
the unionized fruit vendors,
with their baskets of fruits and
    vegetables;
the masons, the production groups
who have also learned to read;
the organized cattlemen, the
    militia-members
with their guns and military clothing
marching to the barracks;
the junior high and elementary
    school teachers
with classnotes about the New
    History.
My companeros, the shoemakers,
the taxi-drivers, the vendors,
the miners working in the
    nationalized mines,
the washerwomen, tortilla-makers,
    salesgirls,
tailors, nurses, journalists,
    engineers,
carpenters, doctors, pharmacists
                all organized.
And one works, produces, studies.
(The Revolution is individual when
    we work,
The Revolution is collective
  when one works for the benefit of
    all.
The Revolution is individual when
    we study.
The Revolution is collective
when one studies for the benefit of
    all.
The Revolution is individual when
    we produce.
The Revolution is collective when
    one produces
    for the benefit of all.)
Nicaraguan children go to school
and ask with interest
who Sandino and Fonseca were;
they sing the hymn of the FSLN,
they love the Revolution.

The sun slowly goes down in the
    West
and everyone returns to work.
They live, love their companeros,
with the love that's part of every
    revolution.
They listen to the radio, think, make
    love,
they love freedom, their
    guerilla-fighter
  girlfriends, their proletarian
    girlfriends,
they go to the Sandinist Defense
    Committee,
watch TV, discuss, read the
    newspaper,
they analyze the revolutionary
process in other countries,
they struggle, suffer in the struggle
against hunger, injustice and
    misery.
Then night falls. The dawn comes.
And I, proletarian and a poet, think
about this total liberation of
    Nicaragua.
And life, history start afresh.

8. Mario Cajina Vega/ THE
    COUNTRY YOU LOVE

Before you dreamed that the
    thunder-blasts
were bombs over Nicaragua
and we trembled in Masaya.
Tranquil now,
both knowing that they breathe
    together,
our daughters in their room,
that the distant bombs are only
    thunder.
And the fresh rain falling on
    Nicaragua.

9. Ernesto Cardenal/ WASLALA

Now all is joyous in Waslala.
        Waslala, lovely name.
(Before the very name spelled
    terror).
Now the peasants no longer come
    bandaged and tied up.
Nightfall no longer brings
heart-rending groans
but the sound of guitars.
Without those souls who shouted:
"Long live the Guard, down with the
    people."
The girls from Cua have come, so
    happy,
  with flowers in their hair.
Now the nightmare is over:
    "Waslala."
Waslala is joyous, the capital of
    terror
and death for the peasants of the
    north.
The seat of the entire
    counterinsurgency plan,
the strategic site for guerilla
    annihilation.
The worst "strategic hamlet"
of peasant repression.
They're no longer there with
    German shepherds
to track down revolutionaries.
This pleasant valley in the
    mountains
that was the darkest in Nicaragua's
    night.
They killed everyone at the farm.
  They burned them alive at the
    farm.
Waslala now without beasts.
These lands meant for growing corn
    were silent cemeteries.
    Sometimes entire families buried.
Now Pancho is there with his
    machete

weeding the cornfield.
You don't have to ask the garrison
permission to bathe in the river.
The Waslala school will have
  teachers
  and not Security Force members.
Soldiers dressed in olive-green
  play with the children.
The fields are no longer
  concentration camps.
The helicopter no longer
roars over the hills
carrying peasants, returning later
with just the crew,
to this place they brought people
  from Dudu, from Kubal,
  from Kuskawas, from Wanawas
  from Zinica, from Zapote.
Here were the lock ups, the
  underground jails,
there were pits holding men,
  women,
  children and the elderly.
The hills are now without beasts
  dressed in camouflage uniforms.
The peasants who come from the
  other side
  sleep in the garrison.
  The night lasted five years.
How beautiful the mountain is this
  morning,
the mountain where so many
  guerilla-fighters

roamed among the monkeys.
In front of the outpost
the children run like hummingbirds.
In front of the CDS the women talk
  between the flowers like toucans.
The red and black flags look like
  birds.
How beautiful the green of the field
  and the green of the companeros.
How lovely the Waslala River flows
  now.
        The day came suddenly.
The coffee crop will be good this
  year.
How joyous Waslala is.

10. Murillo/ MY FRIENDS, THE
    NOISES OF THE STREET

A zenzontle that sings in the
  morning,
a flag floating over the front door,
a woman rushing the pace.
The eyes of that child remind me
of the rainbow's shine
in the mirror of a puddle.
The market open to the morning, to
  life.
A slogan on the wall.
These are the friends of the present.
Attempting the practice of the
  dawn.

11. Coronel Urtecho/ THE PAST WILL NOT RETURN

Now there's not a word that has another meaning
words already have true meanings
What they should mean, not something wanting to hide or falsify
not something which wants to conceal or fake
but simply what they mean
Language was already totally corrupted
a language that was only good for lying
a language that was bad Spanish and bad English at the same time.
Not the Nicaraguan language which Nicaraguans speak.

172

But only gibberish designed to fool and rob and kill
A commercial, Anglo Jargon for exploiting the consumer public.
And above all a way of making the working people's sweat into dollars
But language like everything else was stolen from you.
Like everything else stolen from you in the past.
Finally it's all been recovered.
Now it only depends on you to make it yours.
You'll soon see how your tongue will be reborn purified.
Every word has been passed through fire, treated to the crucible.
Every word has a meaning again.
The meaning of each word, its own feeling
Which it has invented and coined, put into circulation.
Even its original meaning already has new meaning
the meaningless itself already has meaning.
As Joaquin Pasos would say,
in the meaning of meaning and feeling.
Because if there's no meaning, there's no feeling
For the first time in Nicaragua everything has meaning.
Now truth is true, the lie, a lie,
The homeland, a homeland. And Nicaragua, Nicaragua.

CHRONOLOGY: NOVEMBER, 1979 - FEBRUARY, 1980

November: The mining enterprises, many controlled by foreign interests, are nationalized. Eden Pastora represents the FSLN in a meeting with other countries at the Socialist International. On the 17th, the Bishops of Nicaragua publish their "Pastoral Letter" supporting a socialism compatible with Christianity in Nicaragua, and calling for a "Christian commitment to the revolutionary process." Carlos Fonseca Amador's burial site is moved to Managua's Plaza of the Revolution, in ceremonies that honor all those who have fallen in the struggle.

December: All liberal-to-progressive groups in El Salvador's "reform junta" have resigned, as mounting repressions overwhelm promised reforms. In Mexico, Nicaraguan officials begin renegotiating their nation's debt with the private International Bank, to which Somoza had accrued a debt of $500 million. (By 1982, the renegotiation will be completed, establishing favorable repayment terms which exclude any Nicaraguan debt for arms acquired by the Somoza regime.) 700 women hold the first "Assembly of Campesina Women," providing a national forum for women to reflect on their role in society and seek common solutions to problems. Child care on state farms is declared a priority, and the Women's Association begins to work with the Ministry of Agricultural Development (MIDA) to address this need and others. Just before Christmas, the Association of Field Workers (the ATC), representing thousands of peasants and others involved in field labor, holds its first public assembly and sets forth initial demands to meet members' needs. First changes in governmental structures are announced, giving the FSLN more power in state decisions and operations. Tomas Borge becomes Minister of Interior, Henry Ruiz becomes Minister of Planning. Bourgeois discontent grows.

January: The four principal popular vanguard organizations in El Salvador form a strategic alliance called the Coordinadora Nacional. The USSR sets up its embassy in Managua in the confiscated home of former National Guard general Jose Somoza. The extreme left opposition newspaper *El Pueblo* is closed and its machinery confiscated. Some of its editors, also members of the *Frente Obrero* (the Workers' Front), are jailed and accused of violating the Law of Public Order. The journal ceases to circulate, although some of its associates integrate themselves with the Reconstruction process. Late in the month, Mexican President Lopez Portillo, arrives in Managua to confirm his country's solidarity with the new government.

February: The Junta declares Nicaragua's rights to territories located on its continental platform, which include some islands belonging to Colombia. A law is passed regulating the price of land rents for agricultural workers, with the aim of stimulating production. Another new law stresses confiscation as a means of preventing the growing decapitalization and flight of capital by the private sector. Late in the month, the U.S. approves a $75 million loan for Nicaragua, most of the money designated for promoting private sector investment.

Section 2. Remembering the Fallen

1. Jorge Eduardo Arellano/ ABOUT HEROES & MARTYRS

The heroes and martyrs
belong to all the people
But each one of us has our own.
You, who would you have like to
    mention?
I'll list mine for you:
Carlos Fonseca, generosity become a
    torch
German Pomares ("El Danto")
conquering the night
Arlen Siu and her guitar in the
mountains.
And those truly mine:
Rene Tejada and his daring words
still echoing in my ears
Julian Roque, who shared books
and passions and rebel music
(I can still see him dancing
at the "Solar de Monimbo" club.)
Leonel Rugama, shy like a seminary
    student
but born to keep on living
(I used to invite him
to go have coffee at the University)
Francisco, Pancho Moreno,

pure like an ear of corn (a neighbor
of mine in old Managua)
and Selin Shible, more than a
    brother
to me in my birthplace, Granada.

2. Carlos Calero, Ernesto Castillo
    Poetry Workshop, Managua/
    SANDINO AND FONSECA

Without having known them
we remember Sandino after a battle
exhausted and wearing boots
    dripping mud
his uniform dirty and sweaty
opening the path in the Segovia
    Mountains
(maybe remembering Blanca Arauz)
that big hat, those hands
terribly wet from the cold
                in the Segovias.
We also remember
the tall and thin man
                Carlos Fonseca
who crossed the mountains
his arm breaking from his gun's
    weight
teaching peasants to read
so they could read Sandino
building the new road of Revolution
in the mountains.
Also with terribly wet hands from
    the cold
(and maybe remembering his
    children in Cuba).

3. Cony Pacheco, Subtiava Poetry
    Workshop/ CARLOS FONSECA

Stay there, calm mockingbird,
this quaking sound of machine-guns
making you shake out your wings to
    ready
for flight (stay there, don't be

afraid)
even though the machine-gun says
    MADE IN USA
the people fire it with love
because right now they're lowering,
into the grave in Revolution Plaza,
    the body of Carlos Fonseca
who you saw cross paths so many
    times
to go up to the mountains,
he who carried the sky in his eyes.

4. Rosario Murillo/ YOUR DEATH
    WAS MINE
        (To Camilo Ortega)

Your death was mine
before you belonged to death
and your silence was mine
before seeing you dumb,
    your steps detained
and your caress was mine
before seeing your hand detonating
    your last grenade.
Nothing of you has died
all of you is alive
in the wide green of the fields
in the harvests that come blooming
in the furious malinche trees,
in the birds
in the boy's happy games
in the woman, in the man
that hammer hope hard
nothing of you has died
the lemon and pine trees
sing your freedoms
and you "animal of the galaxy"
enveloped, displayed, distinct
on the other side of dreams,
on the other side of the world,
my hair uncombed, my body
    awakened
daring, stubborn,
from whatever piece of your name
the tedious solemnity of the dead.

5. Bosco Centeno/ TO ELVIS
CHAVARRIA

We're not going to remember you
with your guitar
on moonlit nights,
singing serenades on neighboring
islands
nor your uncommon agility in sports
nor your strawberry-wood fishing
pole
on the "Isla del Padre," nor your
hunting iguanas with precise
stone-throws.
We're going to remember you,
brother,
in the laughter of Oscar,
Pocho and Chica's children
running and laughing, full of health,
through the fields of our country.

6. Arnoldo Toribio Cerda, Garca
Laviana Poetry Workshop/
MANUEL DE JESUS RIVERA

We saw you make your way
through the rocky streets of
Diriamba,
You went through the streets
behind the vehicles shouting
LA PRENSA
EL CENTROAMERICANO
you also sold chewing gum
at the Gonzalez Theater,
you were a leader among the barrio
kids
you surprised us when you faced the
BECAT
with only a 22 pistol and two
contact bombs.
On the corners you shouted
FREE HOMELAND OR DEATH
calling the people to the Insurrection
organizing the kids.
You dressed in an olive green shirt.

When the neighborhoods were taken
in September
by the FSLN, by the kids.
The Guards trembled when they
heard your name.
They didn't know you were a child
of twelve.
A market woman betrayed you.
A "compa" arrived at our Security
House
crying and tears fell for your fall.
You had been ambushed in the
market,
child-fighter.

7. Calero/ CHAVELO

The afternoon almost without noise
or people, almost without birds
and calm, there at San Jeronimo.
I remember the afternoon
(Operation Clean-Up)
when they murdered Chavelo.
(Masaya was taken by the Guard.)
Near the cathedral of Masaya
the guerilla-fighter fell.
Two machine-gun riffs
and then a huge silence.
The insurrection was over
1978, September 12th.
The guerilla-fighter fell.
The child for whom Carlos fought
to raise him in schools
with healthy and happy children
with parks, universities, hospitals
THE NEW NICARAGUA
was in the womb of Bernarda, his
wife,
who cried desperately after his death.
And Chavelo's mother, Dona
Guillermina,
cried but in silence.
In those days the Revolution was A
HOPE.

8. Centeno/ FELIPE PENA

Your song is in the endless rain
of San Juan del Norte, in your
    image
as a proud and heroic
    guerilla-fighter
that afternoon at the camp
carrying your gun and backpack like
    a poster
from a solidarity committee
when leaving for the New Guinea
    campaign
with your Indian look
as if scrutinizing the future
with your smile
and your shout of Free Homeland or
    Death.

9. Maritza Padilla, Monimbo Poetry Workshop/ JAVIER

I would have liked to see you
behind the barricade gripping your
    rifle
firing against the Guards.
That's how I imagined you
without knowing you had died
and when they told me I didn't
    believe it.
Since then I remember you
talking to me in Miskitu
and how you got confused doing it
and you serious and standoffish
as if your silence were
what you committed to our people.
Serious, that's how I knew you
and how you were
when you gave me your poems.

10. Gloria Marina Lopez, Schick Subdivision Poetry Workshop/ SEGUNDO CHAVEZ

People called him Chundo
when he went down the streets
of the Schick Subdivision.
An illiterate,
he would discuss the FSLN with his
    friends
and at night would paint signs
on the walls and hand out leaflets.
In May while he sought medicine
for the sick people from his
    neighborhood,
a Guardsman killed him
at the corner of September 15th
    Street.
I can still hear him
shouting in the night,
"Free Homeland or Death."

11. Laura Isabel Morales (Age 11), Niquinohomo Poetry Workshop/ YURI

Yuri was a boy
guerilla fighter 16 years of age.
They killed him with a bullet
                in the head.
His girlfriend was Amparo.

12. Dr. Fernando Silva, Ministry of Health/ GIRL GUERILLA FIGHTER

You're there alone, girl
in the midst of the gunfire,
lying on the battleground
of Chinandega.
The night has erased the sky
like the blackboard
when the 5th-grade classroom was
    closed.

You'd hardly taken off your school
   uniform
when you put on your guerilla uniform
and in the school yard
a hopscotch of shadows stayed
   behind
where only your heart plays.
Here in Chinandega gunshots are
   heard
all around
and you crouch right here, girl,
as if you were behind a desk.
Now everything is death,
but you were life.
What will your father say,
your mother. Your brothers--
that you were the only girl--
love falls to the ground
like when a blindman
   bumps into trees.
Because the most brutal, most
   savage,
can tear the wings
off an angel with its claws.
And you crouch down right there,
   girl.
Behind the barricades you're lying
and instead of being in bed
       at this time of night,
you're here, girl,
with your cold legs
and torn knees and
the shoe that came off your foot
is over there on its side
like a boat that might have sunk.
Why, girl...?
For whom? ...The only boyfriend
   you had
was here in the trenches,
a rifle,
the only thing you touched to your
   cheek
with love.
All of this is too sad, unbearable;
       as if the sky were a well.
   You're alone there, girl,

in the midst of the gunfire.
   Lying on the ground
   in your reddened blouse.

13. Xiomara Espinoza Mais, Garcia
    Laviana Battalion Poetry
    Workshop/ JUAN ERRE

It was June 8th when you fell dead
next to a barricade.
I only remember how your body
   was
your charred face.
I only recall when I saw you
I approached you and I cried,
cried, cried
I grabbed your rifle and went on.

14. Mario Olivas, Condega Poetry
    Workshop/ TO MILAGROS
    CATIN "REBECA"

I hear the rain dripping
on the zinc roof over my room
and I remember your smile
and your olive-green uniform
(which you brought back after
your last battle in Leon)
and your words
(which you used to say to me when
we would meet on the street
of our town).
The town feels empty today.
I still can't believe you're dead.

15. Magdalena de Rodriguez/ JUNE
    26

Early in the morning
I went with two companeros
to gather roses for the dead guerilla
   fighter.
She fell during the assault on the

Cathedral.
Her boldness brought her into
the line of fire. Very imprudent,
the companeros say.
She was beautiful and brave.
She didn't cut her long hair
so she could be recognized from it,
she would say, when she fell.
Opening the gate to someone else's
  garden,
I don't know if I said it or only
  thought it,
"Never have this garden's roses
had a better destiny than these do
  --to lie on the grave
of the beautiful guerilla fighter,
  the one with the long black hair."

16. Roberto Salinas, Colonia
    Centroamerica Poetry Workshop/
    JOSE OMAR HERRERA
    (SAMUEL)

I know that you're dead,
  companero,
but in my memory, you're still alive.
I won't forget our classroom jokes
in the Lyceum
and the Riguero neighborhood secret
  meetings
with "Rene" (the leader).
When we burned a taxi
in front of the Los Angeles Church
and when we "recuperated" that
  truck
and the bombs and spray paintings
and the time we didn't make it to
  class
for fifteen days, the three of us.
I also remember you
when they blew up the bridge
in front of the Baia Hotel
(the one *Joaquin* had burned some
  days before).
The Retreat of July 27th came

and the following day the guard was
  now
entering over the trail of the
  Resistence.
This was the day you fell murdered.
A sonuvabitch sniper
wounded you in the shoulder
and even though you were wounded
you kept on shooting.
Seeing you fall we all fired away,
killing the Korean mercenary.
Afterwards they took you
to the Mexican Experimental
  Hospital
and I couldn't see you
till two in the afternoon
with your blue jeans dirty and
  bloodied
and the dark green jacket
with the torn sleeves,
I saw your pale face,
your half-open eyes
the red and black kerchief on your
  neck.
And I still see the white tennis
  shoes
you came with the day you started
  high school.

17. Cesar Ariel Montoya,
    Centroamerica Poetry Workshop/
    DOMITILA LUGO

I remember you
when we studied together in the
  school.
You were my classmate,
with your blue skirt of paletones
and the worn out white blouse,
your long hair
and your face with some
  blackheads.
I seem to see you seated at a desk
raising your hand
to ask the teacher a question

or talking with our classmates
about the monthly exams.
You were restless and a nuisance in
  class.
You liked songs in English;
I saw you eating green mangos
or raw jacotes at recess;
Domitila, the last time I saw you
was in October of 1977
when we finished the sixth grade,
you were happy
with your grades and your diploma:
we said goodbye
and I never saw you again.
I know that the Guards
killed you in an ambush
in the Santa Clara Neighborhood
(today it's called Domitila Lugo).
You fought with a 38 pistol.

18. Mario Cajina Vega/ FATSO, NOBLE ARTILLERYMAN

"Fatso" noble artilleryman, who
  fought
with a light blue rosary around his
  neck,
after having studied engineering in
  Managua
and leaving his studies for poverty,
  fell
when the National Guard stepped
  up
mortar fire from Coyotepe.
Thirty-three year old "Fatso"
fell towards his 50 machine-gun
which he maneuvered in battle
like an anti-aircraft thistle
perfumed with gunpowder and
  blasphemies.
Tonight, we, his companeros,
will miss his light-blue rosary.

19. Robeto Vargas, German Pomares Poetry Workshop, Matagalpa/ ANDREA

I still can't believe you're dead.
I feel alone and sad with your
  memory.
Coming home and finding our
  daughter
encourages me to go on.
Seeing her grow up lovely and
  honest like you,
full of song and revolution
like when you waved the red and
  black flag
and shouted the watchwords of the
  victory.

20. Juan Ramon Falcon, Tender-Nueva Mecatera Poetry Workshop/ LETTER-POEM FOR NINFA VELEZ, "DIANA"

I saw you tonight on the TV
  documentary
I saw your face behind the scarf
you used during operations.
I couldn't be wrong. It was you.
The hair flying in the wind while
  you ran
was the same hair I wrapped
  around my fingers
the night of your birthday in Esteli,
the same night you told me
about your Sandinist clandestine
  work.
Ninfa, I couldn't forget you, how can
  I?
If even after you're dead
I feel you're the same,
if I still love you this way
and I feel you created this
  Revolution;
maybe that's why I love it so much
as if by channelling my love into it

I could be closer to you.
Loving the Revolution is the most
    direct way
  I have of being faithful to you,
it's the best way to love you.
I'm sure you'd be happy to see the
    advances,
the participation in all tasks,
teaching reading to the peasants
in the northern mountains.
"They are ours, we must be for
    them,"
you told me your birthday night
while we danced.
I realized something that night,
more than loving you, I admired you
(that was my revolutionary way of
    loving you).
You talked and fixed your eyes on
    the heavens
(the same eyes I would see shine
one rainy night in Condega's park
when we said our final goodbye).
That's why when I see a member of
    the brigade
wearing a gray shirt and backpack,
my mind's view of you as a
    guerilla-fighter
is replaced by the image of a
    literacy teacher, and I imagine
    you happy telling me all you've
    done,
always relating your tasks to our
    love,
as you used to.
It's inconceivable for me to think
    you're dead.
And for me you aren't.
Nobody dies in a revolution.
Dying in a revolution is
    revolutionizing life.
it's loving, feeling, living life more
    deeply,
and you, Ninfa, have been born
    again
because you live there,

there where all the revolutionaries
    live
        like Ernesto Castillo
Camilo Torres   Jose Benito
    Escobar.
That's why just as I saw you
running with raised gun
(looking for a revolution)
your physical beauty shining
    through
on the television screen,
is the way I often feel that I see you
and that I meet up with you
and that you come running
with your hair down, wind-blown,
and with your arms open to
    embrace me
and that we kiss,
like the night when we said
    good-bye.
Ninfa, I love the Revolution
that's the only way of telling you
that I love you.

21. Alba Azucena Torres, Juigalpa
    Poetry Workshop/ MONCHO
    OBANDO

It's Sunday,
the stadium in Tecolostote is full.
A river passes by left field
and the children cross it
to get to the stadium
where there's no grass or Coca-Cola
    signs,
and none for Ron Plata,
or Belmont or Windsor cigarettes
or Victoria beer.
You hear the children's hands
happily hitting the zinc
(home of long home-runs).
Hernan, Luis Tito, Manuel
are all on the field, ready to win.
The townspeople have confidence
in their players.

The same ones who took arms
for the Sandinist Front,
well-aware that the Guardsmen
would come look for them at their
  houses
(that's why they went
  underground).
The team isn't all here.
Moncho Obando's missing,
the pitcher who became a hero
(the one with the blue motorcycle
who fell alongside of Cuizaltepe
by the raised monolith
you can see on the side of the road
going to Managua or Camoapa)
when the city was taken
by these guerilla-fighters.

22. Zeneida Zambrano, Elvis
    Chavarria Poetry Workshop
    (Managua)/ CARLOS FONG

Companero.
We were friends during our
  adolescence.
You died fighting in El Naranjo
with a rifle in your hands.
Your wife Eneida
educates the children,
forming them as revolutionaries
as you would have wanted it.
They will grow up
and study the true history of
  Nicaragua.
They'll also defend the revolution
about which you dreamed.

23. Mirna Ojeda, Schick Subdivision
    Poetry Workshop/ TO THE
    UNKNOWN FIGHTER

On the road to San Isidro

surrounded by the mountains,
sunny and silent,
I saw the grave of a fighter.
He had fallen there
with no witnesses
but the emotionless faces
of the Guardsmen who killed him.
No peasant recognized him.
No one knew who he was.
His photograph won't be published
in the papers
nor will his name be
on the list of heroes and martyrs,
but his tomb will be here,
as a symbol of his struggle,
surrounded by wild flowers,
under a heap of dry earth
and a rustic cross
on which a peasant would write:
"unknown fighter."

24. Gerrardo Torrente, September
    14th Colony Poetry Workshop/
    THE TISCARA HILL

All is humanity,
the humanity of humankind.
From the main shore of the lagoon
I see all of Managua.
The lake, the Chiltepe peninsula,
the Plaza of the Revolution,
the ruins are children's parks,
new avenues.
Those who were prisoners on this
  hill,
tortured, naked, hooded,
in rooms air-conditioned to the hilt
they were never seen again
because they are dead.
The Reconstruction moves forward
like the force of air that escapes
from the green depths of the lagoon.

CHRONOLOGY: MARCH - JULY, 1980

March: Weeks of preparation culminate in the official opening of the Great Literacy crusade on March 23. Aimed at bringing literacy to more than half the adult population, the crusade involves thousands of students, teachers and workers who begin to work as literacy brigadists in the mountains, cities and towns of the country. As the crusade begins, Monsenor Oscar Arnulfo Romero is assassinated in El Salvador, and the GNR declares an official day of mourning.

April: Operation "Quincho Barrilete" begins, with the object of bringing literacy to the children who work in the streets and of beginning a pilot aid project with them. On April 12, the Sandinista Popular Militias are officially formed, made up of field and city workers who receive military training in the city and the mountains. On the same day, Violeta Barrios de Chamorro, citing health problems, resigns from the government junta. Later in the month, workers employed by *La Prensa,* take the facilities of the newspaper to protest the firing of director Xavier Chamorro. Within a few days, 80 per cent of the *Prensa* workers join in founding a new paper, *El Nuevo Diario.* Meanwhile, Alfonso Robelo Callejas resigns from the government junta accusing the other members of trying to implant a leftwing dictatorship. Robelo's departure is linked to the *Prensa* struggle, and to opposition from sectors of COSEP to the formation of a state council dominated by popular organizations sympathetic with the FSLN, and to the political dimensions of the literacy crusade.

May: Twenty-nine organizations participate in the official opening of the State Council on the "Day of National Dignity" (5/4). Bernardo Larios and Carlos Garcia, former GNR members and leaders of FAD, an opposition organization, are detained and charged with sabotage, assassination attempts and other counterrevolutionary activities. Doctor Arturo Cruz and Rafael Cordova Rivas join national junta replacing Chamorro and Robelo. Xavier Chamorro takes on position as editor of *El Nuevo Diario.* The USSR agrees to join Mexico, Spain, France, Cuba and other countries in providing assistance to national reconstruction efforts. A young brigadist, Georgino Andrade, is killed, the first victim of counterrevolutionary bands attempting to sabotage the literacy crusade, which is now in full swing throughout the country.

June: Several leaders of the *Frente Obrero,* who also edit the newspaper *El Pueblo,* are arrested. Meanwhile, the literacy crusade reaches its peak, and counterrevolutionaries continue their hit-run tactics throughout the countryside. Petroleum importation and distribution are nationalized, and the GNR signs new petroleum accords with Venezuela.

July: As the first anniversary of the Revolution approaches, Fidel Castro, Yassir Arrafat and Grenada's Maurice Bishop arrive to participate in the celebrations. An enormous crowd from all over Nicaragua joins in dedicating the new July 19th Plaza and celebrating the 1979 victory.

Section 3. The Literacy Crusade and Year's End

1. Jose Coronel Urtecho/ THE PAST WILL NOT RETURN

For the first time freedom is
  freedom.
Soon now words will be themselves
  again
Soon now things and words will be
  the same
Soon the word and the thing
  will be the same thing
As words and acts will be the same
As Saint Teresa said, their words
  are actions.
Soon will come the refinement of
  words
The redefinition of words
The redefinition of the word
  revolution
The redefinition of the word
  democracy
The redefinition of the word
  sandinista
(Sandinista means national--
    defined by Tomas Borge
Sandinista means Nicaraguan--
    defined by Tomas Borge)
And the Revolution will define
what is Nicaragua
As the people will define what is
  revolution
As the past is already the past and
  the future
is already coming from the

Revolution.
As from now on everything will be
from the Revolution's work.

2. Thelma Sanchez Perez, Schick Subdivision Poetry Workshop/ THE DAY WE TOOK THE OATH

On March 22 we were in the Plaza
of the Revolution
and together we took the oath.
Later we went happily with the
  other companeros
drinking fruitdrinks and eating
  fruits.
From there you went to the school
and confirmed your resolve
to leave the next day
  (without my knowing it).
When I went by the school
Alberto told me that you'd left at
  dawn
for Matagalpa, and I began to cry.
Later I saw you,
  with hat and jacket on,
carrying your knapsack,
we met, there at the bus stop.
Neither you nor I said anything
a stare was our farewell.
I remained alone in Managua
aware of the work you would do,
in solidarity with you.

184

And now before I go off
  in the Literacy Crusade
I read the letter you left me
and when I fulfill
this task of the Revolution
I feel you at my side, Manuel.

3. Manuel Adolfo Mongalo, Camilo
   Ortega Saavedra Battalion Poetry
   Workshop (Diriamba)/ THE
   BRIGADISTAS

I saw how parents were kissing
   and hugging
their children who were saying:
"I'll be back soon."
Everything was laughter and
  weeping.
The streets seemed to be left
  isolated,
the neighborhoods alone.
My sister Rosibel made her goodbye
  and cried;
I was calm,
she carried her joy with her to that
  place
where she would teach the people to
  read;
I felt the urge to go,
but I'm in the Sandinist People's
  Army.

4. Salvador Velazquez, Military
   Engineering Battalion Poetry
   Workshop, Sandinist People's
   Army/ REMEMBERING NYLDA
   GARCIA (BRIGADISTA)

Nylda,
your straight hair upon your
  shoulder,
your black, happy eyes,
those words of friendship:
dark, barely fifteen years old.

That's how I remember you,
and that's how I loved you.
Also I remember your last letter
where you told me you were leaving
to teach the people to read.
I felt happy because I knew you'd
   be
doing something beautiful for the
  Revolution
which is growing stronger here in
  Nicaragua;
and I felt sad because you'd suffer
for a time in the countryside, for
  always
having lived in the center of Somoto.
Neither you nor I could've avoided
  it,
        you went away,
and on March 30th of 1980,
        near El Espino
in an accident, teaching the people
  to read,
        you died.
I was left with a letter for you
and you were left with one for me,
but I managed to pull myself
  together, Nylda.
I remembered you,
I'll always remember you,
because you gave your life for the
  Revolution,
for a Nicaragua free from illiteracy
that you, Nylda, never were able to
  see.

5. Francisco Martinez, U.P.E. (Unit
   of Embassy Security &
   Protection) Poetry Workshop/ TO
   A READING INSTRUCTOR
   WHO DIED (MAY, 1980)

In school I knew you well.
We studied two years together
and you were a friend and
  companion.

I knew you wouldn't remain behind
in March when
the literacy brigades departed.
You got your reading primer,
your uniform and went away
far from your home
with the knowledge
of the dangers you'd be facing.
Today I found out about your death
and I felt strange.
In an instant
all the experiences we lived together
passed through my mind and I
     thought
about your revolutionary qualities;
the comfort of your home,
the car your father gave you,
the parties,
your wife and your son
weren't a pretext
to not make that decision.
Now you form part of history,
teaching the people to read
in the Revolution.

6. Isidoro Tercero, State Security
   Poetry Workshop/ THE
   BRIGADISTA

Soil upon your neck,
the cotton shirt of the brigadista
stuck to your body,
your breasts repainted with sweat.
You gave off a foreign perfume,
the smell of a peasant woman,
you were returning from cutting
     cotton.
You understood our struggle, the
     Revolution,
the struggle of our dead...

7. Ariel Rodriguez, Sandinist Traffic
   Police Workshop (Managua)/
   BRIGADE WORKER

I seem to hear your revolutionary
     words
talking to me of the literacy
     crusade.
I seem to see you running
with your hair all wild
frightened by a cow.
I seem to see you
scolding the peasants for not
     bathing daily
happy, full of optimism,
and I seem to see you looking sad
gazing toward Managua
thinking about Urania, your mom
and your sister Betty
and perhaps, maybe, in me.
I also imagine you coming down
from this huge Puerta del Cielo hill
bathing in the Coco River waters
with your short pants faded
sometimes arguing
with some indiscrete peasants
because in passing by, Nincho
     Hernandez
stopped on seeing your body and
     your legs.
You must have left that peasant
     paralyzed
thinking who knows what things
about your beauty.
I also imagine you with your feet
     muddy
and your pants rolled up to the
     knees
steering the cows toward the corral
and I think of the face you make
when you touch the teets of the
     cows
   --you tell me they make you sick.
When you left on Monday, June 1st
at six in the morning I kept still
watching the microbus that would

take you
to Wiwili and later to Salamar
    province
where you're alphabetizing.
I remember the night I spent with
    you
in the Alpino Hotel in Esteli,
I took off your shorts
and left you with only your panties.
All excited, I looked without
    touching you.
I feel a profound love for you.

8. Jose Antonio Rodriguez, Esteli
   Poetry Workshop/ TO YOU,
   ELSA

Girl literacy worker,
who came to alphabetize the
    Horcones community,
the sun already falling to hide itself
in the mountains, I remember.
From my house I saw you go by
literacy books in your revolutionary
    hand.
On your birthday
I gave you a poem
and when I saw you again
you told me you liked my verses.
That afternoon of goodbyes
after the dinner we danced, Elsa.
My hands rested on your body
and as it did on every evening
    when you came,
the sun hid behind the mountains.

9. Jose Garcia, German Pomares
   Poetry Workshop (Matagalpa)/
   COMPANERA BRIGADEERS

There in San Rafael del Norte
in the month of June, 1980
I saw the brigade companeras
    teaching.

From the moment I started talking
    with them
I saw their dedication to the
    Revolution.
And since then I dream
and hear their literacy songs.
On seeing their smiles and being
    close to them
I feel my heart beating fast and
    know that
each day the Revolution is more
    consolidated
and my heart beats on seeing them
fulfilling our revolutionary tasks.

10. Victor Manuel Gomez Pineda,
    German Pomares Battalion
    Poetry Workshop (Matagalpa)/
    ROSA ARGENTINA MONTES

On the night of June 16, 1980
wearing a gray shirt and blue pants
you were in your students' house
sitting on a wood bench
in front of a small, wobbly table
lit by a kerosene lamp
explaining Nicaraguan history,
teaching reading and writing
correcting mistakes.

11. Eliseo Jerez Guadamuz,
    September 14th Neighborhood
    Poetry Workshop (Managua)/
    THE RETURN

I wait for you very contented
because you'll return to our side,
to the home you left one day
without caring about the small
    discomforts.
You went off with your unbreakable
    and happy decision.
You disregarded the rain,
    the mud, the rivers and the cold.

"Only an illness," you said,
would take me out of the mountains."
I felt proud when I heard that you
    belonged
to the Eduardo Contreras Zero
    Squadron.
Now I imagine you've learned quite
    a bit.
Our peasant companero was your
    teacher
teaching you how to plant,
how to keep time by the song of the
    roosters
and know where you are by the
    stars.
You'll come back with a brigadista's
    awareness.
Us parents are happy
(though there are also some
    who lost their children).
And for all this,
when I see you in the July 19th
    Plaza
on the 23rd of August,
then, I'll say: my daughter's come
    home.

12. Santiago Lopez, Pancasan
    Poetry Workshop/ A YEAR
    AFTER THE FINAL
    INSURRECTION

A year has passed
since the final insurrection
    and it doesn't seem possible.
During these nights
the memories of my companeros
    come to me
those who died before the
    insurrection
without seeing our Sandinist victory.
Mariano, William, Yemin
their way of talking
their way of walking.
Today they're dead.

Not dead like many
but alive in the people.
Mariano, age 19, his trips to the
    UNAN--
and he would tell me about meetings
    there
about the companeros who thought
    differently
(from how you thought)
his way of explaining things
his hair combed back.
Yemin, twenty-two years old,
his fast comings and goings
from house to house
    from meeting to meeting
wearing two different shirts
one on top of the other
to try to confuse the Guardsmen
(who were after you from what you
    said)
those sneakers to be able to run
    more
    and silently
and escape from the National Guard.
Today I try to remember all their
    diligence,
all their discipline.
I try to imitate them with every
    day
    that passes with their memory.

13. Gioconda Belli/ JULY 19, 1980:
    IN THE MIDST OF THIS
    GRAND & PORTENTOUS
    SILENCE

One year later, dawn came,
the same day and the same hour,
and we await the morning
walking over mountains and on
    highways,
joining together in the streets and
    avenues
before the startled stare of the birds.
It was not magic,

188

the FSLN billboard on Motastepe
  hill,
the flags,
the beautiful portraits of Sandino
  and Fonseca.
It was not magic,
the river of colors marching toward
  the plaza,
the raving sun not wishing to miss
  the Fiesta.
There were the congested hearts,
the sweat of the bodies,
the hands made to raise barricades,
raising red and black flags
and our eyes grown to contented
united by the hands in the air.
There the familiar faces,
the ones that a year ago were dirty
  and dusty,
now with implacable, gallant
  uniforms
and the troop heads, the
  underground fighters,
the ones who later organized the
  masses
and they gave form to the disorder
and planted the earth
and set the machines ablaze.
There the children
running with flags and flowers
and the slow old ones who were
  awake
at the end of dreams.
There were the excited old friends,
those who we had never before
  received openly.
There our Miskitu brothers,
the forgotten Ramas and Sumos,
their bodies dancing
to the sound of daring drums.
There was the force overwhelming
  the view,
the people's courage
splayed out in slogans and smiles.

And there, all at once,

the impressive silence:
  a people respecting the word
  more eloquent than canons and
    thunderclaps.
And this multitude of squeezed
  bodies
we were alone--each one before all--
alone to think of this human mass
demanding love and sacrifice,
demanding revolution
in their grand portentous silence;
revolution of machetes, plows and
  pistons,
revolution of new attitudes;
demanding tenderness and seriousness
in work, at home, in laughter,
in the way of brandishing love,
  of treating children,
of loving a woman, a man,
revolution from inside toward out,
from outside to within,
revolution in the midst of sweat,
of sun, of fatigue,
wanting to shout with joy
like outrageous horsemen of the
  future.
In the space of my multitudinous
  intimacy,
surrounded by silent cries,
I wanted a morning where I could
  feel myself
blood worthy of this giant people,
blood washed, clean, stream of
  work,
skirt to shelter young corn,
woman proud, new,
full of this greatness from within.

14. Coronel Urtecho/ THE PAST
  WILL NOT RETURN

The past is exactly what has been
  defeated
The past is exactly what's been
  abolished

The past is exactly what's been
　finished.
Now the past has truly passed.
Now the past is truly past
The present present the future
　future
Before the present was
　the past present
It was impossible to separate the
present
from the past
The past the present the future
　were only the past
But the past has already
　even changed its meaning
All the past has been judged and
　condemned
The past will not return.

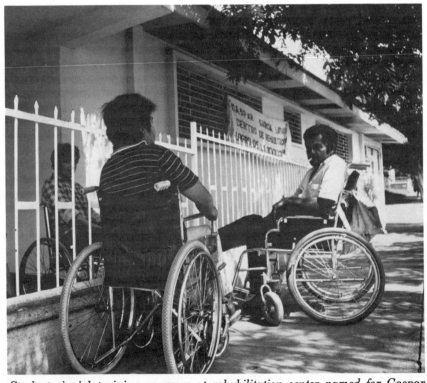

Students in job-training program at rehabilitation center named for Gaspar Garcia Laviana, Sandinista priest, poet and combatant killed in the Insurrection. Managua, August 1983. Photo by Loretta Smith.

Book II, PART II. THE NEW ORDER & NEW CRISES
(JULY, 1980 - JULY, 1982)

*Introduction: Internal Developments, The Church,
The Atlantic Coast, Health & Education*

1. What this Part Contains

This part of Book II covers the two years of the Reconstruction during which, coming out of the Literacy Crusade, and extending through the various campaigns, mobilizations, innovations, confrontations, crises and intensified commitments to carry on, the Sandinistas built their mass organizational base and struggled to keep faith with their initial promises in the face of mounting external and internal forces of opposition. The Revolution made many advances, but it was wracked by many problems stemming from internal opposition by the private sector, the Church hierarchy and others, in combination with ex-Somocista guardsmen operating out of Honduran camps and an increasingly belligerent North American government. Many of the plans for the Reconstruction had to be modified, delayed or shelved completely in view of the threats of economic destabilization and intervention. On the other hand, the growing crisis situation emerging over the course of the two year period could only galvanize deeper commitment among the vast majority of Nicaraguans, especially among those who fought for and hoped to benefit from the Revolution.

The poetic collage presented is perhaps more a witness to this spirit than it is to the total array of events and issues constituting the historical process. Nevertheless, it is true that the four sections comprising Book II, Part II present an ample view of many of the key occurrences and preoccupations. Based completely on poems by young soldiers and militia volunteers, Section 1 portrays the emergence of the military--first the Sandinista Army, then the militias: the raw volunteers going off to military training, experiences and feelings in the school, in the training camp, and in the first missions and vigils as the situation of national emergency develops; but also the themes of love and eros--the goodbyes to sweethearts, the waiting for telephone calls or letters that may or may not come, that may be assuring or downright rejecting, and then the new loves that emerge in the course of service--in conflict or complementary with duty and patriotic elan.

Overlapping in time with Section 1, our second section covers some of the major events of the 1980-81 period, including the uprising in Bluefields and emerging problems with the indigenous people on the Atlantic Coast, volunteer work, etc.; but above all, the recurring thread or motif is the question of the religious struggle--or namely the people's religion as opposed to the perspective of the church hierarchy. Section 3 pays witness to the spirit and values involved in the important health campaigns of 1981-82, mainly through excerpts from the poems of a young medical worker, Juan Herrera Salazar. And Section 4 covers major events of the second year, once again starting with problems--above all, the problem of Eden Pastora and the deepening aggression against the Revolution. However the section also pays homage to the transformations in education and the aspirations of the young people for a better world in the future.

As with our previous introduction, the purpose of this one is to provide a more rigorous understanding of the period and issues to be treated. Our general introduction describes the dominant force of opposition to Sandinista hegemony and the direction of the GNR, as it developed and matured throughout this two year period and beyond. Here, only reviewing the Reaganite campaign in passing, we will then touch on internal Nicaraguan developments as affected by and responding to that campaign's growing force and determination. Then, our overall context established, we will turn to the core themes of our poetic material: the religious question, problems on the Atlantic Coast, and developments in health and education.

2. Nicaraguan Economic Policy, New Institutions & the Private Sector

Early on in this period, financial setbacks contributed to a rise in inflation. Foreign aid and soft credits diminished, problems of efficiency abounded in the public sector, and decapitalization increased because of the negative attitude of certain private sector groups. But the government continued granting significant credits and low interest rates to public and private sector enterprises. Inevitably the 1981 Economic Plan stressed austerity and efficiency. Standard Fruit, the key company of Nicaragua's banana industry, threatened to withdraw from the country. COSEP strongly opposed a GNR decree imposing strong penalties for hoarding and speculation. Lack of foreign financing and the international economic crisis aggravated by Reagan's policies made the national economy suffer all the more. The GNR began a process of regionalization in hopes of stabilizing and streamlining the economy. In the First Popular Health Campaign (Spring, 1981), economic policies based on grassroots participation and organization were revived and fortified.

During the next period, new laws created new possibilities and new disputes. Fierce polemics raged over the expropriation of unused or underused land, as the right spoke of tyranny, and the left argued that more lands should be confiscated. The new Law Against Decapitalization made it hard for some companies to obtain foreign credit; and strong anti-black market measures created unhappiness among profiteers. The Social and Economic Emergency Law meant overall control of foreign currency, luxury importation restrictions, frozen budget costs, a temporary freeze on strikes and the promotion of labor agreements, as well as ever stronger restrictions on the flight of capital. The Foreign Investment law and a policy of economic incentives to cooperating private sector entities entered initial stages, but the Emergency Law obliged the GNR to set aside large sums for defense. Then, in May, 1982, storms brought on Nicaragua's heaviest flooding of the century, causing losses of over $360 million (more than half the nation's budget for the year), mainly in the most productive Pacific Coast areas. Military attacks and the drought which followed the floods meant great deviations in the 1982 Economic Plan, with the immediate consequence of higher unemployment and inflation.

Large numbers signed up to participate in defense tasks as members of the newly formed Popular Sandinista Militia, a volunteer army reinforcing the EPS. In February, 1981 and the months that followed, the Militia joined with the army in repelling counterrevolutionary attacks. Meanwhile, the GNR junta was reduced from five to three members, including Sergio Ramirez, Rafael Cordova Rivas and Daniel Ortega, the Coordinator. The revamped junta launched the National Food Project aimed at rationalizing national grain production and distribution, as well as developing national self-sufficiency that would enable Nicaragua to export corn and beans. The junta also established special courts and regional committees to promote, implement and coordinate production under the Agrarian Reform Law. But by the spring of 1982, interventionist attacks forced the GNR to give priority to defense, as the government declared the National State of Emergency and instituted censorship.

Clearly a major target of emerging GNR-FSLN moves was the private sector, large portions of which increasingly opposed the direction of national development, with some members engaged directly or indirectly in counter-revolutionary activity. Although the new production commissions created for each product involved the private sector, many business people exhibited ever-greater distrust in the process.

Even very early into the two-year period under consideration, various, supposedly non-Somoza businessmen were found implicated in an armed anti-government conspiracy, against which the GNR had to stand firm. When the GNR or FSLN took action, of course, private representatives shouted foul play and dictatorship. Inevitably the loudest protests against the GNR came from the private sector's champions, Robelo's National Democratic Movement, *La Prensa* and COSEP, all three of which were becoming defined by their opposition to the revolutionary process. Technicians identifying with COSEP abandoned their government posts.

In response, the FSLN attempted to create a national forum with various political organizations to discuss national problems and achieve minimal accords beneficial to national unity. The organizations included the Popular Christian, Independent Liberal and Nicaraguan Socialist Parties, as well as such openly oppositional entities as the Constitutionalist Liberal Movement, the Social Democrat Party and even the MDN. Then too, the new Agrarian Reform Law facilitated an alliance of the GNR and large numbers of agrarian owners, since the government protected well-exploited lands and guaranteed financing for productive improvements. However animosities between the more dissident business sectors and the GNR flared when the latter declared the Law of Emergency. *La Prensa* launched fierce attacks and was closed five times. Members of COSEP, as well as members of the Communist Party, were arrested for violating the law.

The national emergency deepened throughout the winter of 1982. At the most critical moment, Eden Pastora surfaced publicly in Costa Rica declaring his open opposition to the Revolution, and Alfonso Robelo left the country, siding with Pastora. Almost immediately, business sectors formed an opposition front which joined with key Nicaraguan businessmen who had already left the country after decapitalizing their enterprises, in appealing to the U.S. for support in armed struggle against the GNR. Arrested COSEP leaders finished their sentences and were released. But investment dropped, as the government held to the principles of the mixed economy and financial support to those private owners who continued to invest in the country.

3. The Revolution and Grassroots Organizations

If many of the State's economic and political measures responded to popular needs in the midst of problems created by inherited structural weaknesses and mounting pressures from internal and external capitalist forces, the poor people of Nicaragua reciprocated through their development and transformation of popular organizations, their assumption of difficult tasks and their intensifying commitment to making revolution in the face of all the dangers and crises.

As the Literacy Crusade came to a successful end, mass work became focused on forming Popular Education Collectives to carry on continuing adult education, and on setting up agricultural cooperatives throughout every area of the country. The CDS's took on the work of distributing basic staples. The newly created National Farmers and Cattle Raisers' Union (UNAG) promoted the interests of small and medium farmers. Participation in the military and the new Militias, in the voluntary work brigades and the emerging Health Campaigns (one in 1980, another in 1981) grew day by day, month by month. On the negative side, UNAG developments caused conflicts between small and medium farmers in the Matagalpa coffee zones; separatist demands emerged among Atlantic Coast indigenous groups; and, as Somocista incursions across the Honduran border mounted, the GNR ordered the relocation of Miskitu border area villages.

In the first months of 1982, the Ministry of Commerce developed a network of locally run neighborhood grocery stores which provided basic food product subsidies for the rural poor. Furthermore, UNAG began to overcome initial problems, to grow in size and force. But as spring came on, defense against counterrevolution began to dominate mass participation. The CDS's increasingly served as mobilization and support points for the increasing numbers who joined the Militia; and overall, the grassroots organizations reached new highs in participation and militancy, as the quantity and quality of border incursions steadily mounted and militia battalions began to move out toward the conflict areas.

4. The Church Hierarchy and the Government

For the two years in question, FSLN and GNR problems deepened not only with the business sector, but that sector's allies in the Church hierarchy. Indeed, the class polarization between private and mass, bourgeois and proletarian, found acute expression in the struggle that raged between the Church hierarchy and the State, as well as between the Church hierarchy and the priests of the poor.

On the whole, Nicaragua's religious organizations maintained their traditional role of helping the poor with basic housing, education and health needs. But whereas past humanitarian programs tended to be isolated or limited, or when guided by progressive impulses, subject to constant harassment, cooperative efforts between progressive parish priests and Sandinistas showed early signs of heightening the effectiveness of social welfare programs, in rural base communities as well as in urban neighborhoods.

Clearly, many of the orientations of the Reconstruction developed through an alliance between Sandinists and those religious workers identified with "liberation theology"; meanwhile relations between the FSLN and the religious hierarchy were less close. Those relations began to deteriorate in almost inverse proportion to the growing degree in which increasing numbers of priests and church lay workers identified their priorities with those of the Revolution, and the degree to which they might only adhere to the policies of a Church superior if they did not contradict Sandinista imperatives. This potential challenge to Church authority only became more threatening to the hierarchy in the wake of the struggles with the private sector during the first year of the Reconstruction. The challenge came to center most specifically on the question of the four highest ranking priests directly holding key government offices, Father Fernando Cardenal, coordinator of key education projects, and Fathers Ernesto Cardenal, Miguel D'Escoto and Edgar Parrales, respectively serving as Ministers of Culture, Foreign Affairs and Social Welfare.

Even during the previous year, Nicaragua's bishops raised the issue of the continued work of these priests in the government. The new year began inauspiciously as the bishops purposely snubbed the massive closing ceremony of the Literacy Crusade. Attempting conciliation, the FSLN sent a communique reaffirming respect for religious beliefs and religious freedom. But the Bishops' Conference answered with a highly critical document, accusing the Sandinistas of attempting to distort Christian language and traditions for their own purposes. Church-State relations cooled progressively, as Bishop Obando grew increasingly negative about the Reconstruction process. On the other hand, the majority of the nation's clergy supported the FSLN and worked in the national health campaigns, helping to train thousands of health workers to carry out vaccination programs, conduct cleanup programs and teach basic sanitation and preventive health care to village residents throughout the country. As the Church-State controversy grew more intense, and as criticisms were leveled against them, many of these priests entered into fierce polemic with the hierarchy. When a new nuncio arrived from the Vatican to mediate Church disputes, debates on religious themes, heavily laden with ideological and political overtones, raged in the newspapers.

Then, in June, 1981, the national Conference of Bishops announced that priests continuing to hold government posts would be considered in "open rebellion and subject to ecclesiastical sanctions." This virtual ultimatum unleashed massive demonstrations in support of the government priests. Famous international theologians wrote letters supporting the priests and criticizing the bishops' stance. As the priests in question refused to resign, the Managua Archdiocese began removing priests judged as Sandinistas from pastoral activities. And it was at this point, that the GNR priests made their carefully worded but unequivocal and definitive response to the bishops. Whereas the bishops argued that clergy could not fulfill priestly duties while serving partisan interests, the priests answered that there could be no contradiction between their Christian vocation to serve the poor and their service within the Nicaraguan government. This answer, cut as verse in Section 2, only exacerbated existing tensions.

In fact, from the Winter, 1981 on, Obando stepped up his contacts with opposition groups and his public protests against the Sandinistas. The bishops refused to participate in the second anniversary celebrations; and throughout the summer and fall of 1982, the hierarchy persisted in its stance against the priests.

Fearing a widening split within the Catholic Church, the base communities called for a meeting between the priests and the bishops. A provisional compromise was reached by which the priests agreed to abstain from all public exercise of their priestly functions while they continued in their government posts; to not attempt to legitimize state decisions by invoking their priesthood; and to maintain communication with the hierarchy, with an end to eventually relinquishing their posts and re-entering church work once the greater difficulties of state consolidation were resolved.

However, this understanding did not end the problem of the government priests, as Church pressure for their resignations continued, and as the Pope became continually embroiled in the dispute. As if to counter the provisional tolerance of the priests in government, the Hierarchy placed more and more restrictions and pressures on radical priests and religious Sandinistas; in response, demonstrations against the Church hierarchy broke out in Managua and in the Christian communities.

Initially, the Vatican refused to enter into the dispute and encouraged dialogue between the two sides. In the first months of 1982, the Vatican named the conservative Monsenor Bosco Vivas as assistant bishop of Managua. Monsenor Obando travelled to Venezuela, and then, invited by a "new right" church group, to the U.S., speaking out against Sandinista church policies. Subsequently the bishops published a harsh criticism of the Miskitu resettlement project, and the GNR appealed to the nuncio, publishing a statement which attacked the bishops' position and their persecution of Sandinista priests.

Reconsidering its previous stance in the light of Nicaraguan hierarchy pressures, the Vatican sent still another delegation to deal with the question of the government priests. The delegation transfered Bishop Barni to Leon; Bishop Santi was named for Matagalpa; and Monsenor Vilchez was named Prelate of Jinotega. But the government priests stayed on in their posts.

In sum, the two year period in question was one of continually intensifying tension between the Catholic hierarchy and the FSLN, and their respective supporters. While large numbers of Nicaraguan Catholics wanted an organic relation between a Church and government committed to the basic needs of the impoverished majority, others saw the Sandinists as hypocritically and demagogically coopting religious rites, symbols and discourse for their own political ends. Meanwhile some Sandinist supporters came to see the Church hierarchy as attempting to maintain a split between worldly and spiritual life which historically only served reactionary worldly ends; they accused Church leaders of fearing the FSLN as a threat to their traditional moral authority and their role as paternalistic welfare providers to poor people who remain poor.

The Sandinist/Church tension would only intensify further after the Declaration of a State of Emergency in March, 1982. Although the new Nicaraguan constitution guaranteed freedom of religious practice, the FSLN's principal orientation was evident in their slogan, "As long as there are Christian revolutionaries in Nicaragua, there will be Christians within the Sandinista Front." Furthermore, when the GNR proposed rotating Archbishop Obando y Bravo's weekly television program among seven priests, the archbishop and *La Prensa* accused the FSLN of attempting to harass the Church and undermine hierarchical authority. There can be no question that the controversy reflected deeper strains between the FSLN and the Archbishop, but they also reflected tensions within the Church itself, as the Archbishop continually refused to heed grassroots church organizations disputing his role and perspective. Splits at both levels would become even more severe in 1983, as the Pope's visit to the country made the struggle over Church in the Revolution a matter of worldwide knowledge and comment.

With all the problems, controversies and areas of growing conflict, questions remained as to the future character of the Church establishments and to what degree their exercise of moral authority and their work on behalf of the poor would complement or conflict with the Sandinists. What was clear by the time of the response by the government priests to the Bishops of Nicaragua has remained true as these pages go to press, that there are many Nicaraguans who see an identity between the Revolution and true Christianity, and there are many who do not; and the outcome of struggle between these two groups of people is central to the future of the Revolution.

5. *The Atlantic Coast and Misurasata*

Part and parcel of the Church conflict, as well as the overall intervention in Nicaragua, but worthy nevertheless of separate treatment is the question of the Revolution's problems with the Atlantic coast often referred to previously, but only the specific subject of one poetic text, by Sandinista official William Ramirez, in Section 2 of this part of our book.

For centuries the Miskitu Indians had made their home along the Coco River which flows between Honduras and Nicaragua, crossing back and forth freely between the two countries. After Somoza's defeat in 1979, the many ex-National Guards who had fled to camps in Honduras began their incursions into Nicaragua. Many Sandinista soldiers and Nicaraguan civilians, including several Miskitus had already died in attacks by the *contras* by early 1981; and the rate of killings rose when the U.S. launched its covert action plan. In February, 1982, the FSLN decided it had to relocate roughly 8,000 Miskitus from their border homes to protect them from the

Somocista bands, and to prevent those Miskitus sympathetic with them from further exacerbating the border problem. The relocation created an international furor, as the U.S. press distorted and manipulated the facts of the matter, viewing it as one of cultural and military aggression against a national minority. The issue of the Miskitus and the relocation move is a complex one which requires an understanding of the tactics of U.S. intervention, as well as of the complex historical dynamics involved, that is far more nuanced than the explanations propagated in the press.

Nicaraguan Atlantic and Pacific coasts differ from each other in culture, geography, ethnic composition, language and political history. A region of jungle and savannah, the Atlantic Coast comprises the eastern half of Nicaragua and holds only 12% of the national population. The Miskitu and Sumu Indians (24 and 2.5% respectively of the Coast population) live in the northern area, each group maintaining its own language and culture. The Black English-speaking Creole population (10%), which came as slaves, runaways and then as Jamaican migrant workers contracted by foreign companies, lives further south in and around the town of Bluefields. The Rama (.24%) and the Garifuna (.47%) are two other indigenous peoples in the region, while the remaining 63% consists of Spanish-speaking mestizos who migrated from the Pacific side mainly during the past 30 years.

Unlike the Pacific tribes, the Sumu and Miskitu defended themselves, their culture and the land against the Spanish, trading for weapons with pirates and the English and developing a militantly defensive group elan, which the British and then the North Americans were able to exploit by making the Miskitus the regional police force protecting their trading interests. During the early century, a boom of relatively high-paying jobs improved Coastal living conditions. Depleted natural resources and the Depression brought this situation to an end just as Sandino was launching his campaign in the mountains. Indeed the coastal peoples identified their job losses with Sandino's guerilla attacks and never identified with him as a national hero.

The Somozas generally ignored the Coastal peoples. No roads or communications systems connected the two coasts, but, inversely, doors were opened for the exploitation of natural resources (gold, forest, bananas and marine life). By the 1950s, over-exploitation had exhausted many of these resources; the area was subject to erosion and flooding, and foreign capital began to withdraw, leaving the coastal population to face unemployment and hunger. Many migrated from the area, while most continued to rely on bare subsistence farming, fishing and hunting.

While doing little for the area's economy, Somoza did impact the Coast's political life by recognizing and granting favors to the local leaders and joining with the most reactionary elements in the Moravian Church which dominated the area, in launching anti-communist, anti-Cuban crusades aimed at discrediting any progressive, dissident tendency which might emerge from the misery and squalor endemic to much of the area. Until the last years of the dynasty, when the National Guard carried out genocidal missions against Indian villages aiding the guerillas (see Cardenal's poem, "Waslala" in Part II, Section I), the Sandinista movement barely touched the region, except for the mining areas, where repression was severe. Those Coastal youth who fought for the FSLN were mainly Creole students from Managua, while most of the Miskitus remained uninvolved in the insurrection.

After July 1979, the GNR viewed the Coast as in a state of absolute decay and neglect. They saw the people there as the most exploited and alienated in Nicaragua. Natural resourses and productive machinery were a shambles; employment, nutrition, health facilities and care, literacy, housing, etc. were minimal; communications and transportations systems were non-existent, except for small barges or canoes travelling through a network of narrow rivers. Food supplies came by airlift or boat. The FSLN believed that confronting the economic problems of the region and overcoming its isolation would eliminate the material basis for the racist discrimination to which the Coast people had been subjected over the years. However, Coastal leaders felt threatened by a new authority which they saw as interfering with their power base, and they played upon the fears of Coastal dwellers that these new Spanish-speaking conquerors would impose their radical order upon them.

In the early months of the Reconstruction, the GNR pursued its policy for regional development, sending international solidarity teachers, social workers and doctors, among them many Cubans, to the area. The Black Creole and Indian populations were included in every dimension of the Reconstruction program, including the Literacy Crusade, which was carried out in Spanish, English, Miskitu and Sumu and reached the remotest areas. The Sandinists viewed their efforts to "awaken the sleeping giant of the Coast" and to integrate the area into national life with naive as well as perhaps complacent and condescending optimism, without recognizing how the peoples of the area might resent the benefits of Sandinista civilization as much as any other brand of Ladino power.

The first overt, rude awakening occurred during Christmas, 1980, when Blacks in Bluefields rioted against the presence of Cuban doctors and technicians and the imposition of new, Sandinista-appointed leaders who were not recognized by the local community. Clearly counterrevolutionary leaders, many with Somocista connections, had stirred up the people. The riot blew over, but the Sandinists were made aware of how difficult it would be to work out the underlying problems. Indeed, it did not take long for a deeper, more extensive and troubling situation to emerge with respect to the Indian population, their organization and their leaders.

Before the Victory, Atlantic Coast indigenous peoples formed an organization, ALPROMISU, to advocate their rights. Although coopted by Somoza, the organization was an important vehicle for expressing and negotiating Indian concerns. After the victory, a new organization was formed under the name of "Miskitu, Sumu, Rama and Sandinistas Together"--or Misurasata. Misurasata grew quickly and gained a representative on the new State Council. Steadman Fagoth Mueller, the organization's leader and representative, claimed to be the guardian of Indian interests against the Sandinists. By 1981, Misurasata, developing under Fagoth's tutelage, pressed for extensive demands, including exclusive rights to 38% of the national territory. The indigenous people's perceived rights to land came up against Sandinista plans for national economic development, and the tension between the two forces increased.

On February 18, 1981, Fagoth and other Misurasata leaders were arrested on the charge of planning armed actions to foment a separatist uprising by the end of the month. The other leaders were arrested in a short time, but Fagoth was held for another two and a half months when it was discovered he had been an informer for Somoza. During his imprisonment fear, ideological differences and confusion sent many young Miskitu across the border into Honduras. On his release in May, Fagoth joined them and led them into an active collaboration with counterrevolutionary Somocista forces.

During November 1981 and February 1982, the Reagan administration sped up its anti-Sandinista propaganda by making distorted claims about the Miskitu situation. Then, in February, former Moravian pastor Efran Wilson was arrested and revealed a plot called "Red Christmas" whose aim was to generate a Miskitu uprising to form a separate state on the Atlantic Coast. According to Wilson, many Miskitus went to Honduras for military training with former National Guardsmen who received aid from training camps in Florida and California and from the Honduran military. Wilson also alluded to the presence of Argentine and U.S. military advisors.

The disclosure of "Red Christmas" and the mounting toll of deaths from border attacks spurred the FSLN to build up military defenses along the easily crossable and attack-vulnerable Coco River. The FSLN decided they could only defend the border by creating a free-fire zone. This involved the relocation of the river village inhabitants who were already suffering from supply cutoffs stemming from Somocista incursions. This relocation became the source of heightened anti-Sandinist propaganda, but as Moravian bishop John Wilson put it, "The moving of the Miskitu communities to more secure areas, though it was painful, was necessary."

Many impartial international observers, including representatives for the U.S. American Indian Movement, were witnesses to the humane implementation of the FSLN military decision. The Sandinistas had planned the relocation areas as model settlements. Church World Service and the UN Food and Agricultural Organization were immediately engaged to participate in emergency relief aid and in planning agricultural development. Delegates from international human rights groups attested to the peaceful and cooperative conditions in the resettlement villages. Even key Moravian Church leaders agreed that this was a disturbing but necessary defensive step against Somocista attacks, and Church pastors continued working with the GNR to restore religious life in the settlement areas.

In the first four years of the Reconstruction, the GNR devoted considerable resources to improving conditions in the Atlantic region. Health care problems, for example, remain numerous, but free medical attention is now available and every town over 2,000, as well as every resettlement village, has at least one resident doctor. Campaigns were waged to prevent dengue, malaria and other common diseases. Work began on a new major hospital in Bluefields. Great progress was made on a highway linking the two coasts, and potable water and electricity began reaching areas which never had them before.

But these changes have been accompanied by serious problems which progressively fed into the U.S. interventionist campaign. Miskitus resented what they considered Sandinist efforts at cultural assimilation and their instances of cultural insensitivity. Many resented the August 1981 "Declaration of Principles with Regard to the Indigenous Communities of the Atlantic Coast," which proclaimed the unity of Nicaragua as one nation with one government that would work to preserve the cultures of the coastal peoples.

In the months which followed the relocation and the international clamor resulting from it, Misurasata developed schisms, with Miskitu Brooklyn Rivera becoming official head and developing a counterrevolutionary contingency operating out of Costa Rica, while Fagoth and those loyal to him continued to base his activities in Honduras, in close cooperation with ex-National Guards. A dialogue on the issues would develop, but many of the Miskitus would join the counterrevolutionaries; and by June, 1983, over five hundred were in government jails.

While great numbers of Nicaragua's indigenous people still remained in the fold, still only time would tell if the Sandinistas could adequately address their grievances and demands--or if in fact the U.S. and their allies would be able to manipulate Ladino-Indian tensions to the benefit of destabilization and counterrevolution. The challenge for the Sandinists would remain nation-building and border protecting while safeguarding the rights of the indigenous peoples. As in many other instances, the "national question," like the "peasant question," continued to plague socialist revolutionary development.

6. Advances in Health

The GNR made great promises to improve the quality of health care and education in the new Nicaragua; and as noted, Sections 3 and 4 of this Part focus respectively on these themes.

With regard to health care, an offical government study of the decade between 1966 and 1976 found that 83 per cent of Nicaraguan children suffered from malnutrition at some point in their lives. Only 17 per cent were of normal height and weight for their age. Prior to 1979, the official figure for life expectancy was 52. But this figure was computed by counting deaths from two years of age on instead of in the usual way, from day of birth. In fact, the latter method placed life expectancy at 32. The very incidence of infant deaths was the result of widespread malnutrition, disease and lack of hygiene. As in many other parts of Latin America, the conviction among many campesinos and indigenous peoples was that the death of infants was out of their control, in the hands of God and the forces of nature.

One of the secondary goals of the Literacy Crusade was to introduce people to the idea that their health conditions were not beyond human remedy. In addition all literacy workers and special health brigades compiled statistics on the diseases, sanitary conditions, health needs, etc. in preparation for a major 1981 health campaign.

By the time of the first health campaign, great changes had already occurred in Nicaraguan health care. First, severe shortages were occurring in medical supplies, key drugs and basic equipment, partially through payment problems, partially through informal U.S. blockade. Second, several of the established Nicaraguan doctors had left the country, or, delaying their departure awhile, occupied their time by fraudulently confiscating government-issued supplies for their use in private practice. Third, volunteer doctors from Mexico, Cuba and elsewhere were already doing important work in extending health care to the rural areas, but were meeting with resistance, especially from the Black and Indian groups, who viewed their presence as an interference in traditional customs.

The health campaigns of 1981 and 1982, along with the overall restructuring of the health services system, led to great improvements throughout the country, in spite of the multiple problems of scarcity of supplies and health providers. Young people joined doctors in the rural areas, to build clinics and sanitation centers, assist in vaccinations and train paramedics, as well as aids in carrying out basic measures of preventive medicine. There were specific campaigns against polio, dengue and a whole series of tropical illnesses.

In the meantime, the GNR worked with the Ministry of Health to improve medical and health conditions throughout the country. In fact, the Ministry's report of 1982 detailed innumerable successes in various aspects essential to a people's health. Since the revolutionary victory, 110 new health posts and 16 health centers had been constructed, with new hospitals on their way in Managua, Masaya, Rivas, Matagalpa and Bluefields. Comparing services with the dictatorship's best year (1977), the Ministry reported a rise of 451%, with an 82.3% increase in vaccinations.

The health campaigns against dengue and malaria had all but wiped out these diseases. And the campaign against polio, involving more than 1,461,000 shots, resulted in a virtual halt to this disease as well. In addition, the Ministry could point to the consolidation of 12 regional nursing aid centers, with more on the way. Twelve hundred health professionals, aides and technicians were sent out on obligatory rural health service. Several specialists graduated in the revamped medical school program, and the Ministry took steps to upgrade the qualifications of all practicing doctors.

Speaking on July 19, 1983, Daniel Ortega could point to "serious and grave deficiencies that still occur in the health sector in the supply of medicines and, above all, in the poor service given to the public." Clearly health services development had been affected severely by U.S. intervention. But Ortega could nevertheless point to "improvements throughout the nation, doubling the number of visits or public services," lower numbers of measles, and above all "successes that have reduced infant mortality." Considerably more work had to be done on health in Nicaragua; and only a revolutionary perspective such as that set forth in our poetry on health could lead to major transformations in this area. But the Somoza era had begun to fade in this as in other social dimensions, and the future lay in young and willing hands.

7. Advances in Education and the Hopes for Children

Especially after the 1980 Literacy Crusade, improvements in education paralleled and in some respects exceeded those in health. Of slightly more than 400,000 children of primary school age, 272,000 were registered for school in 1976. Half of those registered dropped out by the end of the first year. For every 20 students who entered primary school in the countryside, only one completed all six grades. In urban areas, 50 per cent graduated from primary school.

Of the total secondary age population, classrooms were available for only 18 per cent, and half of these were in private schools. In more advanced educational situations, including the universities, there were 17,789 students, with the amount for education provided by the state equivalent to $1,178 per year. These figures of course tell us nothing about the large numbers of people who were illiterate or only semi-literate, nor do they say anything about the content and quality of education under Somoza.

Suffice it say that education in Nicaragua was a privilege for the few. The quality for that few varied from place to place, institution to institution, with genuinely rigorous education mainly the province of well-funded private entities. Most textbooks of a general nature were translations of U.S. texts. Local and national history were of course completely shaped by the exigencies of *somocismo*.

Even as most social and pedagogical energies went into preparing for and then implementing the massive Literacy Crusade, the Ministry of Education and the National Higher Education Council worked with administrators, teachers and grassroots representatives to begin transforming the educational system throughout the country. Much of the first year of the Revolution was spent in comparing different national models seeking the right combination for Nicaragua's circumstances. Teachers and administrators at all levels worked on curriculum reform and structural changes.

In addition, the Ministry made plans for followup literacy work in Miskitu, Sumo and Creole English, for the Atlantic Coast, and for a post-literacy adult education program, both of which were to begin in the fall of 1980. In the midst of the growing problems in the Atlantic Coastal area, the Literacy Crusade brought minimal education to over 1,200,000 people and reduced native language illiteracy to the new national average of 12%.

By July, 1982, more than 18,000 coordinators and 3,000 promoters, including many former literacy workers, were involved in over 18,000 Education collectives attended by more than 163,000 students, many of them recently alphabetized, in different levels of basic popular education. Meanwhile, educational services involving the creation of over 20,000 additional jobs were extended to all school levels and all age groups. In addition to the child development centers developed by AMNLAE and other grassroots organizations, the number of children involved in formal, Ministry-administered pre-schools rose from a pre-Insurrection high of 9,000 to 41,215. And a variety of new pre-school centers were developed throughout the country.

The number of elementary school students rose to over 530,000, or 82%, as compared to the pre-revolutionary high of 65.5%. The number of elementary schools doubled, and over 2,700 new regular teaching positions were created. The Nicaraguan equivalent to junior high school education rose by 50%. Various normal and agrarian technical schools were founded throughout the country, innumerable new resources and services (scholarships, libraries, work-study programs, etc.) were developed in old and new education centers.

In sum, the number of students involved in various forms of high school education rose enormously. Grassroots organizations were involved in every aspect of national education, and had their greatest impact in giving impulse to the Program Promoting the Development of Communal Education (PRODECO), establishing specialized vocational schools in various provincial areas, the Educational Regionalization Plan and the 1981 Consultation over the Ends and Objectives of Education, which set the framework for future improvement of the total educational system.

As for higher education, the number of students in 1982 was double the number in 1976, while the amount invested in each student rose by 199.2% to $5,280.80. The main sector represented in the rise were working class students who previously would not have had access to higher education. In addition, largescale curriculum changes transformed the nature and quality of education for all students, including many who would take their new orientation into teaching positions at all levels. And great strides were made in providing popular access to higher education through the opening of community college-style technical programs in health, agriculture and industry, as well as through a 28-million cordoba scholarship program providing 1,600 scholarships for priority careers in health, agriculture and education.

The number of professors employed in higher education rose by 159% above the pre-Insurrection level, or over 300% in terms of those employed on a fulltime basis, while the number of teaching hours tripled in the same period. Large sums were spent on higher education construction, including residences for scholarship students in Managua and Leon. But to relieve some of the strain on the national economy, as well as to project a richer national future, the National Council of Higher Education arranged for 1,000 scholarships to deserving students to study fields necessary for revolutionary progress in universities throughout the world.

By March, 1983, public school enrollment was up by an additional 129,199 students above the 1982 totals, and it was estimated that one million Nicaraguans were studying at one level or another. Adult education was up by 10,000 with a total enrollment of 183,000; primary school enrollment rose from 369,000 to 579,000; and pre-school enrollment had now risen from 41 to 63,000, or 7 times the number registered before the revolution.

In his fourth anniversary speech, Daniel Ortega summarized some of the advances in education from a later point in time: "We have created 2,639 educational centers, 1252 new school buildings... and 16,975 Popular Adult Education Collectives. ... Compared with 500,000 students ... in 1978, we presently have 1,500,318 students." Ortega also pointed to problems in the education system. But the achievements stood out as remarkable.

Indeed, all the extraordinary advances in education cited here, advances occurring in the midst of the most difficult conditions, are a tribute to the Nicaraguan people, as well as to the GNR and the FSLN, for keeping promises made on taking power. And we should note that these advances must be joined by ones made by the Ministry of Culture in establishing poetry workshops, libraries and cultural centers which are not included in national education statistics.

The poetry on education which predominates in the final section of this part of our book testifies to the human side of what is described statistically in this introduction. The workshop poems are themselves products of the total national effort in education. One poem addresses the question of adult education, but the majority focuses on the question of the education and future of children as crucial to the nation. In the phrase of Orlando Pastora, director of one the many local popular cultural centers with special writing programs for young children (cited by Imuris, in "Nicaragua's Cultural Renewal," *Nicaraguan Perspectives*, 5 [Winter, 1983], p. 15), "The old values collapse and transmute into new values which find nests in the souls of children ... "

Companeros. Managua, August 1983. Photo by Loretta Smith.

CHRONOLOGY: AUGUST, 1980 - JANUARY, 1981

August: Brigades return from the countryside as the first stage of the Literacy Crusade concludes, and the literacy workers are greeted as heroes in the July 19th Plaza. Several young people have been assassinated by counterrevolutionaries. But the illiteracy rate has fallen from over 50% in 1979 to roughly 12% after the Crusade. Commander Humberto Ortega announces the formation of a Militia Brigade whose mission will be to fight against counterrevolutionaries in the mountains. Eden Pastora is named to head the Brigade.

September: A squad assassinates Anastacio Somoza in Asuncion, Paraguay. A day of national celebration is declared. Meanwhile, there are stirrings in Nicaragua, as propaganda mounts against Cuban medical workers and technicians mounts. On September 28, a large protest against supposed "Cuban penetration" takes place in Bluefields, on the Atlantic Coast. Several demonstrators are arrested as "separatists." Doctor Cordova Rivas underlines the participation of counterrevolutionary elements from the F.A.D. (the Armed Democratic Forces) in the disturbance. Government officials admit having made several tactical errors in developing the GNR's relation with the Black and Indian coastal populations, but point to a better future. However, the Revolution is being sorely tested on this front. Simultaneously, throughout September, the Church hierarchy intensifies its criticisms of the Revolution, and *La Prensa* attempts to mobilize a virtual religious war against the FSLN, as the ideological struggle deepens.

October: Meeting in a national conference, 500 religious leaders representing the majority of evangelicals in the country declare their support for the Revolution. The FSLN states its own position with respect to Religion, recognizing the participation of Christians in the Revolution and in the Reconstruction organizations. Religion and Christianity are not opiates of the people, but have shown to play an important role in the struggle for people's liberation. The communique declares the FSLN's respect for freedom of worship and belief, and promises that the FSLN will honor the people's religious traditions, and impede the use of religion against the people's interests.

November: The Conference of Bishops responds bitterly to the FSLN communique on religion, accusing the FSLN of attempting to use and distort Christian concepts to legitimize revolutionary goals and Sandinista hegemony. The Bishops criticize the continued presence of priests in key government and cabinet positions, and say they must resign. Those priests involved, Ernesto and Fernando Cardenal, Miguel D'Escoto and Edgar Parrales, send a response to the Bishops, declaring the religious validity of the revolutionary process and refusing to resign their posts. Relations between the bishops and those supporting the Revolution continue to deteriorate. Salazar, head of COSEP, the private sector organization which serves as the major body of business resistance to the Revolution, is killed by Sandinistas while resisting arrest in El Crucero. The FSLN claims he was involved with business leaders and former Somoza Guards in a counterrevolutionary conspiracy against the GNR. CONAPRO, one of the key organizations of COSEP, resigns from the State Council. Meanwhile, the Union Coordinating Committee, unifying peasant and worker organizations, officially begins to operate.

December. The GNR announces that by year's end, 31 rural popular stores will have opened. The stores provide services and goods at protected prices to those with limited means. Students throughout the country participate in a pre-Christmas work-study program, carrying out a variety of community projects. Shaken by news that three North American nuns and a lay worker have been assassinated in El Salvador, members of the GNR join the people in giving additional dimension to the nationwide pre-Christmas *Purisima* celebration. COSEP members abandon the State Council in protest when their bid to discuss the Salazar case is voted down.

January. Standard Fruit threatens to withdraw from Nicaragua because of the GNR's policies, and state representatives travel to California to negotiate a new accord. The Patriotic Revolutionary Front organizes a "Day of National Unity" to honor Pedro Joaquin Chamorro's memory by activating political pluralism and rallying the people against foreign intervention. The threat of such intervention grows as the now united left forces in El Salvador call for a General Offensive. As Nicaraguans closely follow the struggle next door, the U.S. acuses the GNR of sending arms to the Salvadoran guerrillas, and suspends $15 million of the $75 million promised to Nicaragua. In the face of this, the FSLN reconfirms its solidarity with the Salvadoran struggle, and denounces U.S. agressive plans and manueovers. Rightists respond by attacking the Nicaraguan Embassy in San Salvador. Internally, the GNR passes a law against peculation and waste, involving fines and prison terms for the guilty. Also, a National Consultation is held to establish the objectives and characteristics of education in the new Nicaragua. All sectors of the country meet and debate the issues heatedly. The Episcopal Conference insists that Christianity should be at the core, and not merely another aspect, of any new educational scheme.

Section 1. The Army, The Police, The Military, Love & Revolution

1. Porfirio Salgado, Blindado
   Battalion Poetry Workshop/ A
   QUESTION OF APPEARANCES

We go to our military training
with our camping kits
and study materials,
all happy and joking.
And when we go down
the city streets
we see people
looking at us surprised
since now we're
the ones wearing the helmets
and military uniforms.
We look like National Guardsmen,
but no, because the uniform
and the helmet
protect the Sandinist soldier
in military training
to defend the Revolution
for the same people
who watch us go down
Managua's streets.

2. Fernando Silva (Son)/ MILITIA
   SOLDIERS WALKING DOWN
   THE STREET

Some militia soldiers come by
with their olive-green uniforms
hello one says to me
 sweaty/ tired/ contented
they seem to me like birds that
 come down
to the patio of my house in the
 afternooons
their boots are too big
and their pants are wrinkled in the
 back
the Militia soldiers

are not elegant in any way
the old man who sells greens
 in his little wagon
approaches me smiling
 there you are he tells me
 these are the men
And this is certain
it's certain these Militia soldiers
are the people
preparing to defend the Revolution.

3. Gerardo Gadea, Ernesto Castillo
   Poetry Workshop (Managua)/ AT
   MILITARY SCHOOL

I was on duty
The companeros went marching by
in long rows going to class.
A mockingbird landed on a branch
to share some shade with me.
He warbled, raised his black feathers,
shook himself out,
without stopping his warble.
This month the malinches are in
 bloom
and the air smells of its flower.
Like birds when winter comes,
that's how happy we are at Military
 School;
the companeros play guitar,
sing revolutionary songs,
we shout slogans to Sandino
 to German Pomares
 to Fonseca
 to the Revolution.
Those who arrived three months ago
to study at the Carlos Aguero School
along with the militia members
and are now officer-instructors
of the Popular Sandinist Army
militarily and in columns

leave for their areas
to defend the Revolution
but other students keep on coming
with guitars, slogans, songs and
    poems
to the Carlos Aguero
(like birds when winter comes).

4. Carlos Manuel Galan, Ajax
    Delgado Police Complex Poetry
    Workshop/ CARMEN

For every question of yours
a kiss of mine
and your voice returns
to break the silence.
I caress your cheeks
and on saying
        "When you come back"
I always take your hands
I give you a strong embrace
You know I'm a Sandinist
    Policeman
and that I've given myself
to the Revolution.
I don't want to say things
that will sadden you.
The farewell is
  between kisses/ sad
and I leave, Carmen,
with the hope of returning.

5. Gerardo Torrente, September
    14th Neighborhood Poetry
    Workshop (Managua)/ THE
    MISSION

Five in the morning.
The new infantry recruits
ready to complete another mission
after three months of training.
No one knew where we were going
 --only the top leaders--.
We left the military school in trucks

chanting slogans
and we heard the happy song of the
    larks
leaping from one laurel tree to
    another.
In the Sandinista Air Force
the motors on.
The fighters
rising in squadrons.
One plane,
        another plane,
until they are lost
from view in the clouds.
In the midst of two mountains
we land on a dirt runway.
The people, joyful,
came up to us
asking where we came from.

6. Camilo Monge, Garcia Laviana
    Battalion Poetry Workshop
    (Managua)/ DISCIPLINE

I'm in the Garcia Laviana Battalion
and this morning
as on almost every day
we did our drills.
Later we ate breakfast
and we went to remove forgotten
    books
    from an old room.
They were medical books
along with military books
(I think they taught them
how to kill in English)
and the tasks came one after
    another
removing boards, lifting mattresses,
bringing brooms, sweeping,
collecting old garbage
along with the leaves
that fell last night.

7. Mario Bolanos, Sandinist Police
Poetry Workshop (Leon)/
COMPANERA MILITIA
WOMAN

Today when you find yourself so far
away from Somotillo/ forming part
of the Veronica Lacayo Battalion
I wanted to put an arrow-pierced
heart
in the letter I sent you.
But I thought it better
to write you a note on a wall
--like the ones written
before the Insurrection--
with poorly formed letters
that said:
FREE HOMELAND OR DEATH.

8. Manuel Urtecho, FUNDECI
Workers Poetry Workshop/ HERE
ON THE BORDER

The Negro River
where we bathed together
in the dawn hours,
the birds/ the blackberry brambles
the mountains full of strange noises
the ground wet because of the rain
and I standing post
thinking of you, Malvina.

9. Hugo Torres/ PERSONA

I'm thinking about you
now that it's my day on the watch.
And I have entire units
under my command,
battalions, regions,
artillery, infantry,
thousands of men,
light, medium, heavy weapons,
a whole army
(again I look at the telephone).
If only you'd call me.

10. Modesto Silva, Palacaguina
Poetry Workshop/ MIRIAM

My joy was so great
when I got your letter
that when I read it for the first time
I didn't realize
that you'd written in it
that you didn't love me.

11. John Taylor, Bluefields Poetry
Workshop/ MILITIA WOMAN

I dreamed of you,
in my hands,
a rose, a lily
and a captive bird.
I walked in pastures
with rabbits, owls,
swallows and gulls.
I looked into you,
your olive green, the jacket
you wore when we met.
I released the bird
and went to find you.
The lily and rose
I placed in your hand
were as if to say
    I love you, militia woman.

12. Anonymous/ ALBA LUZ
ACUNA

I saw you at 12 noon
your hair black/ your eyes brown
and your lips painted red,
dressed in black boots,
khaki shirt, green pants
you felt proud to have your uniform.
You'd just arrived and you told me
to make you an acrostic
and I did one about you.
You took the telephone
in the information office

with your low voice
that's impossible to forget,
but our talk was cut off
because I had to go on a mission
but always thinking of you.

13. Aura Sofia Sanchez,
    Palacaguina Poetry Workshop/ I
    REMEMBER

I remember when you explained to
    me
the work we would do during the
    day.
I listened to you
you watched me when I sat down to
    write.
In the end we fell in love
and you told me you had a girlfriend
you couldn't abandon
who went with you into the
    mountains
and who you loved very much.
You wouldn't tell me her name
until our companeros
told me it was H-K-21.

14. Nidia Taylor Ellis, Garcia
    Laviana Battalion Poetry
    Workshop (Managua)/ TO
    COMBATANT JUAN
    BUSTAMANTE ON THE
    SOUTHERN FRONT

It was six in the evening on
    February 17th,
when I fell in love with you, Juan.
With your camouflage uniform
and your GALIL on top of the desk
fulfilling your 24-hour watch turn
I drew near you
and touched your chocolate-colored
    skin.

15. Erwin Antonio Alvarado,
    Camilo Ortega Saavedra Poetry
    Workshop (Diriamba)/ YOUR
    DEPARTURE

Alone with your B-Z rifle
with your gaze fixed on the green
    shrubs
in your marksman's trench
alert, standing watch over the firing
    range
under the sun/ in the Amayito
    Military Base
  this morning/ I went up to you
and you told me your name was
    Yelba Fatima.
Having you close by, I contemplated
    your face
your cats' eyes, your short hair,
your white skin bronzed by the
    strong sun
your lips dry.
Sunday came. You left for Jinotega.
It was sad to know you were leaving
(I had fallen in love with you).
The time I knew you was so short
and I didn't know when I would see
    you again.

16. Pedro Pablo Benavides, Esteli
    Poetry Workshop (EPS Member)/
    TO THE MILITIA WOMAN
    WHOSE NAME I NEVER KNEW

That day I saw you drilling and
    marching
here on the military base,
every one admired you
    (you're the only woman
    among all the militia soldiers).
I admired your routines
the elegance of your marching
and I also admired your body
your short hair, your lively eyes.
That evening while we ate dinner

I kept looking at you,
and when you were in formation
I sought your gaze to tell you with
    my eyes
that I liked you.
The next day in the evening
after you came back from the
    parade in Esteli,
you went to my company's bunk,
I greeted you and you smiled
(I didn't know what to say).
Afterwards you went home.
Today when the Popular Militias
    came down
off the truck back from a mission,
I looked for you, but you weren't
    there.
The Militias went off
and I kept thinking of you
just wanting to see you again.

17. Luis Santiago del Palacio
    Gomez, E.P.S. Infantry Battalion
    Medical Services/ ON LEAVE

Here you have me,
my love,
with my body
bit by fleas all over,
robbing two days
from the Homeland
to be with you
and renew myself
with tenderness.

18. Salgado/ IT'S NOT THE
    REVOLUTION THAT'S
    SEPARATING US

Love,
how many times have I told you

how much I love you
and you don't believe me,
I don't know why you think I'm
    lying to you.
You don't know how much it hurts
    me
when you say things
that are counterrevolutionary.
Revolution is such a great word to
    me.
I wish you thought like me.
I haven't abandoned you.
You know that my time is for the
    Revolution
and I don't want to leave it
even though I see that I'm
slowly losing you.
All this time
since we met in that church
you're putting it aside
without caring how much you hurt
    me.
Many times I've doubted your love.
It's that I wouldn't want to hear you
    say,
only to make you mine,
"It doesn't matter how much time
you give to the Revolution, my
    love,"
and then never repeat those words
    again.
It's hard to believe
that everything could end this way.
That's why I tell you
"The Revolution isn't what's
    separating us
but rather it's you
for wanting to have me always
and I'm a revolutionary soldier
who will continue loving you
wherever I may be."

19. Bernardo Fuentes Telica,
    Ernesto Castillo Poetry
    Workshop, (Managua)/ THE
    "COMPAS"

I see them every day
passing by on the sidewalk
in front of my house
headed toward the Luis Uriza Post.
(In their faces I see love for
    Nicaragua).
One has his arm around the other's
    shoulder
and they enjoy themselves as they
    walk
with their Fal and Galil
"Because today weapons are
to defend the sovereignty of the
    people."
I see them in the jeeps
watching over the city even at
    dawn, chatting and laughing and
    alert.
Their young faces:
students' faces,
simple faces, peasants'
or workers' dark skin.
Nicaragua looks so pretty full of
    soldiers,
militia soldiers and friendly police.
(It is the people themselves, armed,
aiming at the enemy.)
And one can walk calmly.
And we know that the compas are
    young
but worthy of our respect.

20. Monge/ DISCIPLINE

Every day the companeros
have been going out on missions.
I don't know what there'll be for
    tomorrow,
that's why I think of the future
because in the past

this has cost many lives.

21. Juan Antonio Lira, Condega
    Poetry Workshop/ CDS NIGHT
    WATCH

The first call of the watch
in the Cantagallo section of
    Condega,
it was my turn to do it one June
    night
with you, Daniel.
And in low voices (very low)
we were watchful,
remembering the life of a fighter,
days lived in bad weather with
    empty stomachs,
ragged, bearded, sick
bitten by the mosquitos.
And in the camps: the sidesaddles,
    and the chest blows,
    and the lizards,
    and the mountain jumps,
    and the target practice,
    and the dragging,
    and the target positions,
    and the crawling ones,
    and the attack simulations...
And the orders:
    take arms,
    present arms
    at ease.
And once in a while when we
    ambushed the Guard
and took towns in the North,
and the "we have to leave today at
    midnight,
be careful, compa."
This was in Cantagallo
(the mountains of Condega where
the Carlos Fonseca Amador
Northern Front would be).
Now, my brother, the watch will be:
Aiming and firing at
    counterrevolution.

22. Jorge Vega (EPS Member), El Bluff Poetry Workshop/ IN THE
   DEFENSE

And there are Revolutions
like Chile's with Salvador Allende
who didn't arm his people
during the triumphant days
of the Popular Unity
and the workers and laborers
cut off, marginalized

when they fell once again
into the exploiters' hands.
That's why in Nicaragua
we have battalions of kids
of students/ of peasants/ of workers
the people ready to defend
themselves.

CHRONOLOGY: FEBRUARY - JULY, 1981

February: Faced with a paid manpower shortage, the GNR calls upon students throughout the country to join volunteer brigades that work to bring in the nation's cotton crop. CONAPRO "Heroes and Martyrs" forms, made up of professionals who support the Revolution; and the Ezequiel Brigade, a military group, is established to fight increasingly active counterrevolutionary bands operating in Nicaragua's Northern zone. European newspapers report that Jose Esteban Gonzalez, Vice President of Nicaragua's Christian Socialist Party and Coordinator of the Human Rights Commission, has complained of Human Rights violations by the GNR and the FSLN. On his arrival at the Managua airport, Gonzalez is detained and taken before the court charged with violating the Law of Order and Public Security. However, he declares that the European press misreported his comments and is released. The U.S. State Department issues its "White Paper," which claims that Nicaragua is the center for arms shipments to Salvadoran rebels. The U.S. begins to cutting off all economic loans and credits for Nicaragua. The GNR calls for joint Honduran-Nicaraguan border patrols to curb any suspected arms flow.

March: The GRN Junta is reduced from 5 to 3 members, as Arturo Cruz becomes Ambassador to the U.S. and Moises Hasan becomes Minister of National Construction. Daniel Ortega is named Junta coordinator. The World Peace Council announces that Nicaragua will receive the "Ho Chi Min Prize" for its revolutionary triumph and its efforts to achieve world peace. Alfonso Robelo's MDN announces plans for an anti-FSLN demonstration in Nandaime. The FSLN denies permission for the event, and comes under attack from several anti-Sandinista radio stations. The Managua chapter of the Christian Socialist Party and three of the radio stations are assaulted by crowds which *La Prensa* claims were incited by the Sandinistas. The Sandinistas put a stop to the riots and prevent an attack on

218

still another station. They then recommend that *La Prensa* suspend publication for 48 hours. The MDN demonstration is marked by rioting. Christian groups supporting the Sandinista revolution commemorate the anniversary of Monsenor Romero's assassination in El Salvador by making public a document entitled "Christian Fidelity to the Process in Nicaragua." Meanwhile, *Parade Magazine* discloses that ex-Somoza guardsmen are being trained in the U.S. for paramilitary attacks on Nicaragua.

April: The U.S. suspends a loan to Nicaragua for the purchase of wheat. Popular organizations mobilize to express their indignation, coining the motto, "Bread with Dignity." Other countries respond by sending wheat in great quantities. Meanwhile, the CIA's plans for training mercenaries to carry out counterrevolutionary sabotage acts lead to public outcry and the mobilization of the Sandinista Popular Army and the militias. The GNR sends a letter protesting the aid cuts and threatened aggression. The letter stresses the hope for "respectful and stable relations with all countries in the world, including the U.S. We reaffirm our wish that the Central American area become a zone of peace and security." Just a few days later, bloody anti-Sandinista riots break out among the Indian populations of the Atlantic Coast. Steadman Fagoth and other Miskitu leaders are accused of inciting the riots to promote a plan for Indian separatism. A former secret service collaborator for Somoza, Fagoth admits to heading the Separatist movement of opposition to the FSLN. The GNR urges Honduras to stop paramilitary attacks on Nicaragua. Honduran President Policarpo Paz agrees to meet with Daniel Ortega.

May: The GRN restructures the State Council, providing seats to four additional organizations, the Liberal Constitutionalist Party, CONAPRO, the *Eje Ecumenico*, and the National Union of Farmers and Herders. The nation celebrates a Corn Fair to promote homegrown corn consumption in view of the wheat crisis. Meanwhile, Misurasata Director Steadman Fagoth is granted conditional freedom and returned to the Atlantic Coast, to calm his Miskitu supporters. On arrival, he escapes to Honduras with large numbers of Miskitus, and joins the Somocista counterrevolutionaries. Speaking over a clandestine radio program, Fagoth calls upon the Miskitu population to rise up against the FSLN. General Policarpo Paz and Daniel Ortega meet in Guasaule, Nicaragua to discuss border tensions. Paz promises to restrain paramilitary supporters in the Honduran army. Sergio Ramirez, a member of Nicaragua's governing junta, meets with Costa Rican President Carazo Odio in San Jose, where the two agree to strengthen peaceful relations between their countries.

June: The Nicaraguan Bishops issue an ultimatum to four priests who lend their services to the GNR. The ultimatum declares that if the priests do not leave their state offices as soon as possible, they will be declared in rebellion against the Church and sanctioned accordingly. Christian sectors supporting the GNR protest, demanding that the Bishops withdraw their ultimatum. The GNR makes preparations to send a delegation to the Vatican to discuss the matter. The National Assembly of Rural and Urban Base Ecclesiastic Communities writes a letter to the Bishops supporting the presence of priests in the GNR. A Forum on the National Problematic, involving representatives and parties opposed to and supportive of the FSLN begins. Various encounters between Sandinistas and counterrevolutionaries are reported by the Ministry of the Interior. One incident involves a group of prisoners who assault prison custodians, take their arms and hold them hostage, killing several in the process. Responding to widespread rejection of White Paper charges against Nicaragua, the U.S. State Department makes a new charge, that Nicaragua has received Soviet tanks. Press criticism of White Paper allegations comes to a halt. Even as Nicaragua and Costa Rica sign a joint declaration establishing bases of peace and respect between the two countries, Colombia threatens Nicaragua for making claims to Colombian-held islands off the Nicaraguan Atlantic Coast. Various evangelical organizations promote a day dedicated to peace, to counter the threats of invasion made against Nicaragua.

July: Frank Bendana, President of UCAFENIC (the private association of coffee growers), is deported for counterrevolutionary activities. Comandantes Eden Pastora and Jose Valdivia leave Nicaragua asserting that they will dedicate themselves to the liberation struggles of other Latin American countries. The Defense Ministry annouces that the two comandantes will no longer be serving in the Sandinista Popular Army. The dialogue between the Bishops and the four priests in the GNR, requested by the Vatican, concludes, with it understood that as long as the priests continue in the government, they are not to carry out public or private priestly functions inside or outside of Nicargua. The GNR and the Episcopal Conference agree to create a mechanism for constant communication. On the second anniversary of the July 19th Victory, the GRN proclaims new laws, and announces the confiscation of La Prego, La Perfecta, Ancasa, Camino de Oriente, Plaza Esperanza and other private sector factories accused of decapitalization. A profundization of the Agrarian Reform is also announced, involving the development of the National Food Program (PAN) and a further redistribution of land based on the Agrarian Reform Law. As the month comes to an end, the GNR proclaims a state of emergency with respect to a growing epidemic of dengue.

220

Section 2. First Problems, Advances and Faith in the Future

1. Rosario Murillo/ TO THIS OTHER SON

Bone to bone
drop by drop
stone over stone goes this temple
sweat on sweat they raise this altar
where the newest prayers rise up
and each day they try to realize the
    sacred:
the right of the people...

2. Walter Lopez, State Security Poetry Workshop/ IN LEON

On getting up
I see the sky and become nostalgic.
I can hear the song of birds,
the racket of cars
along these sreets of Leon,
the cry of vendors,
the news on the radio,
the excitement of a new day.
The progress of our Revolution.

3. Lopez/ CHINANDEGA

I go out into the streets of
    Chinandega,
I see long-haired foreigners,
they're walking around in short
    pants,
with moccasins on, open shirts,
dark glasses and big backpacks,
I see an old man on a street corner
of the Central Market
with an earthen pot filled with
    scraps,
an inflamed foot covered by a dirty
    rag;
and with his crutch he scares off the

dogs
which sniff at his foot covered with
    flies
    ...and we're in Revolution!
I see kids on another corner,
    shoeshine boys,
shoeshine boys, with rings of soil
around their necks, shirts
    unbuttoned,
their bodies stained, scabby
    ...and we're in Revolution!
In the market a pregnant woman
is carrying a quintal of beans.
The Callejas girls are passing by
    there
talking about fashions
that haven't yet come to Nicaragua,
the Navarros discussing what color
    hair
they'll ask for at the beauty salon,
the Montealegres planning their
    Miami trip
and the car they'll buy this
    Christmas
    ...and we're in Revolution!
We're in Revolution,
workers and peasants united,
in order to change these things.
These things from the past.

4. William Ramirez/ SING, SIMON, SING

We always thought, and sometimes
    felt,
that the coast
was so-o-o very far away from us.
And still it's hard to get to the coast,
to discover it, love it, feel it.
Now that the dawn's no longer a
    temptation,
let's undertake tasks of unity
with our brothers

trying to correct our mistakes,
learning their customs, languages,
  culture
because they speak Miskitu, Rama,
Spanish and English
they dance their own dances,
including the May Pole...
And what's learned by the rest of
  Nicaragua
soon the rest of the world will learn,
that our problem is not
between races and colors
but our problem is between rich and
  poor,
between those who want
to keep on exploiting the poor
and those of us who don't want
to let them exploit us
because the Black peasant of the sea
was exploited not for being Black
but for being poor and a fisherman,
and the Miskitu was exploited
not for being a peasant
but for being a poor peasant;
and then we'll realize
that in spite of the hardships
our country's poverty creates,
we'll make advances,
though little by little,
because the problem of the Coast
is a serious problem,
a challenge for the Revolution
But we will solve it all together
because we already took the first
  step.

5. Fathers Miguel D'Escoto,
   Ernesto Cardenal, Edgar
   Parrales, Fernando Cardenal/
   RESPONSE TO THE BISHOPS
   OF NICARAGUA*

As first response to the
  communication
of the Episcopal conference of
Nicaragua
we wish to say to the Bishops of
  Nicaragua,
to our brother priests and faithful
  Catholics,
to our brothers in the faith of
  Christ,
to our compatriots,
to all people of good will:
That we believe in God the Father,
Creator of the world and of humans,
we believe in Jesus Christ, Son of God,
    our brother and savior,
we believe in the Church,
visible body of Christ to which we
  belong,
we believe in justice,
basis of human living together,
we believe in love,
first and principal mandate of Jesus,
we believe in our priesthood,
which is our vocation
    to serve our brothers,
we believe in our homeland, the
  great family
to which we belong and are indebted
we believe in the popular
  Revolution,
made for the people, to overthrow
  tyranny
  and implant justice and love
we believe in the poor, who will be
  those
  who will construct a more just
  homeland
and will help us to save ourselves.
This is our faith and our hope,
and in accord with our beliefs we
  have wished
to serve our compatriots
in the positions that they have
  designated
and we will keep doing so in
  whatever place
where our presence and service are
  needed,

222

because they have given us our
  duties
--the power to serve,
not the power to dominate,
  --the power to give up our
  comforts,
    not the power to enrich ourselves,
--the power to liken ourselves to
    Christ
  in the service of our brothers,
  --the power to fullfil our priesthood,
  not to separate ourselves from our
  vocation,
  --the power to be ready to
  hear and obey the voice of God.
To maintain ourselves firm in our
  faith, hope and love,
as in our intentions to serve,
we count with the good will, the
  understanding,
the advice, the prayer of brother
Bishops, priests and lay people.
Finally, we declare
our unbreakable commitment to
the Popular Sandinist Revolution,
in fidelity with our people,
which is the same as saying:
in fidelity with the will of God.

6. Fernando Rodriguez/
    POLITICAL WORK IN CIUDAD
    DARIO

Without holding back a tear
a gaze fixed, thoughtful, sad
on Ernesto Velazquez, on Cecilia
  Matamoros
thinking of our fallen Sandinist
  brothers,
not without a strong, unexpected
  embrace
a squeeze of the hands
some pats on the back/ the
  conversations
      in the Pre-Party Study Circles

in the July 19th Sandinist Youth
in the CDS's
are about our people.
And we spend our days off in
  Maunica
    Ispangual/   Wiscanal
with Espiridion, Micayla, Ambrosio,
Lencho and others
who always wait for us
because now our talks
are more interesting.
We speak about the orientations,
the political lines,
and the tasks within our reality.
Now the differences begin to
  disappear
we students live with the peasants.
When we arrive in the valleys,
hamlets, provinces,
they're always waiting for us.

7. Segundino Ramos, Sandinist Air
    Force Poetry Workshop/ EMILIA
    RAMOS

You worked in the coffee harvest
in the Santa Isabel Hacienda
that belonged to the landlord Jose
  Arevalo
  and today belongs to the people.
You planted corn, picked beans,
  weeded rice.
You didn't understand clearly
  how you were exploited,
but it made me happy when you
  said
"Everything will be different
when the Revolution triumphs"
Because Manuel Lezama,
a Sandinist, made you see it.
Afterwards you felt proud
because I participated in the
  struggle.
Today you work as a volunteer
in the construction of a school

In this way you contribute
as Arlen Siu did
as the beautiful literacy workers did
making reality of Carlos Fonseca's
   dream,
like the women who give their best
   days
to fire rifles in El Salvador,
   Uruguay,
Chile and Paraguay,
like the women of Cua and Blanca
   Arauz
who fought at Sandino's side.
That's how you are, mom.

8. Ernesto Cardenal/ MYSTIC
   VISION ABOUT THE LETTERS
   "FSLN"

On top of Motastepe Hill,
   on the outskirts of Managua
a large advertisement in white
   letters
                     ROLTER
could be seen from many Managua
   streets
and the little boy Juan
while riding in an automobile
asked me what did those big letters
   mean
                     ROLTER
And I told him a brand of shoes
and it was so people would buy
   those shoes.
"But when the Revolution triumphs
there won't be ads, right?" the boy
   asked me.

It was a few days before the
   October Offensive
which he didn't know about
                     anxious days for me.
That afternoon he played Sandinists
   and Guardsmen with other children
but the problem was, they said,
   nobody wanted to be a Guardsman.
Many times after the triumph the
   large letters
made me remember Juan's words,
   even though
         /they didn't come true
For a year now from many
   Managua streets
instead of those letters on the hill
   we see others:·   FSLN
And I many times also recall
   the child's words with joy.
It was a Sunday at noon with an
   overcast sky.
And there are days when one asks
   for a sign.
Very intimate solitudes.
 Like when Santa Teresa upon her
   deathbed
would feel doubts about whether
   God existed.
Then from the car I looked
at the large letters on the hill
and from within God spoke to me:
 "Behold what I did for you,
      for your people even.
Behold those letters, and never
   doubt me,
 have faith, man of so little faith
you jerk."

9. Coronel Urtecho/ THE PAST WILL NOT RETURN

   It's the first time in Nicaragua that a revolution is the Revolution
   The first revolution against the entire past
   The first one which has really overthrown the past
   The first one to immediately erase it from Nicaragua's map

To clear the slate or, in other words, leave the blackboard black.
A black opening, a black gap, a black hole, like in space
That's what's left from the whole past
For that reason, only those from the past live in the past
Only those from the past long for the past
But don't be mistaken. No one will be fooled in Nicaragua anymore.
The past will not return.

10. Francisco de Asis Fernandez/ JULY 19TH

--To all who made this joy
possible...

These parks, these factories, these
   children,
this Anniversary and those to come
already were shining like a
   firmament
of suns put in the hearth,
the secret meetings, the weapons
   transfers,
the heavy and despairing silence
 at the farewells to the fallen.
The blind were and will still be
   others,
inhabitants of a dark republic.
They don't even have or want to
   have a partner
to whom they can passionately say,
You're my Republic, we're a free
   you
and a free me on the streets,
 in the workshop and in bed.
They saw and see without seeing.
They hear without hearing.
They struck out, fanning
   themselves.
The ball was painfully coming
 from the distant past,
just as this joy, these parks,
these factories, these children
and this brilliant light of this
   anniversary
come to us from the future.

11. Carlos Escorcia, Pastor of Assemblies of God (Managua)/ FAITH ON THE MARCH°*

Faith made Moses
leave the Pharoh's palace
and lead his people out of Egypt.
Faith led the slaves away
from their oppressors' land.
We in Nicaragua
have crossed the Red Sea.
Now we are crossing the desert
marching toward a land
that flows with milk
and honey for all.
Those of little faith
want to turn back.
But we would rather voice
the hopes of the poor
than the fears of the rich.
And we shall never,
ever go back
to the Pharoh's palace.

CHRONOLOGY: AUGUST, 1981 - JANUARY, 1982

August: Official mourning for Torrijos of Panama, dead in a plane accident. After repeated requests by the GNR for talks with U.S. officials about improving relations, Reagan sends Assistant Secratary of State for Latin America, Thomas Enders, for tight-lipped discussions with Foreign Minister D'Escoto. In the face of "increasingly deteriorating relations," D'Escoto affirms the GNR's wish to find a "*modus vivendi.*" During this same month, *La Prensa* is closed for 48 hours, after D'Escoto denies severe criticisms of Archbishop Obando Bravo that are attributed to the Foreign Minister. Christians supporting the FSLN protest the Archbishop's stance against pro-Sandinista priest Manuel Batalla. The Venezuelan government gives the Archbishop a vote of confidence by awarding him an honorary decoration. *La Prensa* dedicates a special issue to him, including photographs and paid tributes, especially from professionals and private sector representatives. Honduras grants the U.S. permission to build a military base in the Gulf of Fonseca.

September: Twelve people, including Vice Minister Leonel Poveda and other GNR functionaries who had fought on the Southern Front, are charged with conspiring against the government and arrested. Several religious base community organizations affirm their Catholic identity in the face of bitter accusations made by conservative sectors of the Church hierarchy. A judge in Jinotega fines 20 businessmen 725,000 cordobas in slander damages against another businessman. A conjunctivitis epidemic having severe effects on crops causes problems throughout the country, and a nationwide socio-economic State of Emergency is declared. The Presidents of Mexico and Venezuela call upon Honduras, Nicaragua and the U.S. to explore ways of halting the escalation of hostilities in the region. France and Mexico conjointly recognize the FDR/FMLN as a "representative political force in El Salvador." FDR president Guillermo Ungo travels to the U.S. to "test international reaction" to the French-Mexican declaration, stating that "the door is now open" for talks with the U.S. However, Reaganite officials indicate that the French-Mexican declaration will not cause the U.S. to re-evaluate its opposition to negotiations.

October: U.S.-Honduran Halcon Vista military operations aimed at intimidating the FSLN begin on the Honduran coast very close to Nicaragua. The Sandinistas respond with popular demonstrations and military mobilizations. An anti-interventionist/anti-imperialist program named for Benjamin Zeledon is held throughout Nicaragua. In the U.N. General Assembly, Daniel Ortega reads a proposal by El Salvador's FLMN-FDR calling for a political solution of the Salvadoran crisis. Ortega supports a peace plan for El Salvador which calls for negotiations without pre-conditions. Nicaraguan Ambassador to the U.S. Arturo Cruz reiterates his country's desire for a "positive and harmonious" relation with the U.S., declaring that "Nicaragua has not permitted and will not permit its sovereign territory to be used as a staging point for any direct or indirect military intervention in the affairs of El Salvador, or of any other country." Cruz adds that Nicaragua "has fully endorsed the joint French-Mexican proposal for a peaceful and negotiated solution in El Salvador." Meanwhile COSEP sends a letter to the GNR junta questioning the revolutionary process and accusing the FSLN of preparing "a new genocide." Two days later, four signers of the letter are caught in a conspiracy against the government, while other conspirators leave the country, and leaders of the CAUS and the Communist Party (including Eli Altamirano) are arrested for publishing a slanderous document designed to discredit the FSLN. Sandinista supporters occupy Alfonso Robelo's house, as class strife intensifies by the day.

November: Chontales Catholics direct a letter to the Nuncio and the Bishops lamenting the persecution of pro-Sandinista priests and Christians by their bishop, Monsenor Pablo A. Vega. Monsenor Bosco Vivas, a faithful collaborator of Mons. Obando is named Auxilary Bishop of Managua. Communist Party members accused of violating the Law of Public Order and Security are turned over to the authorities. The FSLN proposes a law governing the conduct and relations of the nation's diverse political parties to the Council of State. Opposition parties meet later in the month to discuss the proposed law. The next day, Tomas Borge leads the Nicaraguan delegation to the COPPPAL, in Panama, to analyze the "problem of Nicaragua." Mexican President Lopez Portillo reaffirms his country's support of the Nicaraguan government and his plan for U.S.-Nicaraguan dialogue. The Reagan administration intensifies charges and threats against Nicaragua. Secretary of State Haig tells Congress that Nicaragua is becoming a powerful totalitarian state which threatens U.S. interests; he refuses to rule out military action against the Sandinistas. Regular Honduran troops attack the Nicaragua border post at Guasaule on two separate occasions using machine guns and mortors. In communiques with Honduras, Foreign Minister D'Escoto protests attacks on Nicaragua, noting that "provocations of this nature only tend to obstruct Nicaraguan efforts to lessen tensions in Central America and avoid them between our two countries." D'Escoto urgently requests the Honduran government to honor the May 1981 agreements for continued dialogue and cooperation. Popular Honduran organizations charge that the counterrevolutionary station, Radio September 15th, operates out of San Marcos, Colon, Honduras, under the direction of Coronel Carlos Rodriguez. Dr. Roberto Suazo Cordoba is elected president of Honduras, but the military keeps its control. Dr. Arturo Cruz resigns as Nicaraguan Ambassador to Washington.

December: The second period of Council of State sessions closes after passing 73 new laws, including several related to urban reform, and one law which provides land titles to 80,000 families. Four hundred priests and lay leaders in Nicaragua write letters to the Pope calling for peace in Central America. The evangelical churches dedicate December to the cause of peace, as religious fervor sweeps the country during the Purisima celebrations. D'Escoto and Haig meet in Santa Lucia at the Eleventh Assembly of the O.A.S., and D'Escoto accuses the U.S. of seeking to intervene in Nicaragua. Counterrevolutionaries sabotage an Aeronica Boeing 727 plane in the Mexico City airport. The Ministry of the Interior reports the killing of 15 *contras* in San Carlos, Zelaya Norte, and Rio Coco, as well as damage to a FAS helicopter and the disappearance of more than 20 FSLN fighters through the actions of counterrevolutionary elements. A Honduran Air Force jet carrying Steadman Fagoth force-lands in Puerto Limpira (the Honduran Miskitu area), and Nicaragua protests the support for counterrevolutionary activity by the Honduran military. The Associated Press exposes the existence of 6 counterrevolutionary training camps in the Miami area. Still under wraps is Reagan's authorization during this month of the $19-million CIA-directed plan for paramilitary and terrorist operations against the FSLN. In apparent initial implementation of this plan, terrorist attacks, code-named "Red Christmas," are launched in Nicargua's remote northeast border area.

January: Two Sandinista Air Force members attempting to steal a plane are killed resisting arrest. The FSLN exposes plot by ex-National Guards and foreigners to blow up Nicaragua's only oil refinery and cement plant. Many conspirators are captured, including William Baltodano, who reveals many details to media reporters, *e.g.*, the participation of various foreign diplomats (in some cases, directly representing the wishes of their governments) in the plot. Implicated Venezuelan diplomats are ousted from the country, and Venezuela sends a note of protest, demanding explanations. The FSLN also reveals that France is selling helicopters and patrol launches to Nicaragua. Members of the July 19th Sandinista Youth clash with opposition party members in the Occidental Cemetery on the anniversary of the assassination of Pedro Joaquin Chamorro. *La Prensa* supporters fire on demonstrators protesting the stance of the newspaper in the face of a mounting intervention. Two people are seriously wounded, and the paper closes for a few days for "security reasons." By mid-month, Bishop Obando concludes his trip in the U.S. FSLN members and supporters are outraged at Obando's acceptance of homages paid him by a Reagan-related institution and the Bishop's comments on the Revolution. Efforts by the Base Communities organization of Managua to dialogue with Mons. Obando collapse because of the hierarchy's hostility toward lowly, rebellious priests. The bishops and the Ministry of the Interior exchange angry public communiques about the deportation of two Capuchin priests and three North American laypeople working on the Atlantic Coast. Also, near the coast, the Rio Coco area is declared a "military zone," and the GNR decides to move various Miskitu border communities toward the interior of the Atlantic sector, in the face of constant incursions of counterrevolutionary bands

228

in Zelaya Norte. After six days on the march, the Miskitus set up in "Tasba Pry." The resettlement of roughly 8,500 Miskitus in an area 60 kilometers from their old one immediately becomes a matter of a major U.S. propaganda campaign. After meetings with U.S. Under-Secretary of State James Buckley in San Jose, the foreign ministers of Costa Rica, El Salvador and Honduras announce the surprise formation of the "Central American Democratic Community," a "triple alliance" which conspicuously excludes Panama, Nicaragua and other Central American governments. As the month ends, intellectuals from all over the world gathered for the Ruben Dario conference proclaim their principles of "Cultural Independence," and Daniel Ortega attends the inauguration of Roberto Suarzo Cordoba as the elected president of Honduras.

Section 3. The Health Campaigns

1. Aura Sofia Sanchez, Palacaguina
   Poetry Workshop/ YOUR
   LESSON NOTEBOOKS

In the health brigades
I see you
with your lesson notebooks
where for the first time
you wrote my name
after the literacy crusade.

2. Juan Herrera Salazar, Jinotega
   Poetry Workshop/ LEONEL
   RUGAMA

I met you yesterday Leonel.
I read your poems.
You called
"to the blind who beg at the bus
   stops
to the consumptives from the
   stadium
to the deaf and dumb by birth."
Today I was in the Guillermo
   Matute
   Medical Office
The office filled with children

Children from Ducali
Los Robles/ Asturias
Fantasma/ El Cua
and from Bocaycito
The shoeshine kids from the Otto
   Casco Plaza
   with sore throats
The fruitselling kids from the park.
Efrain, with nosebleed
old child with spittle
and Demetrio who suffers from
   cramps.
You could have read your poems
                    like a saint.
I'm going to tell you what we do
now that I don't know where you
   are
now that we live in Revolution.
The peasants line up to refill their
   medicines
in the house of the people
the pregnant women wait
from Monday through Friday
for their pre-natal exams
the pork vender/ the fried banana
   seller
the cook from La Enchilada
get in line to carry their samples

to the Amin Halum Hospital
laboratory.
There are also lines for remedies
injections
to visit the oculist
the gynecologist
the ears-nose-and-throat specialist
The Red Cross workers start
another course
the Juan Ramon Turcios Nursing
School
will have its second promotion,
we multiply the workshops
for health promoters,
we carry out
a national anti-polio vaccination
campaign
the handicapped are integrated into
society,
the dogs are vaccinated against
rabies
there's already a home for the aged
in Jinotega.

3. Herrera/ AMIN HALUM
HOSPITAL

The Amin Halum
is a hospital of the people.
Today it's a hospital of 180 beds
with admission rights for every one.
We paint the hospital corridors blue
the medicine room clear yellow
at the end of the room
we put the photo of Lina Herrera
Martyr of the Revolution.
For the patients awaiting their
appointments
we paint the benches brown
with white letters that say:
SURGERY ROOM/
MATERNITY ROOM
I think of the problems
of hospital organization
of the laboratory

of the isolation room
of the control room
with its burnt sterilizers,
of the flight of hospital supplies
of the sabotage the
counterrevolutinaries
carried out in the Operation Room,
of the flies in the laundry room
of the flies in the kitchen.
I carefully consider
the steps we take in organizing our
union
I think about the last assembly
with a hundred health workers
united to defend our process.
I'm happy to know
we've doctors in the vanguard.
The inhuman treatment of patients
will never recur.
They'll never humiliate the cleanup
crew again.
Before the insurrection
they kicked over the bucket of
placentas.
They drenched the floor in blood
and with "sons-of-bitches"
and other choice words,
called the porter to mop it up.
Now we make pinatas for the
children
in pediatrics and nutrition.
Peasant mothers will never suffer
humiliation
in this hospital.
I see the future with jubilation.
There'll be no more flies.
We'll wax the back patio, we'll have
clothing in Pediatrics and Nutrition.

4. Herrera/ MEDICUS MINISTER
NON MAGISTER NATURAE

A doctor is only a minister
not a master of nature.
That's what they taught me in

Medical School.
I have heard some doctors
  at the Amin Halum Hospital
send prayers to the Lord
I have seen them go to mass.
They give the impression
of having understood the Latin
  aphorism.
I have heard the same doctors
explain to their patients
the nature of their illness
their prognosis and their treatment.
They explain the nature of the
  illness
              according to the client
the prognosis and treatment
              according to the wallet.
These are the doctors who bring us
              the pack of specialists
              cosmetic therapy
              symptomatic therapy
              basic therapy
              and definitive therapy
if the client can afford the bill.
I think
these doctors give you aphorisms
  if you don't have money
  Medicus minister et magister if
    you do.
Yesterday in the monthly assembly
of the Jinotega Medical Society
we discussed professional ethics
              the people's interests
              the union's interests.
Some withdrew from the meeting.
They maintained the positions of
  COSEP
(the Supreme Council of Private
  Enterprise).
These doctors are the same ones
who go to church.
The rest of us doctors pronounced
  our support
for HEROES AND MARTYRS OF
  FESOMENIC
(the Nicaraguan Federation

of Medical Societies).
We decided to initiate
the Moral Reconstruction of the
  Union.
We decided to elaborate
  the code of professional ethics.
They cannot be permitted
to sack the state hospital
to carry the serums
the syringes, the antibiotics
that are the people's property
to their private clinics.
They can't keep on charging
              for transfusions.
We won't let them advance in their
  conspiracy
We won't be accomplices
in the pain others cause
We want clean medicine
for strong humans
for clear humans
for humans from the Sandinist
  Front.
We want the medicine that is born
with the Revolution.
We want doctors who don't hide the
  truth.
We want a medicine with ministers
  for the peasants
  for the workers
  for the students.
We want doctors who are
  ministers for every one.
  In writing this poem
I   don't violate professional ethics
I don't betray my colleagues.
I simply interpret my rights
the rights of the masses
the rights of my brothers in the
  mountains.
Now is the time for saying who
  we're with.
Who are the doctors of the
  Revolution
and who are the doctors
  of the counterrevolution

Medicus Minister I am
of the poor
of the peasants
of the students.

5. Herrera/ LEONEL RUGAMA

We think of the indices of perinatal
  mortality
of the indices of infant mortality.
We examine the figures from Zaire
Guatemala, Haiti.
The representatives of Mead
  Johnson
invade the clinics
with sample catalogs full of lies
with photos of rosy children
with photos of green and blue-eyed
  children.
They invent slogans
and sell us malnutrition:
When she doesn't have enough milk
      NESTLE
When she can't keep her milk down
      NESTLE
When she doesn't want to
  breast-feed
      NESTLE
When the breast is dry
      NESTLE
Four, five, seven bottles a day
always with NESTLE milk.
We are resisting imperialist
  propaganda
We doctors demand that the OAS
the FAO, UNICEF
and the World Health Organization
defend the children.
Let's march, shoemakers,
  bartenders,
carpenters, cutters,
cabinet makers, fishers
let's shout:
WE DON'T WANT NIDO MILK
WE DON'T WANT PELARGON
Let's go with our wives

with our brothers
with our children
to expel EATON
MEAD JOHNSON, NESTLE.

I listen to the cry of the children
in the Amin Halum Hospital
the cry of the children from Yal
  of the children from Jinotega
the cry of the children from
  Nicaragua.
Now we don't want Nido milk
Now we don't want Pelargon milk
Now we don't want Enfamil
No more Sustageno
No more Nestogeno
      Shit on NESTLE.

6. Herrera/ THE PEOPLE SHOULD KNOW

We leaf through the P.L.M.
Dictionary of Pharmaceutical
  Specialties
22,500 specialties
for businesses like Ciba, Roche and
  Schering.
But the basic list of medications
of the O.M.S. (World Health
  Organization)
doesn't reach 250.
It's time we explain to the people
  the reason for these lies.
The people should know
why Neurobion
    Deboyecta
    Venadon
are used.
The people should know why
  Trimetoprin Sulpha
bears three different names:
    Bactrim
    Lidaprim
    Eusaprim
with each name the price changes.

232

The French give the name of
    Cloroquina
to Nivaquina
that witch's brew
the capitalists call
        an "Industrial Secret"
We will not fool our brothers
in the mountains
companero peasant
I tell you these things
because we are in Revolution.
Aderogyl C is not a miraculous
    vitamin.
Our children need:
milk, cheese, eggs
meat, green vegetables, fruits,
potatoes and rice.
Who said milk causes diarrhea?
Who taught that fish brings joy
that oranges are bad
and pineapples are frozen?
Food doesn't cause parasites.
So that the children don't get
    parasites
give them: shoes
                drinkable water
                decent sewers
                houses of cement
                        of brick
                paved streets.
Give them agrarian reform.
Our children need the Revolution to
    continue.
Companero peasant
they withdrew plain aspirin from
    the market.
What will happen with your tooth
    aches
            with your ear aches
What will you do when your body's
    all loose?
            when it pierces you
            when it jabs you.
Now they prescribe Flanax for you

and you can't buy it.
Look around you
look at Felicita
    at Afrania
with lice and malnutrition.
I will always repeat:
            better eggs/ better meat
don't use capsules of Venadon.
We augment the wealth of the people
we help the Ministry of Health.
We make our prescriptions for
    malnutrition
        Agrarian Reform.
We make an end to diarrheas
with sewers and drinkable water.
We carry out sanitary education
we create our people's pharmacies
we speak with the Ministers
we forge the Nicaraguan A.P.P.
        the People's Property Area.
Only in this way will I be sure
that my prescription
will impel the Revolution.

7. Avelio Lopez Pabon, San Juan
    de Oriente Poetry Workshop/ IN
    THE HEALTH BRIGADE

In San Juan de Oriente we are
    organizing
to eliminate polio and typhoid.
We've received orientations
in the health workshop.
In zone 5 you can see houses of
    adobe,
of palm leaves, or of quarry stones.
The terrain is wavy.
Jocotes, guayabas and oranges
    abound.
Organized young people
vaccinating house to house,
we are the people
wiping out sickness.

CHRONOLOGY: FEBRUARY - JULY, 1982

February: The Second Sandinist Assembly reaffirms political pluralism, the mixed economy and defense of the Revolution. The GNR releases a plan of incentives for export production, offering greater benefits to the private sector. New schedules are set for different groups of workers to relieve urban transportation problems. COSEP leaders are released from prison. Miguel D'Escoto holds a bitter tv debate with U.S. U.N. Ambassador Jeane Kirkpatrick. Meanwhile, in Managua, Commander Bayardo Arce denounces the open participation of the U.S. in aggression against Nicaragua, as the State Security Forces expose the "Red Christmas" counterrevolutionary plot to create a beachhead in the Playa area of the Atlantic Coast. Miskitu leader Efrain Omier exposes the ties of religious representatives in the plans of Miami and Honduras-based Somocistas. Revealing details of the counterrevolutionary plans, and presenting a list of 60 soldiers and civilians killed by *contra* bands in Zelaya Norte, the Defense Department also sets forth evidence confirming the participation of religious leaders in the "Red Christmas" conspiracy. On February 19, the Episcopal Conference of Nicaragua publishes a document accusing the GNR of human rights violations with respect to the Miskitu relocation process. The GNR appeals to the apostolic Nuncio, claiming the bishops' accusations are without foundation and calling for the visit of a delegation from the Vatican to discuss future relations between the government and the bishops. On the same day, Security Forces reveal a counterrevolutionary plot to blow up bridges and cotton gins in Chinandega and Corinto; and the GNR puts forth proposals for a negotiated peace with the U.S. at the first session of the COPPPAL, a confederation of Latin American political parties meeting in Managua. On February 20, Mexican President Lopez Portillo, speaking at COPPPAL, proposes a regional peace plan with three main points: the U.S. should cease its threats and military actions against Nicaragua; if the paramilitary units operating from Honduras are disbanded, Nicaragua should reduce the size of its armed forces; the various affected countries should enter into mutual non-aggression pacts. The GNR welcomes the proposal and prepares to award Lopez Portillo the Augusto Cesar Sandino order in the Plaza of the Revolution. Just as the COPPPAL conference comes to a close, a dynamite-filled valise explodes in the Sandino Airport, killing three people.

March: Commander Jaime Wheelock heads a delegation to the U.S. to answer alarming accusations about Sandinista treatment of the Miskitus, while Alexander Haig pressures the U.S. Senate to approve largescale operations against Nicaragua. Meanwhile, discussions of the Political Parties Law bog down in the face of potential invasion, as word leaks out confirming the U.S.'s $19 million covert action project. Humberto Ortega calls on the people to organize civil defense and make preparations in every barrio as part of a general alert. The young Nicaraguan Orlando Tardencilla, captured in El Salvador and accused of participating in the Salvadoran guerrilla struggle makes a laughing stock of the U.S. State Department which brings him to Washington to verify their story about Sandinista complicity in arms shipments to El Salvador. Tardencilla publicly denies the charges, denounces tortures suffered in El Salvador and accuses the State Department of wanting to blackmail him into speaking against the Nicaraguan Revolution. The GNR demands he be returned to his country, and two days later he is received in Managua as a hero. On the very next day (March 15), the CIA covert action plot now public knowledge, the GNR decrees a State of Emergency for the entire country. In the days which follow, press censorship and other measures are taken; nine members of the Jehovah's Witnesses are accused of violating the State of Emergency and expelled from the country. Peace marches are held in every city and town, and the GNR reaffirms its peace initiatives. U.S. officials thwart Mexican hopes for April negotiations; and Daniel Ortega's speech before the U.N Security Council, exposing U.S. intervention and inviting immediate and unconditional negotiations, is ignored by U.S. officials.

April: Twelve of the fifteen countries in the U.N. Security Council vote in favor of Nicaragua's stance vis-à-vis U.S. aggression; but the U.S. exerts its veto powers, and counterrevolutionary bands attack posts on the Honduran and Costa Rican borders. In the face of invasion threats, the GNR suspends Holy Week vacations, a move which the Church hierarchy interprets as sacrilege. At midmonth, speaking to reporters in a luxurious Costa Rican hotel, Eden Pastora denounces the "totalitarian nature" of the Sandinist Revolution and pledges to oust the Sandinistas from power. Answering Pastora, the FSLN points to the coincidence between Pastora's position and U.S. CIA aggression projections. Commander Jose Valdivia, Pastora's closest associate, returns to Nicaragua and accuses his old comrade in arms of having betrayed Sandinista ideals, the Revolution and the people. The State of Emergency is extended another thirty days, as it will be again and again in the months which follow.

May: The May Day rally emphasizes socialist construction, as Tomas Borge promises that the Sandinistas will continue with the Reconstruction. Luis Carrion denounces the existence of a counterrevolutionary, clandestine radio station called "The Voice of Sandino." Sixteen people, including ex-Human Rights Commissioner Jose Francisco Cardenal, ex- *Prensa* reporter Adriana Guillen and ex-commander Chamorro Rapacioli are found guilty of counterrevolutionary activities. $320 million in loans for developing projects come to Nicaragua as a result of trips by Daniel Ortega to the USSR and Sergio Ramirez to various European countries. Mexican officials express pessimism about the likelihood of U.S.-Nicaraguan talks. A U.S. official reports, "We were cool to the Mexican initiative from the beginning, but we were effectively ambushed by Congress and public opinion. We had to agree to negotiate or appear unreasonable." The U.S. and Nicaragua exchange negotiating positions, even as U.S. official Stephen Boxworth denies that the State Department is footdragging on possible negotiations. Despite Nicaraguan readiness to negotiate, the U.S. stalls, with one official telling the *New York Times* that "we want to do some more probing to make sure they're serious." The GNR declares a broad stretch of the Pacific coast a disaster area because of the floods that leave more than 100 dead and thousands homeless. The government seeks international aid, and the first delegation to evaluate the damage comes from Cuba, headed by Raul Castro Ruiz.

June: The GNR announces that the flood damages require rethinking the nation's economic situation. The Ministry of Internal Commerce (MICOIN) places harsh sanctions on merchants who change the prices of basic foods or speculate with the people's hunger. More than 250 business people are fined in a day. Commander Borge questions reactionary and dogmatic Christians at the closing ceremony of the Second Encounter of Christians for Peace in Latin America and the Caribbean. Alfonso Robelo, head of the MDN, declares that he will struggle alongside with Eden Pastora in the counterrevolutionary organization, the *Frente Revolucionario Sandinista* (the FRS). Robelo accuses the GNR of turning totalitarian and following the developmental lines of Cuba. Counterrevolutionary media broadcasting into Nicaragua increase with the augmentation of radio stations September 15th from Honduras and "Voz Sandino" in Costa Rica, as well as the installation of Channel 5 on Honduran tv. On the other hand, the GNR denounces the presence of a U.S. ship in its territorial waters in the Gulf of Fonseca; the state of emergency is prolonged another 30 days, and seven news stations are reopened.

July: Paramilitary attacks on Nicaragua increase dramatically as the Revolution's third anniversary approaches. The anniversary celebration involves the mobilization of the people in the face of economic and laboral problems. Meanwhile joint U.S.-Honduran military maneuvers are held near Nicaragua's remote northern border. U.S. planes move equipment and a battalion of Hondurans troops moves to a new permanent base in the border area.

Section 4. New Problems, Pastora, Education & the Children of Nicaragua

1. Aldo Solorzano, Sandinist Traffic
    Police Poetry Workshop
    (Managua)/ DON'T REST

The change is slow,
sweat upon sweat,
anxiety upon anxiety.
My anguish in making this new
    poetry.
All will be new in Nicaragua.

2. Virgilio Pavon, September 14th
    Neighborhood Poetry Workshop
    (Diriamba)/ THE
    NEIGHBORHOOD DRUNKS

Rosa, German, Esperanza and
    Humberto
get drunk
every Saturday and Sunday.
The neighbors can't sleep.
Rosa make a scandal until dawn
and shouts and cries are heard
when she whore-this's and that's
    her girls.
Humberto beats his wife,
because he doesn't find his supper.
Esperanza, drunk, tells her husband
she has other men
and German, who's calmer,
is too hung over to work the next
    day.
Only Rosa says she's a
    revolutionary
but sells booze at forbidden hours
and thinks that by belonging to the
    C.D.S.
she won't be punished
by the revolutionary laws.

3. Gioconda Belli/ THERE SHALL
   BE NO PARDON

There shall be no pardon, Eden, for
    your back
        turned against the people
for the barrel of your rifle aligned
    with enemy rifles.
There shall be no pardon for your
    own image
for the face that you will daily have
to confront in the mirror.
We shall not forget your false
    promises,
your dazzling decorated uniform
that never quenched your pride.
We shall judge you harshly
as traitors are judged
and you shall go wandering like
    Judas
without homeland or people,
at night hearing the applause of
    before
turned into slogans of repudiation;
because this people Eden, as it made
you a man
Now tears off your medals
and burns your signature on the
    sidewalks
because if you were something
it was because of the FSLN
whose sons now efface you forever
as you have chosen to erase yourself
            for all times
with all the hearts that once
admired your arm raised
on the gangway of a plane
    --without a doubt you were a fine
    poster--
Those of us who made you a man,
Eden, we unman you;
you are only a zero in history.

4. Julio Valle-Castillo/
    NOTIFICATION TO EDEN

I   should discharge my poem in
    your back
as it would be fitting for a traitor.
--Eden Pastora you sold out
my Commander Zero
when he was going toward
    someplace in America
            and to the lowest bidder.
You're an infiltrator and,
    he didn't detect you.
--Eden Pastora you shit
    on the image of Commander Zero,
that is, on the August photo
at the door of the plane, about
to consummate the act, with his
    beret
framing the clearest
and widest head of that sky
pomegranate garlands on his neck
and victorious arms with his G-3
    raised
--Eden, you shit--
on the image of Commander Zero,
as if in a crown of laurel leaves,
militarily saluting
    in the 1st Anniversary parade
before the Armed Forces of our
    hope.
--Eden Pastora you shit on
    yourself,
because Commander Zero will
    continue being ours
and you're not even your own.
    Others
will be Commander Zero, those who
    govern
their madness and give form to their
    fire
and raise them like a single column
to my people and their song
in the center of the plaza.
These will be the Zeros of the

Commander.
Zeros will be those who in order to
    live
on this land die, those who
    understand
that an authentic Revolution is
    always
better than its errors and defects.
Look out, Eden, one day you'll come
    up against
the solitary star of Commander Zero
and until this encounter occurs,
you can betray who and what you
    want.
Talk and lie; but know that in
    Nicaragua
no one has prohibited or erased your
    name
from our History,
that it was you and not Commander
    Zero,
who went against History
    and History erased you.

5. Daniel Ortega/ IN SPITE OF
    EVERYTHING*

We have advanced, but the route is
    large
and we have to keep opening roads,
in spite of the aggressions,
in spite of the slanders.

6. Salvador Velazquez, Engineering
    Battalion Poetry Workshop, EPS
    (Managua)/ FROM THE
    ENGINEERING MILITARY
    BATTALION

Seeing you study at night inspires
    me.
Your workday ended:
The night arrives.
You don't tire because,

notebook under your arm, Ester,
you go to the Maestro Gabriel High
 School.
Always in a hurry. And I observe
 you from here in my Military
 Unit:
You talk, you laugh, you move your
 hands.
It's as if you see me.
I keep looking at you
and lose you among my companeros.
There you take history classes:
Sandino's thought
             your future
             the Revolution.

7. Ervin Garcia, Masaya Poetry
    Workshop/ YOU DON'T KNOW

The little school today has new
 desks
and more students
Miguel, the kids are big now!
and they whitewashed Dona Sara's
 house
where I did literacy work.

8. Gerardo Gadea, Ernesto Castillo
   Poetry Workshop, Managua/
   SCHOOL BEFORE THE
   REVOLUTION

When I was twelve,
I stopped going to school.
    I was scared
because once the teacher
Macario Tercero
shut me up in a dark room
and another day I saw him
 punishing
fourteen year old Cleotilde
with a raw leather belt.
He made her get on her knees
and cross her arms.

She sighed and twisted
but she didn't cry
and when she got up
there was a puddle on the floor.
(The boys and girls wanted to cry.)
Mr. Rosendo, Cleotilde's father,
sent her to a farm
and I didn't go back to school.
I went to gather wood
with Lionza Acosta's grandchildren
or Juan Betanco's children
and we would go swimming
in the Chiquito River
 or swing in the rattan
 among the trees.
We would spend the day
there on Pastor Hill
and at dusk
we would all come home
             with a handful of wood.
Today kids gladly go to school
and with their teachers
organize the Rearguard
because the Revolution
belongs to them.

9. Mirna Ojeda, Schick Subdivision
    Poetry Workshop, Managua/ TO
    MY NEPHEW, HAXEL

When I'm seated under the Tiguilote
 tree,
you come to me
and with your big black eyes,
you look at me, you start asking
 questions about one thing
and another, and you make me
 smile.
With your scant three years,
you have memories of the war.
You know it was war
because you heard people talk of
 war,
just as you heard the shouts of
Free Homeland or Death, at night,

and you repeated it, and you knew
that the National Guard was bad.
Now you sympathize with the compas
and when you see them
pass on the street with their Galils,
you shout,
"There go the Sandinista Police,"
and they smile at you.
But you still don't understand some
    things
and that's why you ask.
You fill me with emotion

when you sing of Carlos Fonseca
and making your tiny fist
you shout, "PRESENT."
When you're bigger
and all the proletarian children
study the true history of Nicaragua
in school (healthy and happy),
and when you're all grown up
and there is no longer misery among
    our people,
you'll understand better.

10. Coronel Urtecho/ THE PAST WILL NOT RETURN

It's the first time in Nicaragua that a revolution is the Revolution
The first revolution against the entire past
To clear the slate or, in other words, leave the blackboard black.

11. Juan Herrera Salazar, Jinotega Poetry Workshop/ LEONEL RUGAMA

On July 19,
we'll celebrate
the Revolution's anniversary
Revolutionaries are being formed
    everywhere.
We make revolution in Acahualinca
    in the Maldito neighborhood
    in education/ in culture...

12. Daniel Ortega/ THREE YEARS* (Speech on July 19, 1982)

We have walked for three years
without stopping a single instant,
and we've advanced in spite of the
    obstacles,
like Sandino's guerilla fighters
in the Segovia mountains,

more resolute than the rains,
firmer than the cold,
who learned to fight
against hunger and fatigue,
who knew how to defeat fear
and rise up heroically
against the traitors and invaders,
who barefoot and poorly armed
were not defeated by the Marines
and warplanes of U.S. military
    power,
who were capable of all this
and of willing us dignity, history,
    patriotism
and we're going to need their spirit,
and we're going to need their
    example,
because they were the people
    fighting for the people,
because they were the homeland
    fighting for the homeland,
because they were history making
    history.

13. Nicaraguan Children/ A BETTER WORLD

A 12 YEAR OLD GIRL:
We the children of Nicaragua
speak to the children of the world,
so we can unite
to build a better world.

A 12 YEAR OLD BOY:
What is a better world?
The children ask themselves.
A peasant child answers,
we don't want to be farmworkers
if we're hardly ten
or twelve years old.
A better world

shouts a shoeshine boy
is something clean like my shoes
so bright and I shine them with
love.

AN 11 YEAR OLD GIRL:
Children of the whole world,
let's unite to build a better world,
without war, without exploitation,
with peace;
because the children are the future.
If we unite we'll be happy,
for only united can we overcome all.

Children of Nicaragua. Demonstration at U.S. Embassy against contra kidnappings. Managua, December 1984. Photo by Vicki Grayland.

BOOK II, PART III (*July, 1982 - July, 1983*)

Introduction: Developments During the Year, the New Poetry,
Solidarity & Women in the Revolution

1. *Socio-Economic and Political Developments during a Year of Crisis*

Three main factors, a continuing rise in counterrevolutionary activity, the floods and subsequent summer drought and the overall effort to restructure the Nicaraguan economy in the midst of difficult Central American and world market conditions, combined to shape national development in 1982-83. Like other underdeveloped countries, Nicaragua suffered economic setbacks during this period in part because of the fall in prices for agricultural exports, coupled with rising prices for imports essential to agricultural and overall development. Added to this was the U.S.'s punishing economic war against the country: the withdrawal of Standard Fruit, the prohibition on computer replacement parts from the U.S.; the 90% reduction in Nicaragua's sugar quota, and the threatened suppression of Nicaraguan beef imports. Clearly, the economy suffered from continuing private sector recalcitrance and the public sector continued to suffer from inefficiency and "birth pangs." And to all of this must be added all the economic losses suffered from the counterrevolutionary attacks and the diversion of resources from the productive to the military sphere.

In the face of difficult circumstances, the GNR and mass organizations throughout the country were compelled to restructure institutions and programs, and at times create new ones. Such developments inevitably became the subject of controversy, increasing the level of opposition to the Sandinistas in some quarters. However, overall, the difficult conditions, the external threat and the internal opposition only intensified commitment to the Revolution among the vast majority of Nicaraguans. In spite of everything, a vigilant optimism reigned among the Sandinista bloc, which grew in size and strength throughout the year.

Our general introduction to the Reconstruction outlines most of the major issues and events pertinent to comprehending this period and the poetry which it generated. Below, we will detail a few key matters necessary to giving a fuller understanding of the total national dynamic, passing from economic, political, institutional and class questions to ones that give us a richer grasp of the Sandinista culture which reached new levels of development in the course of this year of crisis.

2. *The Economic Situation*

In his "State of the Nation" talk in May, 1983, Daniel Ortega indicated the main points about the national economy during 1982-83. The gross national product was down 2%, and the foreign debt soared to a record $3,968 million. The fall in international prices for agricultural exports created a $246 million decrease in export earnings--almost half of the total earnings for 1982. These factors, shared throughout Central America and the underdeveloped world, led to inflation and unemployment rises, as well as curtailment of certain plans for improved social services. Inflation rose almost a point over the 1981 rate of 23.9%; unemployment rose from 15.9 to 19.8%, with 185,200 people out of work. Although state factory production rose by 6%, overall manufactured goods production dropped 3%, as efforts were directed more to the crucial agricultural export sector.

For reasons cited, economic production was far from the projected total, and while counterrevolutionary attacks caused great economic losses and diverted resources that could have gone to building the national infrastructure and new sources of economic growth, still the GNR managed to maintain and in some cases multiply public services to the degree that the national standard of living rose, even with high inflation and unemployment. Inevitably, luxury goods consumption declined sharply, weakening middle sector support for the GNR; and while on the whole the poor might be materially better off than before, there might be some question if they felt better off, in a situation fraught with danger and hardship on every side. Indeed, throughout the year, unions and other organizations had to meet and mobilize over food shortages and other basic problems caused by the economic crunch.

As economic and military problems impacted the country, the GNR took several important steps throughout the year to avert deeper crisis. First, recognizing the need for a more efficient coordination of institutions and activities, the GNR decentralized its work and reduced its public sector bureaucracy by dividing the country into six regions and two sub-regions for administrative, military and economic functions.

Subregional Agrarian Reform offices were set up to implement the law at the local level. Then, working with mass organizations in a test of the new structure, the GNR promoted a massive campaign of volunteer work which produced record cotton and coffee harvests later in the year.

Under UNAG's leadership, cooperative and independent agricultural producers met to consider their problems and make recommendations to the

GNR. Demands accepted by the government included indemnification for the basic grain debts of Sandinist agrarian, credit and service cooperatives and individual producers, as well as assumption of debts for those peasants integrated into various units of defense against the *contras*.

Throughout the year, as the people mobilized for harvests and defense, the GNR also struggled against continuing private sector decapitalization and underproduction, enforcing ever stricter penalties against those who actively opposed the national interest. Also, the Government attempted to maintain some private sector support for the process by offering business incentives and assuring private sector participation in the deliberations over the new political parties law, planned to set the course toward electoral politics in the framework of the Revolution. For instance, top-level discussions of November, 1982 counted with the participation of the Revolutionary Patriotic Front and the Ramiro Sacasa Coordinating Committee. During the spring of 1983, new incentives were announced for private meat, cotton, coffee and sesame producers. But as the year came to an end, the polarization of capital and labor continued, as the GNR passed ever harsher laws against those entrepreneurs declared as working against the interests of the Revolution.

This polarization could not help but be reflected in terms of the Church during the period in question.

3. The Church Hierarchy and the Government

In July, offended by a letter from the Pope to the bishops on the theme of church unity, the GNR temporarily prohibited its publication until Christians committed to the Revolution could study it and make constructive criticisms. Bishop Obando provoked a large public demonstration by transferring pro-Sandinist Mons. Arias Caldera from his parish. Tensions mounted as Fr. Carbollo, a spokesman for the Archbishop, was discovered committing adultery and subjected to public humiliation by outraged neighbors, and as Salesian secondary students attacked youths participating in a pro-government demonstration in Masaya. Indeed the month of August was the most critical in Church-State relations since July 1979.

The FSLN attempted to initiate a truce by repeating its principles of respect toward religion, and meetings were held with the bishops. However, problems broke out over the political propaganda certain traditionalist sectors launched with respect to the hierarchy's promotion of the Consecration of the Virgin. Answering FSLN criticisms, the bishops published a statement on the right to a Catholic education. The Pope's proposed visit to Nicaragua in 1983 became a focal point of conflict between conservative sectors and those aligned with the process, as the papal nuncio claimed that the visit might well be contingent on the government priests renouncing their posts. The priests did not resign, and the Pope did come to Nicaragua in the spring, in the midst of an increasingly bitter conflict between the Church hierarchy and Sandinist supporters.

Coming at a time of intensifying war in the country, the Pope enraged Sandinista followers by his failure to honor those who were dying in the struggle and by his blanket condemnation of the FSLN and the revolutionary priests serving in the government. The Pope incited a great outpouring of resentment as thousands of Sandinist supporters saw him attempting to use his religious position to condemn a process for which they had sacrificed and were still risking so much.

Afterward, the Church hierarchy joined the capitalist world in attacking the Sandinista treatment of the Pope, and the Sandinistas retaliated with angry acts of their own. The Pope's confrontational visit and its aftermath then became manipulated by the Western press into a scandalous incident which undoubtedly hurt the Revolution's image in some quarters.

Internal to Nicaragua, the Pope's visit and reception led to a sharpening of the ideological confrontation in Nicaragua. Some sectors were confused and disoriented. People at once supportive of the process and devout Catholics could not differentiate between religious positions and those that were really positions of political opposition. The polemic over the visit caused some religionists to turn from the Revolution. But, meanwhile, many young people began leaving the church, and even those church sectors dominated by liberationist theologians. The Somocistas held masses in "reparation" for what the Sandinists had done to the Pope in Nicaragua, with Somocista bishop Leon Pallais leading the mass assisted by *contra* leaders. It seemed clear that religion would be at the center of the ideological struggle for some time to come.

In May, the GNR incited church wrath by deporting Spanish priest Timoteo Merino for turning peasants against the FSLN and recruiting them for ARDE. ARDE itself increasingly confronted the Revolution on a religious level, attempting to convince peasants to take up arms "not for political reasons, but rather to defend their religion and keep Communism from coming to Nicaragua."

During the same period, leaflets with a picture of the Pope and Jesus and slogans of the FDN were taken from groups of ex-National Guards in the north. The leaflets provoked strong protests throughout the country against the *contras'* manipulation of religious symbols. But the Church hierarchy, led by Bishop Obando y Bravo, persisted in their hostility to the government, attacking the deportation of Merino and other *contra* priests, and moving in ever greater and seemingly irrevocable opposition to the

Revolution. Sandinistas reacted angrily when Obando persisted in not condemning *contra* actions and killings, as the rift widened further.

All in all, 1982-83 was a deeply conflictive and revolutionary year, involving a national crisis that affected every aspect of activity and consciousness. In many ways, the U.S. backed FDN and ARDE campaigns only strengthened support for the Revolution and provided the motive for more efficient and dedicated work, while deflecting blame for economic problems from the government and toward international factors. Defense measures were virtually integrated into daily life, as employees took extra work loads to replace on-duty army reserve members. And the number of people joining the militias rose throughout the year. In the fields and in the factories, the people grew increasingly alert and militant. The majority of the population remained calm, but with a growing awareness of the critical situation precipitated by U.S.-backed aggression. And many families had to mourn lost relatives, as the death toll in fighting for the year rose to 600. But children still attended school, the life and the work of the country continued, and there was still time for celebrations and for developing new modes of expression and communal participation as the new revolutionary culture took on deeper and more determined contours.

4. Intervention, Solidarity & Poetics

In Book II, Part III, less attention is given to day to day occurrences than in earlier units of our text. This is so in part because much of the poetic material covering this period has yet to be published, but it is also because the period depicted is one of great crisis in the revolutionary process, and it seemed important to focus on and underline certain particular themes and motifs which, existing throughout much of the Reconstruction, reach their fruition in this year. In this regard we should underline the fact that the dominant concern in our sections, is not on given events, but on the underlying developments in ideology and culture that accompany those events.

The dominant theme, of course, is intervention and defense, as well as the commitment to the revolution which the attack from without could only incite to its peak among the thousands in Nicaragua who believed in the Revolution. Thus, this part opens with a section which expresses these concerns and feelings, and anticipates our "Epilogue" poetry, where a final crescendo of slogans, shouts and flashback passages will constitute the climax of this volume and of the process by which the most extreme and militant possibilities of Sandinist culture achieve their hegemonic force throughout the country. Much has been said earlier in the book and in this introduction about the events of 1982-83, about the continuing efforts of the government, about the struggle with the private sector and the Church hierarchy, and above all about the intervention itself. Here, after an opening section that deals directly with defense, are three other sections, dealing respectively with poetry, solidarity and women, that are also very important and about which something must be said in this introduction.

Perhaps the question of solidarity requires the least explanation in the context of the international crisis over Nicaragua; in one sense, it is a key to this crisis as it developed from the first days of Reconstruction. The Reagan administration devoted considerable energies to building its justification for aggression against Nicaragua (as well as for its failures in the Salvadoran war), on the basis of Nicaragua's purported service as a conduit of arms to El Salvador. For their part, the Sandinistas have denied the charge while clearly stating their moral support for the Salvadoran insurgents.

In his *Playboy* interview with Claudia Dreifus, Daniel Ortega summed up the FSLN position: "The insurgents have the financial means to buy weapons ...Furthermore, the weapons the insurgents are using have been in their hands for a long time--long before our revolution triumphed here. Now, certainly, we openly *sympathize* with the Salvadorans. But to send them weapons would be to play into the hands of those who want to name Nicaragua as the great arms supplier to El Salvador. ... The principal weapons supplier of the Salvadoran rebels is the North American Government. The arms ... the United States ... had given Salvadoran-government soliders ... inevitably get captured; so the more weapons the United States sends to El Salvador, the more weapons for the revolutionaries (*Playboy* [Sept., 1983], pp. 199-200)."

Our poetic material makes no direct comments about the degree of real material support for other Central American revolutions stemming from the land of Sandino. However, it does portray the Sandinist ethos with respect to people's struggle, international solidarity and imperialist aggression. It shows how these attitudes are part of the newly emerging and crystalizing Sandinist culture, one which of course has its roots in Segovia mountain campaigns of another era but which are now indelibly cast as the hegemonic view in the new Nicaragua. How, it might be asked, could it be otherwise? How could we but expect that a people fired up with their own costly victory over a powerful dictatorship, that a people helped by international solidarity in their own struggle, could not but feel the deepest solidarity for the struggle of neighbors in Guatemala and El Salvador?

The feelings grew with the overthrow of General Romero's regime in October, 1979; they became more intense with the assassination of Bishop Romero; and they grew over the years as the struggles continued in El Salvador and Guatemala, as the U.S. more and more intervened in these processes, and also as others in many parts of the world, including those doing such important work in the U.S., labored in solidarity with the struggles in Central America and against the Reaganite intervention. Solidarity became a cornerstone of the Sandinist vision; in Gioconda Belli's famous phrase, it expressed the "tenderness of the people," the love of one people toward other peoples; it was, in Ernesto Cardenal's macro-vision, a key dimension of the evolutionary and indeed cosmic process of unity.

Belli's poem expresses the ties of this sentiment of solidarity to the Nicaraguan experience in the insurrection. The passages from Cardenal show how solidarity is an issue of state (and of liberation theology as well), pursued in the visits of Nicaraguan officials and representatives to conferences and gatherings in other parts of the world. The *tallerista* poems dealing with El Salvador point to how young Nicaraguans have thought about the struggle raging in their neighboring country. We are fortunate also to have a poem by Orlando Jose Tardencillas, the young Nicaraguan who fought in El Salvador, was imprisoned there and then upset U.S. State Department plans by refusing to parrot U.S. charges of Nicaraguan aid to the Salvadoran guerilla fighters. But perhaps the most interesting selection in this section is the expression of solidarity so tellingly and touchingly set forth in the parable of Antland, written by a young child in Leon. Clearly, solidarity is now firmly inscribed as a dimension of the hegemonic culture, and it is something to be defended at a high cost.

Indeed, it is only fitting that this book of cultural creation emphasizes the cultural dimension in its concluding sections. If anti-imperialism, solidarity and defense of the revolution are the dominant motifs of Part III, these motifs are nevertheless given greater substance by the parts dealing with poetry and women. Our poetry section presents poems and poetic excerpts about poetry, and demonstrates the self-consciousness of cultural producers with respect to the politicization of cultural life in a country undergoing revolution and counterrevolutionary attack. While Rosario Murillo, Vidaluz Meneses and other professional poets are represented in our section, it is dominated by young workshop writers and Sandinista militants, including a health brigade worker and several members of the Sandinista army and the militia.

The connection of this poetry to the period of anti-Somoza struggle is clear in the preoccupation with the model of poet-combatant most centered in the image of Leonel Rugama. That image was actively promoted in the early months of the Reconstruction, and it became more pronounced as the poetry and cultural activities of the nation developed in relation to escalating imperialist aggression. If anything, Sandinista poetry becomes even more militant, more politicized in the context of the Reconstruction and Intervention. As the poems in the poetry section and elsewhere reveal, writing poetry takes on the discursive norms of political language, and political, revolutionary work takes on the discursive norms of the poetic craft; poetry is protrayed as a force of revolutionary vigilance and militancy; revolutionary vigilance and militancy displace and transform the language even of love poetry. In effect, poetry, love and revolution achieve a contradictory, but creatively transformative identity.

We have had much to say about Nicaragua's new poetry elsewhere in this volume. Here, we wish to underline the fact that the developments in poetry and poetic discourse described and depicted throughout the course of this book are only heightened examples from an important, unique but nevertheless not isolated sphere of artistic and cultural creation of the work that has gone on in all the arts. Indeed, while Ministry of Culture-sponsored poetry workshops spread to the police force, the army and the militias, as part of the general dissemination of Sandinista cultural production, so too the Sandinista Association of Cultural Workers, under Rosario Murillo's direction, extended its work in terms of cultural brigades in the mountain and border areas--in fact, whereever Sandinista combatants trained, organized, kept watch or fought. From this perspective, we need only round off our orientation to the new poetry in Nicaragua by citing three related comments, the first two about the workshop poetry, and the final one about poetic production in the context of the cultural brigades involved in the defense against counterrevolutionary incursions.

Says John Beverley, ("Sandinista Poetics," in *The Minnesota Review*, ns 20 [Spring, 1983], pp. 127-134):

> *Poesia de taller* ... is a program, directed by Cardenal, to set up workshops where ordinary folks--soldiers, workers, housewives, children--can learn to write poems in (and about) their workplaces, homes and communities. The goal is the decentralization and disalienation of cultural production. ... Nicaragua is a country of poets, so there is a lively and healthy debate going on about the value of *poesia de taller*. ...

> Who gets translated in *Poesia Libre*, the official poetry journal of Cardenal's Sandinista Ministry of Culture? Brecht, of course; Palestinian poets; Sappho; Sioux and Eskimo songs; but also: Rexroth's collection of Japanese *tanka*; Muriel Rukeyser; Carl Sandburg; Allen Ginsburg; William Carlos Williams (especially Williams). This may seem odd in a country whose revolutionary anthem contains the line "Luchamos contra el yanqui, enemigo de la humanidad" (We fight against the yankee, enemy of all humanity). Yet the Nicaraguan poetry workshops ... seem to be dominated by the spirit of Williams' most prosaic poems or Kenneth Koch's work on teaching poetry to children.

> After reading a bunch of these poems you might get the impression that to write something in a non-W.C. Williams plain-speaking mode might be akin to an ideological crime. But these are small quibbles,

especially when the alternative is the sophisticated alienation of something like U.S. post-modernism. In communism, Marx remarked, there will be no poets as such; only people who, among other things, will write poetry. *Poesia de taller* points in that direction; it is a beginning, like all beginnings naive and wonderful at the same time.

Julio Valle Castillo, Head of the Literature Section in the Ministry of Culture, writes, in his Introduction to an issue of *Poesia Libre*:

Workshop poetry ... is a direct and profound poetry, it is the life of the people with their language, it is physical geography, it is the history of our Sandinista Revolution written in verse. A poetry full of emotions, of testimonial (battles, love) it is the neo-epic. We believe that this poetry in its language, in its way of relating humanity with the world, has a great value: it is a poetry written by the peasants of Niquinohomo, of Condega, of San Juan de Oriente, of Jinotega, Palacaguina; by construction workers; by Monimbo artisans; by militia soldiers, by literacy brigadeers, by members of the Sandinista Workers Center. By the people. The language they use is the same the people use while talking under a manocu tree, in the Cantagallo guerilla camp, in the San Miguelito port, or which they write a letter to Nilda Garcia, a literacy worker who died in Espino. The poetry technique's the same as William Carlos Williams used, or the one used on the Polynesian Islands, or the one used in present-day Salvadoran combat poetry.

Finally, Roberto Jose Leyva, member of the Rolando Orozco Brigrade of the Union of Sandinista Writers, explains in his article, "An Art Ever More Beautiful" (published in *Ventana* [July 9, 1983], p. 9):

[Jose] Marti said: Poetry is durable when it is the work of every one. Those who understand such work are as much the authors as those who create it. In the mountains, this message is encouraging. It provides orientation to artistic and literary work, because it obliges us, it commits us to our people. Its importance is in finding the social, spiritual and human needs of our brothers and sisters, in opening ever more ample roads of possibility for cultural work. There it becomes clear that our work as revolutionary artists in the cultural brigades is to seek the autocthonous, dig it out, and return it to the source from which it came: The People. Art in relation to People's Artists, is a significant example that we should reinforce and enrich, [so that we understand its enormous function] of disposing, recreating and expressing in a beautiful and joyful form, life, as necessity, as the spiritual satisfaction of the people. It is here that the people beautifully creating their culture, producing the definitive encounter between the people and their profoundly revolutionary, eminently humanistic artistic creation. Art as popular recreation, with immediate exigency in the social dimension.

The historical challenge set before us is to be capable of producing an art of quality that satisfies the people's taste, at the same time that it elevates their cultural level, an art rooted in the most beautiful of popular tradition and creation. And this art has its integral content, because by arriving in the mountains with our songs, poems, dances and paintings, we entered into the ideological struggle in the terrain of art responding with firmness and with the development of an art that has to be better, that has to be more beautiful than whatever art produced by the bourgeoisie. And the point is that they cannot produce an art better than ours, because they have nothing new to say, or express in their art. Our slogan of love in the mountains was all of our art for the poetry of life, against aggression and death.

--Drafted July 7, 1983.

5. *Women in the Process*

The question of women in the revolution requires a more extended commentary. For, as often noted, if there is one single dimension of cultural and revolutionary development that may serve as a measure of the whole, it is the emerging role of women. And we know that many revolutionary movements have been greatly hampered or have failed for not having developed this dimension in their struggle.

As noted in the introduction to Book I, the women of Nicaragua played a greater role in the Insurrection than perhaps the women of any other revolutionary struggle. Cutting across social class and sector lines, women's opposition to the dictatorship was an essential dimension of the revolutionary bloc necessary to the revolutionary victory. The pre-victory women's movement started with mothers, wives, sisters, and sweethearts---that is, women acting in a sense as traditional women, from their material base in these womenly social roles. But women as professionals and students gave, by nature of their predominantly middle sector background and orientation, a more independent thrust to the movement, which projected a more autonomous and individuated participation, even as the movement became linked to peasant and working class women.

The insurrection over, the question was what role women would play in the new, emerging order. It is true that cultural contradictions already existant in the pre-insurrectional period made women's active participation possible. But it is also true that people know the difference between their cultural norms and what they tolerate in what is defined as their "emergency situations." And we know that even those oppressed by a given set of norms tend to affirm them, for fear of losing the "secondary rewards" they have accrued in the midst of their oppression, that they are "culturally programmed" to maintain their roles rather than be left out on a limb. This is by no means to deny that the victimizers are those who fight most fiercely to maintain past norms, nor to deny the fact that the victimizers are also victimized, in longrun human terms by the oppressive system which gives them certain advantages that are ultimately crippling.

There is no question but that revolutionary culture in Central and Latin America, while paying some lip service to an elevated role for women, tends to have its machistic dimension, that the Revolution is seen as a situation in which men will cease to be slaves and will become ... men. And "uneven development" in this case can mean that those who are most revolutionary in their values and words in the public sphere are most quick to defend traditional roles and rewards in the private. Nothing could be more revolutionary for the total structure of a society than a transformation in the structure of family and private life. But obviously nothing could be more difficult to attain than this latter transformation, even in a process which like the Nicaraguan Reconstruction, tends to blur and at times eradicate the lines between public and private.

Traditional norms had already gone by the boards in the insurrectional period, but the euphoric weeks after the victory were also a period of uniting families, which is to say reinforcing and reaffirming dimensions of the past, as well as a time of "general copulation" and baby-making. The notion of the revolutionary woman who would carry on in the Reconstruction vied with an image of the *muchacha guerillera*, who, the enemy defeated, lays down her sub-machine gun, puts her uniform in the closet, and, at home in the bosom of the family, begins to take on her roles as sweetheart, wife and mother. But it soon became evident that the "emergency situation" was not over, and that indeed, "emergency" might well become the new norm. Furthermore, lacking "middle cadre" to carry on the tasks of the Revolution, even the most unconsciously and deeply machistic Sandinistas knew that large numbers of women had to be involved in the process to the extent of their capacities and skills.

While the majority of Nicaragua's women had been oppressed in education and the development of advanced practical skills, nevertheless their oppression had provided them with the traditional virtues of patience, discipline and commitment which were important to the process; and indeed many middle sector women, either through their education, professional experience or their roles as home managers, did possess skills necessary to the Revolution.

Finally, as the efforts to keep faith with the primary goal of the Revolution, that is, to build a society meeting the needs of poor people, began to erode the insurrectional bloc, as more and more members of the middle and upper bourgeoisie began to oppose the Revolution, and as U.S. intervention plunged the nation into deeper crisis, the need to compensate for losses by mobilizing every possible sector meant that structurally, and aside from whatever constraints *machismo* might create, women, represented by women's organizations, and stressing the concerns of poor women throughout the country, had to participate in significant ways. This meant, also that while women might be told (and might believe) that their particular issues must play second fiddle to the broader national goals, those issues would be given a certain respect, and would, in cases where the overall national importance of given issues was patent enough, become the basis for legislative and direct action.

Early in the Reconstruction, the insurrectional women's organization AMPRONAC, took on a new name, AMNLAE, the Luisa Amanda Espinoza Association of Nicaraguan Women, after the first FSLN woman to die fighting the National Guard. In the organization's initial phase, the main goal was to incorporate women into the basic tasks of Reconstruction: the literacy and health campaigns, the neighborhood committees, the army and the militias.

Women constituted over 75% of the 50-plus % illiterate in Nicaragua. Thus it is no surprise that thousands of women who could read and write scoured the nation's neighborhoods and villages teaching basic Spanish and basic mathematics. Under Somoza, only 20% of women received consistent health care, so it is not surprising that women came to make up over 80% of the volunteer workers in the health campaigns of 1981 and 1982. In this capacity, they traveled to various communities, giving vaccinations, teaching paramedics and giving families instruction on basic hygiene and preventive health care. In 1982, AMNLAE conducted a thorough self-evaluation of its organizational structure, and decided to change its role from that of a mass organization to a political movement. It identified critical sectors where women worked, studied, organized or cared for their home and children (the markets, factories, farms, schools, homes, neighborhoods, unions, Christian communities, etc.), and sought to develop women's caucuses within these arenas to ensure that women's issues were taken seriously in all of them.

As the national crisis over U.S. interference and intervention emerged, the organization reconstituted itself in function of the following goals: promoting fuller women's participation in every sector; helping women to develop ideological and political clarity; coordinating with other existing organizations; and bringing consciousness and action with respect to *machismo* and women's concerns to the heart of the FSLN. The organization also designated several particular areas of struggle: proposing and advocating for legislation that affects women's lives, dealing with the problem of family abandonment and child support claims, ending women's underemployment; involvement in the militias.

In an effort to formulate legislative proposals on women, AMNLAE spoke to women of all class and occupational sectors to determine what they felt was most important. Then lawyers did legal research to create first drafts for new laws. The drafts were then taken back to the sectors for feedback before final versions were submitted to the Council of State. Utilizing these procedures, AMNLAE succeeded in using its Council membership to wipe out many discriminatory laws and guarantee women's full legal equality. An early victory was the prohibition on publishing and distributing commercial and promotional material which used women as sexual objects. Another was a law assuring the jobs of pregnant women. AMNLAE also promoted a rape law that included measures against rape by husbands.

The question of "parental responsibility" also spurred on several intense debates before legislative proposals were set. The issue was a serious one, given the high frequency of men abandoning families in which their spouses had severely limited economic means or job prospects. Social Welfare Ministry officials complained that "many [male] workers who are ideologically identified with the revolution ... are not so revolutionary at the hour of confronting ... their ... parental responsibility."

One law passed in this area stripped fathers of their automatic authority within the family by mandating that parents living together must share decision-making about the children and that when parents are separated, the authority rests with the parent who lives with the children. A second law, in response to the presence of 40,000 earthquake and war orphans, allowed single people to adopt children. But a third law, forcing men to assume legal and financial responsibility for ther children even if they don't live with them, most directly addressed the most endemically serious problem facing countless Nicaraguan women. Although far from solving the problem or of resolving a large per centage of the male abuses in this area, the law has enabled thousands of women to apply for and receive child support payments. A battle was won, but the struggle continues.

Another major problem affecting women and the nation as a whole is the fact that while many women remain the prime or only economic support of their families, most are employed in marginal sectors of the economy. AMNLAE specifically addressed such primary concerns as the situation of seamstresses, domestic workers and prostitutes. Domestic housework, while a recognized evil, remained a necessary occupation for many women who had been provided with no alternative productive skill. Domestic clothing production is important for a nation geared to cotton exportation, even though it is often a low-pay occupation.

Finally, widespread prostitution, especially in the urban and port areas, has been the basis of support for many children, and has hardly been liquidated by the new revolutionary morality, especially when the women involved are already hardened to the life and have no productive alternative. AMNLAE has attempted to address the first problem by developing projects aimed at the socialization of domestic work. It has given high priority to establishing day care centers and organizing community laundry and dining facilities, and to promoting the concept that child care is not just the responsibility of mothers but of the whole society. With respect to domestic clothing production, AMNLAE has set up sewing collectives nationwide, in which experienced seamstresses teach their skills to other women. As for the problem of prostitution, AMNLAE has established rehabilitation centers and sought to provide counselling, peer support and alternative job training.

It is in the latter area, the generation of higher level job training and employment of women, as well as the ever growing development of unions and other organizational structures to deal with basic questions of women's employment, that AMNLAE seeks long term solutions to the three specific problems mentioned here, and innumerable other problems which face women workers in Nicaragua. Needless to say, the gains that women have won in the legal system, workplace and home are not generalized evenly and smoothly to all sectors and situations. And increasingly, since 1981, U.S. destablization and military intervention have constituted a national emergency which, while helping to sustain certain advances and even recuperate certain others, have nevertheless back-burnered several important matters that require attending to.

While women played major roles in the Insurrectional combat, after the war high-ranking women officers were relegated to strictly political work. Continuing sexism in EPS ranks led AMNLAE leaders to argue that women could not play their full military role within the frame of male-dominated army units. Their argument only achieved success as the national crisis came on. In spite of frequently loud protests at home, women joined the militias in growing numbers. Then in June, 1981, Nicaragua's first all-women battalion left Leon to defend Nicaragua's northern border from *contra* attacks.

Two days later, AMNLAE demonstrated in Esteli, demanding and winning the right to form an all-women's battalion in a town where women already constituted over 60% of all militia members. Since this early period, women have distinguished themselves in national defense.

Without a continuing revolution of the situation of women, there can be no sustained revolution in everyday life and the everyday values which inform every institution and every project of a society. The future of women, and therefore of the revolution itself, is largely dependent on how, even in the midst of class struggle, economic crisis and military aggression, the women themselves find ways to continue their struggle and advance toward full and satisfactory social participation.

Our section of women writing poetry about women depicts the process of women's growing consciousness and field of action from the insurrectional period on into most critical hours of intervention faced during the Reconstruction. Clearly, the growing independent role of women has been paralleled by their ever increasing contribution to political poetry from the late 1960's to the present. And that contribution to poetry ultimately crystalizes in works specifically on the question of women in the Revolution. Indeed, we may say that the increasing proliferation and evolving character of this poetry parallels and reveals much about the development of AMNLAE itself.

Just as AMNLAE grew out of middle sector women's opposition to Somoza and only gradually linked itself with Sandinista peasant and workers' opposition, so early women's political poetry, including poetry on the specific theme of women, was mainly a product of progressive middle sector women. Our section reflects this predominance through the work of Gioconda Belli, Vida Luz Meneses, Rosario Murillo, Cristian Santos and Daisy Zamora (as well as Alfonso Robelo's wife, Indiana Cardenal, whose writing of militant poetry suggests the kind of tensions that have developed and ruptured many bourgeois households). And it was only as we were preparing the final version of this section, that we discovered examples of new emerging people's workshop poetry appropriate for inclusion. Furthermore, just as the theme of intervention dominates all of Nicaraguan life in the period from 1981 on, so it begins to dominate in the final selections of this section. Overall and in the fullest sense, then, this section can be said to express the evolving, ever more committed and militant consciousness of women in the new Nicaragua. Given our view on the advances of women, we may also say that this section symptomizes the cultural and ideological advance of the entire process of the Revolution on the eve of its fourth anniversary.

CHRONOLOGY: AUGUST - OCTOBER, 1982

August: The GNR sends the U.S. a note reiterating its desire for peace talks, and proposing that the points of negotiation put forth by each side the previous spring be the basis for initiating the negotiating process.. The U.S. reduces the Nicaraguan sugar importation quota by 90%. The month is a critical one on the religious front, as Church-State relations reach new levels of crisis.

September: The Presidents of Mexico and Venequela appeal to the heads of state of Honduras, Nicaragua and the U.S., calling for an exploration of ways to halt the escalation of the crisis. One hundred and six Congress members endorse the proposal. Lt. Colonel John Buchanan, USMC (Ret.) briefs a House subcommittee on the critical border tension between Honduras and Nicaragua, indicating that Nicaragua's "military buildup" is "defensive in nature." Pointing to Reagan's exaggerations of Nicaragua's military capacity, Buchanan also warns of a possible Honduran invasion in December and concludes that "the Reagan administration is distorting the facts in order to justify covert operations aimed at overthrowing the Sandinistas and an unprecedented military buildup in Honduras."

October: Attempting to blunt the Mexican-Venezuelan peace initiative, the Reagan administration backs its "forum for peace and democracy" in San Jose, Costa Rica. Nicaragua is excluded from the forum, and Mexico and Venezuela decline to attend. Standard Fruit abandons the country.

Section 1. Defending the Revolution

1. Fernando Rodriguez, Ciudad
   Dario Poetry Workshop/
   REVOLUTIONARY VIGILANCE

I've been keeping revolutionary
   watch
for three nights.
50 meters from my trench is
the church tower with its clocks,
two of them destroyed by an M-50
fired from the Shell station
by the Sandinistas

as they pushed out the guards
who commanded the city from the
   tower.
The clock on the eastern side marks
   2 a.m.
Two bells are heard all over the city
alerting the kids when we keep
   watch
on the neighborhoods of Ciudad
   Dario.

2. Francisco Torres, Masaya Poetry Workshop/ TO MY BROTHER JULIO

I've worked in the popular health campaigns,
repaired desks for the work-study project,
collected books in the Masaya neighborhoods
for the National Library Campaign,
and at night while bourgeois children sleep
I take revolutionary watch turn
and try to be revolutionary.

3. Carlos Pineda, Condega Poetry Workshop/ TO TATIANA ARMIDO

Cantagallo, a mountain of 3,500 feet
above sea level,
northeast of Condega.
It served as a guerrilla camp
before and after the Insurrection.
There is a cave full of moss
damp in all seasons.
In this very cave
your body was conserved
by the mountain cold without decomposing
(you died accidentally while keeping watch, Tatiana).

4. Rosario Garcia, Palacaguina Poetry Workshop/ YOU TOLD ME HOW THEY KILLED YOUR BROTHER

You told me how they killed your brother
and your eyes filled with tears.
--It was the Guards stationed
in Honduras--you said--they nabbed him
and beat him till they got bored
and one of them said it would be better
to slaughter him as if he were an animal.
When your mother arrived to claim him
at a hospital in Tegucigalpa,
she looked at him torn to pieces
with a sign on his chest
that said "Sandino-communist."

5. Cristian Santos/ HONOR GUARD

Four Militia kids
form an honor guard
before the bier of Luis
on their faces
    pain and conviction
and on the face of Luis
eyes and lips half-opened
"We couldn't close them...
through the mountains
till we busted their asses...
later we gathered up his body
and going up against the river's current,
we brought him to his mother."
The kids tell me this with tenderness
when they end their honor guard duty
for Luis.

6. Margaret Randall/ LETTER FROM NICARAGUA

All you want to do is murder us,
    those who have survived
your several dress rehearsals.
It's not that serious yet, most of us

don't meet your person-level:
neither robust nor blue-eyed
nor promising according to your
    current IQ
or the Rorschach
that defines your sense of life
Forgive us if we don't agree
with your definition of the N-Bomb
the binary chemical solution
or the Salvadoran solution
as an adequate pain-killer.
We're sufficiently underdeveloped
to want to deal with
our pain in our own primitive way.
Forgive us too if we can't fully
    answer
your questions about our society,
    define it
as marxist-leninist or
    social-democrat,
agreeably pluralist
or sufficiently free enterprise.
If we insist on the crudity
of exploring our own creative
    process
loving our homeland with the
    passion
50,000 sisters and brothers
root in our throats.
Excuse us, please, we're always
    forgetting
we were supposed to ask permission
to defend our truth
and distribute our laughter as we
    see fit.
Don't bother yourselves trying to
    understand
our teaching our soldiers poetry
    along with defense combat
self respect and how to write their
    names
in ink instead of blood.
When our grandparents scraped
    their living
from this land you sent your
    Marines.

Later you provided us with "one of
    our own":
bought and paid for
by your American Way of Life.
He had a brother and a son, a
    grandson
and infinite pockets.
We said goodbye more than once
but you trained a legion of our
    brothers
bought them off and kept them in
    shape
(to keep us in shape)
and the shape they kept us in
was increasingly pine-boxed and
    horizontal.
Here it was a crime to be young,
and you reminded us daily of that
    crime
committed by so many, and so often.
But we kept forgetting, we fought
    and came up
from your undying friend
and his protective Guard.
We fought and won, we buried
our sisters and brothers (few were
    blond
or met your standards for
    personhood)
and we began the long pain, the
    silent joy,
the impossible made possible by a
    history
of eyes and hands.
We know we don't meet your
general 1982 standards for
    dependent nations.
All you want to do is murder us.
All we want to do is live.

7. Felipe Saenz, EPS/ THE LAST
    WAR

You who in this war
did nothing for the people

and raised your fists
to the height of our eyes,
who saw a sea of blood
    and bones
    in the night
    and, secure,
clasped the dictator's hand.
You, poor animals,
ruled by fear
unable to grasp the true song
of these new days
and not knowing
what was made of your names.
You who smiled
at the hunger of your children
and who unhappy never found
the true road of humanity.
You who were saved from oblivion
    brother assassins
    soldiers of falsehood
You shall not return
we assure you
tearful with joy
    20 years
    40 years
    80 years
  after our victory
  to bloom in these fields
because this is the last cemetery
  of your generations.

8. Isidoro Tercero, Interior Ministry
Poetry Workshop/ BETWEEN
OCOTAL AND SUSUCAYA

Today the rain sprinkles the earth
and the Agrarian Reform arrived
we have the rifles
the schools,
  organized, defeating capitalism.
The cornfields are blooming.

9. Alberto Garcia, Ajax Delgado
Police Complex Poetry Workshop
(Managua)/ IT DOESN'T
MATTER
(*To my companeros crippled in the
war*)

It doesn't matter
that Mario Peralta's fingers are
  mutilated
from a bullet fired by the National
  Guard.
Mario, the one left disabled
after the battle's now in a wheel
  chair.
It doesn't matter that my left leg's
  whithered
from a fracture in my vertebral
  column.
We made a Revolution
and we're going to defend it.

10. Daniel Ortega Saavedra/ WHAT
PEOPLE*

What people is going to cross their
  arms
when they try to take back their
  conquests?
That's why the people are in the
  Militias,
in the Defense Committees, in the
  Police,
in the Ministry of Internal Affairs,
in the reserve battalions,
in the defense of their interests.
It has been our task to consolidate
an entire revolutionary project
of political and economic
  independence,
of justice and freedom,
of non-alignment and defense,
of the people's right to
  self-determination.
All this against the will of U.S.

power,
which tries to kill the Sandinist
  Revolution
and with it hopes for change
in Central America.
We tell our people
we are confident
that reason will prevail
over war-mongering madness,
but we must prepare for the worst,
ready to resist, ready to fight,
ready, whatever way circumstances
  demand,
to defeat imperialist aggression and
  invasion.

11. Mario Martinez, EPS/ THE LAST MARINES

And the struggle my love
          is to end with
the last marines
made in USA: with Soooza
                with Popeye
                with Superman
and the ducks of Walt Disney.

12. Marvin Rios, Ernesto Castillo Poetry Workshop (Managua)/ WAITING

In the distance a vulture flies by
like a push-pull plane set to attack,
turning and turning as it flies
  overhead.
My militia companeros
leave their trails on pastures
and their rifles shine in the sun.
A fighter plane flies over the hill
and in my watch post
I protect the route of my
  companeros.
The plane is ours.
Now I see the columns

keep on advancing
          firm
awaiting the enemy.

13. Juan Ignacio Centeno, Condega Poetry Workshop/ LOVE AMONG THE RESERVES

Mariel
let me now begin to kiss
your cheeks
your lips,
your body.
Perhaps tomorrow will be too late
and the Yankee Marines will be
  here once more.
Then you'll be curing wounded
  companeros,
and I'll be in the line of fire.

14. Giconda Belli/ SONG OF WAR

The war will come, love
and in the combat we'll give no
  quarter
nor put brakes on our song,
but poetry will be born from the
  dark holes
of our rifle barrels.
The war will come, love
and we'll lose ourselves in the
  trenches
digging for the future
on the outskirts of the Homeland
at the point of our hearts and fire
detaining the barbarian hordes
who seek to rob what we are and
  what we love.
The war will come, love
and I'll wrap myself in your
  invincible shadow
like a wild lionness
I'll protect the land of my children
and no one will deny this victory

armed to the teeth with the future.
Although we won't see each other
for so long that our memories may
    die,
I pledge to you clutching Nicaragua

like a baby girl on her mother's
    breast:
THEY'LL NOT PASS, LOVE,
WE SHALL OVERCOME!

CHRONOLOGY: NOVEMBER, 1982 - JANUARY, 1983

November: The GNR declares a military emergency in one fourth of the country as *contra* groups attack northern towns seeking to disrupt harvests. *Newsweek* reveals extensive details of the U.S. paramilitary war on Nicaragua. U.S. officials affirm that the operation is intended to "keep Managua off balance and apply pressure." During a visit to Washington, Costa Rican President Monge warns President Reagan of the dangers U.S. policies might pose for the region. Reagan responds with polite silence. The GNR decrees a Military Emergency in one fourth of the country. Opposition groups, including the Revolutionary Patriotic Front and the Ramiro Sacasa Coordinating Committee, participate in GNR-sponsored discussions over political functioning in the years to come.

December: Reagan designs his Latin American trip to include visits with leaders of all three countries neighboring Nicaragua. GNR junta member Sergio Ramirez points out that U.S. diplomats continue to refuse to see high-level Sandinista officials. The U.S. has still not responded to Nicaragua's diplomatic note of August, 1982 urging peace talks. The U.S. also continues to oppose peace talks between Nicaragua and Honduras, as over 800 troops enter Nicaragua and attempt to take Jalapa.

January: Preparations are made for a new stage in the anti-FSLN campaign. Six task forces of roughly 2,000 armed men begin probing the border areas, attempting to take Rio Blanco, Bismuna and Northern Zelaya, with the goal of then moving into the nation's mining areas. Jeanne Kirkpatrick visits Latin American countries to bolster Reagan's Pro-Peace and Democracy Forum. More than 6,500 health posts are set up for a vaccination campaign, and more than 35,000 volunteers enter a one-month training course. Roughly 20,000 volunteers participate in the cotton harvest; and well over 11,000 join the Matagalpa coffee harvest. Eight persons, including two young children are killed in the harvest, and there are various kidnappings and disappearances. Diplomats from Colombia, Venezuela, Mexico and Panama meet on Contadora Island to begin working on an alternative to the U.S.'s plans for Central America.

262

Section 2. *The Poets & the People*

1. Rosario Murillo/ DEDICATION

"If our lives are needed in the work for liberation we develop among the masses, then let's offer our lives without waiting to be mentioned in the history of generations. But we may rest assured that our bones are the spinal column of this history." --RUGAMA, 11/68

Rest assured, Leonel!
You are the spinal column
of this history!

2. Mayra Jimenez/ IN THE SANDINO AIRPORT

In the Poetry Workshops
they have written poems
about the Masaya lagoon, the Coco River,
the Carlos Aguero Military School, Leon,
Pochomil, Shepherd's Hill in Achuapa...
The new poetry in the Revolution.

3. Juan Herrera Salazar, Jinotega Poetry Workshop/ LEONEL RUGAMA

Poet Leonel Rugama
today in the poetry workshops
we write an epic.
The poets of the militia
the poets of the Sandinist Police
the poets of Condega and Esteli
we shall make known the process of changes.
Poet Isidoro Cantillano will sing
of the border incidents
poet Domingo Moreno,
the mysteries of love in the country.
Yalmar Luna, the quaint people of

his town.
We shall replace the blue prince
and the maidens
we shall speak of the combatants
who pardon the Guards.
I shall continue writing about the war declared
against diarrheas
about the hospital combat against pseudomonas,
we shall replace verses that proclaim
cosmic solitude
glacial abysses
metal noises of fluid sadness
with poetry that seems a kiss
a kiss mouth to mouth
tongue
tongue to talk of the fallen of Pancasan
of the heroes of Raiti and Bocay.
Don't worry
this poetry is born any and everywhere
a whole continent shall listen
to the epic of the Revolution.
Poetry, love and Revolution
are all the same thing.
On the 19th of July
they'll all be in the plaza
all those you called

they shall all be present there to
    talk
            listen and do
            things saints do.

4. Marta Liset Silva, San Judas
    Barrio Poetry Workshop,
    Managua/ YESTERDAY &
    TODAY

In Leon, Masaya, Esteli, Matagalpa
    and Managua
all was tears and anguish.
Mothers on their knees
before the Somoza Guards
so they wouldn't carry off their
    children,
while in the mountains the guerrilla
    fighters
suffered from sleepless nights, from
    hunger,
from fever
in order to liberate the people.
Today we see the happiness of the
    children
and I see the joyful faces of the
    mothers.
Now I study, I go to the cotton
    pickings
I belong to the Association
of Sandinist Children.
I write poetry at the age of
    thirteen.

5. Marlene Falcon Vilchez, Condega
    Poetry Workshop/ IN THE
    OFFICE

I tried to give form to a poem
while I looked at verse after verse
that Fernando had written.
In the office,
everything confused me:
the folders with written pages

and on the right side of the desk
some drawings of Carlos Pineda
(skull on dirty sheets
 with writings on the other side)
and they made me
leave the poem unfinished,
leave it and begin to write other
    things
that made me remember you more,
    Mayra.

6. Indiana Cardenal/ ENCOUNTER
    IN THE WORDS

        "*And the pain I feel
        the longing I have to see her*"
        --LEONEL RUGAMA

I read your poems
your absence takes form
I imprison the intangible
and savor your words
with the rim of my eyes.
I hear your sound, your voice.
I almost feel you.
I don't know you
and I've never seen you.
I want to talk to you, tell you
my things, read you my poems.
I seek you and find you in the
    words.
I only wish to extend myself
in your memory.

7. Murillo/ IT'S TRUE WE'RE
    BUILDING A WORLD

Who can I tell
that I know the laws and priorities
that I recognize poetry in a face,
    in being wide awake, in vigilance
that I understand the importance of
    technique
that I live in anguish

that I dream of solutions
that tears still come to my eyes
that the national anthem gives me
   goose bumps
and that in the eyes
of little boys with big bellies
I find the wise eyes of the dead?
Who can I explain this to
without shame or blame?
Who? Before the homeless people...
the bare hospitals, the benchless
   schools,
the artisans with no materials
to do their work,
the migrating
   peasants...Imperialism.
Who is going to believe
in the urgency of a poem
that makes demands on us
as if it were the only one in the
   world
as if it were building a world?

8. Ana Sofia Martinez, Palacaguina
Poetry Workshop/ A POEM

I like to write about life in the
   Revolution,
about love,
the death of brigade members
and Militia leaders,
about the peasants from the
   National Union
of Farm and Cattle Workers,
about the dawns in the mountains
with birds and butterflies
the sun rising over the post where
   the sentry
watches over the Sandinista Air
   Force base,
about Mombacho in the Lake,
my grandfather sowing the land
going to the runway to see the T-33
   come in,

seeing the children's joy
in the Berta Diaz barrio
playing guerrilla fighters arguing
   who'll be
Sandino, Carlos Fonseca
or Rigoberto Lopez Perez,
about the border guard keeping
   vigil,
the Security Company's change of
   guard
and the soldiers marching,
their rifles shining under a full moon
or about hearing the speeches of
   Tomas Borge
in the July 19th Plaza
remembering the heroes and
   announcing that
the land belongs to the peasant who
   works it.
As if such things were poems.

9. Carlos Calero, Ernesto Castillo
Poetry Workshop, Managua/
NEXT TO YOU

In this revolution life is like writing
   a poem,
the elements are here:
in the streets, in the factory,
participating in the work,
in study, on the job, or better:
being with you--giving you my all--
without saying words;
in the slogans we've shouted
in the Plaza of the Revolution,
in the voluntary work going
in the columns of workers
while the sun comes out over
   Granada Lake.
It's enough to say I love you fully,
that I feel life depends on what all of
   us do.
And learning to die for our people
to have the right to love and be free.

10. Murillo/ SHADOWS AT DAWN

I need to arm the sky with my
    songs
assault memories
and make them rain renewing the
    grass.
I should find a torrent of clear
    water
to wash my knotted hair in the
    morning sun.
I'm going to look for a perfect
    rainbow,
a song that atunes to the madness
    of the poem,
a verb that becomes flesh
and a love unknown, infinite,
that leaves me like a Sunday
    magician
boasting of marvels and mysteries.
I want a tree with flowers
a plaza with flags and choirs
a slogan born of the people
repeated, infinite, dazzling;
the face of Carlos Fonseca in the
    wind
A Sandino, a Rigoberto, a Rugama
I want a love with subject,
predicate and rifle
a familiar refrain
a collective prayer, I want the
    dawn
to initiate these hands still new and
    clumsy
to draw me to the creation of this
    world.

11. Aldo Ramirez, Ajax Delgado Police Complex Poetry Workshop, Managua/ TO FRANCISCO TORRES (CHILD-POET)

When I read your poem
about your fallen brother,
I knew you profoundly.

I want to ask you to let me be your
    brother.
Let me give you materially
what your brother would give you
    today.
When you want a pair of pants, a
    shirt, a book,
come and ask for it without shame.
Let me feel happy.
Let me be your brother.
Come and ask for me.

12. Daisy Zamora/ LETTER TO CORONEL URTECHO

All we spoke of has now become
    certain
and the words are alive and breathe
and for the first time we can clutch
    them
as one clutches a guis, a duck...
not to hurt them, but just to set
    them flying
over the most beautiful summer in
    La Azucena.
The words have acquired
the concrete form of things
and from your San Juan River
    school come to be
    artesanal workshops, agricultural
    production
    and cattle development centers.
Libraries, health centers,
    cooperatives
and the first cultural house in the
    history
of the old port of San Carlos come to
    be
You think now that I've forgotten it
when all these days I've been saying
    to you
these beautiful words that in our old
    walks
were only dreams.
Any way I write them down

so that they're writ
in your history and in mine
(I imagine you now in your
   inevitable beret,
walking stick and white long sleeve
   shirt
reading or conversing or closing the
   door
of your house at six in the afternoon
or perhaps waiting for my arrival
or this letter.)

13. Murillo/ POINT NUMBER 1 ON
   THE AGENDA

Over what tombs
what drownings
over what proud spirit of giving
   birth
does one write Poetry today?

14. Carlos Manuel Galan, Ajax
   Delgado Police Complex Poetry
   Workshop (Managua)/
   COMMANDER CHE

I see you on my white tee-shirt
with your gaze fixed and serene.
Your hair messy and a thought of
   yours
that I wrote below your picture:
"He who works has a right to rest
but can't be a man of the
   vanguard."
That's what I wrote on my white
   tee-shirt,
next to the poem I wrote for you,
   Commander.

15. Falcon/ WHEN I FEEL ALONE

Seated in one of the blue chairs of
   my home
I want to write poems to the

Revolution
like the ones I wrote to Aunner,
to Argentina
to Alonso in the literacy Campaign
to the coffee harvests us students
   worked on
and I want to write about Urlando
   Pineda
(killed in September, '79)
about the militia men and women
   who today
left in their battalions for the
   mountains.
A year ago they themselves went
   dressed
as brigadistas to teach the peasants.
I also think
about the communities of young
   Christians
working for the Revolution,
about the Sandinist Youth,
about the National Literacy Crusade
when at this time all the squadrons,
all of us, came back down to town
sad because we would no longer be
with the peasants playing guitar
   and singing
and the nights telling stories of the
   region,
of Sandino,
sharing everything with them
and happy to find ourselves
with family, boyfriends and friends
recounting our experiences
of the last five months.
I'm done writing
and now I don't feel alone
   I'm with the Revolution.

16. Carlos Gadea/ CARLOS
   AGUERO SCHOOL

I have your last poem in front of
   me
and I'm writing to you
from this military school, my love.

I've also suffered the torment of my
    leaving,
and I've cried like you.
At the end of April I'll come
to start our new life
and then we'll work together in the
    Revolution.
Save your poems in the same folder
    as mine,
    as if they were yours
        poet.

17. Vida Luz Meneses/ TO
    GUILLERMO
    FRONTIERGUARD & HIS
    BROTHERS & SISTERS

Today I heard the poem you
    dedicated to us,
and I grew aware of the nostalgic
    echo
we left you in the chest.
How can I explain that we make
    pact with you
and make you feel even here we
    fight for life?
How can I make this tensed fist
    reach you,
probably with an ensemble of
    weaknesses,
which, united, achieve their vigorous
    force?
With what words can we slip

into your shooting well
to murmur our presence in your ear
and offer you our songs
to fill your watch time?

18. Luis Santiago del Palacio
    Gomez, EPS Infantry Battalion
    Medical Services/ LOVE
    OFFENSIVE

With these verses
I'm trying to locate
the command post
of your feelings
to locate it and launch
a mortar shot of love
and burn your heart
with my presence.

19. Santiago/ TO MY BELOVED
    WIFE

Just as I write you
verses of love,
I would like to create
verses that track,
verses that puncture,
verses that burn,
and make them by the thousand
to launch them
in decisive form
at the heart of the enemy.

CHRONOLOGY: FEBRUARY - APRIL, 1983

February: Over 5,000 troops take part in Honduran Big Pine Operations; other military exercises take place in Panama. The CDS's organize large assemblies and "Face the People" forums to discuss the Housing Law. More than 100,000 participate in a protest in front of the U.S. Embassy. Demonstrations throughout the country for Augusto C. Sandino Ideological Study Week, ending with a demonstration of 50,000 in Ocotal. ANDEN (Nicaraguan National Teachers Association) celebrates its anniversary with a speech by Tomas Borge defending public education in answer to recent Episcopal pronouncements. AMNLAE holds a Commitment Assembly, handing out membership cards to more than 3,000 outstanding women in the Department of Managua. Over 5,000 attend the assembly, which is part of AMNLAE's consolidation process underway throughout the country. The CST (Sandinista Workers Confederation) holds its First National Constitutive Assembly with more than 400 delegates representing factories, industries and trade unions from all over the country. The Assembly elects a National Council and Secretariat, develops proposals for the 1983 operational plan, including revision of salary scale, bargaining power improvements, adult education reforms, etc., as part of a 6-month union democratizing process. On February 26, a march and demonstration are held in Masaya to honor the Militia's fourth anniversary; and the first military training course of 1983 begins the same day. At month's end, counterrevolutionary attacks escalate, with the *contras* terrorizing peasant settlements and making their most significant attack to date, on San Jose de las Mulas. It becomes clear the *contras* are planning a major action as preparations are made for the Pope's visit.

March: Nicaragua sends two protest notes to George Shultz denouncing Somocista actions and the obvious buildup of *contra* forces. The Pope's visit stirs great controversy in Nicaragua and throughout the world. Meanwhile, in Costa Rica, a series of news stories in various newspapers distorts the picture of the war in Nicaragua, using falsified photos and making claims for counterrevolutionary victories that never took place. However, *contra* assaults increase in number and intensity, and it is clear that the situation is becoming progressively serious. FDN forces march into central Matagalpa province, advancing as close as 60 miles from Managua. Simultaneously Miskitu Indians attack on the Atlantic coast, and initial clashes occur between Eden Pastora's ARDE troops and the Nicaraguan army. The U.S. media announce a probable invasion, but Central American sources speak of "probes," "testing actions" or "dress rehearsals" aimed at gauging FSLN mobilizing capacity and the *contras'* ability to coordinate and sustain their own efforts. However, the Sandinista troops and militia counterattack fiercely on various fronts, inflicting heavy casualties and sending *contras* scurrying across the border. Junta member Sergio Ramirez confirms that the GNR will do whatever is needed to preserve the Revolution and continue developing production and services. Defense and production in the search for peace is the nation's current theme.

April: The CIA concludes that "the Sandinistas needed to be considerably weaker before they would start to even teeter, much less topple" (Jack Epstein and J.H. Evans, "Aiming for Jugular in Nicaragua Raids" *In These Times* [Nov. 9-15, 1983], p. 3.) Throughout the month, the FDN and ARDE accelerate their recruitment, swelling insurgent ranks from 4,000 to 7,000 by months' end. *Contras* keep on attacking throughout the month, opening up the Southern Front by sending in roughly two hundred soldiers from Costa Rica. Kidnappings and killings occur in the Tasba Parni area, while there are 12 violations of Nicaraguan air space along the southern border, and attacks on Halouver, Cruz Verde and Sarabiqui. On April 27, Reagan delivers his major address attacking the Revolution and attempting to justify continuing and escalating war against the FSLN. He stresses the "totalitarian nature" of the government, as well as the ubiquitous issue of arms supplies to El Salvador.

Section 3. Imperialism, Solidarity & the Vision of Unity

1. Ernesto Cardenal/ FOUNDING OF THE LATIN AMERICAN HUMAN RIGHTS ASSOCIATION

The row of Latin American flags is just one
mix of borderless national colors.
From the iguana things slowly
    arrived
  at this species
denouncing Fascist regimes from the
    microphone.
We are animal, each one separate,
    individual.
  Animal the same as the iguana.
But together we are NOT animal,
  we are humanity:
humanity defending the rights of
    humanity.
From life in the stalks there's a
    great advance.
We are some strange being:
a being that is diverse and one.
  There's only One.
I remain looking at length at my
    species,
although flash bulbs and spotlights
    blind me.
Solidarity with Bolivia, with El
    Salvador,
is a human endeavor that took off
with our sister the iguana.

2. Benjamin Monge, September 14th Neighborhood Poetry Workshop (Managua)/ ARRIVALS

Helped and financed by Queen
    Isabel of Spain,
Christopher Columbus arrived in
    America
with three ships:
The Pinta, the Nina and the Santa
    Maria.
He sailed seeking the Indies
and losing his way, arrived in
    Guarani
  (today called the Bahamas).
He usurped the native name
  and called it San Salvador.
They raped, brought in venereal
    diseases,
horses and arms to murder the
    Indians
(all of them were Europeans).
Now in another San Salvador, ships
    arrive
bringing howitzers, helicopters,
    planes
to assassinate the Salvadoran
    population.
And they're helped and financed
by the transnational corporations,
    imperialism.

3. Segundo Ramos, Sandinista Air
   Force Poetry Workshop/ HOW
   TO HELP OTHER PEOPLES

I was surprised by the noise
of the Lacsa airplane turbines
taking off for other countries
and I knew it would arrive in El
   Salvador
where the people are fighting in
   Santa Ana,
Perquin, Suchitoto, Guazapa and
   Aguilares.
I would like to be there at this
   moment
firing my rifle, helping this people
but I'm in Nicaragua helping to
   consolidate
the Sandinista Revolution
and I know that this is one of the
   ways
to express my solidarity for other
   peoples
who struggle to be free.

4. Patricia Hernandez, Masaya
   Workers Center Poetry
   Workshop/ IN THE STREETS

Every day the streets of San
   Salvador fill with transients
   looking for jobs.
The stores remain open with the
   shelves
filled with clothes, cosmetics, jewels,
foreign dolls that all say:
MADE IN U.S.A.
The walls of the Sheraton Hotel,
of the Mortgage Bank,
the Siman and Europa department
   stores,
the national palace, the cathedral
--all the walls of San Salvador's
   buildings

have been seized by the slogans
of the FMLN and the FDR.
In the streets the guards
massacre the demonstrators.
On the street of the national palace
there are always corpses.
Afterwards they remain vacant,
the asphalt bloodied.
At night there is no one
on the streets of San Salvador.
After the curfew,
on the streets there are only guards.

5. Orlando Jose Tardéncilla/
   TORTURE CHAMBER
     (*in El Salvador*)

Barefoot, naked.
Hands, thumbs swollen.
Electrodes tied to the balls,
the pain, the fear,
the terror of betrayal.
The dirty, dirt-packed fingernails,
the needles.
The burning and viscous liquids,
the hallucinations.
The badsmelling rubber, the hood.
The anguish closing up in each
   tooth,
the handcuffs.
The jail cold and solitary,
the isolation.
The cockroaches, the rats,
the fear of silence.
The world turned off and mad,
the meditation.
More blows, more tortures,
pain.
More electrodes, ultra-sound,
needles, isolation.
More blows in the balls,
more outrage for being human,
more commitment.
More Free Homeland or Death.

6. Jose Benito Armas, Leon Popular Center Children's Writing Workshop/ BROTHERHOOD*

A long long time ago
many merry and happy families
lived in the village of Antland.
Antland was a little place
on the volcano slopes,
near a forest full of love and
  warmth,
full of gardens and beautiful trees,
that made the dwellers happy.
All the ants worked for themselves
but when one had need,
the others helped as best they could.
One day news came that a huge
  monkey
had come to the nearby village of
  Snailand,
and forced the villagers to give him
  food,
or if not he would kill them.
That afternoon the ants met in the
  park
and decided to help the snails
by pinching him till he had to go.
With the ants' help the little snails
united and beat the great monkey
by hurting him and making him go.
Ever since then the snails and ants
lived very united, merry and happy
  together.
They made a celebration full of joy.

7. Gioconda Belli/ THE TENDERNESS OF THE PEOPLE

I told you that solidarity
is the tenderness of the people.
I told you so after the triumph,
after we'd passed
through the hard times of battles
  and tears;

when all was dreaming and
  dreaming,
awake or asleep,
never once flagging in flaming the
  dream,
until it ceased to be one, until we
  saw
the red --in truth--waving over the
  houses,
the shacks, the trees on the
  highway
and we think of all it befell us to live
and it was like a great jigsaw puzzle
of rages and fire and blood and
  hope...

8. Santiago Lopez/ FREE AS THE BIRDS

Looking through the latticed window
in the front of my room,
I see how the sun comes up
and lights up the leaves of the
  soursop tree.
Figures form on the floor.
A dentiroster alights and sings
on the branch of the plum tree.
It flies off, and returns
singing to the same branch.
I think about that bird
  of Nicaragua.
The Salvadorans, Guatemalans,
  Belizians,
  all of Latin America
will be free like that bird!

9. 12-Year Old Girl/ A BETTER WORLD

We the children of Nicaragua
speak to the children of the world,
so we can unite to build a better
  world...

10. Cardenal/ ECUMENICAL MASS IN DUSSELDORF

So much united song, so many
    throats together
in the words of the song.
And all smiling, so many smiles
    together
like one single smiling face.
One face made out of 2,000 faces.

This is the social being God created
in the beginning, I think, social and
    one,
    "male and female he created them
    one."
All the faces together formed
one single face out of all of them.
And one single face out of one.
"Let there be many Nicaraguas in
    the world."

CHRONOLOGY: MAY - JUNE, 1983

May: Throughout the month, militia recruitment drives and mass organizing on all fronts reach new levels. The Honduran and Costa Rican-based
contras enter into alliance; and the Sandinistas fight against contingents in
Sarabiqui, La Esperanza, El Papayo, Fatima and Las Azucenas. Early in
the month, Jeanne Kirkpatrick praises the Contadora group for the first
time, but the U.S. initiative is mainly to move the group to the right.
While *contra* attacks are set back in Mcarali, Matagalpa and Jinotega, the
U.S. reduces the Nicaraguan sugar importation quota by 90%, potentially
curtailing Nicaraguan annual revenues by $45-60 million. From mid-
month on, the *contras*, including many Miskitus, attempt to invade Llano de
Bawisa, while Eden Pastora leads ARDE forces in the San Juan River
area. Meanwhile, the UN Security Council backs the Nicaraguan position
against the U.S., and the OAS condemns the U.S. unilateral sugar quota
reduction. As the GNR scrambles to find alternative sugar buyers, the
situation of National Emergency pressures tax and other economic measures, including confiscations, that meet mixed reaction throughout the
country. Controversy also rages with the Church over the deportation of
anti-Sandinista priest Timoteo Merino.

June: U.S.-Nicaraguan relations reach a new low, as the GNR expels three U.S. diplomats for their participation in a CIA plot to poison Foreign Minister Miguel D'Escoto, and the U.S. responds by closing all U.S. based Nicaraguan consulates except the one in Washington, and by giving Nicaraguan consuls twenty-four hours to leave the country. *Contra* recruits swell to 10,000; the cross-border incursions continue; and the U.S. propaganda war intensifies. Emphasis in the anti-Sandinista campaign shifts from interdiction of arms to El Salvador to encouraging the Sandinistas to "modify their behavior." But it is becoming ever clearer that the policy really goes far beyond this. In fact, during the month, the CIA elaborates plans to expand the covert operations to become the most extensive since the Vietnam war, including a boost to $43 million in aid to the *contras,* compared to an estimated $30 million during the previous year.

Section 4. Women & the Revolution

1. Rosario Murillo/ I THE WOMAN OF CLAY

Formed and guarded
century on century
I am the headless fury of time
a face without features
the end of loves without mirrors
I live and have lived alive in the
 clay
through the rivers and seasons
geological strata and eruptions
countless cultures that don't die
and those just beginning
in the midst of all the noise
I, woman...

2. Cristian Santos/ SUNDAY DROWSINESS

Saturday, day and night
I washed plates, saucers,
I cleaned floors
and clothes. I...I don't know.

Today, Sunday
at dawn, the children
have already been here,
the floor dirty
saucers and washrags too,
lunch to make
and a Sunday drowsiness
irresistably overcomes
my arms, legs and feet.
Let them wait,
the saucers, the rags
and lunch too.

3. Daisy Zamora/ TO DIONISIO, COMPANERO (1978)

We are closer to ourselves now,
closer than when overwhelmed with
 objects
we moved among all those people
 always foreigners.
We nourished to life
words no one mentioned.
Nothing without sustenance is said

274

now.
I can no longer write you mild
poems
shaded by the acasias
or willows in the yard.
I no longer have a window to see
the sun
setting the gentians on fire.
Our life is something else now. That
life
of which we always spoke
To which we were coming little by
little...
Now we are ourselves
with thousands and thousands of
our own.

4. Indiana Cardenal/ STAMPEDE
(7/79)

The tyrant is no more
The Lake of Managua is dry
I don't have tears to cry
for my dead.
My canals closed from pain
The dust of my land
penetrates my pores
to the bone.
I am with you, peon, worker
peasant loving the soil
you cultivate.
It belongs to you, it's yours
it's your conquest.
The tyrant is no more.

5. Gioconda Belli/ NEW
CONSTRUCTION OF THE
PRESENT

I'm on the cutting edge
of the construction of myself,
worried about cements, structures,
solid walls
to protect the baggage of dreams

I carry on my shoulders,
I require certainties and tranquil
lanes,
firm steps towards my own familiar
homeland.
This clay needs to take form,
become brick.
I've accumulated times like colored
baby blocks
and now the days ask me
to structure their rhythm,
the cadence of my audacious
awakenings,
the sound, the track of my steps.
The time for lone meditation has
gone,
there are choirs where I may join
my voice,
songs springing from thick throats,
inviting arms decoding the earth...
Every day new challenges are born
demanding answers.
In this present made
with so much blood,
we have to trace face contours with
firmness,
we have to reinforce our arms,
tighten our muscles,
rush forth to conquer this ripe
earth,
force the dawn to be born.
Against the skeptics and instigators,
against the baleful prophesies
we must show we have ceased
to be quicksand.

6. Zamora/ REFLECTIONS ON MY
FEET

I have my father's feet
thin, long, pale feet with blue veins
bony men's feet
different from my sisters'
round, soft,
                    slight women's feet.

I see my feet narrow as spatulas
wearing socks and schoolgirl shoes
trafficking corridors, noisy classes
    and breaks.
wearing stockings, fine sandals,
    patent leather,
suede, and my first dance slippers.
These feet have left some traces
in the combat zone
                    some footprints
in the steep streets that rise
and fall in Teguicigalpa
dark at night or deserted at dawn;
in the ever humid, rainy streets of
    San Jose
  at the change of the stoplight
in the hatchway of the underground
    Radio Sandino
in the buses, the streetstands, the
    foodstalls,
the markets, the security houses,
  in the underground hospital.
My feet with mocassins,
tennis shoes and boots
  splashing through puddles
with bluejeans, a shirt and
    ever-damp hair
  --exile is a wet and cold-ridden
    memory...
I see these feet now walking freely
with sandals, heels or militia boots.
They walk through offices, outposts,
    ministries,
they visit art schools, workshops,
    libraries
and cultural centers in Ocotal,
    Camoapa,
Matagalpa, Bluefields, Puerto
    Cabezas,
Siuna and other places.
My instep bone comes from my
    grandfather
and I don't know how far I will walk
the bottoms of my feet planted in
    our land,
this land for everyone given to

everyone
so we can build with it
the future of everyone.

7. Belli/ SONG TO A NEW TIME

I stand up above the fatigue of
    work,
  renegade to my class
born among soft pillows
and illuminated dwellings;
surprised at age 20
by a reality
far from my meshed and spangled
    clothes,
overturned by the ideology
of those without bread and land,
dark forgers of wealth,
men and women with no other
    fortune
than their vigor and brusque
    movements.
I stand up to sing
about the earthquakes
and the screeching, desperate voices
of some of my relatives
demand the rights they have lost
    forever,
raging against the dispossessed
who invade the plazas,
theaters, clubs, schools
and who are displaced now, still
    poor,
but owners of their Homeland
and their fate, proud among the
    proud,
volcanoes emerging from the war
trees grown in the din of the storm.
I stand up
above the fatigue of work,
above the dead still living among us,
with those who never die,
moving toward the mountain peak
exposing my surname, my name,
deserting it in the underbrush,

276

undoing my clothes, my brilliant
    spoils,
to watch the dawn of the workers,
who go forth making roads,
    stunning the day
with the broken chains of centuries
and women in cornskirts cradling
    children
children leaving orphan homes
    behind,
undernourished and parents
    murdered,
come into the time of hope.
The people come laughing
with their load of tomorrows to build
and I sing possessed by the guitars
    of History
awakening pregnant with sweetness
in the belfrys of the towns,
simple victors over darkness
and the tricks of politicos
shouting with neither fear nor
    shame,
lions unleashing the fury
of their beauty to the sun.
I sing, we sing,
smashing the past to bits,
giving birth to the sun,
burning ourselves from within.

8. Santos/ ARS POETICA

It is the hour of silence,
a silence that lets us
hear the smoothness
with which the wind moves
the Tempisque leaves
and the nocturnal crickets,
the time, too, sister
to listen to our thoughts
                with clarity.

9. Vidaluz Meneses/ NOTES FOR
    ANGELA

On this long and elusive Sunday
    afternoon
I write to you
I like to think of you spending this
    time
revising a telex or monitoring
waiting on every word
that threatens our Revolution.
Or have you had some free time
and have you looked for an
    apartment
for when you return to your
    children.
In the time of finding yourself alone
I hope you'll have the strength we
    shared
when we decided, each woman in
    her own time--
to be unlike Lot's wife, attached to
    the past,
but to leave everything
we couldn't take with us
and continue with pain and with
    love
along the road of history.

10. Rosario Romero, Gaspar Garcia
    Laviana Rehabilitation Center
    Poetry Workshop/
    AUXILIADORA ("CARLA")

Today as I see you with this blouse
and skirt
I remember the day you arrived in
    the mountains
with three companeros.
Our leader asked you
if you were off to a fiesta
seeing you dressed like that,
but you talked to me
saying you'd left your high school.
When you read this poem

you'll remember the day you joined
us
the day you became one companera
more
in the Filemon Rivera Northern
Front.

11. Murillo/ BEATING OFF
SHADOWS
To Gioconda

I think of the eyes we have nailed
for a bright star's promise
and the stubborn way
we've talked of perfect times,
strange and blind in the midst of the
night
we kept on scraping at the silence.
We have lullabyed this different
future
loving and securing it
loving and cradling it
singing good mornings
at the threshhold of the door,
still dusty, our hands dirty,
the words still sad,
our backs bent under a cape of night
we harshly insisted on possessing
the future.
The revolution is an act of daily
magic
an armed woman on night watch
a cry on a wall, as naked as a knife
as solid as hope.
We who have talked
of mirror signals aimed at the sun
of everlasting marvels, of constant
miracles
let's go to the center of the world,
let's fabricate large, unknown
futures.

12. Belli/ THUNDERCLAPS &
RAINBOWS

I will start by dreaming once more
of our Moon, of the planet Earth
of the planet Earth
of a very definite place
of the navel of a large continent,
and I will start to tell you
about the sun between the trees,
about the heat, about the jungles,
the song of the birds,
and the lovely voices of the people.
I'll make you songs with
thunderclaps,
I'll tell you about calloused hands,
about the war, about the Triumph,
about what it cost us, what we
suffered,
what we now enjoy, work for, do.
I'll feel the sharp nostalgia
for the damp land,
I'll think of things I've stopped doing
getting wrapped up in dreams,
coming to know planets.
And we'll go along together
gaining from the stars' conjunction.
You'll tell me I was right
that this place is beautiful,
my volcanoes hung over the
countryside
like a woman with disheveled
breasts,
the lakes, the flags, the smiles...
and you'll say:
Work, woman, work, let's work,
so the dream is right here,
in this very place.

278

13. Ester Martinez Z., Monimbo
   Poetry Workshop/ YOU
   REMEMBER

You remember, Ruby
when the streets were dusty
and we played Papa and Mama
in the neighborhood.
When dirty, barefoot
and our hair all wild
we went into Don Venancio's
   backyard.
We robbed the daisies
and took off their petals saying:
I'll get married or I won't.
All this happened before.
Now we're not playing.
Now for sure you're a mama
   at age fourteen.

14. Meneses/ COMPANERA

Throw off your chains with firmness
and their deafening fall
will not make you tremble.
You are going to the encounter
with your infinite personal destiny.
Make your name yours
and plant it like a flag
in conquered territory.
Now nothing can stop you.
Now you yourself recognize your
   own path.
Mistress of your road.
Conscious of the portion of history
that belongs to you, Companera.

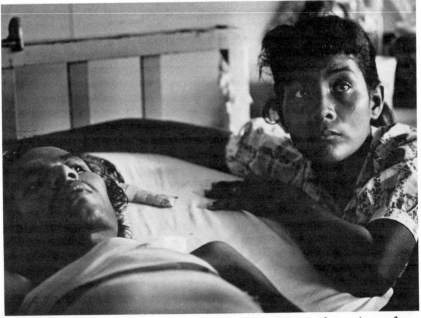

*Wounded campesino and his wife, survivors of contra attacks against a farm-
ing cooperative in eastern Nicaragua. Hospital in Managua, December 1984.
Photo by Vicki Grayland.*

EPILOGUE (1983 - 1985)

Nicaraguans at U.S. Embassy demanding the release of civilians kidnapped by contras backed by the Reagan administration. Managua, December 1984. Photo by Vicki Grayland.

INTRODUCTION: CONTINUED INTERVENTION & SANDINIST LEGITIMATION

by Richard Grossman with Marc Zimmerman

1. The Revolution & Its Crises

Into the second half of its first decade, the Nicaraguan Revolution has begun and developed innumerable basic reform programs, survived years of "covert war," and, with the national elections of 1984, completed the initial stages of consolidation and institutionalization.

By the fourth anniversary celebration in 1983, the trends for the immediate future had emerged. On the one hand, Daniel Ortega, speaking for the government, supported the Contadora peace proposal and offered additional suggestions for easing regional tensions. On the other hand, the Reagan administration, confronted with the continued failures of the *contras*, escalated the conflict, announcing extended military maneuvers in Honduras and stationing a fleet off both Nicaraguan coasts. The maneuvers would be a good cover for increased aid to the *contras*, the militarization of Honduras, and the development of an infrastructure for an actual U.S. invasion of Nicaragua. Then as now, the major question was clearly posed, between regional peace or war.

In the fall of 1983, unmarked planes began attacking the Managua airport and all the nation's seaports, devastating millions of dollars of the national oil reserves, as well as other supplies, in the Corinto harbor. The depth of U.S. involvement in the "covert" war was slowly becoming clear.

The major event of the fall, however, had to be the U.S. invasion of Grenada. The Nicaraguans inevitably took the invasion and subsequent occupation as an obvious warning that Nicaragua might well be next. The era of "gun-boat diplomacy" had returned. The Sandinistas, preparing for a direct U.S. invasion, expanded the militias and started a military draft.

Nicaragua also continued its search for peace, both by supporting the Contadora process and by directly offering draft peace proposals to the U.S. (which the State Department rejected as "deficient"). Within the U.S., a growing anti-interventionist and peace movement brought thousands to rally in Washington against Reagan's Central American and Caribbean policies. The House of Representatives voted to end aid to the *contras*, but this effort was stymied by the Republican-controlled Senate.

At the same time, in the midst of the war, the revolutionary process continued to develop. Nicaragua opened its first geo-thermal plant built mainly with Italian aid. The first class of medical students trained since the Victory graduated. The land reform program continued at a rapid pace, with well over 250,000 acres granted to peasants (or over 30% of the land granted since October 1981) in the last 41 days of 1983.

In the closing session of the Council of State in December 1983, Daniel Ortega expressed the "absolute conviction" of the Sandinistas "that we have never been as strong as today, that never in our history has there been a government as solid and popular as this one." At this moment, several measures were taken: Nicaragua's first free elections were scheduled for 1985; an amnesty was announced for all Miskitus (all those in jail were released), and for all *contras* not directly implicated in war crimes. Furthermore, a dialogue began with internal opposition forces. The process of institutionalizing the revolution had begun.

During 1983, hundreds of Nicaraguans had been killed by *contra* attacks, and economic damage totalled hundreds of millions of dollars. The real tactics of the *contras* may be typified by the testimony of Reverend Jim Feltz, a North American priest whose parish in Central Nicaragua was attacked in early September 1983. "In Ocaguas, the FDN 'freedom fighters' murdered two campesinos. One was stabbed and had his eyes dug out before he was killed. The other was hung from a beam of his own house ... The task force arrived in El Guayabo the next day and killed nine people. One of their victims was a 14-year-old girl who was raped by several men and later decapitated." Still here, as elsewhere in Nicaragua, the determination to move forward persisted. The villages were rebuilt, and the people continued to organize and prepare themselves against further attack. For example, in Feltz's area, participation in the militias jumped 400% after the events described.

As one year ended and a new year began, the *contras* launched new major attacks in the north and south with the aim of disrupting the amnesty program; U.S. harbor minings began, and the Reagan-appointed Kissinger Commission made its report designed to legitimize U.S. strategy. Then in February, Daniel Ortega chose the fiftieth anniversary of Sandino's assassination to announce that Nicaragua's promised elections would take place on November 4th, two days before the U.S. elections. Clearly the election process became the most important internal development in Nicaragua throughout 1984. The Sandinistas saw the process as a way of institutionalizing the Revolution; the Reaganites, the *contras* and sections of the internal political opposition saw the elections as a way to discredit the Sandinistas (especially internationally) through a barrage of accusations and a campaign of electoral boycott.

Clearly another tactic was to maintain and at times step up the war, as a series of revelations pointed again and again to direct U.S. involvement.

By spring, several Dutch, Panamanian, Soviet and other ships had been damaged by mines; and U.S. news media finally accepted Nicaragua's claim that the mines were the work of the CIA and not the *contras*. But even as the Congress debated and decided, the Reagan administration provided the necessary supplies for a major new military offensive. When the invading *contras* were once again set back after losing over 1,000 soldiers, the CIA demanded that the FDN and Arde merge for the sake of better coordination. Seeing that he might be marginalized, Eden Pastora objected only to barely escape an assassination attempt. FDN members were then brought to Costa Rica to begin the merging process. Meanwhile, the U.S. sought to combat pressure from the World Court with respect to Nicaragua's complaints about the harbor mining, and about the overall intervention. The U.S. also continued to pressure the Contadora countries hinting at economic and political reprisals if they did not exert a "more positive" influence on the Sandinistas. There were a series of minor peace gestures directed toward image-making at home and abroad, while the reality remained a two-track policy of war with a peaceful face.

A clear contrast between the U.S. and Nicaragua emerged in their respective demands stemming from Secretary Shultz's June talks with the FSLN leaders. The U.S. insisted that Nicaragua stop the exportation of subversion to other Central American countries; restore military equilibrium to the region through disarmament; remove foreign military advisors from the area; and assure free elections, political pluralism and respect for human rights. For its part, the GNR stressed the importance of dialogue and the need for certain minimal principles: respect for self determination, signing of formal agreements with regard to mutual security, a negotiated solution of the Salvadoran conflict and earnest support for the Contadora group. It was clear that no agreement could be reached between Shultz and the Sandinistas, so long as the U.S. used its peace gestures as a screen for political, economic and military sabotage.

As the fifth anniversary of the Revolution approached, the GNR forces had driven off the latest *contra* attacks, and the country became increasingly mobilized around the elections. In his address on July 19th, 1984, Daniel Ortega reviewed the achievements of the first five years of Reconstruction: the successful literacy campaign and continued gains in education, land reform and health. Health care was especially worthy of note. For example the infant mortality rate had dropped dramatically; almost the entire population had been vaccinated against disease; there were no new cases of polio reported since 1981; measles cases had declined from 3,000 in 1979 to 104 in 1983. In addition, the agrarian reform had been very successful with nearly 2.8 million acres of land being distributed and the formation of thousands of cooperatives totalling over 60,000 members. Still the war had taken its toll with over 7,000 Nicaraguan casualities and $225 million in economic destruction. "In spite of the aggressions," Ortega insisted, "we are committed to consolidating the Revolution's democratic institutions and accordingly, we will hold Nicaragua's first free elections on November 4." So the elections were officially confirmed, and the steps necessary for the electoral process were set forth and later carried out.

In the weeks which followed, the GNR lifted emergency restrictions, developed its amnesty program, and struggled to convince opposition parties that they should participate in the elections. But the *Coordinadora* and other opposition forces developed their strategies and placed great strains on the democratic image the GNR tried to manifest. Perhaps the most important matter was that of the deepening rift with the Catholic Church. The arrest of Father Pena for arms trafficking and conspiracy became the basis for a largescale controversy. At home and abroad, Archbishop Obando y Bravo spoke against the Sandinistas, raising money from private sources to prevent a Communist takeover of Nicaragua. The appointment of Fernando Cardenal as Minister of Education only further fueled the flames of controversy. On the military front, June and July alone saw 516 *contras* and 103 Sandinistas reported as killed in action, and the fighting kept right on through August.

Meanwhile, with the Nicaraguans focused on the first free elections in their history, the U.S. focused only on the boycott of the three small *Coordinadora* parties. Ignoring the unprecedented popular process developing in Nicaragua, the U.S. media lost sight of one of the most remarkable stories in recent Latin American history. The Nicaraguan government and the Supreme Election Council continued to meet with the boycotting parties and even repeatedly extended the registration period for parties to enter their candidates so that the *Coordinadora* could participate. Instead, the *Coordinadora* rejected all attempts at compromise and followed a policy stamped *Made in the U.S.A.* Finally, to round out a summer of insult and injury, the U.S. quickly spurned the Contadora group's 2-years-in-the-making peace treaty, seemingly without bothering to read the document. "We can't win," complained Comandante Bayardo Arce. "For more than a year, the U.S. insisted that we sign Contadora. Now that we announce we would do it, the U.S. says it is no longer good enough." While the Contadora countries have continued to search for an acceptable peace plan, the U.S. rejection of the proposed treaties has seriously undermined Contadora's efforts.

In the early fall, the depth of U.S. participation in counter-revolutionary violence and terror become more and more a matter of public record. The Reagan administration tried to maintain its approach of denying that the U.S. was involved or that U.S. laws were being broken, while government officials simply continued to encourage "private" help for the *contras.* Then, in the October scandal over the CIA's assassination training manual, the administration sought to defend the CIA by imputing the manual to "low-level agents." However, as Foreign Minister Miguel D'Escoto argued in his letter of protest to Secretary of State Shultz, "the manual ... is a new material proof of the official policy of state terrorism that is backed by the North American administration against the Nicaraguan people..."

Of course during the fall the most pervasive instance of U.S. hostility had to do with the strategy behind the all-out effort to discredit the Nicaraguan election process: If the elections were seen as a farce, the Nicaraguan government would not be "legitimate" and hence it would be acceptable to overthrow it. However, the elections could not be dismissed. For weeks, all social sectors throughout the country were mobilized to see that the process was carried out honestly. Every possible concession was made to bring the widest possible participation from groups and parties opposed to the Sandinistas. Every one knew that the very legitimization of the Revolution was at stake. While few doubted that the Sandinistas would win (just as few doubted Reagan would win in the U.S.), the goal was to solidify and institutionalize the space for legitimately participatory and oppositional politics within the framework of a popular revolutionary state. Perhaps there has never been a more extensive effort to combine the best qualities of various governmental forms--and all this done in the midst of economic debilities, a history of dictatorships and the overt hostility of a neighboring government that had at its disposal the most prodigious material and technical resources in the history of the world. All observers (and there were hundreds representing countless international organizations) agreed that the voting process was fair and open.

Just two days after the election of Daniel Ortega and Sergio Ramirez, on the very day that Reagan was re-elected by a voter turnout of just slightly over 50% of those registered, his administration launched the MIG scare. Soviet fighters *might* be on their way to Nicaragua, and if this turned out to be the case, the U.S. reserved the right to stop them. While the Nicaraguans repeatedly denied they were about to receive MIGs, they also insisted on their right to arm themselves with whatever weapons necessary for their defense. Not bothered by the facts, the Reagan administration and the U.S. media continued to speculate on whether Nicaragua was about to receive MIGs and what the U.S. response should be. It was in this atmosphere of growing threat from without that the people mobilized for an allout national defense.

It is simply symptomatic of recent press treatment of the Sandinista Revolution that the Nicaraguan defense mobilization was viewed as a further sign of demagogic opportunism, without a consideration for the international context of events. However, even in the midst of a new national emergency, the Sandinistas continued in their efforts of reconciliation. One of the leaders of the Miskitus in exile, Brooklyn Rivera, temporarily entered Nicaragua to begin negotiations with the GNR about a permanent return. When he attempted to reenter Honduras and meet with the Miskitus,

Rivera was arrested and expelled from the country. Within the Nicaraguan Miskitu community a new organization was formed to give critical support to the Revolution, and several Miskitus ran as FSLN candidates in the elections. The Sandinistas also supported a "National Dialogue" of all the political forces within Nicaragua (including the *Coordinadora* parties, the national business association, the Catholic Church, etc.), to seek an agreement of cooperation for the nation's future development. The collapse of the dialogue meetings after a month was only another of many failed efforts which pointed to the irreconcilable differences generated by a resolutely popular revolution.

The problem of irreconcilables reemerged in its most painful form during December, as the Church/State controversy escalated. On instructions from the Vatican, the Jesuits removed Education Minister Father Fernando Cardenal from their order. In the wake of this event and the controversy it stirred, pressure came to bear on the other government priests, all of whom refused to resign. In a phrase that seemed to speak for them all, the Education Minister stated, "My resignation now would not only be treason to the cause of the poor, but also to my homeland."

Meanwhile, new revelations in the U.S. press continued to expose the U.S. role in the war. Stories appeared on a secret U.S. military unit that had been involved in attacks in Central America; and other stories appeared indicating that a number of American soldiers had been killed, their deaths being listed by the Pentagon as accidental. There were also reports of U.S. helicopters having attacked Nicaragua at least twice in 1984, the first one in January over the town of Potosi, and the second in March over San Juan del Sur. The Council on Hemispheric Affairs released a report at the end of 1984 calling the *contras* among the worst human rights violators in the hemisphere. The report stated that "over 800 non-combatants have been killed by the *contras* after capture, and hundreds more have died as a result of *contra* attacks."

The war continued throughout December and into 1985. As for 1984, it was in sum a year of deepening U.S. involvement. There can be no doubt about the extent of U.S. attempts to overthrow the Nicaraguan Revolutions--the U.S. mined the harbors; it armed, financed and trained a ruthless, mercenary army; it prepared and threatened a direct and massive military invasion. The war had brought great hardship to the Nicaraguan people, with thousands killed, the economy severely damaged, and much needed social programs slowed down or postponed because of the allocation of monies and energies for defense. Since the war began, over 1,300 children and adolescents had been killed. During the course of 1984 alone, 5,600 Nicaraguans were killed, including 3,000 *contras*, 2,000 government soldiers and 600 civilians.

Still 1984 also showed the determination of the Nicaraguan people. Hundreds of thousands now directly participated in the defense. The mass organizations continued to grow in vitality and capacity. The social reforms managed to continue; and by the end of year, the land reform program had distributed over 10 million acres of land, representing 37.5% of all arable land, to over 45,000 families. Cultural programs of all kinds continued to expand. Under attack, the Revolution had succeeded in further consolidating. Preparing for the second major phase of the Reconstruction, now with an elected president and vice-president, the Nicaraguan people had spoken: *No pasaran!*

2. *Final Thoughts & the New Poetry*

By the time this book appears it will be out of date. Each effort to bring it up to date before publication will fail, and every successive reader of the text will be more frustrated than the last seeing how obsolete the book has become, how it must be supplemented by other perspectives, other works. The July 19th Victory provided a fitting conclusion to *Nicaragua in Revolution: The Poets Speak.* In the course of finishing this book, there were moments when it seemed that a massive intervention and counterrevolution might provide an unwanted ending. Indeed, as this passage was drafted and printed on the page, there was no way of knowing how many Nicaraguans involved in this book (poets, collaborators, people mentioned--so many who had struggled so hard for this Revolution) might be in prison, in exile or dead as the result of a massive foreign intervention. It is some consolation that thus far such fears have proven unwarranted. However, there is no question but that the counterrevolution has continued and that it will continue, and there is no question but that "progressive forces" have been and will be hard put to stem the oppressive tide. Finally, of course, there is no question but that the great mass of the Nicaraguan people will stand with the Sandinistas and resist. But who knows in detail what will happen and what the outcome of present developments may be? Who knows what the situation will be when *you* read these words?

At least history provided us with a climax at once chronological, dramatic and definitive. The November elections and the December mobilizations point to the institutionalization of the Revolution and the end of the first major phase of the Reconstruction. Above all, they point to the legitimacy and consolidation of the more militant anti-imperialist Sandinista tendencies, as the ones brought to domination by the counterrevolution itself. Events in January and February, 1985 only confirmed the sense of escalating war efforts by the U.S. So, although Bishop Pablo Antonio Vega of the Bishop's Conference was a guest at Daniel Ortega's inauguration, the Pope toured Latin America attacking liberation theology, and the Vatican undertook moves that led to the suspension of Ernesto Cardenal, and to the announcement by Edgar Parrales that he was prepared to resign from the priesthood rather than to surrender his active role with the people. And so, just as Daniel Ortega took office, the Reagan administration sought to step up the covert war by claiming that the Sandinists were working closely with terrorist organizations from the Middle East, that the government was completely in the Soviet sphere, and that the U.S. had to provide more aid to the *contras*, until the totalitarian Sandinists cried "Uncle." In the face of continuing problems, Ortega pointed to the following year as one of even greater economic problems than ever before.

Our final poet collage attempts to at least touch on all the key issues of 1983-84 and the beginnings of 1985. Of the collage materials, it should be noted that what we set forth represents the smallest fraction of what has been written in the past few years. We have the good fortune to have statements on recent events by key voices: the old master poet Jose Coronel Urtecho on the elections; the U.S.-based Nicaraguan cultural attache Roberto Vargas on the MIG confrontation; Fernando Cardenal on his ejection from the Jesuit Order. Indicative of the very essence of Nicaragua's new poetry, Daisy Zamora makes a poem from a variety of news headlines and reports. Daniel Ortega and Omar Cabezas are simply two of many political figures whose speeches verge on poetry; most of the young poets represented write verse that suggests prose. And we even have a checklist of CIA "dirty tricks" from the famous "Manual"--a list, which, *made in USA*, but translated here from the Nicaraguan Spanish of our source, may well come to stand as the quintessential *contra* poem giving the proper objective presentational balance to this volume.

But perhaps most striking to a student of Nicaraguan poetic and political discourse is the powerful return to the core of the Nicaraguan poetic tradition: the reemergence of the theme "and if I don't return," from Edwin Castro after the "execution" of Somoza Garcia; the conscious evocation of the line by Fernando Gordillo now made a slogan of the national alert: "After one hundred years, the enemy is the same." And Gordillo's famous phrase, cited by Gioconda Belli, serves as a powerful affirmation of the logic behind this volume: "Struggle is the highest song."

Nothing could be truer of the story of Nicaragua and the spirit of this book than Gordillo's statement.

In Part III, Section I above, in this Epilogue, and in this volume as a whole, song, speech and verse blend in the growing dialectical unity of discourse that is a constituent and expressive form of the evolving Sandinista social bloc and its struggle for survival and hegemony. The collage of prosaic poetry, poetic speeches, slogans, shouts and flashback phrases which closes this text and projects far beyond the fifth anniversary of the Victory is an expression of the unity forged throughout the years of insurrection and reconstruction. The negative past will not return, but the past of struggle which the Somoza past attempted to repress returns with a fullness that expresses a continuing intensification of faith in the possibilities of fundamental human change.

Defense, the Election & the Future (July, 1983--)

****

1. Luis Santiago del Palacio Gomez, E.P.S. Infantry Battalion Medical Services/ IN SUICE

Brilliant firefly
here in Suice
and tonight
don't approach me,
for I'm on postwatch
and I don't want
our position
discovered by the enemy.

****
****

2. Daisy Zamora/ NEWSPAPER SELLER

"Zero Polio Rate
134,000 Acres Granted to Peasants
15,600 Plots and Homes for the Poor"

3. Luis Santiago/ 120 MM.

120 mm. mortar shots
make a deafening noise
but we launch them with rage
because there go the hospitals
the schools and the parks
that we can't build
because we have to defend
ourselves.

July 1983: Early in the month, the CIA plan is leaked to the press as the Congress gears up to debate a bill to cut off covert aid. The leak forces the CIA to speed ahead with its plans. By midmonth, CIA officials testify that they intend to train and arm up to 15,000 *contras*, twice the number of Salvadoran guerillas. *Contra* leaders Robelo and Rivera admit wanting to increase coordination and cooperation with FDN Somocistas; Pastora reveals that funds from unnamed sources have enabled his forces to resume fighting. On July 19th, the FSLN espouses the Contadora peace proposal, calling for an end to foreign arms shipments and military bases, as well as a peace treaty between Nicaragua and Honduras, etc. Washington responds by announcing plans for joint U.S.-Honduran military maneuvers involving 20,000 U.S. troops and entailing the refinement and testing of plans for a naval quarantine of Nicaragua. On July 28, the House votes 228-195 to cut off covert aid, an almost empty symbolic gesture since the bill is not only ignored by the Senate, but also authorizes $50 million in overt aid to the *contras*.

4. Pablo Martinez Tellez, "El
Guadalupano"/ THE FOURTH
ANNIVERSARY (Song)

On our fourth anniversary
we're forging our history
defending our conquests,
defending our nation,
this Sandinista homeland.
And we proudly tell our leaders
that we've upped production levels,
that we're organized
throughout the nation
and we're set to beat
the invaders who want
to take us from power.

5. Daniel Ortega/ A YEAR OF
STRUGGLE FOR PEACE &
SOVEREIGNTY* (From Speech
on July 19, 1983, in Leon)

We truly want peace
to keep on building schools,
we want peace
to keep on raising

production levels
we want peace
to improve health care
for the people
we want peace
to wipe out hunger and misery
we want peace.
So that mothers, children,
brothers and families
should not have to live
the martyrdom of war,
we want peace.
But we don't want
a peace of graves,
we don't want a cowardly peace,
in that case we'd prefer to suffer,
we'd prefer to fight,
we'd prefer to die...
To defend the land,
ALL ARMS TO THE PEOPLE
To defend the conquests
of the Revolution,
ALL ARMS TO THE PEOPLE
To defend this new society,
ALL ARMS TO THE PEOPLE
To defend this
FREE HOMELAND OR DEATH.

August 1983: Statements by key figures begin to suggest the CIA's new timetable for Nicaragua. General Paul Gorman, commander of the U.S. Southern Command in Panama, tells the press that 5,175 U.S. troops and 6,000 Honduran soldiers would train to stop infiltrators, counteract guerillas and repel artillery and tank attacks. Maneuvers would build toward joint field exercises in December 1983. FDN representatives announce expectations for a major push in November or December, and Robelo claims that by December ARDE will link with Fagoth's Miskitu forces fighting in the north in an effort to seize control of the Atlantic coast. On August 23rd, U.S. warships carrying more than 16,000 military personnel appear off both coasts of Nicaragua.

6. Anon./ KEEPING WATCH

Keeping watch
night and day

to spot our enemies
and stop them
from advancing
and destroying

what we have built
with such heroism,
with such joy!

7. Zamora/ NEWSPAPER SELLER

*"Thousands Join in Coffee Harvest
1,000 Somocistas Attack from
    Honduras"*

8. Rene Castilla R., Frontier Guard Troops/ I'LL BE HERE

And,
when I go,
I won't say good-bye,
because I'll return,
I'll be here;
I'll return in the first drops
of winter,
in our child's
first smile,
when the last invader falls...

September 1983: On the eighth, in an action claimed by ARDE, a twin-engine Cessna 404, later traced to a CIA leasing company, attacks Managua's Sandino International Airport, firing two rockets which damage the control tower, two hangers and the main terminal building. The same day, FDN frogmen hit Puerto Sandino, and 1,000 FDN troops open an offensive on the Northern border. Later this month, General Gorman announces that the U.S. military will build a network of roads in Costa Rica along the Nicaraguan border, matching similar construction in Honduras by U.S. servicemen.

9. Guillermo Perez Leiva, Frontier Guard ADE Troops/ THE LEONEL RUGAMA BRIGADE

From a distance
I see the IFA going off.
Off they go.
I gradually lose them from view
I still hear their laughter...
    Songs...Poems...
that resound like echos
in my heart, in my ears.
Their joy floats in the air.
Some vehicles go, others arrive
and the road they went on
loses itself in the mountains.
I don't know when they'll return,
but I know they'll return.
    Marta, Rosa,
        Cristina, Vidaluz,

Auxilliadora--
All of them:
The Leonel Rugama Brigade.
I keep looking toward the distance,
now with a knot in my throat,
a void in my heart and a
"TILL THE FINAL VICTORY,
        BROTHERS!"

10. Zamora/ NEWSPAPER SELLER

*"Blood of 65 Children Spilled in
    Mountains
Blood of 75 Children Spilled in
    Mountains
As Battles Rage, Coffee Harvest Goes
    On"*

11. Mario Montenegro/ LITTLE PARAKEET FRONTIER GUARD

And if I don't return, love,
look for me in songs,
look for me in the earth.
Look for me in the swamps,
in the birds and mountains,
in the laughter of children,

there I'll be.
On the hilltops,
in the dust of the road,
in the gaze always fixed,
against the aggressors.

October 1983: FDN leader Edgardo Chamorro Coronel warns that Mexican tankers carrying petroleum to the Sandinistas will be sunk. Esso Standard, a subsidiary of Exxon, decides to stop leasing its tankers to Mexico, which supplies nearly all of Nicaragua's fuel. CONDECA, the Central American defense pact involving troops from Guatemala, El Salvador and Honduras, is revived to confront "Marxist-Leninist aggression." General Gorman represents the U.S. at the first conference. *The New York Times* reports that the CIA resupplies the *contras* from Salvadoran airbases. The Sandinistas shoot down a U.S. registered DC-3 ferrying supplies to *contras* inside Nicaragua. The plane's pilot and co-pilot, both former Somoza officers, describe how they fly regular U.S.-coordinated missions from Honduran bases. ARDE speedboats attack the Benjamin Zeledon fuel storage facility on the Atlantic coast and destroy 380,000 gallons of gasoline. A few days later, FDN speedboats launched from a CIA "mother ship" and driven by mercenaries (not *contras*) attack Puerto Sandino on the Pacific coast destroying 400,000 gallons of diesel fuel and gasoline along with the main pipeline connecting an offshore oil platform to the onshore refinery. Five days later, Corinto fuel tanks are destroyed, as Kissinger meets with Robelo in Costa Rica after refusing to meet with Salvadoran FMLN representative Guillermo Ungo in Panama. Three days later, FDN planes severely damage the repaired oil pipeline and loading buoy at Puerto Sandino. Finally, at mid-month, Reagan administration officials proudly admit the CIA recommended and helped plan the fuel storage attacks and predict more strikes against industrial installations. On October 20, the FDN engages the Sandinista army and militia in a northern village and causes more than $2 million in damages and 32 civilian lives. Atlantic coast Miskitus make a speedboat attack on a freighter in Puerto Cabezas. The U.S. rejects Nicaragua's latest peace proposals, as it has rejected all previous offers to negotiate. The House votes to ban covert aid by the same majority as on July 28, and with the same stipulations. Robelo lobbies in Washington for continued aid and a slice of any overt funds; he privately recognizes that the Somocista-infested FDN must have a role in any post-Sandinista government. Then, *contras* attack and damage a newly inaugurated $14 million geothermal power plant 34 miles west of Managua. Just a few days later, U.S. Marines and Army Rangers invade and occupy Grenada. CIA Director William Casey reportedly tells the Senate Intelligence Committee that Nicaragua, like Grenada, is not immune from U.S. military intervention.

292

Nicaraguan army reserves and civilian militia are mobilized immediately on receiving notice of the action. Washington calls an urgent meeting of CONDECA, which could easily serve as a multi-national invading force in the same way Caribbean troops are employed in Grenada.

12. Aquile Gonzalez Ruiz/ I PROCLAIM IN MY TESTIMONY THAT...

I have heard your stories
of Jalapa, El Carbon, La Mia,
of Escambray, and El Portillo,
of Teote...
I have heard the mortar shots,
the machinegun trills,
and one shot or another
and I have heard the rumors
and I have seen the fires,
and I have seen the signs;
I have seen the night ablaze.

13. Roberto Vargas (Nic. Embassy in USA)/ OF SUPERSONIC SECRETS

Today 35,000 Nicaraguenses
evacuated out of Port Corinto
firebombed by CIA frogmen
in the Washington autumn.

14. Gonzalez Ruiz/ I PROCLAIM

But today, amidst innocent laughter,
in the clownsplay with the children,
amidst the poems,
the dances and the songs,

I have seen your pain, your rage,
I have seen your urgency,
your obstinacy.
*Today I have seen your flesh
opened...*

15. Vargas/ SUPERSONIC SECRETS

In Grenada "rescue," intelligent
agents
and "the proud and the few"
dropped
from friendly skies, were shocked to
find black people speaking English
and Spanish like themselves, alleged
tourist
airport really a tourist airport,
a reported mental hospital fortress
full of patients DEAD from their
saviour's sanity and "success."

16. Gonzalez Ruiz/ I PROCLAIM

And today, Nicaragua,
with your lessons of love,
I have committed myself
to your history
I have put my signature
to your flags, your borders,
with the point of my rifle.

November 1983: Sandinista troops destroy perhaps the main *contra* camp in the key Jinotega region. At the same time, American troops arrive in Honduras for a new phase in the Big Pine II military maneuvers. On November 10th, Richard Stone visits several countries in the region, clearly bypassing Nicaragua and the Contadora countries. A week afterwards, a supposedly decisive Contadora group meeting ends with a resolution to meet again on December 14th. Later on, Daniel Ortega visits the presidents of the Contadora nations and presents new negotiating proposals.

17. Zamora/ NEWSPAPER
   SELLER

"*Soap, Oil and Flour*
Distribution Nationalized
Tenants Will Have Their Own Home
Cotton and Coffee Harvest
Battalion Enlistments
A Triumph for the People"

18. Jose Coronel Urtecho/
   ANNOTATIONS*

The Sandinista Revolution
is our bet
for another culture,
another civilization,
another kind of humanity.

December 1983: The Nicaraguan government decrees amnesty for all Nicaraguans who have taken up arms against the Revolution, with the exception of former members of Somoza's National Guard, and Contra leaders responsible for terrorist attacks. A special amnesty is included for the Miskitus, and a national commission is set up to start the reparation process. The *contras* launch a new offensive both on the northern border and the Atlantic Coast, with the intention of disrupting the amnesty program. U.S. Vice President Bush refuses to meet with Daniel Ortega, when both are present in Buenos Aires to attend Alfonsin's inauguration. The Kissinger Commission visits Mexico and Venezuela, and pressures the Nicaraguan government to "solve the internal conflicts through dialog with the Somocistas." The meeting of the Contadora group is postponed until January 7th. However, the foreign ministers decide to meet by themselves, drafting a document entitled "Norms for Carrying out the Commitments and Objectives of Contadora."

19. Zamora/ NEWSPAPER
   SELLER

52,000 Families to Get Drinking
   Water
13,000 Acquire Energy
Lands Appropriated in Past
Returned to Sumos and Miskitus.

20. Erwin Areas/ THE CHILDREN,
   THE TANKS, EVERYTHING IS
   READY

The children, the tanks
and all the people
waiting for them,
the children play
mounted up on the tanks
and talk about the war
like it's a game
they don't deserve.
But that's how it is.
The yankees menace,

and now the children
climb up on the tanks
and we all wait

with tanks, with rifles
with all the people
waiting for them.

January 1984: The *contras* step up their heavy attacks in the north. Once again they attack the town of Jalapa, and one again they are beaten, losing 300 in the process. A U.S. reconnaissance helicopter is shot down over Nicaragua, crashing a few yards over on the Honduras side. The first official death of a U.S. soldier results from the crash. On the same day, the Kissinger Commission issues its report, calling for more of the same military program, but attempting to revitalize the Central American economy through structural transformation and the infusion of capital. Daniel Ortega confirms that national elections will be held in the near future, and the CIA begins to mine Nicaragua's harbors.

21. Gioconda Belli/ REFLECTIONS

My heart has been reborn
from high mountains,
thawed by fire, by sparrows,
by moons with mirrors in the face,
because "struggle
  is the highest song"
and if I err, I can learn,
and if I'm naked,
I can dress myself in love,
and If I'm silent, I can speak,
and all this in seeing
the lakes that surround life.

22. Coronel Urtecho/
     ANNOTATIONS*

I can't stop admiring
how now
each day in Nicaragua
all the people are present.

23. Belli/ REFLECTIONS

This time of deaths,
is also a time of valuing life,
of forgetting disgust
and fighting it,
of struggling against vices
and eradicating bad habits,
of purging ourselves
like crystal purified
in this pure fire
of the Revolution,
taking it lovingly,
giving of ourselves,
opening ourselves
to this life we have chosen,
finding ourselves
in our own small and greatness,
trusting like a child
in the light of the morning,
without ceasing to hammer
the anvil on the forge
  --though at times
the strokes pain us,
when we look within ourselves
and see the great uprooting
of ourselves
that remains to be done.

February 1984: This month marks the end of the Big Pine II military maneuvers, and the announcement, by the Reagan administration, of new military maneuvers, Granadero I, to begin in May 1984. The anti-Sandinistas, reorganized after the defeats of November and December, begin an intensified penetration into the country. On February 21st (the fiftieth anniversary of Sandino's assassination), Daniel Ortega announces that the elections will be held November 4th. All officially recognized and registered political parties will have the right to present a candidate to be elected for the presidency. The FDN, however, will be excluded from the elections, according to the Statute of the Republic (approved July 1979), which prohibits the return of Somocism. The Emergency Law in effect in Nicaragua, which partially restricts the freedom of communication and mobility for political rallies, is said to be revised to grant the amount of freedom necessary to develop a meaningful electoral campaign. The FSLN proposes the presence of international observers (the Contadora Group, the Socialist International, among others) who would testify to the fairness of the election.

24. Coronel Urtecho/
     ANNOTATIONS*

The immense variety
Nicaraguan life is starting
to show
through the Revolution.

25. Belli/ REFLECTIONS

This is life
with its contradictions,
the dream after we awaken,
the wounds of time that mark us,
the wounds of war we still lack.

26. Coronel Urtecho/
     ANNOTATIONS*

Today at least,
the touchstone of all
is politics.
(False to think that,
at this time
art and poetry
could be non-political.)

27. Belli/ REFLECTIONS

In these evenings
of the menaced homeland,
poems are born from these hands,
these rifles, these faces,
that look at us as if to say:
Sister, brother, while I die,
what are you doing?

March 1984: The Nicaraguan ports of Corinto and Sandino are attacked. The anti-Sandinistas claim responsibility. Nicaragua convokes an emergency meeting of the U.N. Security Council, to condemn the attacks. Meanwhile, in the U.S., the Senate approves $21 millions for couterrevolutionaries and $67 millions in emergency aid for El Salvador. In that country, elections are held, and Napoleon Duarte, the U.S.-backed candidate, wins as expected. Concrete steps towards the approval of the Electoral Law are taken, as the Electoral Council initiates its work.

28. Coronel Urtecho/ ANNOTATIONS*

The grotesque irony
that the United States
spends millions of dollars
with the object
of reducing us to misery.
    ****
While Reagan insists stubbornly

in his way,
we can't separate ourselves
from our way.
    ****
Those who find Reagan normal
don't know they're subject
to an aberration.

April 1984: The Nicaraguan electoral process moves forward while political parties work toward alliances. However, the rightist parties seem to be vacillating between participation and abstention. News of harbor minings hits the U.S. press, creating a major debate in the Congress over the extent of the U.S. participation in the war. Both the House and Senate pass resolutions condemning the minings, and Congress finally votes to stop funding the *contras*. But even as the congressional debate continues, some ten thousand U.S.-supplied *contras* invade the country while the U.S. launches new maneuvers off the Nicaraguan coast.

29. Erwin Areas/ AND ALL THE PEOPLE

The truth is this
my love.
The dogs of war
hope to invade us
(it's not the first time
in this century).
But they don't imagine
that the tanks, the rifles
our arms,

everything is ready:
    the anger
    the closed fist
    the love
    the last kiss
    the word in the ear.
The dogs of war
don't know, love,
that EVERYTHING IS READY.

May 1984: The strong attacks by anti-Sandinista, sometimes with help from the campesinos, continue. Political parties still debate over abstention or participation in the coming elections. The Independent Liberal Party, Communist Party, Socialist Party and the Popular Social Christian Party reaffirm their decision to take part in the elections. Nicaragua goes to the World Court to protest the harbor minings and the U.S. war. The Court unanimously demands that the U.S. end its mining, but the Reaganites refuse to recognize the Court's jurisdiction. Nicaragua negotiates a pact with Costa Rica to attempt halting cross-border attacks.

30. Omar Cabezas/ THE UNITED STATES & WHAT WE BELIEVE*

The U.S. government
has made Central America
a granade that can explode.
We don't wish to give reign
to the horsemen of the Apocalypse
galloping over our brains.
We wish rather to trust
in the species, in humanity,
to believe that beings
given life and reason
will not allow it,
that the North American people
will not permit genocide.
We believe in life.
We trust life will win over death.
That good will win over evil,
positive is better than negative,

and love stronger than hate.
But we need help
so the dream does not die,
so hope will not disappear.
We want peace,
and we want them
to leave us in peace,
to let us build a paradise
in this small Nicaragua.
Let us keep on building roads
and children's parks,
hospitals and homes for the aged,
don't deprive the Central American
people of their dreams.
Let us for once prove
it is possible to build
the Kingdom of God on Earth.

June 1984: Secretary of State Shultz flies to Managua ostensibly on a mission of "peace and dialogue." Ex-CIA agent David MacMichaels, whose job had been to analyze evidence of the GNR supplying arms to El Salvador, indicates that there is no such evidence. The GNR moves to break up an "internal front" of the Catholic hierarchy for planning sabotage in Managua. Father Pena is video-taped participating in a *contra* bomb-planning meeting, and is then arrested while transporting a bag of explosives. The government stresses that it is acting against an individual, but the hierarchy sees itself under attack, and Obando y Bravo calls for a demonstration. Only 300 people attend, but the event is widely publicized on the Voice of America and elsewhere; and the GNR responds by cancelling the visas of ten foreign priests who supported the demonstrations. The small conservative parties based in the Democratic Coordinating Committee (or

Coordinadora) announce their intent to boycott the Nicaraguan elections; Reagan calls the elections a "Soviet-style farce."

31. Coronel Urtecho/
ANNOTATIONS*

For the exploiting bourgeoisie,
and for the bourgeois clergy as well,
religion is nothing more
than another form of exploitation.

32. Daniel Ortega/ ON RELIGION*

This revolution respects religion,
affirms that the Church
is the people,
and that the voice of the people
is the voice of God.
But some shut themselves up
in the temples
and plug their ears:
Christ called them hypocrites
and cast them out of their temples.

July 1984: Hundreds of thousands rally in support of the Revolution, as its fifth anniversary celebration comes and goes in the midst of great mobilization over the intervention and the national elections. In answer to growing problems with the Church hierarchy and the Church's pressure for the resignation of the "Sandinista priests" in the GNR, Daniel Ortega tells the cheering crowd that Father Fernando Cardenal has been appointed Minister of Education. The election law is completed, and emergency restrictions on freedom of press, travel, assembly, etc., are lifted for the election period. The Amnesty Law for *contra* soldiers is extended in an effort to encourage them to return and participate in the elections. By the end of the deadline to register candidates, seven parties have done so. These include the FSLN, and the parties of the left and right opposition: on the left, the Marxist-Leninist Popular Action Movement (MAP-ML), the Nicaraguan Communist Party (PCN), the Popular Social Christian Party (PPSC), and the Socialist Party of Nicaragua (PSN); on the right, the Independent Liberal Party (PLI) and the Democratic Conservative Party (PCD). The Social Christian, Social Democrat and Constitutionalist Liberal Parties grouped in the *Coordinadora* join Reagan in calling for a national dialogue with the *contras*. The FSLN agrees to many *Coordinadora* terms to guarantee a genuinely free election, but they refuse to accept the integration of the *contras* into the electoral process. In turn, the *Coordinadora* officially announces its boycott, and Arturo Cruz, unofficial *Coordinadora* non-candidate for president, returns to Nicaragua from the U.S. to lead the boycott. Roughly 1.6 million people (or 94% of those eligible) sign up to vote during the registration period of July 27-30.

33. Anon./ IT WILL ALWAYS BE
THE 19TH

We pledge to defend our victory
with every drop of guerilla blood
every bullet and red-and-black life.
*No technical or human force
can detain an armed people
peasant, worker, student militias
we'll defend the Revolution!*

34. Daniel Ortega (At Celebration,
July, 1984)/ FIVE YEARS AGO*

Five years ago
we won victory,
we buried
the reign of nightmares.
Five years ago
songs of roosters and birds
proclaimed the triumph,
the reign of dreams and hope.
Five years ago
the bells rang out
the guns and rifles
glittered and vibrated
announcing the good news,
the birth of a free people.
All of Nicaragua began
to compose the most beautiful
    poems,
with verses on literacy training,
on education, culture, health, sports,
the nationalization
of the banks and exports,
the recuperation
of the people's riches,
the right to work, organize, mobilize,
the right to housing and to land,
the rights of women and children,
the young and old.
But these verses
broke the snoring of Goliath,
the Goliath who for so long
had held our homeland in chains,

the Goliath who thought
he had killed off David
when he murdered Sandino...
Goliath once more
unleashed his fury
against the workers,
against the peasants,
against the youth and women,
against the children,
against the heroic people
of Nicaragua.
The war drums pound again,
the same aggressor as before
has launched his pawns
to kill, to rape,
to torture, to destroy--
to try and reimpose
the reign of death on Nicaragua.

35. Anon./ IT WILL ALWAYS BE
THE 19TH

From north to south,
from sea to sea,
there'll be no unwatched corner
of our homeland
It will always be the 19th,
it will always be heroic July,
ever advancing, never retreating.
*Today we defend life
the bursting harvest,
The Revolution.*

36. Ortega/ FIVE YEARS AGO*

Sandino once said,
"if I die one day,
the ants will come
to tell me
that Nicaragua is free."
Sandino,
father of the Homeland
and of the Revolution,
here are your ants!

they are the Indians, Blacks,
Miskitus, mestizos and whites,
the artisans, artists and journalists,
the soldiers, the militia,
the elderly...
Here are your people,
those who revived you from the
   grave,
the imprisoned heart of Nicaragua.

Sandino, here you are resurrected,
at the front of the Sandinista Front,
at the front of our combatants,
at the front of our heroes and
   martyrs,
at the front of Nicaragua,
immortal guerrilla
with your eternal slogan,
Free Homeland or Death!

August 1984: The election campaign starts, with each party given 9 million cordobas to campaign with, and guaranteed a supply of printing materials and gasoline, as well as access to the media. All parties have thirty minutes per week of television time to present their programs. As promised, the right to strike and freedom of the press are largely restored, and many parties begin holding meetings and rallies, but the three small parties of the *Coordinadora* still refuse to participate, in spite of constant Sandinista efforts to bring them into the process.

37. Coronel Urtecho/
   ANNOTATIONS*

In the electoral campaign
it became patently clear
that to the degree
the parties opposed to Sandinism
put forth their ideas
they were empty ones.

38. Vargas/ SUPERSONIC
   SECRETS

The liberation of Nicaragua

is engendered
by our father Sandino and by our
love for liberty as in the way we
vote with our rifles and our poetry.

39. Coronel Urtecho/
   ANNOTATIONS*

The Revolution's not only
the government
but all the people
(That's the reality
the reaction doesn't accept).

September 1984: Two U.S. mercenaries are killed in an attack over Nicaragua. The Contadora Group presents its draft peace treaty. Nicaragua immediately accept it, but the U.S. rejects the plan. Also this month two U.S. mercenaries are killed after their helicopter is shot down while participating in an attack launched from a U.S. airbase in Honduras and carried out with U.S. arms, supplies and planes, which results in the death of four Nicaraguan civilians, including three children.

40. The People/ SLOGANS

We beat them in the insurrection
and now in the election.

Let's march to the front
with the front.

Voting is a right for all.

2 elections there'll
be in November,
which of the two'll
be better?

Not with bullets
not with votes
can they overthrow
this revolutionary power.

October 1984: U.S. newspapers reveal the existance of a CIA-prepared manual for teaching the *contras* how to better carry out their terrorism against Nicaragua, and involving the "neutralization" of FSLN officials. As part of the continuing campaign to discredit the Nicaraguan elections, U.S. Embassy officials meet with opposition leaders still running and urges them to join the *Coordinadora* boycott. Virgilio Godoy, the PLI presidential candidate, withdraws, but the vice-presidential candidate does not agree, and continues to campaign. The election campaign ends in Nicaragua with a Sandinista rally of 300,000 people.

41. Vargas/ SUPERSONIC SECRETS

Mr. Reagan's ace in the sleeve
"deficits" are discovered/
20 billion$
over his dead body tax promises
   ...as he-autographs
murder manuals to "Dogmocratize"
Managua again/where is Anastasio
Somoza the III?
where is Tacho III?

42. CIA/ FREEDOM FIGHTER'S MANUAL
(*Guide to what the free Nicaraguan
can do to tie down Marxist tyranny
with minimal risk for the combatant*)

don't do maintenance work

*throw tools into sewers
come late to work
call in sick
leave lights on
plant flowers on state farms
leave water taps on
hoard and steal food
leave open state farm corral doors
spread rumors
call in false hotel reservations
spill liquids
drop typewriters
steal, hide key documents
threaten the boss by phone
call in false fire and crime alarms
damage books
break light bulbs and windows
cut telephone cables
cut alarm system cables
paint anti-sandinista slogans
("Long Live the Pope")...*

43. Vargas/ SUPERSONIC
   SECRETS

No one buys the CIA publication
in broken Spanish for "neutralizing"
baby clinics or "bibles of Babylon"

44. CIA/ FREEDOM FIGHTER'S
   MANUAL

put nails on roads and highways
put nails next to tires
put dirt in gasoline tanks
put water in gasoline tanks
cut vehicle upholstery
break wipers and headlights
cut and perforate tires
break the distributor coil
steal the rotor cap
invert battery cable connections
cut down trees onto highways
put rocks on the roads
dig ditches in the highways

45. Anon./ NOTICE FOR THE
   YEAR 3000

The distinguished gentleman
Don Virgilio Godoy says
he'll not run
in next year's elections
"because the conditions
are still wanting."
Don Virgilio is of the opinion that
"there will only be proper conditions
when they guarantee me I won't
   lose."
Good luck we wish
to the "stainless gentleman"
in the elections of the year 3000.

46. Coronel Urtecho/
   ANNOTATIONS*

The elections grew
visible, audible, palpable,
not only at the urns,
but at vespers,
at the enormous rally
of the Sandinista people of Managua
in the Heroes and Martyrs
Park Plaza
on the first of November.

November 1984: Nicaragua holds its election on November 4. About 75% of the registered voters cast their ballots, with 67% of their votes going to the FSLN, 14% to the PCD, 9% to the PLI and the other 10% split aong the other parties. Newly elected President Daniel Ortega declares, "This is a historic moment for our people. These are our first free elections." Two days later, on the day of the U.S. elections, the Reagan administration announces the possibility that Soviet MIG jets are being delivered to Nicaragua in suspicious-looking crates that await unloading in the port of Corinto. The Sandinistas deny they are about to receive MIGs, but urge the people to mobilize in defense against possible U.S. invasion. Tanks are deployed around Managua and each neighborhood prepares to meet the invasion by digging trenches and preparing civil defense procedures. Meanwhile, a group of *contras* kills fourteen peasants in an assault on the farm cooperative at La Sorpresa, and the same group then attacks another neighboring cooperative, this time without success. The U.S. keeps the pressure on by sending spy planes over Nicaragua, which break the sound barrier and cause sonic booms. On November 30, the month-long "National Dialogue" between the FSLN and legal opposition leaders breaks down for lack of agreement on crucial questions.

47. Coronel Urtecho/
ANNOTATIONS*

Never were there elections so true,
not to say so lovely
like the celebrated ones
of November 4th in Nicaragua
in spite of the official
Central American hostility
and the imperialist aggression.

48. Vargas/ SUPERSONIC
SECRETS

Some fundamentalist zealots may
believe Cmte. Daniel Ortega played
a (typical Sandinist trick)
Cmte. Daniel
gathered the networks' finest
over Managua press breakfast
a few days after elections and
began to speak in the tongue
of our "martyrs and heroes."
Their vote deposited in the
mountains and barrios of
as he spoke, our collective truth
was punctuated by a hole in the
sky/Managua skies raped by
SR71 supersonic swat teams/in
front of evening news cameras
****
'MIGS GO TO MANAGUA'
****
...liars dice in Corinto
with the "public credibility"/CIA
shell games//MIGS we see them
Mine you don't/credibility
slump for U.S. "intelligence"
communities whose responsibility

it now remains the verification
of Sonic/Boom
be it Sandinistas in MIGS
or U.S. mugs in SR71 surprise.
****
...crates in fogged
out fotographs/stuck/
between election finals
and a fool's moon/
crates filled thigh hi
with MIG 21 or 69 fantasies lipstick
and laced, from Russia w/love--
abt. to be spread out
...and mined Corinto port/
supersonic voyeurs
call their stock market analysts
to place bets
as Soviet ships underline
Monroe Doctrine
delusions/CIA visionaries negate
****
watch for Mr. T. goes to Managua
in a trojan horse cartoon
for Christmas present
and future viewing/
****
my unarmed people ... now pillars
of our own process and sunrise/
who will not be upstaged by CIA
MIG macho supersonic saberrattling
****
secret to all who desire it/
covert to none/
and they watch over the crates
that stick like corn between
the gold teeth of imperialism/
that reflect the image
of a big dog chasing them
biting its own "deficit" tales/
Soviet style crates

304

that reap the reward of media
in full genuflect to MIGless crates
****

for this they wd. reduce us to ashes
    and solidarity posters/
Where is your MIG u see/
    mine u don't
****

"the emperor wore no clothes"/
between the East/West conflict

and "wheres the MIG" commercials
****
...Now voting with shovels a trench
voting with anti-aircraft guns
    your "intelligent" planes
voting for your "intelligence" a
    candle
full of alleluyahs and gun powder
to punctuate your supersonic
    secrets/

December 1984: Twenty-one civilian coffee harvest volunteers from TELCOR, the Nicaraguan telephone agency, are shot dead or burnt to death as *contras* attack the truck carrying them with machine guns and hand granades. The direct military action abates somewhat as Christmas and the January inauguration of Daniel Ortega and Sergio Ramirez draw near. However, the Church-State struggle heats up, as the Vatican removes Fernando Cardenal from the Jesuit order because of his refusal to abandon his government post. There are new revelations about the U.S. intervention in Nicaragua, even as President Napoleon Duarte meets with revolutionaries in El Salvador.

49. Fernando Cardenal/ LETTER
    TO MY FRIENDS

My commitment to the cause
of the poor is from God
and from God is my desire
to not abandon my work.
For me to be true to the Gospel
and the plan of God
for my life is
to keep on with my present duties.
I can't conceive of a God
who would ask me to abandon
my commitment to the people.

50. Zamora/ NEWSPAPER
    SELLER

"*Stop Aggressions from Honduran
    Territory
18 Sandinista Army Brothers Fall in
    North*"

51. Raul Gavarrete, San Judas
    Neighborhood Poetry Workshop/
    FROM THE BALCONY OF THE
    RUBEN DARIO POPULAR
    THEATER

From the theater balcony
on my feet and firm
while we all listened
to the National Anthem
I thought in those who died
and who now live within us,
    within the Revolution.
I imagined the market sellers
who sold in the stinking
and tiny stalls
of the Oriental Market
and today sell in new markets
with walkways and gardens
that seem like parks.
I remembered the earthquake ruins
now turned into
the Luis Alfonso Velasquez Park,
the barricades raised

during the Insurrection,
the brigade workers leaving for the
    mountains;
the past and the present,
from Sandino to what will come.
I could imagine the Nicaragua
of the future.
Managua rebuilt with recreation
    centers
where the children will play,
where couples will talk of their love,
broad avenues with trees,
workers with worthy homes,
buses in good condition
    cared for by the people
and libraries and sports centers.
All the cities like new.
In the countryside
the peasants living better
with electric light
in good health, with good schools.
Then I felt what it is

to love this land;
I thought in what has been done
to live in peace. All this I thought
while I heard the National Anthem.

52. Fernando Cardenal/ LETTER TO MY FRIENDS

My conscience brings me
to this irreducible,
irrevocable and irreversible
commitment to the people.
This is what God asks of me,
this is what God wants.
And I am ready to go to my death
to fulfill this.
And nothing and no one
can shake my resolve.
Whatever goes against
my commitment to the people
for me clearly goes against
the will of God and would be a sin.

January 1985: Nicaragua's new National Assembly is sworn in on January 9th, and elects its new officers including delegates from five of the seven parties with Assembly representation. Priorities of the Assembly are seen as writing a new constitution, and matters pertaining to the continuing war and the economic crisis. The first act of the Assembly is to declare a general amnesty for all *contras* willing to integrate themselves in the national process. On January 10 (the seventh Anniversary of the assassination of Pedro Joaquin Chamorro), Daniel Ortega and Sergio Ramirez are sworn in as new President and Vice President. Before a crowd of 80,000, Ortega reaffirms Nicaragua's support of the Contadora process and the World Court's effort to bring the U.S. to a legal position with respect to Nicaragua. Ortega confirms the Assembly's amnesty offer; he also spells out a program for improved relations with MISURASATA and other rebelling Atlantic Coast groups. But he indicates that the months to come will be difficult because of the intervention. He promises to continue implementing agrarian reform as well as programs in education, child protection, the emancipation of women, Atlantic Coast development, etc., to the degree the continuing war makes it possible to do so. Bishop Pablo Antonio Vega attends the inauguration, and some bishops denounce *contra* terror for the first time. There is now some Church recognition of the government's legitimacy, as a new dialogue opens between FSLN leaders and the bishops. However, Church officials continue their pressure on the priests in the government, with Edgar Parrales indicating his intention to forsake his

Church position rather than stop serving the people. The Reagan administration escalates the war throughout the month, breaking off bilateral talks with Nicaragua, rejecting the World Court stance on the intervention issue, sabotaging the Contadora process and ending all efforts at negotiations. Reagan charges that the Sandinistas are criminals allied with Middle East terrorists; he asks for increased aid to the *contras*.

53. Vargas/ SUPERSONIC SECRETS

A people and country 100 times the
   size
of Nicaragua u still choose to either
A stoop 100 times as low to kick
   our tiny
     uppity asses   or
B raise your military budgets and
   flag

    100 times higher to wave in
    the face
of Nicaraguenses defending from
   her
    last volcano our right
    to be or not to be
    there is no question!!!

February-March 1985: As the Pope tours South America attacking liberation theology, the Church moves to suspend Ernesto Cardenal. U.S. pressure causes the "indefinite postponement" of Contadora meetings scheduled for mid-month, although the pretext is Nicaragua's supposed kidnapping of a draft resister seeking asylum in the Costa Rican Embassy. Arguing for increased aid to the counterrevolution, Secretary of State Shultz argues that Nicaragua is now behind the Iron Curtain, and Reagan, speaking on national tv, makes his sharpest attack on the Sandinistas and his clearest statement of intent to overthrow the Revolution. Calling the *contra* mercenaries "freedom fighters" and "our brothers," Reagan urges support in his efforts to pressure the Sandinists until they have to say "Uncle." In an effort to revive Contadora negotiations, President Daniel Ortega offers to send home 100 Cuban military advisers, forego a scheduled delivery of Soviet planes, and release the draft resister whose arrest has been used to justify the Contadora breakdown. When Reagan officials label his offer a bogus effort to influence Congressional discussions of economic aid to the *contras*, Ortega reiterates his recent urging for resistance in the face of one of the most difficult periods in the nation's history. He meets briefly with George Shultz in Uruguay, and they at least agree that the Contadora process should be resumed. But the Reaganites continue their verbal attacks on the Sandinistas, in an effort to convince a very reluctant Congress to renew aid to the *contras*. A well-accredited human rights group releases a report of continuing and escalating *contra* atrocities; and the Reaganites, facing increased Congressional opposition to their funding proposals, begin to consider alternative ways to finance the war.

54. Fernando Gordillo/ ANDRES
(*Slogan of Defense Brigades*)

At a century's distance,
the enemy is still the same.

55. Zamora/ NEWSPAPER
SELLER

"*Drying our tears,*

refining our marksmanship,
justice shall be done
and it shall be definitive."

56. Edwin Castro/ AMBUSH

Sandino is in the mountains!
Sandino is in the towns!
Sandino is...! Sandino...!
Sandino is Nicaragua!

April-June 1985: Those opposed to U.S. intervention mobilize against Reagan's proposal of a $14 million *contra* "humanitarian aid" package, which stipulates that the aid could be used for military purposes if the obviously doomed talks he demands between the FSLN and the *contras* should fail. But in spite of all the Reaganite pressures and manipulations, Congress accedes to the growing opposition and refuses to fuel the *contras*. Anticipating further Reagan moves in the wake of his Congressional defeat, the Sandinists reach out to still friendly nations as *contra* atrocities continue (including an attack on Bishop Salvador Shlaefer), and U.S. actions push Nicaragua's economy into deeper crisis. Sergio Ramirez travels to Western Europe, but all media attention goes toward Daniel Ortega's visit to the Soviet Union. As long expected, Reagan declares an embargo on Nicaraguan trade and curtails direct flights to Nicaragua. Country after country expresses disapproval of Reagan's move, and the embargo is condemned in the U.N. But the U.S. persists in what is virtually a declaration of war. The Pope pays off the *contras* by making Bishop Obando a Cardinal; Ernesto Cardenal tours the U.S. affirming that the embargo will not end U.S.-Nicaraguan cultural exchanges. In rallies and meetings, the Nicaraguan people express their will to continue with the Revolution.

57. The People/ SLOGANS

The use of force
doesn't resolve
but only aggravates
the tensions in the region.

A people's sovereignty
is not discussed
but defended
with arms in hand.

We're ready to raise
a wall of rifles

where the aggressors
will be smashed.

58. Juan Carlos Tefel/ THE
DAMAGES WILL BE PAID.

59. Coronel Urtecho/
THE PAST SHALL NOT RETURN.

60. Grupo Libertad/ FRANCISCO
MEZA BRIGADE

An echo in the mountains:
Our enemies SHALL NOT PASS!

CLARIBEL ALEGRIA. Born in Esteli in 1924, she soon went to live in El Salvador and identifies hereself as Salvadoran. She wrote several volumes of fairly subjective poetry but went through a process of politicization to the point that today she figures as one of Central America's militant poets. Now a resident of Managua, she has also written novels and important books on the Nicaraguan and Salvadoran revolutions with her husband, North American Darwin Flakoll. She shared the 1978 Casa de las Americas prize with Gioconda Belli, and a collection of her work translated by Carolyn Forche has recently been published by the University of Pittsburgh Press.

JORGE EDUARDO ARELLANO. Poet and literary scholar, Arellano is the author of *Panorama de la Literatura Nicaraguense* (1977) as well as bibliographies and articles on Nicaraguan writers. He was born in Granada in 1946 and is author of many poems.

CARLOS ARROYO PINEDA. A well-known Sandinista who fell on October 17, 1977. He was a law student at the UNAN and his poetry has appeared in *Barricada.* The cultural house in his native Matagalpa bears his name.

GIOCONDA BELLI. Born in 1948, she became known for a poetry that combined erotocism and politics. She published *Sobre la Grama* (1975) and *Linea de Fuego* (1978),

the second work winning her Cuba's Casa de las Americas prize. She has been a major Sandinist essayist and poet since the victory.

ALEJANDRO BRAVO. A young poet who served as co-editor of *Taller,* an important student journal of the UNAN. Winner of the 1980 Leonel Rugama prize for his volume, *Tambor con luna.*

TOMAS BORGE. One of the three founders of the FSLN and Interior Minister of the New Nicaragua, Borge wrote poems which master poet Carlos Martinez Rivas considers as among the few examples of surrealist writing in Nicaragua.

JAIME BUITRAGO GIL. A university student from Leon, he first published in *La Prensa Literaria.*

MARIO CAJINA VEGA. A professional graphic editor, he was born in Masaya in 1929. He attended college in Spain and took typography clases in London and the U.S. He has published many short stories and poems, and his books include *Tribu* (1961), *Lugares* (1964), *Familia de Cuentos* (1969) and *El Hijo* (1976).

ERNESTO CARDENAL. Born in Granada in 1925, Cardenal was imprisoned for his early opposition to the Somoza dynasty; and after his ordination as a priest, he founded his famous commune in Solentiname in Lake Granada. He worked very hard to win solidarity to the Sandinist cause during the insurrectional period, and has served as Minister of Culture since that time. Among his many works are *Hora Cero, Canto Nacional* (*1970*), *Oraculo sobre Managua* (*1973*), and *Vuelos de Victoria* (*1984*).

EDWIN CASTRO. Born in Leon into an anti-Somocista family, he joined in the conspiracy which led to the assassination of Somoza Garcia. Captured, imprisoned and tortured, he wrote several memorable poems before being murdered in prison in 1960.

ERNESTO CASTILLO. Nephew of Ernesto Cardenal, Castillo died heroically at age 20 during the Leon insurrection in September, 1978. A hero to young workshop poets.

BOSCO CENTENO. Born in Solentiname and a workshop poet in Cardenal's commune, Centeno served in the Sandinista Army during the Insurrection.

JOSE CORONEL URTECHO. Born in Granada in 1906, he was one of the major innovators of the Vanguard Poetry movement in the 1920s. His poetic work is brought together in *pol la da Nanta Katanta Paranta*, published by the UNAN. He has also published *Rapido Transito* and *Reflexiones sobre la Historia de Nicaragua*.

PABLO ANTONIO CUADRA. Born in Granada in 1912 and a major figure of the Vanguard, Cuadra's work includes poetry, theater and the essay. During the Somoza

years he moved from an early flirtation with Fascism to Pedro Joaquin Chamorro's liberal opposition to the Somoza dictatorship. Through his work as editor of the journal, *El Pez y la Serpienta* and the literary supplement of *La Prensa*, Cuadra introduced many new young political poets and did much to help form the revolutionary counter-culture so important to the Insurrection. After July 1979, he continued on the staff of *La Prensa*, clearly opposed to the FSLN.

JOSE BENITO ESCOBAR. An important Sandinista who died in the 1970s.

FRANCISCO DE ASIS FERNANDEZ. Born in Granada in 1945, he published two collections of poetry and edited *Antologia de Poesia Politica Nicaraguense* (Mexico, 1979).

GASPAR GARCIA LAVIANA. A Sandinista priest who fell in 1978. He was Spanish, but so important to the Sandinista struggle that he merits inclusion in this book and these notes.

FERNANDO GORDILLO. Born in 1940, he spent much of his life as an invalid, suffering from an illness that finally killed him in 1967. Founder and director of the journal *Ventana*, he wrote essays, stories and poems. A few of the latter are still models for Nicaragua's young poets, and Gordillo is remembered in the dedication of buildings and organizations that emerge in the Reconstruction process.

MAYRA JIMENEZ. A poet from Costa Rica, she worked with Ernesto Cardenal in the Solentiname poetry workshops and directed the Ministry of Culture's poetry workshops during the first years of the Reconstruction.

RIGOBERTO LOPEZ PEREZ. Born in Leon in 1929, he killed Somoza Garcia on September 21, 1956 and was killed in the process. He wrote several poems, some of them explaining his motivation in the violent events that led to his death. He is now considered a national hero.

CARLOS MEJIA GODOY. An excellent composer, singer and musician, he and his brother Luis Enrique forged the new song movement that played such a major role in the Insurrection and continues to play a major role in the Reconstruction.

ERNESTO MEJIA SANCHEZ. Born in Masaya in 1923, he was an arch opponent of Somoza Garcia and went into exile in Mexico during the 1950s. A literature professor at the UNAM in Mexico, he became well known for his poetry and essays. His major works of poetry were published in the volume, Recoleccion. After the Sandinista victory, he was appointed Nicaraguan ambassador to Spain.

VIDA LUZ MENESES. Born in Masaya in 1945, she published Cuando yo me case and Llama Guardada in the years prior to the Insurrection. During the Reconstruction, she has become one of the major women poets.

RICARDO MORALES AVILES. Sandinist militant, theorist and poet, he was born in Diriamba in 1939, graduated at the national university in Mexico and became an FSLN member in the 1960s. playing a major role in the Frente Estudiantil Revolucionario. He was imprisoned in 1968 and subjected to mistreatment and torture until his release in 1971. He was killed in action in 1973. Companero of FSLN militant Doris Tijerino, he wrote several poems while in prison, many of them dedicated to her.

ROSARIO MURILLO. Born in Managua in 1951, she wrote increasingly militant poems and became a revolutionary in the late 1970s. Her earlier volumes of poetry were republished after the Victory as Amar es Combatir. And she won the Leonel Rugama Young Poet's prize with her volume, Un Deber de Cantar. Head of the Sandinista Association of Cultural Workers, she is also a member of the Sandinista Popular Militia.

MICHELE NAJLIS. Born in Granada in 1946, she attended the UNAN and became a friend of Fernando Gordillo and Sergio Ramirez, with whom she founded Frente Ventana, a committed writer's group. The first woman to write fully militant anti-Somocista poetry, she published El viento armado and became an influential university professor speaking out and helping to organize students against the dictatorship. With the victory, she took charge of the Office of Immigration.

DANIEL ORTEGA. One of the major Sandinista leaders, he joined the Insurrectional tendency and is the FSLN member who has served in the governmental Junta since the first days of the Insurrection. Nicaragua's new president, also a writer of political poems.

FELIPE PENA. One of the Solentiname poets, he was killed in 1979 in Nueva Guinea a few months before the final victory.

OSCAR ANTONIO ROBELO. A young Sandinista killed by the National Guard in 1978.

LUIS ROCHA. Born in Granada in 1942, he published Domus Aurea (1968) and worked on many magazines and newspapers, including La Prensa.

MAGDALENA DE RODRIGUEZ. A schoolteacher, housewife and mother of five children, she kept a prose and verse diary of the Insurrection seen from the perspective of her hometown of Esteli.

LEONEL RUGAMA. Born in Esteli in 1950, he attended a Catholic seminary, started a chess club, dabbled in poetry and then joined the FSLN in 1967. A victim of foco theory romanticism, he fell in a shootout with the National Guard in 1970. He left a handful of outstanding political poems and is revered in Nicaragua today as the model of the militant poet.

CRISTIAN SANTOS DE PRASLIN. A young poet from Managua, her anti-Somocista poetry began to appear in La Prensa Literaria during the final insurrection.

FERNANDO SILVA. A doctor by profession, he was born in Granada in 1927. Author of the novel, El Comandante and many short stories, he is also a wellknown poet. Most of his energies in the Reconstruction have been devoted to medical questions.

FERNANDO ANTONIO SILVA. Son of Fernando Silva, he was born in 1957 and has published poems in newspapers and magazines.

PEDRO XAVIER SOLIS. Young poet who began publishing his poems during the Insurrection. A brigade worker during the Literacy Crusade, he lives in Managua.

RICARDO SU AGUILAR. Born in the Riguero Neighborhood of Managua, he fell in 1979 on the highway to Masaya.

DORA MARIA TELLEZ. Commander Two during the National Palace takeover of 1978 and leader on the Rigoberto Lopez Perez Western Front during the 1979 insurrection. A national heroine, she was born in Leon in 1958 and has been very active during the Reconstruction.

ORLANDO JOSE TARDENCILLA. At age 19, he became known to every one for his confrontation with the U.S. State Department, when officials had pulled him out of a Salvadoran prison and expected him to attack Nicaragua in front of the tv

312

cameras.

ALBA AZUCENA TORRES. Born in 1959 in Tecolostote, Chontales, she has published in *Poesia Libre* and *Barricada*. She served in the Gregorio Aguilar Barea Popular Culture Center and worked especially hard as a Delegate of the Chontales Literacy Commission.

HUGO TORRES. Participant in the National Palace takeover, the Insurrection and now the struggle against the Counterrevolution, he has only recently published some of the poems he has written in the past few years.

JULIO VALLE-CASTILLO. Born in Masaya in 1952, he studied Spanish Language and Literature at the UNAM in Mexico. A student of Ernesto Mejia Sanchez, before the Victory he edited the volume, *Los Modernistas en Nicaragua* (1978) and two books of poetry, *Las Armas Iniciales* (1977) and *Formas Migratorias* (1979). Since 1980, he has worked as Coordinator of the Ministry of Culture's Literature Section.

ROBERT VARGAS. A long-time resident of San Francisco, California, he has written poetry in Spanish and English in solidarity with his fellow Nicaraguans, as well as with U.S. Chicanos. He fought during the Insurrection and is currently serving as Cultural and Labor Counselor of the Nicaraguan Embassy in Washington. He is no relation to the workshop poet named Roberto Vargas.

LUIS VEGA. Poet and student, he participated as a combatant in the Final Insurrection and published his testimonial war poems in *La Prensa Literaria*.

JUAN VELAZQUEZ. Born in Managua in 1943, he has published poems in magazines and literary supplements. After the Insurrection, he worked in the Literature Section of the Ministry of Culture.

DAISY ZAMORA. Born in Managua in 1950, she won the Mariano Fiallos Gil Poetry Prize in 1978. She has published her tightly crafted poems in a variety of publications. Her poetry grew more political as the Insurrection unfolded and as she became involved in ever more serious Sandinista work. She was one of the prime people involved with Radio Sandino, and she became Vice Minister of Culture during the Reconstruction.

MARC ZIMMERMAN. General editor of this volume, he published many articles of socio-literary theory and criticism and worked in Nicaragua's Ministry of Culture during 1979-80. His books include: *Nicaragua in Revolution: The Poets Speak* (Mpls: MEP, 1980); *Processes of Unity in Caribbean Societies, Ideologies & Literature* (Mpls.: I&L, 1983) and *Flights of Victory*, a trans./ed. of Ernesto Cardenal's recent poetry (N.Y.: Orbis, 1985); also, *Lucien Goldmann y La Sociologia de la Creacion Cultural* (forth.).

A SHORT BIBLIOGRAPHY OF KEY BOOKS ON NICARAGUA IN ENGLISH

Prepared by Richard Grossman

Aldaraca, Bridget, Edward Baker, Ileana Rodriguez & Marc Zimmerman, ed. *Nicaragua in Revolution: The Poets Speak/ Nicaragua en Revolucion: Los Poetas Hablan* (MEP: Minneapolis, 1980).

Black, George. *Triumph of the People* (London: Zed Press, 1981). Overall history of Nicaragua and the Sandinistas through 1980.

Booth, John. *The End & the Beginning: The Nicaraguan Revolution* (Boulder, Colorado: Westview Press, 1982).

Borge, Tomas. *Carlos, the Dawn is No Longer Beyond Our Reach* (Vancouver, Canada: New Star Books, 1984).

_____, et al., *Sandinistas Speak* (N.Y.: Pathfinder Press, 1982). Collection of speeches by Sandinista leaders.

Cabestreo, Teofilo. *Ministers of God, Ministers of the People* (Maryknoll, N.Y.: Orbis Press, 1983). Interviews with priests in government.

Cardenal, Ernesto. *Apocalypse and Other Poems* (N.Y.: New Directions, 1977).

_____. *Flights of Victory/ Vuelos de Victoria: Songs in Celebration of the Nicaraguan Revolution* (Maryknoll, N.Y.: Orbis, 1985).

_____. *In Cuba* (N.Y.: New Directions, 1976).

_____. *With Walker in Nicaragua and Other Early Poems* (Mid 'on, Conn.: Wesleyan University Press, 1984).

_____. *Zero Hour and Other Documentary Poems* (N.Y.: New Directions, 1980). Almost all the major pre-victory political poems (1960-1979).

Collins, Joseph. *What a Difference Could a Revolution Make?* (San Francisco: Institute for Food and Development Policy, 1982). Analysis of agrarian reform.

_____ & Frances Moore Lappe. *Now We Can Speak* (San Francisco, Institute for Food and Development Policy, 1982). Intro. to the Revolution.

Ferlinghetti, Lawrence. *Seven Days in Nicaragua Libre* (San Francisco: City Lights, 1984).

Hirshon, Sheryl. *And Also Teach Them to Read* (Westport, Conn.: Lawrence Hill, 1983). On Nicaragua's Literacy Crusade.

Meiselas, Susan. *Nicaragua: June 1978-July 1979* (N.Y.: Pantheon, 1981).

Millet, Richard. *Guardians of the Dynasty* (Maryknoll, N.Y.: Orbis, 1977).

Nolan, David. *The Ideology of the Sandinistas and the Nicaraguan Revolution* (Coral Gables, Florida: University of Miami, 1984).

Randall, Margaret. *Christians in the Nicaraguan Revolution* (Vancouver: New Star Books, 1983).

_____. *Risking a Somersault in the Air: Conversations with Nicaraguan Writers* (San Francisco: Solidarity Publications, 1984).

_____. *Sandino's Daughters* (Vancouver: New Star Books, 1981).

Rius. *Nicaragua for Beginners* (New York & London: Writers & Readers, 1982).

Selser, Gregorio. *Sandino* (N.Y.: Monthly Review Press, 1981).

Tijerino, Doris/ Margaret Randall. *Inside the Nicaraguan Revolution* (Vancouver: New Star Books, 1978).

Walker, Thomas. *Nicaragua: The Land of Sandino* (Boulder, Colorado: Westview Press, 1981).

_____, ed. *Nicaragua in Revolution: An Anthology* (N.Y.: Praeger, 1981).

Weber, Henri. *Nicargua: The Sandinista Revolution* (London: Verso, 1981).

Wheaton, Phillip/ Yvonne Dilling. *Nicargua: A People's Revolution* (Washington: EPICA Task Force, 1980).

Wheelock Roman, Jaime. *The Great Challenge* (Managua: Alternative Views, 1984).

White, Steven F., ed. *Poets of Nicaragua: A Bilingual Anthology* (Greensboro, N.C.: Unicorn Press, 1983).